History of American Education Reform:

Lessons for the Future

Gregg B. Jackson

Vardquest Publishing

History of American Education Reform: Lessons for the Future

by Gregg B. Jackson

Copyright © 2008 by Gregg B. Jackson

All rights reserved. Reproduction by any means is limited to the fair-use provisions under U.S. copyright law and international copyright treaties and conventions, unless written permission is secured from the author. Purchasers of an electronic download of the book are hereby granted permission to make one personal electronic archive copy and to print out one copy of parts or all of the file for their personal use.

Vardquest Publishing
United States of America
Vardquest.com

Printed in the United States of America

ISBN: 978-0-578-02669-5

LCCN: 2008906701

To my students who made this necessary and possible.

Table of Contents

CHAPTER 1: Introduction 1
Gregg B. Jackson

CHAPTER 2: Universal Public Schooling 9
Nina de las Alas and Gregg B. Jackson

CHAPTER 3: Secularization of Public Education 45
Gregg B. Jackson

CHAPTER 4: Progressive Education 69
Gregg B. Jackson, Sean B. Kelly, and
Maria Soledad MacKinnon

CHAPTER 5: Professionalization of Teaching 101
Gregg B. Jackson

CHAPTER 6: Special Education 133
Gregg B. Jackson and John Y. Jones

CHAPTER 7: Compensatory Education 163
Beth Antunez and Gregg B. Jackson

CHAPTER 8: Multicultural Education 195
Daniel C. Padolsky

CHAPTER 9: Lessons from the Past 233
Gregg B. Jackson

CHAPTER 10: Prospects of the Early 21st Century Reforms 269
Gregg B. Jackson

Author Bios 307

1

Introduction

Gregg B. Jackson

American education has changed dramatically over the past two centuries. In the early 1700s, American schools emphasized the teaching of religious beliefs and children were lashed for recitation errors. During the early 1800s, education began to play a key role in preparing citizens for democracy and commerce, but most teachers had only an elementary school education and many had not mastered their own lessons. By the early 1900s, almost all children were attending elementary school but only about 15 percent continued on to high school.

This book examines the forces that have propelled and resisted public elementary and secondary school reforms. It explores what motivated the reformers and their opponents; what social, economic, and political forces aided and resisted reform efforts; what strategies were used to advance the reforms and to oppose them; and what the consequences have been—both positive and negative. From examination of these past reforms, lessons are inferred and then applied to major education reform efforts under way at the dawn of the 21st century. What are their prospects for success? What might be done to improve their chances of success?

The history of education reform involves stories of noble ambitions, colorful personalities, prolonged conflicts, skillful maneuvering, repeated setbacks, and gradually achieved success. Thomas Jefferson helped father our nation but his several attempts at education reform were stillborn until he achieved a grand success in old age. Horace Mann doubted his abilities and was constantly under attack but became known as the father of universal public education. John Dewey introduced democratic practices into the classroom but was criticized by teachers and parents for dictatorial direction of his school. Lyndon Johnson hoped to use federal aid to equalize funding among public schools but, when that appeared politically impossible, he maneuvered legislation through Congress that established compensatory education services for low-achieving youth.

This book examines seven reform efforts in a parallel manner, with the intent of identifying factors that contribute to reform success. Each of Chapters 2-8 addresses one major education reform effort:

- Universal public education—opening schools to all, regardless of the families' means
- Secularization of education—removing religious instruction and practices from public classrooms
- Progressive education—urging a curriculum that provides a broad preparation for life and a pedagogy that is based on child psychology
- Professionalization of teaching—preparing teachers for complex instructional responsibilities
- Special education—adapting instruction to the needs of students with disabilities
- Compensatory education—making available extra educational services for those who begin school with inadequate preparation
- Multicultural education—promoting schools that teach and value the contributions of all major racial/ethnic groups within society

These seven reforms were chosen because they aspired to make big changes in education, they were eventually initiated throughout most of the country, and they have been long maintained. They are not without critics but they have changed the face and character of American education.

The book was written for all who are concerned about education—those who are leading reform efforts, the parents and teachers who find themselves in the crossfire of reform battles, and those who are interested observers. It is hoped that the book will provide the reader with a "way of orienting the present moment, so that you know where you are and where we have come from...so you can make decisions based to some extent on what has gone before."[1]

This book is partly a mapping of what is known and partly a voyage of discovery. Such voyages are fraught with difficulties and risks—even more than history suggests— for many of the failures sink without leaving a trace. Despite that, human nature impels exploration, understanding, and the pursuit of envisioned futures. The authors of these chapters have prepared them with both trepidation and boldness.

The trepidation looms from the complexities of assessing education reform. There has long been, and continues to be, considerable disagreement about the aims of education. Publicly announced goals sometimes mask self-interest with a façade of nobility. Many forces affect education reforms, including chance events, and these forces interact in complex ways. The conflict over reforms often continues beyond the decision-making, affecting both the implementation and evaluation of the program results. In addition, the historical record of major education reforms suffers many gaps.

The authors' boldness springs from several sources. We share the modern western conviction that progress is possible and desirable—although we are acutely aware that success is not assured by good intentions. We think that education is important—for students as individuals and for the economic and social well being of our nation. We are pained by the fact that American education is not working well for millions of young people. We have evidence that dramatic strides have been made by several reform efforts. We are hopeful that the mapping and discovery undertaken for this book will assist us and others to contribute more effectively to the enhancement of American education.

Education and Reform

Education is a deliberate, systematic, and sustained effort to transmit knowledge, develop skills, forge habits, and instill values. This book focuses on education in public elementary, middle, and high schools. These will often be referred to collectively as "K-12 schools" (with the "K" representing kindergarten). The focus will not include private schools, because over the past century these schools have enrolled only about seven to eleven percent of students.[2] Private schools have sometimes started innovations that moved to public schools, and they have sometimes adopted innovations initiated in public schools. Their pivotal roles in the progressive education reform and special education reform will be indicated.

The control of public schools in the U.S. has always been highly decentralized. The federal government provided only about six to nine percent of the K-12 public school budget over the latter half of the 20th century.[3] It has important influence in only a few domains of education, particularly civil rights, special education, compensatory education, and very recently, in standardized testing and accountability. Most decisions about the structure of public education, the curriculum, and the pedagogy are shared by 50 state governments and by 15,000 boards of local school districts, most of which are elected. In addition, the administrators and Parent-Teacher Associations at individual schools make decisions affecting the nature of education at those schools. Finally, teachers are the front line implementers, and they may carry out reforms as intended, may adapt them in ways they think are desirable, may fumble them because of a lack of training and support, and may resist implementation when they consider a reform useless, harmful or against their personal interests.

This book focuses on deliberate and sustained education reform efforts that spread throughout most of the country. The book is not about gradual evolutions in education such as declining classroom sizes or refinements of curriculum and textbooks. Similarly, it is not about modest innovations in existing practices, such as the installation of blackboards in classrooms, the "new math" of the post-Sputnik era, or training teachers to add higher-order questioning to their repertoire.

Analysis of Education Reforms

To examine education reforms, the authors use both historical and policy analysis. Most of the reforms examined in this book have played out for more than a century. Historical analysis is essential for examining their progression. Policy analysis provides a focus on the problems or opportunities that were perceived, the alternative responses considered, the factors affecting the decision-making, implementation of new approaches, and evaluation of the changes.

Several of the reforms discussed in this book have been the subject of an entire book. No one chapter can cover any reform thoroughly. Instead, we have focused on describing a few pivotal battles in the campaign for reform and then briefly outline how the reform played out across the country.

For historical sources, we have drawn upon early histories and recent ones, because perspectives about history change over time. Both traditional and revisionist histories have been consulted. The former tend to focus on the progress achieved in American education while the latter tend to focus on the shortcomings, particularly in serving racial/ethnic minorities and lower class students. Considerable use is made of social and educational statistics, but most data series were not first collected until the 1860s or later. At times, data on two related matters must be reported for different periods because the data series were not collected at the same points in time.

Although a few of the reforms discussed in the following chapters had important antecedents in Europe, the European developments will not be described. Rather, brief mention will be made of ideas and practices that were imported by American reformers.

A common analytical structure is used in each of Chapters 2-8. First, we describe the initial conditions of education that the reform strove to change, focusing on the nature of education at the time and its perceived shortcomings. That section will describe who went to school and who did not, the main objectives of schooling, the nature of the curriculum and instruction, the levels of teacher preparation, and sometimes the effects of those conditions on students.

In each chapter we seek to identify and describe changing social-economic-political contexts that were associated with the reform. For instance, the decision that the governance of our country was to be by citizens, rather than by monarchs and bishops, created a problem because the citizenry had little knowledge or experience in making governance decisions, and thus provided an impetus for the creation of universal education systems. The civil rights movement of the 1950s and 60s popularized the ideal of equal educational opportunity, which in turn helped precipitate federal legislation mandating special education for all children needing it. In this second example the changes did not create the problem of learning disabilities, but they heightened concern about a long-existing problem. The 19th century spawned new philosophies and the new science of psychology, which in turn sparked progressive education pedagogy. In this case the changing context did not create a problem but rather an opportunity.

Next, the campaign for the reform is described, identifying key reform leaders, their motives, and their strategies. Usually there is substantial conflict over education reform proposals because they involve major changes to important public institutions. Indeed, opposition is the most predictable response to reform initiatives. It emanates from several factors including ideology differences, self-interests, costs, and fear of the unknown. There are many possible goals of education, and even when people agree on the priority goals, they may disagree about the best means for achieving them.

The conflict over education reforms can serve useful functions. Giandomenico Majone explains:

> Public discussion mobilizes the knowledge, experience, and interest of many people. . . . Each participant is encouraged to adjust his view of reality, and even to change his values, as a result of the process of reciprocal persuasion. In this way, discussion can produce results that are beyond the capabilities of authoritarian or technocratic methods of policy-making.[4]

Opposition to change may be inevitable, but it need not prevail. Advocates of reforms can marshal supporters by publicizing the severity of the problem, explaining how their reform will solve the problem, countering the objections, and discrediting the opposition by revealing its hidden self-interests.

Power is always brought to bear in the advocacy of a reform and in the opposition to it. Power can emanate from personality—charm, intelligence, and skill as a public speaker. It can arise from property—land, business ownership, and other wealth. It can also be based on organization—political parties, interest groups, and bureaucracies.[5] Often all three forms of power are used in promoting and resisting reforms. While the wealthy have more property, the middle class and poor have more votes.

When deciding whether to adopt a reform proposal, decision makers usually consider whether the goals and objectives are desirable (which is a value judgment), whether there is the capacity to implement the proposal, whether the proposal is likely to achieve the objectives and goals, whether the reform is likely to have undesirable side effects (partly a value judgment), and whether the costs are affordable. Officials also may consider their self interests—what will be the reactions of their important political supporters and the general electorate, what will be the implications for their range of authority, and how will the reform affect their work life. Sometimes a reform is adopted by formal policymaking procedures, and other times it slowly permeates into practice. Universal public education was adopted by formal policy, but multicultural education was diffused by scholars, community activists, professional associations, and teacher education institutions.

The chapters also describe the implementation of reforms after they have been formally adopted. Implementation is usually more difficult than the advocates and decision makers anticipate. There is likely to be foot-dragging, resistance, and even sabotage during implementation. Substantial changes in institutions and operating practices exacerbate difficulties. Weak leadership and management, inadequate resources, and a lack of incentives for compliance will compromise implementation. If the preliminary impacts are less than expected, or there are noticeable negative side effects, implementation may stall.

Each chapter analyzes the success of the reform effort. There are several possible criteria by which the success of an education reform effort could be judged, including: (1) whether the reform has been adopted widely throughout the country, (2) whether it has been implemented largely as intended, (3) whether the implemented reform has long been maintained, (4) whether the reform has achieved its short-term objectives, (5) whether it has achieved its long-run goals, (6) what types of positive and negative side effects have resulted, and (7) whether the value of the net benefits (benefits minus disadvantages) exceeds the cost of the reform. All but the latter will be assessed in the following chapters. Short-term objectives are usually intended impacts on students that should occur while they are still in school. The goals are longer-term ends that are desired by the reformers. For instance, the objectives of compensatory education are personal and social development and basic academic skill acquisition, but the goals are to prepare disadvantaged kids to benefit fully from their subsequent education and the opportunities of adult life.

Most reforms are subject to informal evaluations, and at times, formal ones. Evaluations can focus on any of the criteria of success enumerated above.[6] Assessing the success of a reform can be difficult, time consuming, and expensive. Only one reform discussed in this book has been subject to comprehensive national evaluations. Several have been subject to smaller-scale evaluations, and a few have gone largely unevaluated. Advocates hope the evaluations show success, and will use that result to maintain support for the reform and to expand it to other schools, districts, and states. Opponents hope the evaluations show failure, and use evidence of that to revisit the policy with a hope of scaling it back, modifying it, or terminating it.

Even if a reform succeeds, it is not clear that the reform was the only feasible response to the targeted problem. The counterfactual question, what other reform responses might have been undertaken and why did one prevail, can provide insight to a given reform effort and its future.

Each of the seven reforms examined in this book has been widely implemented and retained—in some cases retained for more than a century, but that does not assure that they will endure perpetually. One of the reforms (secularization of education) is strongly opposed by a portion of the population, two other reforms have never escaped controversy (progressive education and multi-cultural education), one is under mounting attack (universal public education), and the others have regularly been subject to debates about how to best implement them. The future of each reform will be assessed.

Concluding Chapters

Some have argued that education has become a relic of the past as America has otherwise rapidly modernized. We doubt anyone will believe that after reading this book. The reforms examined in the book clearly indicate, contrary to some popular opinion, that major education reform can be achieved in the United States, can partially achieve the targeted objectives, and can long endure.

The book concludes with two chapters of analysis and synthesis. Chapter 9 presents ten lessons about reform success that are inferred from the examined reforms and from other scholarly literature. What contributions to success were common in these reforms? What hurdles did reformers often encounter and what strategies were most commonly used to overcome them? These lessons can be used to assess the prospects of an incipient reform and also to guide formulation and implementation of a reform so to increase its chances of success.

In Chapter 10, the inferred lessons are used to assess the prospects of three high-profile education reform efforts currently under way— comprehensive school reform, test-based accountability, and school choice. Are they likely to be widely implemented, long retained, effective in achieving their objectives and goals, and without serious adverse side effects?

The authors strive to help readers understand the complexity of school reform efforts, the sustained effort that is required, the slippery and bumpy slope that must be traveled, the confluence of factors that affect the outcome, and the progress that American education has achieved because of these efforts—even though serious shortcomings and problems remain. Historiographers Jacques Barzun and Henry Graff assert, "History moves minds by what it inspires."[7] The authors of this book are writing about the past but looking toward the future.

For those who wish to explore further the history of American education reform, a website with guidance and resource materials has been developed at AmericanEdReform.info It includes an annotated bibliography of key print and web sources and a comprehensive conceptual framework of factors that can affect education reforms.

---

[1] Bernard Bailyn, *On the Teaching and Writing of History* (Hanover, NH: University Press of New England, 1994), 12.

[2] Calculated from U.S. Department of Education, National Center for Education Statistics, *120 Years of American Education: A Statistical Portrait* (Washington DC: author, 1993), 36-37.

[3] Calculated from U.S. Department of Education, National Center for Education Statistics, *Digest of Education Statistics: 2001* (Washington DC: Government Printing Office, 2002), 178.

[4] Giandomenico Majone, *Evidence, Argument, & Persuasion in the Policy Process* (New Haven, CT: Yale University Press, 1989), 2.

[5] John Kenneth Galbraith, *The Anatomy of Power* (Boston, MA: Houghton Mifflin, 1983).

[6] Carol H. Weiss, *Evaluation*, 2nd ed. (Upper Saddle River, NJ: Prentice Hall, 1998), 12.

[7] Jacques Barzun, & Henry F. Graff, *The Modern Researcher*, 5th ed. (Fort Worth, TX: Harcourt Brace Jovanowich Collge Publishers, 1992), 38.

2

Universal Public Schooling

Nina de las Alas and Gregg B. Jackson

As the thirteen colonies were at war for their independence, Thomas Jefferson introduced a bill in the Virginia House of Burgesses for the creation of a statewide system of public education. Much to his consternation, the bill was soundly rejected. A half-century would elapse before other leaders would succeed in establishing such systems.

What came to prevail as universal public schooling involved three basic components. First, the schooling is open to all, regardless of religion, financial means, gender, or race; and the school is attended by a wide spectrum of the children in a given community. Second, the schools are controlled by the government and supported with public funds—primarily by local property taxes and state income or sales taxes. Third, core knowledge, skills, and values are conveyed in all the schools within a given district or state, for the benefit of the child, the community, and society.

INITIAL CONDITIONS

On the eve of the American Revolution, every colony had elementary and secondary schools. Access, however, depended on race, geographic location, the financial means of one's family, and whether a "charity school" was within the reach of the poor. The school year was often three to five months. Attendance was erratic. Few children went on from elementary to secondary schools, and most of those did not remain long. The nature of schooling varied by region, depending on the economy, culture, and religion. The New England colonies had the most extensive provision of public education and the southern colonies had the least.

Established by Pilgrims in 1620, the Massachusetts colony had a strong religious foundation for education. The Pilgrims were adherents of Calvinism and had come to America to escape religious discrimination and persecution. To protect their religious beliefs and create moral societies, they established town theocracies that melded religion, government and education. The colonists considered education to be a private family matter but soon recognized a need for public intervention. In 1642, in response to "the great neglect of many persons and masters in training up their children in learning and labor," the Massachusetts General Court passed a law requiring town selectmen to "take account from time to time of all parents and masters of their children ... especially of their ability to read and understand the principles of religion and the capital laws of this country."[1] Compliance with the statute was erratic. Four years later the colony passed the first public education law, The Old Deluder of Satan Act of 1647, which mandated that every town of fifty households must provide instruction in reading and writing, being that "one chief project of the old deluder Satan [is] to keep men from the knowledge of the Scriptures."[2] The law also provided that all towns of a hundred households must provide instruction in Latin grammar to prepare youth for university study. There were, however, no provisions mandating that children be sent to school.

From the mid 1700s through the early 1800s, New England students attended several types of elementary schools. Young boys of wealth were often tutored. Students of modest means could attend locally controlled public "common schools" that required a moderate fee or could attend "dame schools" run by women who provided basic instruction in their homes for a small fee. A portion of impoverished children attended free "charity schools" established by churches and philanthropic organizations.[3] These organizations also created "Sunday schools" to provide basic academic instruction for impoverished children who worked during the week. It was common for philanthropic schools, private schools, and even church schools to receive subsidies from public sources. That could be in the form of land for the school, buildings, and even contributions to operating costs.

In elementary schools, the curriculum focused on the four R's—then defined as reading, writing (penmanship), arithmetic, and religion. Instruction emphasized memorizing texts, learning prayers, and reading the Bible.

Boys of wealth often continued their education at Latin grammar boarding schools, where they learned Latin and Greek in preparation for college admission. Middle class boys and girls might continue their education at academies, which combined study of the classics with practical subjects such English grammar, algebra, geometry, bookkeeping, surveying, homemaking, and teaching. Children of impoverished families rarely continued their formal education beyond the elementary level, but they might be apprenticed to learn a trade.

During the late colonial period, religious and charitable groups, especially the Quakers, created a few schools for African American children. Several African American leaders also created small pay schools, often within their homes. Boston allowed African Americans to attend the city's public schools, but poverty and a hostile reception by white children dissuaded most.[4] Otherwise, there were few educational opportunities for African Americans in the north.

The cultural roots of education in Virginia differed from those of Massachusetts. Virginia was settled by the sons of the British gentry, hoping to make a fortune from large estates deeded by the British Crown. Fertile lands worked by indentured servants and slaves yielded bountiful harvests of cotton and tobacco for export to Britain. The Anglican Church, the official church of England and of Virginia, was less emphatic about the need to read Scripture than was Calvinism and thus provided less incentive for education. In addition, the southern populations were more dispersed than those in New England, making access to schools more difficult.

In 1618 the charter of the founding Virginia Company made provision for schools and set aside funds for education. Seven years later, when the Company was dissolved, the colony fell under the direct jurisdiction of England, which passed laws requiring all children to have religious instruction but provided little funding for implementing the laws.

Wealthy plantation owners believed one was "better never born than ill-bred."[5] They hired tutors to educate their children and sometimes the children of the plantation manager. The tutors were Anglican ministers, educated indentured Scots, or former schoolmasters. Tutors taught Greek and Roman classics, French, history, philosophy, political thought, music and painting, architecture, medicine, and natural sciences. The focus was on preparing the sons of the elite for the private secondary schools, the universities of England, and the practical business of running an estate.[6] Those not sent to England for their secondary education attended Latin grammar schools or academies in Virginia. Daughters were taught the fine arts befitting ladies of that day.

White students with lesser means might find dame schools, as in New England, or "old field schools" or "pauper schools." Old field schools were built on unproductive fields. Often headed by Anglican ministers, they charged fees but usually had provisions to admit impoverished students at no charge. Pauper schools for orphans and the poor were established by some churches and philanthropic institutions. They taught religion, reading and arithmetic, and sometimes history and agriculture.

Slave children were excluded from southern schools in the 1700s. Several southern colonies, including North Carolina and Georgia, had laws making it a crime to teach slaves to read. It is estimated that about five percent of slave children did learn to read, some taught by slave owners or their children and others by literate adult slaves.

The middle colonies of New York, New Jersey, Delaware, Pennsylvania, and Maryland had far more diverse populations, in terms of national origin, religion, and language, than did the New England or southern colonies. Not surprisingly, they adopted a broad range of schooling arrangements, including most of those found in New England and the South.

CHANGING CONTEXTS THAT PUSHED UNIVERSAL EDUCATION

During the 1800s, dramatic changes in American society pushed the expansion of educational opportunity. The very establishment of a democratic nation spurred reform for universal public schools, as did massive immigration, rapid industrialization, and the growing role of local and state governments.

Establishment of a Democratic Nation

Europeans colonists had occupied the eastern seaboard of North America for a century and a half before declaring independence from England. The kindling for the revolution was the European Enlightenment with its ideas about the natural rights of man, the ability of human reason to guide social affairs, and democratic governance. The sparks that ignited the revolution were Britain's imposition of new taxes on the colonies, restrictions on American trade, prohibition of town meetings without the permission of the British governor, and the granting of land to Quebec that the New England colonies considered their frontier.

The new country was conceived by the Declaration of Independence and the Constitution of the United States. It was a marriage of opposites. The Declaration of 1776 was an optimistic and idealistic proclamation of human rights and individual freedom:

> We hold these rights to be self-evident, that all men are created equal, that they are endowed by their Creator with certain unalienable rights, that among these are life, liberty, and the pursuit of happiness....That whenever any form of government becomes destructive of these ends, it is the right of the people to alter or to abolish it, and to institute new government.

The Constitution of 1788, on the other hand, was a cautious and pragmatic plan of democratic governance that separated power among three branches, so that each might counter abuses of the other. This duality in the founding of the country, between optimism and caution, idealism and pragmatism, and individual freedom and government power, is an enduring legacy that has influenced education reform.

The United States was not initially as bold an experiment in democracy as the rhetoric of the day suggested. The Constitution was silent about who could vote. All the initial states imposed some restrictions on white male voting, most requiring a "freehold" of land valued at $300-500 (equal to three or four years of a craftsman's earnings). Former slaves and other males of color did not secure the vote until 1870, and even after that they were often illegally prevented from voting. Women would not acquire the vote until one and a half centuries after the founding of the country. Despite these restrictions, the new country had begun with wider suffrage than any other. As the frontier states entered the union, their state constitutions were free of restrictions on voting by white males, and gradually most of the original states adopted similar provisions.

From the beginning, the founding fathers worried about whether the expanded electorate would exercise the vote wisely. Education was widely perceived as important for responsible civic participation and for the general development of the country. George Washington's first message to Congress declared, "Knowledge is in every country the surest basis of public happiness."[7] Noah Webster, however, observed in 1790, "The constitutions are republican, and the laws of education are monarchial. The former extend the civil rights to every honest and industrious man; the latter deprive a large portion of the citizens of a most valuable privilege."[8]

The events of the French revolution provided a vivid reminder that the common man could be a threat.[9] While the American revolution had been carried out by a coalition of elites, middle class and working class colonists,[10] one wave of French revolution was led by the working class and peasants, who targeted not only the monarchy but unleashed a "reign of terror" on all citizens of property, arresting 300,000 people and executing an estimated 17,000-40,000. Many in the middle and upper classes of the new United States feared that there could be a similar revolution against them if the common man did not have a stake in the government.

Without widespread education, there was a disquieting prospect that democracy would bring ignorance and impulse to the voting booths. As James Madison warned, "A popular government without popular information or the means of acquiring it is but a prologue to a farce or tragedy, or perhaps to both."[11]

Despite those concerns, the United State had no official means of providing that education. Neither the Constitution nor the Bill of Rights made any mention of education, leaving the matter to states and local jurisdictions. By 1800, only seven of the fifteen state constitutions mentioned education. While several of the statements were very general, others, such as those of Vermont, Massachusetts, Pennsylvania, and Georgia called for a school to be established in each town or county.[12] By the early 1830s most northeastern states were operating or subsidizing elementary schools for the poor.

Massive Immigration

The faces of the nation changed dramatically in the nineteenth century. During the 1820s, an average of 13,000 European immigrants entered the United States each year. During the 1830s, about 50,000 arrived each year. Twenty years later, the numbers of new arrivals more than quadrupled. By the 1880s, annual immigration averaged 500,000.[13] In 1845, thirty-five percent of New York City's population was foreign-born, and a decade later it would be about 50 percent. Other eastern cities experienced similar trends. Irish immigrants predominated through the first half of the 19th century, and Germans predominated during the latter half.[14] That was unlike the early settlement of the colonies, which had been primarily from England.

The Irish crowded into northeastern cities, where they were widely disdained for their accent, culture, religion and poverty. Irish gregariousness offended Anglo-Saxon reserve. The Catholic Church in which the Irish worshiped was the one against which Protestants had rebelled a few centuries earlier. Many of the Irish immigrants were poor, and the few who arrived with modest savings were sometimes fleeced by agents, employers, and rooming house proprietors.[15] Native-born workers resented the immigrants because they were willing to work for lower wages, but at various times the immigrants' rates of arrival exceeded the demand for labor and left them unemployed. The Irish were also widely perceived to be prone to intoxication, immorality, and crime.

The Germans brought a different language and culture. Most immigrants from southern Germany were Catholic and most from the north were Lutheran. Many German immigrants located in the countryside as farmers and tradesmen. They were often perceived to prosper quickly, which drew envy and resentment. Some were also adamant about preserving their language and passing it on to their children.

There was a widespread perception that the immigrants needed to be Americanized—acculturated in the values, habits, and mannerisms of the dominant Anglo-Americans. Universal schooling was seen as a means for that end. It was also to provide children of the poor with moral training, with the hope of raising them to be "industrious, sober, punctual, God-fearing citizens."[16] Michael Katz, a historian, notes that American values in the 19th century made it far more acceptable to redress poverty by trying to improve the character of the poor than by directly providing for their material needs.[17]

Rapid Mechanization and Industrialization

Mechanization and industrialization in the nineteenth century changed North America as much as immigration. In the mid-1700s, there were small factories with water-powered machinery for making various staples of life. By the mid-1800s, large textile mills arose in the northeast, processing cotton grown in the south. The introduction of steam engines to factories boosted productivity further. Thirty thousand miles of railroad track crisscrossed the nation, greatly facilitating the transportation of raw materials and finished goods. Steel prices dropped by 80 percent over just fifteen years. Oil began being pumped from the ground. Both steel and oil were essential for internal combustion engines, trucks, and motorized farm equipment.

Industrialization supported universal education in several ways. It generated financial support. It sparked urbanization that both facilitated physical access to schools and exacerbated social ills. It provided a model for organizing and managing large systems of schools. Equally important, it created a demand for new skills.

Universal public schooling is expensive. There are the direct costs of the buildings, staff, and supplies that have to be paid with public funds. There are also the "opportunity costs" incurred when children attending school are not helping with the work of family enterprises or earning wages from employment. Early mechanization and industrialization dramatically increased productivity, wealth, and wages. The value added from manufacturing rose ten-fold over the forty years between 1839 and 1879.[18] Average daily wages in the northeastern part of the country increased 67 percent over the decade of the 1860s, even though the average workday declined from 11 hours to 10.5 hours.[19] The introduction of cast-iron plows, reapers, and combines boosted farm productivity about 40 percent between 1800 and 1840.[20] The resulting new wealth could be taxed to support schools. The higher farm earnings and worker wages also made families less dependent on their children's labor for survival. Birth rates dropped 20 percent between 1820 and 1860, leaving families with fewer children to support through years of formal education.[21] The productivity improvements on farms and in manufacturing allowed fewer people to produce more material output, and that freed up a portion of the workforce to engage in service occupations such as teaching.

The urbanization associated with industrialization also helped spur universal public education. Existing cities grew and new ones sprouted. In 1780 there were only 10 cities with more than 8,000 people; by 1860 there were 282. Over the same period, the percentage of population living in cities rose from 2.7 percent to 16.1 percent.[22]

The high population densities of urban areas facilitated universal schooling. The close proximity of many people made it easier to plan and administer schools. There was a wider supply of potential teachers. Textbooks and building maintenance were easier to arrange. Finally, urbanization made it easier for students to reach the schools, substituting walks of a few blocks for those of several miles.

Urbanization made people more inter-dependent, exacerbating social ills and making them more visible. Human waste and garbage that had been dumped at a distance from farmhouses created a vile stench in the early cities. Adolescent males, who in rural life would be working along side their fathers or uncles, could no longer do that. As a result, they were denied their normal means of learning an occupation and adult roles. Some went to school, some took mindless jobs in factories, and others roamed the streets and gravitated to delinquency. Crime was exacerbated by the close proximity of many people without family ties. The pathologies of mental illness, alcoholism, and violence, which were largely hidden by widely dispersed farm life, became visible to all in the cities.[23] These conditions spurred social reformers to improve urban life. They thought education could save society from delinquency and subsequent adult crime by re-socializing lower class youth.[24]

Industrialization raised the demand for education in several ways. It created many new skilled occupations—machinists, engineers, accountants, salesmen, and managers—to which young people could aspire and for which they needed formal education. Whereas farmers and craftspeople had often provided occupational preparation as their children worked along their side, a factory worker could not do that. Formal education, therefore, became all the more important for children's futures. Finally, the inventors, engineers, and entrepreneurs who forged an industrial America were self-made men, and that suggested that social mobility was achievable if one acquired the right skills and worked hard.[25]

New industry spawned new forms of management. Successful factory owners often branched out, establishing other factories in different parts of the country. Several also integrated their businesses vertically, acquiring suppliers of their raw materials and retail outlets that sold their products. To manage these far-flung enterprises, hierarchical bureaucratic structures with a chain of command were created. The most able and experienced managers were to serve at the top, with their influence extending through successive levels of the bureaucracy. This model of management would be adopted for the universal public school systems in the 1800s as growing cities required multiple schools and hundreds of teachers for thousands of students.

By the late 1800s, increasing numbers of industrial workers had joined labor unions and workingmen's political parties in an effort to improve their wages and work conditions. These organizations generally supported the creation and expansion of universal public education, partly to increase the economic and political opportunities of their children and partly to discourage child labor, which lowered the wages of adult workers.[26]

Expanding Government Action

During the 1800s, federal, state, and local governments gradually assumed more responsibilities in many spheres of American life. That provided precedents for initiatives in public education.

By the mid-1800s, booming cities were symbols of American progress but also housed wretched poverty, serious health hazards, and rampant crime. Books such as *How the Other Half Lives, The Battle of the Slum, and The Shame of the Cities* publicized these urban ills and demanded responses. Municipal governments gradually assumed responsibility for social services, including the supply of water, sanitation services, and fire and police protection.[27] Several also established public health departments.

Throughout the 1800s, one state after another had created asylums for the insane and reformatories for delinquent youth. That became a precedent for state establishment of universal public education systems.[28]

The Northwest Ordinance of 1787, which was aimed at spurring settlement of mid-western lands, had provided land grants for the establishment of educational institutions. The federal government had little other involvement in education until almost a century later, when the First Morrill Act of 1862 provided additional land grants for the establishment and maintenance of agricultural and mechanical colleges. Then, in 1867, the Department of Education Act authorized what now would be called a small bureau of education to:

> ... collect such statistics and facts as shall show the condition and progress of education in the several States and Territories, and of diffusing such information respecting the organization and management of schools and school systems, and the methods of teaching as shall aid the people of the United States in the establishment and maintenance of efficient school systems.[29]

THE CAMPAIGN FOR UNIVERSAL PUBLIC EDUCATION

Ellwood Cubberley, the first serious historian of American education, noted that the campaign for universal public education was contentious:

> Excepting the battle for the abolition of slavery, perhaps no question has ever been before the American people for settlement which caused so much feeling or aroused such bitter antagonisms. Old friends and business associates parted company over the question, lodges were forced to taboo the subject to avoid disruption, ministers and their

congregations often quarreled over the question of free schools, and politicians avoided the issue.[30]

Proponents of universal public education systems claimed that the patchwork quilt of church, private, and charity schools had proven inadequate. They asserted that education was a natural right of all children. They argued that public education systems would diffuse knowledge widely for the benefit of the state and country, prepare all white males for the wise exercise of their vote, minimize status distinctions in society, "Americanize" immigrants, morally uplift the poor, and alleviate the social ills of poverty.

Opponents protested that the current arrangements provided adequate education for those who needed it. They claimed that universal public education systems would bankrupt existing private and religious schools, undermine local control, interfere with rights of parents to raise their children as they saw fit, provide more education than many children could absorb, and replace native language instruction with English instruction.[31] They added that public schools would be too expensive to sustain and would impose an unjust tax on the industrious and childless to benefit the indolent and those with children. It was argued that the state's forcible taking of one man's property, through taxes, to educate another man's children was no different than taking one man's plow to work another man's field.

Two of the highest profile proponents of universal public education were Thomas Jefferson and Horace Mann. Jefferson led a campaign within his home state of Virginia in the late 1700s and early 1800s. Mann began soon thereafter in Massachusetts, but he also advised others throughout the country and later became known as the "father" of American public education.

Jefferson: The First Initiative
For A Statewide System

The historian Bernard Bailyn describes Thomas Jefferson as dignified and humorless; a man who simplistically perceived only evil in the European monarchies and only good in the Enlightenment; but also a superb master of public affairs, who "was as unconventional, as imaginative, resourceful, and tough as the best ... and more adroit than most...."[32] Jefferson launched the first campaign for a state system of universal public education. Afraid that the new nation would fall prey to the same concentration of wealth and power that had led to tyranny in Britain after its initial democratization efforts, he noted:

> Every government degenerates when trusted to the rulers of the people alone. The people themselves therefore are its only safe depositories.

And to render even them safe, their minds must be improved to a certain degree.... An amendment of our [Virginia] constitution must here come in aid of the public education.[33]

Jefferson desired a school system that would allow everyone the basic education necessary to participate effectively in the new democracy. He expected elementary education to teach reading and writing, improve mental faculties and moral discipline, convey the rights and responsibilities of citizens, and prepare young people to engage judiciously in the democratic processes of the new nation.[34] Believing that superior intelligence was not limited to the affluent but was distributed through all classes of white men, Jefferson sought to create an educational system that would assure those of outstanding intelligence could achieve the highest levels of education, regardless of their financial means, thus allowing their talents to contribute fully to the nation's development.[35]

In 1778, while the Revolutionary War raged, Jefferson introduced legislation in the Virginia House of Burgesses entitled "Bill for the More General Diffusion of Knowledge." It called for three years of free elementary education for all white children, both male and female, regardless of wealth or status. Counties would be divided into units, each of which would establish a school. The children would study reading, writing and arithmetic, and they would become familiar with the history of Greece, Rome, England and America.

Boys of families that were so inclined and financially able would continue on to one of 20 "Latin grammar" schools to be established throughout Virginia. Here, students would study Greek and Latin, English grammar, geography, and advanced arithmetic for up to six years, according to their abilities and desires. In addition, annually, the most promising boy of poor parents from each county would continue from elementary into grammar school. All of his expenses would be paid out of public funds. At the end of one year of grammar school, following rigorous examinations, one-third of the *public* scholars who showed the "least promising genius and disposition" would be discontinued. After the second year of attendance, all but the most able public scholar in each grammar school would be discontinued, and the remaining boy would continue his studies at public expense for the full six years. Of those 20 scholars completing the six years of grammar school, the superior half would be selected to attend William and Mary College at public expense.[36]

Jefferson realized that his ambitious proposal would face resistance, but he was adept at forging compromises and he was not accustomed to losing. In 1779 the bill was introduced in the Virginia House of Burgesses but was not acted upon. Two years later, it was reintroduced, and again not acted upon. After modifications it was introduced five years later and won a vote in the House but died in the Senate. When introduced in the House the following year, it was again not enacted. In 1796, eighteen years after the initial introduction, an eviscerated version of the bill, with only provisions for elementary education, passed both chambers, but provisions for local discretion assured it would not be implemented.[37] In 1817 Jefferson tried again with "A Bill for Establishing A System of Public Education," which also failed to win passage.

Jefferson's trail-blazing effort failed for several reasons. The vote in Virginia was still limited mostly to plantation owners. The heavy Irish immigration, which helped prompt the creation of public school systems, did not begin until the early 1800s and went mostly to the northeastern cities, not to Virginia. The south lagged considerably behind the north in industrialization and urbanization. The Commonwealth of Virginia was inclined to very limited government action and was still straining from the debt incurred during War of Independence. Any proposal for new taxes provoked opposition. Furthermore, Jefferson was abroad as the U.S. ambassador to France for most of the time his bills were introduced in the legislature, and thus could not personally engage in the debate about them. Jefferson attributed the defeat of his 1779 bill to the tax burdens it would have imposed, but he attributed the defeat of the final bill in 1817 to "ignorance, malice, egoism, fanaticism, [and] religious, political and local perversities."[38]

In addition, some who were supportive of public education were opposed to the provision in Jefferson's bill that would offer publicly-paid schooling at successively higher levels only to the best students. As one scholar explained, "the American people ... were inherently hostile to any notion of educating one group of children at public expense for a longer period of time than all the others."[39] Be that as it may, Jefferson's proposal would have assured that a small number of boys of the common folk would rise to the highest levels of education. No state in the Union would achieve that for another 100 years.

Jefferson initiated three other education reform efforts. He tried to modernize the curriculum of William and Mary College, which had been established by a royal charter to assure preparation of Anglican clergymen. He urged that it add courses in science and western European languages but failed in that effort.[40] He also introduced a bill to create a public library and art gallery in Virginia, and that too failed. Only in his old age, after serving two terms as the third President of the United States, did Jefferson finally achieve a success in education reform. That was the establishment of the University of Virginia, the first public university in the eastern United States. The effort consumed his attention and he micro-managed every detail, designing the buildings, specifying the modern curriculum, and hiring the professors.[41]

Horace Mann: Impassioned Leadership

In the early 1800s Horace Mann had observed the expansion of the franchise, heavy Irish immigration into Boston, the first booms of the industrial revolution, and an expanding government role. When he moved to Boston, he witnessed rioting and a gang tried to set fire to his office. Massachusetts already had state laws mandating the local provision of public schooling, but local jurisdictions often ignored the laws.

Mann held a dualistic conception of human nature. He wrote, "Human nature occupies the vast intermediate space between the angels and the demon. It may ascend to the one; it may fall to the other."[42] Having rejected the tenets of Calvinism, he looked to law and then to education for the salvation of society. He believed that "The mobs, the riots, the burning, the lynchings, perpetrated by the men of present day, are perpetrated, because of their vicious or defective education when children."[43] He thought that the state could and should take an active role in improving the lives of all people, and he felt such efforts would be best directed at children, noting, "Men are cast iron; but children are wax. Strength expended upon the latter may be effectual, which would make no impression upon the former."[44] Mann's vision of public schools was not just to rescue the poor from mean circumstances. He thought that education could help men and women discern the ethical demands of natural law, asking, "Are they so educated that, when they grow up, they will make better philanthropists and Christians, or only grander savages?"[45]

Mann served in the state senate. When a proposal was introduced to create a state board of education to help improve education, Mann enthusiastically supported it. The bill failed but was introduced again in 1837 and passed. The Board's powers were to be limited to gathering and disseminating information about education throughout the state. It would have only one staff member, an executive secretary to be appointed by the governor.

Mann was surprised when Governor Everett asked him to lead the new Board. He accepted the post, even though it meant a loss of status and prestige. He was also racked by doubts about his ability to perform the responsibilities. Mann's moral earnestness was sometimes accompanied by righteousness that he knew he could alienate people. He counseled to himself with the following admonishment,

> I must not irritate. I must not humble, I must not degrade any one in his own eyes.... I must be a fluid sort of man, adapting myself to tastes, opinions, habits, manners so far as this can be done without hypocrisy or insincerity, or a compromise of principle.[46]

Mann threw himself into a task that would require all his faculties. Immediately he toured throughout Massachusetts, traveling 500 miles on horseback to observe the schools, introduce the people to the role of the new state board, and impress upon them the importance of education. In the Massachusetts Senate, Mann had gained fame for his use of facts and statistics in persuasive oration. As head of the Board, he used that approach in his speeches and official reports to turn a spotlight on the shortcomings of the current system and provoke public outcry.

In long annual reports, Mann blamed three factors for the many shortcomings in the state's public education: decentralization, meager financial support for the schools, and the inherent contempt that common schools received from the upper class.[47] He reported that school committees rarely visited their schools (only one-sixth of the committees had done so in 1837), had provided spartan facilities and not maintained them, and rarely examined teachers for their knowledge of the subjects to be taught.[48] He indicated that almost half of all students were absent on a given day and one out of ten schools experienced student rebellions that led to their closing before the end of the term.[49] He noted that 17 percent of students in school attended private schools, suggesting substantial dissatisfaction with the public schools. Mann traced the poor quality of instruction in common schools to the low wages and low social standing of teachers, both of which he claimed repelled talented people.[50]

These indictments brought him a torrent of criticism. He was variously accused of being a utopian dreamer, a base materialist, a public menace, and an atheist.[51] Mann responded to his critics with righteous conviction and consummate rhetoric. His proposals were supported by liberal public officials, some ministers, many educators, most workingmen's associations, and a small portion of industrialists, landowners, and rich merchants. His opponents differed so much in their opinions and interests that they could not form a cohesive coalition to defend the existing system or to offer an alternative to Mann's proposals.

Mann proposed several bills that the legislature quickly voted into law. One statute required the extension of the school term to a full six months, longer than had been the case in many districts. A second gave the state board power to draw up a list of approved books to be included in each school library. Child labor in factories was limited. Local school committees were required to keep better records and submit an annual report to the state board. Equally important, three state-controlled "normal schools" were established to prepare teachers. In each case Mann was careful to recommend funding to support these measures. He urged a modest state-paid stipend to compensate local school committee members for the reporting burdens. He had the state appropriate funds to support local school libraries. He also secured a substantial private donation for the establishment of "normal schools" to prepare teachers and then asked the legislature to match it.[52] Local school committees were encouraged to raise more funds by a state offer to match the increase.[53]

Mann's legislation continued to draw criticism as he undertook implementation and enforcement. The opposition came from many directions. Local school committees felt that their powers were being usurped by the state Board of Education. Several even claimed that this was the first step toward Prussian centralization or socialism. Other opponents feared the education would interfere with farm work and child employment, family discipline, or religion.[54] There was widespread concern about the increased taxes that would have to be paid. Several opponents claimed that the new taxes would infringe on the rights of those choosing to use private schools. Some argued that expanding public schools would create unfair competition against private schools. Still others worried that children would not appreciate a free education and that it would make them grow up lazy and idle.[55]

In 1840, three years into Mann's tenure as secretary of the state Board, the Democratic party wrested control of the state legislature from the Whigs. Mann had been a Whig. The Whigs had represented affluent Americans and generally favored state and federal intervention to build the country, whereas the Democrats of that era represented the common man and advocated individual liberties and local populism. The victorious Democrats immediately introduced a bill to eliminate the state Board of Education, claiming it was unjustly regulating local education. The bill failed by a substantial margin, demonstrating widespread support for Mann's public education system.[56]

That did not end the criticism. For instance, in 1844, Boston schoolmasters criticized Mann for his efforts to reform the practice of teaching. They had been trained in the classics and theology, and they opposed efforts to replace that with the secular and scientific learning of the industrial age. They also denounced his efforts to remove corporal punishment as a means of disciplining students and scoffed at his proposed alternative—to use love to win affection of the students—as impractical and soft.[57]

Mann's views did not always prevail, but he pushed forward wherever he could. During his 12 years as state superintendent, Mann made considerable progress in expanding and enhancing the quality of public education in Massachusetts. Enrollments increased by about 36 percent.[58] State appropriations for education were doubled. Two million dollars, a huge sum in those days, was allocated for building new schools. Teachers' salaries were increased by 50 percent. A month was added to the school year. Textbooks were re-written. The use of harsh corporal punishment was reduced. Supervision of teaching was improved. School libraries were enlarged. In addition, three state normal schools were established to prepare better teachers.[59]

Mann noted that all these changes were having little effect in the poorer parts of the state, which led him to support proposals for compulsory education. In 1852 the legislature passed a law requiring students between the age of 8 and 14 to attend school for at least 12 weeks a year—if the local public school remained open that long. There were exemptions if the parents were poor (and thus needed the child's labor), the child was ill, or the child was being educated outside of schools. This was the first such law in the nation and the crowning accomplishment of Horace Mann, even though the law was weak and compliance would come later.[60]

Twelve years of 15-hour days and relentless hammering by his foes took their toll on Mann's health. He stepped down from the Board in 1849. After a respite, he was elected to the U.S. House of Representatives, where he advocated for the abolishment of slavery, national support for railways, and a host of other means he thought would better the country. At a college commencement address, Mann admonished the new graduates, "be ashamed to die until you have won some victory for humanity."[61]

Mann's success was partly based on his ability to see education with a systemic perspective. To achieve his goals, he perceived that much more was needed than the establishment of universal public schooling. Indeed his work anticipated three other reform efforts described in later chapters of this book: the secularization of education, progressive education, and the professionalization of teaching. He was mindful that most of his reforms would add to the costs of education, and he sought to use state funding as an incentive for local compliance. He also used research to inform legislation, was adroit at working with legislators, and understood legislation would be for naught if he did not win the hearts and minds of the local people responsible for implementing it.

Expansion of Universal Education

Mann's influence spread far beyond Massachusetts. He founded *The Common School Journal* to reach teachers, school board members, and the public. He advised leaders in several states and traveled on speaking tours. He inspired a network of reform leaders, several of whom organized associations like the American Institute of Instruction and the American Lyceum, which drew more supporters for the effort. Mann's counterparts found sympathetic ears with additional publications like the *American Journal of Education* and the *Common School Advocate*. As "friends of education," they spread ideas for public education.[62]

The Massachusetts system of universal public education was largely replicated, with some lags, variations, and backsliding, throughout the northeastern states, then in the mid-west and finally in the far west and south.⁶³ In the northeastern states, an existing patchwork of schools was gradually replaced and expanded with the state and local tax-supported system, but in the far west public school systems were built from the ground up.

The reformers encountered not only enthusiasm but also apathy, opposition, and retrenchment. Some western cities' initial reaction was populist disdain for the eastern elites' initiatives, but other western cities saw public education systems as a magnet to draw settlers, as a means of socio-economic development, and as a status symbol. In the mid-1800s southerners sometimes associated universal public schooling, even only for whites, as an undesirable "northern" institution. As the historian Lawrence Cremin summarizes:

> The fight for free schools was a bitter one, and for 25 years the outcome was uncertain. Local elections were fought, won, and lost on the school issue. The tide of educational reform flowed in one state, only to ebb in another. Legislation passed one year was sometimes repealed the next. State laws requiring public schools were ignored by the local communities that were supposed to build them. Time and again the partisans of popular education encountered the bitter disappointments.... Yet by 1860 a design had begun to appear, and it bore upon it the marks of Mann's ideal.⁶⁴

The leaders of the universal public school reform effort were from the upper-middle class and were able to connect with the people of power and influence.⁶⁵ They drew direct support from social elites with humanitarian sympathies as well as those worried about the unruly masses. The reformers appealed to diverse audiences, arguing that public schools could serve the interests of many different groups. For the poor and working class, reformers offered a pathway for upward mobility. For property owners, they promised social stability. For businessmen, they would provide a literate and disciplined workforce. For the cultured, they promised to scrub the baseness off the masses. And for taxpayers at all levels they proffered an investment in the economic and social development of the town, the state, and the country. Reformers also appealed to the new country's sense of nationalism. The 19th century was a time of distinguishing the United States from Britain and creating a unique identity; universal public education was a tool for that purpose.⁶⁶

By 1861, nineteen of the 34 existing states had regular state school officers. Nine others had ex-officio state school officers who headed the state education structures.⁶⁷ At this time, most state boards of education averaged just one staff person.⁶⁸ Board activities were limited to collecting and publishing data, but they had the ear of the governor and state legislature. Increasingly they also had the authority to withhold state funds from non-complying local districts. Over the following decades, their roles and resources would expand considerably.

Under each state school officer, there were city or county districts. Most urban districts acquired superintendents who supervised several elementary schools and often one high school. Those schools began to be subdivided into several classrooms, ordered into ascending grade levels, with supervision provided by a principal. Each level in the hierarchy imposed some regulation on the next level. Rural districts often operated just a single one-room elementary school well into the 20th century, with an estimated 200,000 such schools remaining in 1916.[69]

Many of the public schools initially charged modest fees, called "rate bills," although many waived them for poor parents. Parents were expected to provide the textbooks. Gradually full public funding came to support the cost of schools and textbooks were purchased by the district. By 1890, the states provided an average of about 20 percent of the funding for public education, and the rest was provided by the local jurisdictions.[70]

This structure has remained remarkably consistent since, with only a few modest changes. Through much of the 20th century, many small local districts consolidated with other districts to achieve administrative efficiencies and to provide broader curriculum options in their high schools. Starting in the 1970s, the states began to assert more control over local districts and began to pay a larger share of public education expenses, with the average state share rising to 45 percent at the end of the century. In the mid-1900s the federal government began exercising power over the states and local districts, first through federal court orders for school desegregation and then through federal grant programs that provided funding for various educational services.

Evolution of the System

While the structure of public education systems was set early, three subsequent changes over the following half-century dramatically expanded the influence of universal public education. Compulsory education laws were enacted and gradually enforced. Universal education expanded to include high schools. And finally, public education belatedly opened its doors to Native American, African American, and Mexican American students.

Compulsory Education

Universal public education systems were often in place for several decades before the passage of compulsory education laws. It was one thing to offer educational opportunity to all, and quite another to mandate schooling for every child. Two forces spurred this change. First, as we have seen, the desire for an informed and deliberative electorate, the drive to

Americanize immigrants, and the hope of countering the ills of urban poverty had pushed the adoption of universal public schooling; but there would be little chance of achieving those purposes without the participation of the children least likely to enroll—those of the poor and immigrants. Second, following the Civil War, there was increased public willingness to use coercive government powers to counter social evils in the south and later elsewhere.[71] Compulsory education laws were first applied to elementary schooling and gradually the mandated upper age was raised to force most adolescents into high schools.

These laws did not come easily. Opponents charged that some students could not benefit from education, that some parents needed their children's labor, that states should not interfere with local control of schools, that the laws would create a dangerous new precedent of state intervention in family life, and that school attendance was already on the upswing without such laws. Educators often opposed these laws for the reasons just cited and because of the overcrowding of schools, their desire to avoid coerced and rebellious students in their classrooms, and a fear that the laws might spark a backlash against the new universal public school systems.[72] By 1880, only 16 states had compulsory education laws. Another 18 adopted them by 1900, and the rest, mostly southern and southwestern states, did so during the following two decades.[73] Compliance was initially weak but was gradually achieved.[74] Laws limiting child labor were often adopted about the same time as compulsory education laws, and enforcement of the former aided compliance with the latter.

High Schools

High schools existed in Mann's time, but secondary education enrolled only a small percentage of adolescents and was provided mostly by "Latin grammar" schools and private academies. The initial proponents of public high schools included the liberal elite, some businessmen, some of the middle class, and education reformers. They argued that high schools would extend the benefits of elementary education, prepare skilled workmen for industry and provide channels for upward mobility. Opponents considered high schools a waste of money. With most jurisdictions struggling to support public elementary schools, many taxpayers were reluctant to take on new burdens. The poor and the working class were often initially disinterested, seeing college preparatory programs as irrelevant to their children's lives, but some associations of workingmen supported high schools as a means of allowing their children to share one of the privileges of the upper classes.[75] After Kalamazoo, Michigan had voted in 1827 to establish public high schools and levy additional taxes for their support, several indignant citizens sued in court to prevent the tax. The court ruled against them.[76]

High schools expanded rapidly during the first half of the 20th century. Many early public high schools focused on providing preparation for college, much as the Latin grammar schools had. Others focused on providing practical arts and occupational skills—including the preparation of teachers. In the early 1900s, "comprehensive high schools" began to be established, aiming to serve a broad spectrum of adolescents, offering three curriculums: college preparatory, general, and vocational.[77] As high schools proliferated, districts also began assigning the last two or three grades of the traditional eight-grade elementary schools to separate junior high or middle schools.

Many white girls had access to elementary education from early colonial times, although practice varied considerably during the period.[78] By 1850, the first year in which national data were collected, the percentage of girls age 5-19 enrolled in school was only six points less than for boys of the same age group.[79] Girls were not permitted to go on to the Latin grammar schools or to college, because those institutions prepared religious and civic leaders, roles denied women of that era. However, as academies became popular in the northeastern colonies, some served middle class and upper class adolescent women, providing more advanced education in the humanities, the domestic arts, and occupational skills.

Native American Students

The Naturalization Act of 1790 had denied Native Americans citizenship in the United States, and they would not regain it until the early 20th century. In 1819 the Superintendent of Indian Trade convinced Congress to pass the Civilization Fund Act to support schools for the Indian tribes adjacent to white settlements. It authorized the employment of "capable persons of good moral character, to instruct them [Native Americans] in the mode of agriculture suited to their situation; and for teaching their children in reading, writing, and arithmetic."[80] The money was used to subsidize missionary groups that established elementary schools. The plan was to teach Indian children white men's ways and Christianity.[81] The federal government had hoped that education would convince Native Americans to sell their lands to the rapidly expanding white population. When the tribes showed little inclination to do so, President Jackson asked Congress to pass the Indian Removal Act of 1830 that ordered most southeastern tribes to relocate west of the Mississippi River. When they refused to move, Jackson used the U.S. Army to herd them west on what became known as the "Trail of Tears."

Despite their uprooting and humiliation, several tribes established their own schools, often initially with the help of missionaries. The schools taught their tribal language and culture, as well as English and academic subjects. In the mid-1800s the Cherokee school system reportedly had achieved almost 100 percent literacy within the tribe—a higher rate than prevailed among white communities. The Indian schools were successful enough to send a few graduates to eastern colleges.[82]

As the white settlers moved further west during the mid-1800s and began to cross the Mississippi River, the federal government declared that the earlier assignment of western land to Indians had been "too great an extent of country, to be held in common [by the Indians]."[83] It decided to relocate the former eastern Indians and the indigenous western Indians into designated reservations, leaving the rest of the land to white settlers. This time the Indians fought fiercely but were overwhelmed by the Army forces. The federal government had promised the establishment of schools on the reservations but often instead established elementary boarding schools off the reservations, thinking them more conducive of transferring the children's allegiance to the federal government. Thus many Native Americans did have government funded elementary education starting in the late 1800s, but it was not controlled by their local communities. It was not until 1975, with President Nixon's urging, that Congress passed the Indian Self-Determination and Education Assistance Act, returning substantial control over reservation schools and community colleges to the Indian tribes. By then, however, most Indian people lived off the reservations.

African American Students

By the early 1800s several southern states had rescinded laws banning slaves from being taught to read, but African American children were excluded from schools serving white children. White evangelical groups and African American community leaders established some schools for African American children. As tensions grew between the North and South, many southern jurisdictions again adopted laws prohibiting the education of slave children.[84] In 1850 about 56 percent of whites age 5-19 were in school, but only two percent of nonwhites were enrolled.[85] Following the Civil War, the federal government's Freedmen's Bureau built several thousand schools in the south for African American children. Church groups and benevolent societies provided the teachers—10,000 by 1869, serving about 200,000 children. As a condition for readmission to the United States, southern states were required to adopt new constitutions assuring non-segregation of public schools, but most adopted vague provisions, and before the century closed, all 11 states of the Confederacy had constitutional or legislative provisions enforcing segregation in the public schools.[86]

As the northern states created universal public school systems, they sometimes excluded African American children altogether and sometimes established segregated schools for them. African American leaders were generally staunch advocates of education. A Negro national convention in 1832 resolved, "If we ever expect to see the influence of prejudice decrease and ourselves respected, it must be by the blessings of an enlightened education."[87] In Connecticut, and probably elsewhere, white townspeople often argued against providing any schooling for African Americans for fear that such opportunities would attract more African Americans to the town.[88] In 1847 the New York state legislature had appropriated special funds for villages that set up separate schools for the estimated 11,000 African American children in the state but only $396 was requested.[89] The new mid-western states often initially excluded African American children, but by the 1850s most relented, establishing segregated systems.[90] By 1860 every non-southern state had public education for African American children, although often in dilapidated facilities and with the most rudimentary curriculum.[91]

Many African American leaders and white abolitionists campaigned to eliminate the segregation, claiming that it was inherently unjust and that the schools for African Americans had inferior facilities, teachers, and other resources. White leaders generally resisted the calls for desegregation, arguing, in the words of one group, that African Americans' "peculiar physical, mental, and moral structure require an educational treatment different" from whites.[92] Some African American leaders also opposed desegregation, arguing that segregated schools protected their children from the low expectations of the white teachers and the racist insults of white children. They also noted that segregated schools provided jobs for African American teachers, who in desegregated systems would lose those jobs because few whites would allow them to teach white children.[93] Between 1855 and 1880, eighteen states gradually enacted laws prohibiting segregation by race, color or religious opinion in the public schools. Compliance varied--usually better in the small communities than the large cities.[94]

The arrest of Homer Plessy, who was one-eighth African American and seven-eighths white, for riding in a white coach of a train in Louisiana, would have momentous consequences. His conviction was appealed, and in 1896 the U.S. Supreme Court ruled in *Plessy v. Ferguson* that separate but equal facilities for African Americans were legal.[95] That precedent stood for a half-century and was applied to all types of facilities and services, including public schools.

In the mid-1900s the National Association for the Advancement of Colored People (NAACP) sought through the courts to improve the opportunities of African Americans. At first, using the *Plessy* decision, it succeeded in getting several African Americans admitted to all-white colleges by showing that there were no equal facilities available to them elsewhere. Then the NAACP reversed direction and challenged the *Plessy* decision head-on, seeking to demonstrate that separate was inherently unequal, even if the facilities and services were identical, because the forced separation had a stigmatizing effect. That bold strategy succeeded in the unanimous 1954 Supreme Court decision of *Brown v. Board of Education of Topeka,* which declared:

> Today education is perhaps the most important function of state and local governments.... It is required in the performance of the most basic public responsibilities, even service in the armed forces.... To separate (children) from others of similar age and qualifications solely because of their race, generates a feeling of inferiority as to their status in the community that may affect their hearts and minds in a way unlikely to ever be undone.... We conclude that in the field of public education the doctrine of 'separate but equal' has no place. Separate educational facilities are inherently unequal. [96]

A few days later, President Eisenhower urged compliance with the ruling, even though he doubted the ways of the south could be changed by court edict. While several states and big cities moved quickly to eliminate segregation, Virginia and most deep southern states stonewalled.

One year after the decision, the Court announced that compliance with the *Brown* ruling should move "with all deliberate speed." In response, white citizens' councils were formed to combat the implementation and to "prevent the mongrelization" of the Caucasian race. Southern states abolished compulsory schooling, denied state funds to biracial schools, and offered tuition grants to students who attended segregated private schools. Prince Edward County, in Virginia, closed its entire public school system for two years. Governor Faubus of Arkansas called out the state National Guard to prevent desegregation, and Governor Wallace personally stood on the steps of the University of Alabama to block desegregation there.

African American leaders responded by pressuring local officials to comply with the law. With the new invention of television, the whole country watched as peaceful African Americans participating in non-violent demonstrations organized by Martin Luther King Jr. and others were brutalized by southern police using attack dogs, batons, and water hoses. A boycott and demonstrations in Montgomery, Alabama, succeeded in forcing the local bus company to desegregate. Civil rights leaders used similar strategies elsewhere, often with success, but the progress was slow and piecemeal because of widespread southern defiance.

Mexican American Students

In the 1830s, white settlers from the United States had moved into the Mexican territory that is now Texas. Skirmishes with the local Mexicans escalated to war, and before the decade was out Mexico had ceded land to the aspiring independent nation of Texas. In the 1840s, white settlers moved into what are now California and New Mexico, and further skirmishes ensued. In 1846, the United States declared war on Mexico and invaded as far south as Mexico City. Former President and General Ulysses Grant later wrote this had been "the most unjust war ever waged by a stronger against a weaker nation."[97] With the Treaty of Guadalupe Hidalgo, the U.S. expanded its boundaries, gaining most of what is today Texas, New Mexico, Arizona, California, Nevada, and Utah in exchange for $15,000,000. Mexico lost almost half of its landmass. The treaty promised eventual U.S. citizenship to those Mexicans who chose to remain in the new U.S. lands, but a decade later the whites of several Texas counties physically drove out their entire Mexican American populations.[98]

Whites (called "Anglos") streamed into the southwestern part of the continent and claimed most of the land not retained by the federal government, establishing large farms and ranches. Mexican-Americans were mostly relegated to farm labor, ranch hand jobs, and other manual labor, although a few owned their own farms and others ran small businesses. Farm and ranch owners generally were against educating Mexican-American children because they valued their inexpensive labor and feared that education might raise their aspirations. Public officials, on the other hand, generally wanted these children in school so that they could be Americanized.[99]

From the late 1800s and onward, Mexican Americans were often relegated to segregated schools. A 1930s survey of school districts in the southwest found 85 percent reported being segregated.[100] Generally the rationale given for this practice was that it would benefit Mexican American children—it would aid in Americanizing them. The schools often had inferior facilities and were sent textbooks discarded by the Anglo schools. Students in the Mexican American schools were often even barred from competing in athletic leagues of the Anglo schools.[101]

There was also selective enforcement of compulsory education laws, with some jurisdictions overlooking non-attendance by Mexican Americans. In one Texas county, in 1921, only 31 percent of Mexican American school age youth were in school. One school superintendent reported that school board would probably fire him if he were to encourage these children to attend school.[102]

The League of United Latin American Citizens (LULAC) challenged Texas segregation as early as 1930 and the anti-Mexican bias of its textbooks as early as 1939, sometimes with success but often with defeat.[103] Mexican-American advocacy groups in other southwestern states did likewise. The Supreme Court decision in *Brown v. Board of Education of Topeka* proved crucial to reducing government-induced segregation of Mexican American schoolchildren.

SUCCESS OF THE REFORM EFFORT

Universal public education was adopted throughout the United States by the late 1800s. Publicly governed and supported education was available to almost all except children with severe disabilities. Core knowledge, skills, and values were taught in the schools with the intent of benefiting both the child and the state.

Not only was education universally available, but by 1900 virtually all children except those with severe disabilities were enrolled from age five to about 13.[104] The intensity of exposure to elementary schooling also increased substantially. Between 1870 and 1900, the length of the school term increased from 132 to 144 days and average absenteeism dropped from 41 to 31 percent, resulting in a 26 percent increase in the average number of days of attendance.[105] Illiteracy among those 14 years old and older is estimated to have dropped from 20 percent to 11 percent over the same period.[106]

Implementing universal high schooling required the better part of another century. In 1900 only 10 percent of 14- to 17-year-olds in the country were enrolled in secondary schools. By 1935, in the midst of the Great Depression, with one-fourth of the adult workforce unemployed, 60 percent of adolescents were enrolled in high school, and that figure rose to 90 percent by 1970.[107] The percent of 17-year-olds with high school diplomas rose from 6.4 percent in 1900 to 76 percent in 1990.[108] The percentage of the youth aged 18-24 who were enrolled in college rose from 2.3 percent in 1900 to 51 percent in 1990.[109]

There is an interesting and important question about universal public education that is not well addressed by most histories of 19th century schools. If the poor, immigrants, and the working classes, who were widely perceived as uncouth and even dangerous, were brought into the universal public school system, how did the system leaders succeed in convincing middle class families to move their children from private schools to public schools, where they would commingle with these undesirables? A substantial shift in enrollment from private to public schools over that period has been documented.[110] Our speculation suggests part of the answer is that the commingling of social classes was limited. In the cities and large villages, social class and ethnic segregation by neighborhoods probably was common, and most elementary schools in the mid 19th century were still one-room schools serving a small neighborhood.[111] As neighborhoods changed, gerrymandering of attendance zones was probably used to "protect" middle and upper-middle class schools from threatening encroachments. Rural areas received far fewer immigrants than the northeastern cities, and those who arrived were often relatives of the locals. Native Americans and African Americans, if they were admitted, were usually assigned to separate schools. City high schools were bigger than elementary schools, and because they enrolled only a small percentage of all adolescents, they had to serve many neighborhoods. There are reports that the school districts often aimed to build first-rate high schools deliberately to attract students from the Latin grammar schools and the academies, and that they also attracted some of the sons of skilled craftsmen, but it is clear that few of the poor went to high school until well into the 20th century.[112] Thus, it seems likely that what evolved in the mid 19th century were universal public school systems, each centrally managed and with a core curriculum taught in all schools, but with social class and ethnic segregation by school.

Achievement of Goals

Universal education had several grand goals that are not easily assessed. Neither Thomas Jefferson nor Horace Mann was content merely to provide education for all. Instead they hoped to provide good quality education that would help all citizens and the nation achieve their potential.

The quality of elementary public education throughout the 19th century was often although not universally low, as will be documented in the following chapters of this book. Ever since colonial Massachusetts mandated that each town fund its own school, the quality of education was associated partly with affluence of the local communities. Several historians have noted there were high failure rates and dropout rates from public schools throughout much of the 1800s, and that the children of the poor and the immigrants failed and dropped out at notably higher rates than the children of affluent families.[113]

Education disparities continue to this day. In some public schools, students master rigorous courses in literature, history, mathematics and sciences; study music, theater or graphic arts; and develop skills in the civic responsibilities of a democracy. In other schools where the opportunities are offered, substantial percentages of students are not learning well. In still other schools, some of these opportunities are not even offered. The questions of who is responsible for this and what should be done about it dominate current debates about American education.

The initial purposes of universal public education were to prepare an able electorate, Americanize immigrants, and uplift the poor. Later it was to serve industrialization and economic advance. Did universal public education meet these varied objectives?

Has public education helped youth to understand their rights and civic responsibilities, intelligently exercise the duties of citizenship, and resist demagoguery? Probably, but only modestly. Most Americans have a general sense of their rights and responsibilities, although their familiarity with the Constitution and its amendments is spotty. Americans participate in elections at lower rates than in most democratic nations. The United States has spurned both Fascist and Communist demagoguery, which prevailed in countries with noticeably weaker public education systems, although the countries that succumbed to those ideologies differed from the U.S. in several geopolitical and cultural ways that may have affected their fates.

There is no doubt that public education did help acculturate successive waves of immigrants to American values, teach them the English language, and prepare them for the changing workplace. The common schools also contributed to intermarriage among ethnic and religious groups.

Has public education eliminated poverty, deprivation, and an underclass? Obviously not. Despite unprecedented economic growth over the past two centuries, about nine percent of the American families remain in poverty, and African American and Hispanic families suffer more than twice that rate of poverty. [114] Yet, public education has facilitated upward mobility for millions of Americans in each generation. A review of the literature on career and social mobility suggests there were increasing mobility rates in America during the latter half of the 19th century, with about 20-50 percent mobility toward the end of the century--about two-thirds of the mobile people moving up and one-third descending.[115] Both widespread education and industrialization contributed to this mobility.[116] Despite that, Marxist-oriented scholars argue that the affluent leaders of the country have used public education to limit the progress of the lower class by instilling middle class values so effectively that the poor have been unable to rise in revolt.[117]

Has public education fostered the intellectual development and the technical skills that America needs to succeed in industry and international trade? Almost certainly, but again unequally. Students remain in school far longer than in colonial times and the 19th century, and the curriculum is more advanced except in the study of the classical languages. Schools teach English composition rather than just spelling and penmanship, higher levels of mathematics, both physical and biological sciences, geography, and history.[118] In addition, public high schools feed into public universities, which were created with federal incentives and state initiatives because the private universities of the late 1700s and early 1800s refused to teach the practical subjects of science, engineering, and agronomy, considering them unbefitting gentlemen.

Even if public schooling has not fulfilled the loftiest goals set by reformers, it is not an exceptional failure in the quest for progress. It is difficult to identify a single American institution with a broad purpose that has fully achieved its goal. For instance, during the Great Depression of the 1930s, the federal government created a Security Exchange Commission, a Federal Deposit Insurance Corporation, and a Social Security system, and began more aggressive use of monetary and fiscal policy to smooth out the ravages of business cycles, and yet despite those efforts the economy has periodically suffered serious recessions. Similarly, federal, state, and municipal health agencies have made real contributions to the productivity and quality of life in this country even though they have fallen far short of eliminating disease. Universal public education has benefited millions of Americans in each generation, but it has also failed to prepare many students for the opportunities and challenges of adult life.

Unintended Side Effects

The most obvious side effect of universal public education systems has been the crowding out of private school options at the K-12 level. The reformers quite deliberately aimed to bring most children into the public systems, for without that, they would have been meagerly funded and suffered from low status, just as had the charity schools of the past. As the public systems expanded, the burden on taxpayers also increased substantially. It became difficult for the working class to pay their taxes and also afford the option of private schools. From 1890 until the end of the 20th century, private K-12 school enrollment ranged from 7 to 11 percent of total enrollments.[119] Some current reformers would like to make it easier for all families to afford the option of private schools, and that will be discussed in Chapter 10.

WAS UNIVERSAL EDUCATION INEVITABLE?

Was universal education the only possible response to the changing contexts from which it arose? Did there have to be a public education system, or could education have been left to families much as housing and employment were? If public support and control of education was inevitable, did it have to take the form of universal public education systems?

As this chapter has indicated, several cities first provided public subsidies for church controlled schools and charity schools. Education for all children who would hold the franchise in adulthood appears to have been imperative for the survival of the new democratic country with a large influx of immigrants. Expanding government funding to private schools so that they could educate all students was precluded by events described in the next chapter: Catholics' desires for public funding of religious schools and the anti-Catholic sentiments of 19th century Protestants. Limiting public support to schools for the poor, however they might have been organized, would have created status differentiation between public and private schools, offending both proponents of equity and the voting poor. Clearly the development of universal public schools served the nation's needs better than the alternatives that had formerly been tried.

FUTURE OF THE REFORM

When policymakers are confronted with a mix of success and failure in an important enterprise, they have four basic options. They can react to the failure by abandoning the effort. They can content themselves with the limited success and continue the enterprise unchanged. They can look for ways to improve the enterprise. Or they can consider alternative approaches to achieve the same goals. There are some signs suggesting that universal public schooling will continue to expand over the next few decades and there are some signs indicating that it might contract.

The expansion, if it comes, will be mainly at the pre-school (pre-kindergarten) level or the postsecondary level. Publicly provided preschool began on a limited scale with the Head Start program in the mid-1960s (see Chapter 7) and there has been growing interest since in making it universally available. In 1985 there were only 96,000 children in public elementary schools' pre-kindergarten classes but by 2005 there were more than 10 times as many, even though total public elementary enrollments had increased only 23 percent.[120]

There is plenty of room for increases in undergraduate college-going rates. If current reform efforts succeed in improving the academic achievement of the lower half of students, expanded college-going rates would be a natural consequence of that. Considerable expansion might also occur at the graduate levels, where enrollments in master's degree and doctoral degree programs have risen rapidly but still involve only a modest percentage of those earning bachelor's degrees.

If there is a contraction of public education in the United States, it is likely to be at the K-12 level. Since the 1970s there has been a growing popular desire to offer all parents, or at least poor parents, the option of a publicly funded voucher that they could use at the private school of their choice. The potential of that reform effort will be discussed in Chapter 10. The widespread frustration with disruptive students in public school could also spark proposals to lower age at which education is no longer compulsory.

---

[1] Quoted in Adolphe E. Meyer, *An Educational History of the American People* (New York: McGraw Hill, 1957), 30.

[2] Quoted in Adolphe E. Meyer, *An Educational History of the American People* (New York: McGraw Hill, 1957), 30.

[3] Ellwood P. Cubberley, *Public Education in the United States: A Study and Interpretation of American Educational History*, rev. and enl. ed. (Boston: Houghton Mifflin, 1934), 54.

[4] Stanley Schultz, *The Culture Factory: Boston Public Schools, 1780-1860* (New York, Oxford University Press, 1973.

[5] Merle Curti, *The Growth of American Thought*, 2nd ed. (New York: Harper & Brothers, 1951), 28.

[6] Merle Curti, *The Growth of American Thought*, 2nd ed. (New York: Harper & Brothers, 1951), 28.

[7] Quoted in Adolphe E Meyer, *An Educational History of the American People* (New York: McGraw Hill, 1957), 102.

[8] Quoted in Allen O. Hansen, *Liberalism and American Education in the Eighteenth Century* (New York: Crowell-Collier and Macmillan, 1926), 235.

[9] Merle Curti, *The Social Ideas of American Educators* (Patterson, NJ: Pageant Books, 1959), 55.

[10] R. Freeman Butts, *Public Education in the United States: From Revolution to Reform* (New York: Holt, Rinehart and Winston, 1978), 6.

[11] Quoted in Merle Curti, *The Social Ideas of American Educators* (Patterson, NJ: Pageant Books, 1959), 55-56.

[12] Adolphe E. Meyer, *An Educational History of the American People* (New York: McGraw Hill, 1957), 97.

[13] U. S. Department of Commerce, Bureau of the Census, *Historical Statistics of the United States: Colonial Times to 1957* (Washington, DC: Government Printing Office, 1960), 57.

[14] U. S. Department of Commerce, Bureau of the Census, *Historical Statistics of the United States. Colonial Times to 1957* (Washington, DC: Government Printing Office, 1960), 56-57.

[15] Carl F. Kaestle, *The Evolution of an Urban School System New York City, 1750 – 1850* (Cambridge, MA: Harvard University Press, 1973), 139.

[16] Carl F. Kaestle, *The Evolution of an Urban School System: New York City, 1750 – 1850* (Cambridge, MA: Harvard University Press, 1973), 112.

[17] Michael B. Katz, *Improving Poor People: The Welfare State, the "Underclass," and Urban Schools as History* (Princeton, NJ: Princeton University Press, 1995), 3-4.

[18] U. S. Department of Commerce, Bureau of the Census, *Historical Statistics of the United States: Colonial Times to 1957* (Washington, DC: Government Printing Office, 1960), 402.

[19] U. S. Department of Commerce, Bureau of the Census, *Historical Statistics of the United States: Colonial Times to 1957* (Washington, DC: Government Printing Office, 1960), 90.

[20] U. S. Department of Commerce, Bureau of the Census, *Historical Statistics of the United States: Colonial Times to 1957* (Washington, DC: Government Printing Office, 1960), 281.

[21] U. S. Department of Commerce, Bureau of the Census, *Historical Statistics of the United States: Colonial Times to 1957* (Washington, DC: Government Printing Office, 1960), 23.

[22] Ellwood P. Cubberley, *Public Education in the United States: A Study and Interpretation of American Educational History*, rev. and enl. ed. (Boston: Houghton Mifflin, 1934), 143.

[23] Ellwood P. Cubberley, *Public Education in the United States: A Study and Interpretation of American Educational History*, rev. and enl. ed. (Boston: Houghton Mifflin, 1934), 142-143, 148-150; Karl F. Kaestle, *Pillars of the Republic: Common Schools and American Society, 1780-1860* (New York: Hill and Wang,1983), 32, 65, 70; Richard Pratte, *The Public School Movement: A Critical Study* (New York: David McKay Co., 1973.), 51-52; David B. Tyack, *The One Best System: A History of American Urban Education* Cambridge, MA: Harvard University Press, 1974), 30-33.

[24] Michael B. Katz, *Restructuring American Education* (Cambridge, MA: Harvard University Press, 1987), 17.

[25] James B. Conant, *Thomas Jefferson and the Development of American Public Education* (Berkeley, CA: University of California Press, 1963), 59-60.

[26] Harry G. Good, *A History of American Education*, 2nd ed. (Toronto: The Macmillan Company, 1962), 38;
Adolphe E. Meyer, *An Educational History of the American People* (New York: McGraw Hill, 1957), 152; Joel Spring, *The American School: 1642-2000*. 5th ed. (Boston: McGraw-Hill, 2001), 115.

[27] Merle Curti, *The Growth of American Thought*, 2nd ed. (New York: Harpers & Brothers, 1951), 298.

[28] John G. Richardson, "Common, Delinquent, and Special: On the Formalization of Common Schooling in the American States," *American Educational Research Journal* 31 (Winter 1994): 695-723.

[29] Richard C. Atkinson and Gregg B. Jackson, eds., *Research and Education Reform: Roles for the Office of Educational Research and Improvement* (Washington DC: National Academy Press, 1992), 55.

[30] Ellwood P. Cubberley, *Public Education in the United States: A Study and Interpretation of American Educational History*, rev. and enl. ed. (Boston: Houghton Mifflin, 1934), 164.

[31] Ellwood P. Cubberley, *Public Education in the United States: A Study and Interpretation of American Educational History*, rev. and enl. ed. (Boston: Houghton Mifflin, 1934), 165-166.

[32] Bernard Bailyn, *Faces of Revolution: Personalities and Themes in the Struggle for American Independence* (New York: Alfred A. Knopf, 1990), 29-34, 35.

[33] Thomas Jefferson, *Notes on the State of Virginia* (1787), quoted in Merril D. Peterson, ed., *Writings: Thomas Jefferson* (New York: Literary Classics of the United States, 1984) 274-275.

[34] Thomas Jefferson, *On the Objects of Primary Education*, quoted in Frederick Mayer, *A History of American Thought: An Introduction* (Dubuque, Iowa: Wm. C. Brown,1951), 111.

[35] Merle Curti, *Human Nature in American Thought: A History* (Madison, WI: University of Wisconsin Press, 1980), 81.

[36] Thomas Jefferson, "A Bill for the More General Diffusion of Knowledge," (1778; reprinted in *The Papers of Thomas Jefferson, Vol. 2*, Julian P. Boyd, ed., Princeton, NJ: Princeton University Press, 1950), 526-533.

[37] Julian P. Boyd, ed. *The Papers of Thomas Jefferson, Vol. 2*, (Princeton, NJ: Princeton University Press, 1950) 534-535.

[38] Karl F. Kaestle, *Pillars of the Republic: Common Schools and American Society, 1780-1860* (New York: Hill and Wang,1983), 9.

[39] James B. Conant, *Thomas Jefferson and the Development of American Public Education* (Berkeley, CA: University of California Press, 1963), 7.
[40] James B. Conant, *Thomas Jefferson and the Development of American Public Education* (Berkeley, CA: University of California Press, 1963), 274-275.
[41] Adolphe E. Meyer, *An Educational History of the American People* (New York: McGraw Hill, 1957), 105.
[42] Quoted in Merle Curti, *Human Nature in American Thought: A History* (Madison, WI: University of Wisconsin Press, 1980), 147.
[43] Quoted in Henry J. Perkinson, *Two Hundred Years of American Educational Thought* (New York: David McKay Company, 1976), 63.
[44] Quoted in Henry J. Perkinson, *Two Hundred Years of American Educational Thought* (New York: David McKay Company, 1976), 63.
[45] Quoted in Merle Curti, *The Social Ideas of American Educators* (Patterson, NJ: Pageant Books, 1959) 132-133.
[46] Quoted in David Tyack & Elisabeth Hansot, *Managers of Virtue: Public School Leadership in America, 1820-1980* (New York: Basic Books, 1982), 62.
[47] (Robert B. Downs, *Horace Mann: Champion of Public Schools* (New York: Twayne Publishers, 1974), 36.
[48] Henry J. Perkinson, *Two Hundred Years of American Educational Thought* (New York: David McKay Company, 1976), 65-66.
[49] Harry G. Good, *A History of American Education*, 2nd ed. (Toronto, Ontario: The Macmillan Company, 1962), 159.
[50] Robert B. Downs, *Horace Mann: Champion of Public Schools* (New York: Twayne Publishers, 1974), 42-43.
[51] Adolphe E. Meyer, *An Educational History of the American People* (New York: McGraw Hill, 1957), 162.
[52] Henry J. Perkinson, *Two Hundred Years of American Educational Thought* (New York: David McKay Company, 1976), 66.
[53] Jonathan Messerli, *Horace Mann: A Biography* (New York: Alfred A. Knopf, 1971), 226.
[54] Merle Curti, *The Social Ideas of American Educators* (Patterson, NJ: Pageant Books, 1959), 87-88; Harry G. Good, *A History of American Education* 2nd ed. (Toronto: The Macmillan Company, 1962), 162-163.
[55] Merle Curti, *The Social Ideas of American Educators* (Patterson, NJ: Pageant Books, 1959), 87-88; Harry G. Good, *A History of American Education*, 2nd ed. (Toronto: The Macmillan Company, 1962), 162-163.
[56] David Tyack & Elisabeth Hansot, *Managers of Virtue: Public School Leadership in America, 1820-1980* (New York: Basic Books, 1982), 60.
[57] Robert B. Downs, *Horace Mann: Champion of Public Schools* (New York: Twayne Publishers, 1974), 100-101.
[58] Michael Katz, *The Irony of Early Educational Reform: Educational Innovation in Mid-Nineteenth Century Massachusetts* (Boston: Beacon Press, 1968), 224.
[59] Adolphe E. Meyer, *An Educational History of the American People* (New York: McGraw Hill, 1957), 163.
[60] Harry G. Good, *A History of American Education*, 2nd ed. (Toronto, Ontario: The Macmillan Company, 1962), 376-377.
[61] Horace Mann, Antioch college commencement oration, 1859; quoted in George Seldes, ed., *The Great Quotations* (Secaucus, NJ: The Citadel Press, 1983), 463.

[62] Lawrence A. Cremin, American Education: The National Experience: 1783-1876 (New York: Harper & Row, 1980), 177.
[63] Richard Pratte, *The Public School Movement: A Critical Study* (New York: David McKay Co., 1973), 52-60.
[64] Lawrence A. Cremin, *The Transformation of the School: Progressivism in American Education* (New York: Alfred A. Knopf, 1961), 13.
[65] David Tyack & Elisabeth Hansot, *Managers of Virtue: Public School Leadership in America, 1820-1980* (New York: Basic Books, 1982), 45-46.
[66] John G. Boswell, *The Role of National Development in Determining the Policy and Structure of Education.* Retrieved 11/26/02 from www.gwu.edu/~manuscript/contents.htm. [See Chapter 1.4: "The State and National Identity"]
[67] Elmer Harrison Wilds and Kenneth V. Lottich, *The Foundations of Modern Education*, 4th ed. (1970 New York: Holt, Rinehart and Winston, 1970), 343
[68] David Tyack & Elisabeth Hansot, *Managers of Virtue: Public School Leadership in America, 1820-1980* (New York: Basic Books, 1982), 18.
[69] U. S. Department of Commerce, Bureau of the Census, *Historical Statistics of the United States: Colonial Times to 1957* (Washington, DC: Government Printing Office), 208.
[70] U. S. Department of Education, National Center for Education Statistics, *120 years of American Education: A Statistical Portrait* (Washington DC: Government Printing Office, 1993), 32.
[71] Stephen J. Provasnik, "Compulsory Schooling, From Idea to Institution: A Case Study of the Development of Compulsory Attendance in Illinois, 1857-1907" (Ph.D. diss., University of Chicago, 1999), 309.
[72] Stephen J. Provasnik, "Compulsory Schooling, From Idea to Institution: A Case Study of the Development of Compulsory Attendance in Illinois, 1857-1907" (Ph.D. diss., University of Chicago, 1999), 32-66, 148-182; David B. Tyack, "Ways of Seeing: An Essay on the History of Compulsory Schooling," in *History, Education, and Public Policy,* ed. Donald R. Warren (Berkeley, CA: McCutchan, 1978), 55-89.
[73] John G. Richardson, "Common , Delinquent, and Special: On the Formalization of Common Schooling in the American States," *American Educational Research Journal* 31 (winter 1994): 695-723.
[74] Harry G. Good, *A History of American Education*, 2nd ed. (Toronto: The Macmillan Company, 1962), 377-78
[75] Michael Katz, *The Irony of Early Educational Reform: Educational Innovation in Mid-Nineteenth Century Massachusetts* (Boston: Beacon Press, 1968), 48-50; David Cohen, "The American Common School: A Divided Vision" *Education and Urban Society 16* (May 1984), 253-261.
[76] Charles E. Stuart and others v. School District No. 1 of the Village of Kalamazoo and others, 30 Michigan (1874), 84.
[77] Harry G. Good, *A History of American Education*, 2nd ed. (Toronto: The Macmillan Company, 1962), 233-255.
[78] Ellwood P. Cubberley, *Public Education in the United States: A Study and Interpretation of American Educational History*, rev. and enl. ed. (Boston: Houghton Mifflin, 1934), 12, 21, 52; see the illustrations in Clifton Johnson, *Old-Time Schools and School-Books* (1904; reprinted New York: Dover, 1963), 25, 55, 94, 131-132, 133; Karl F. Kaestle, *Pillars of the Republic: Common Schools and American Society, 1780-1860* (New York: Hill and Wang,1983), 27-28.

[79] U. S. Department of Commerce, Bureau of the Census, *Historical Statistics of the United States: Colonial Times to 1957* (Washington, DC: Government Printing Office, 1960), 213.

[80] Joel Spring, *Deculturalization and the Struggle for Equity*, 3rd ed. (Boston: McGraw-Hill, 2001), 19.

[81] Joel Spring, *Deculturalization and the Struggle for Equity*, 3rd ed. (Boston: McGraw-Hill, 2001),18-23.

[82] Joel Spring, *Deculturalization and the Struggle for Equity*, 3rd ed. (Boston: McGraw-Hill, 2001), 23-26, 98-100.

[83] Joel Spring, *Deculturalization and the Struggle for Equity*, 3rd ed. (Boston: McGraw-Hill, 2001), 26.

[84] R. Freeman Butts, *Public Education in the United States: From Revolution to Reform* (New York: Holt, Rinehart and Winston, 1978), 61-62.

[85] U. S. Department of Commerce, Bureau of the Census, *Historical Statistics of the United States: Colonial Times to 1957* (Washington, DC: Government Printing Office, 1960), 213.

[86] R. Freeman Butts, *Public Education in the United States: From Revolution to Reform* (New York: Holt, Rinehart and Winston, 1978), 143-148.

[87] Quoted in Leon Litwack, "Education: Separate and Unequal," in *Education in American History*, ed. Michael B. Katz (New York: Praeger, 1973) 253-266. pg. 253

[88] Leon Litwack, "Education: Separate and Unequal," in *Education in American History*, ed. Michael B. Katz (New York: Praeger, 1973) 253-266. pg. 256

[89] David B. Tyack, *The One Best System: A History of American Urban Education* Cambridge, MA: Harvard University Press, 1974), 112.

[90] R. Freeman Butts, *Public Education in the United States: From Revolution to Reform* (New York: Holt, Rinehart and Winston, 1978), 60-61, 138-39.

[91] Leon Litwack, "Education: Separate and Unequal," in *Education in American History*, ed. Michael B. Katz (New York: Praeger, 1973) 253-266. pg 255, 259

[92] Carl F. Kaestle, *Pillars of the Republic: Common Schools and American Society, 1780-1860* (New York: Hill and Wang, 1983), 177.

[93] See: Carl F. Kaestle, *Pillars of the Republic: Common Schools and American Society, 1780-1860* (New York: Hill and Wang, 1983), 175-176; Leon Litwack, "Education: Separate and Unequal," in *Education in American History*, ed. Michael B. Katz (New York: Praeger, 1973) 253-266. pg. 261

[94] R. Freeman Butts, *Public Education in the United States: From Revolution to Reform* (New York: Holt, Rinehart and Winston, 1978), 139-142.

[95] 163 U.S. 537 (1896).

[96] 347 U.S. 483 (1954).

[97] Joel Spring, *The American School: 1642-2000* (Boston: McGraw-Hill, 2001), 194.

[98] David Montejano, *Anglos and Mexicans in the Making of Texas, 1836-1986* (Austin: University of Texas Press, 1987), 25.

[99] Joel Spring, *The American School: 1642-2000* (Boston: McGraw-Hill, 2001), 201.

[100] Gilbert Gonzalez, *Chicano Education in the Era of Segregation* (Philadelphia, PA: Balch Institute Press, 1990) 21-22.

[101] David Montejano, *Anglos and Mexicans in the Making of Texas, 1836-1986* (Austin: University of Texas Press, 1987), 230.

[102] Guadalupe San Miguel, Jr., *"Let All of Them Take Heed": Mexican Americans and the Campaign for Educational Equality in Texas, 1910-1981* (Austin, TX: University of Texas Press, 1987) 47-50.

[103] Guadalupe San Miguel, Jr., *"Let All of Them Take Heed": Mexican Americans and the Campaign for Educational Equality in Texas, 1910-1981* (Austin, TX: University of Texas Press, 1987) 76-82.

[104] U. S. Department of Education, National Center for Education Statistics, *120 years of American Education: A Statistical Portrait* (Washington DC: Government Printing Office, 1993), 26-27.

[105] U. S. Department of Education, National Center for Education Statistics, *120 years of American Education: A Statistical Portrait* (Washington DC: Government Printing Office, 1993), 34.

[106] U. S. Department of Education, National Center for Education Statistics, *120 years of American Education: A Statistical Portrait* (Washington DC: Government Printing Office, 1993), 21

[107] U. S. Department of Education, National Center for Education Statistics, *120 years of American Education: A Statistical Portrait* (Washington DC: U. S. Government Printing Office, 1993), 27.

[108] U. S. Department of Education, National Center for Education Statistics, *120 years of American Education: A Statistical Portrait* (Washington DC: U. S. Government Printing Office, 1993), 55.

[109] U. S. Department of Education, National Center for Education Statistics, *120 years of American Education: A Statistical Portrait* (Washington DC: U. S. Government Printing Office, 1993), 76

[110] Carl F. Kaestle, *Pillars of the Republic: Common Schools and American Society, 1780-1860* (New York: Hill and Wang, 1983),116-117; U. S. Department of Education, National Center for Education Statistics, *120 years of American Education: A Statistical Portrait* (Washington DC: U. S. Government Printing Office, 1993), 36.

[111] Barbara Finkelstein, *Governing the Young: Teacher Behavior in Popular Primary Schools in Nineteenth-Century United States* (New York: Falmer Press, 1989), 22.

[112] Carl F. Kaestle, *Pillars of the Republic: Common Schools and American Society, 1780-1860* (New York: Hill and Wang, 1983),121

[113] See: Colin Greer, *The Great School Legend: A Revisionist Interpretation of American Public Education* (New York: Basic Books, 1972), 107-109; Stephen J. Provasnik, "Compulsory Schooling, From Idea to Institution: A Case Study of the Development of Compulsory Attendance in Illinois, 1857-1907" (Ph.D. diss., University of Chicago, 1999), 302-305; David B. Tyack, *The One Best System: A History of American Urban Education* (Cambridge, MA: Harvard University Press, 1974), 11.

[114] U.S. Department of Commerce, Bureau of the Census, *Statistical Abstract of the United States: 2001, 121st ed.* (Austin, TX: Hoover's Business Press, 2002), 445.

[115] Hartmut Kaelble, *Social Mobility In the 19th and 20th Centuries: Europe and America in Comparative Perspective* (Leamington, Spa, (UK): Berg, 1985), 9-20.

[116] Seymour Martin Lipset and Reinhard Bendix, *Social Mobility in Industrial Society* (Berkeley, CA: University of California Press, 1967), 35,38, 60, 99-100, 229.

[117] Colin Greer, *The Great School Legend: A revisionist Interpretation of American Public Education* (New York: Basic Books, 1972), 55-59.

[118] Clifton Johnson, *Old-Time Schools and School-Books* (New York: Dover Publications, 1904 (reissued 1963), 14, 40, 45, 50-53, 63-66, 69, 110-111, 121, 301-308, 318, 371.

[119] Calculated from: U.S. Department of Education, National Center for Education Statistics, *120 years of American Education: A Statistical Portrait* (Washington DC: U.S. Government Printing Office, 1993), 36-37.

[120] U.S. Department of Education, National Center for Education Statistics, *Digest of Education Statistics, 2007* (Washington DC: U.S. Government Printing Office, 2008), 66.

3

Secularization of Public Education

Gregg B. Jackson

The personal writings of the nation's founding fathers amply demonstrate that they were god-fearing men. Yet the Constitution makes only one reference to a Divine Being and is silent about religion except to prohibit any "religious Test" for the holding of public office.

Education that seeks to instill religious beliefs and practices of one particular faith is said to be "sectarian." Education that seeks to instill the religious beliefs and practices that are common to several related religious denominations, usually Protestant, is said to be "nonsectarian" Education that avoids any religious instruction or practice, but may teach about the histories and belief systems of the world's major religions is said to be "secular."

INITIAL CONDITIONS

Many of those who settled early in the New England had fled religious discrimination and persecution. Mostly Calvinists, they had come to America not to establish religious tolerance for all men and women, but rather with the dream of creating their own religious utopias. When puritan villages discovered Quakers within their midst, they sometimes flogged, jailed, and even hanged them.[1] The holding of office and the right to vote were limited to church members,[2] and town government largely served the church.[3] As noted in Chapter 2, in 1647 the Massachusetts General Court mandated that towns provide education under The Old Deluder of Satan Act. A 1789 Massachusetts law required that clergy participate in the supervision of public schools and certification of teachers.[4]

Unlike New England, the middle colonies were settled by people of several different faiths. Despite that diversity, New York's 1700 Law of the Province called for life imprisonment of Roman Catholic priests caught performing religious rights.[5] The schools of the Lutheran and German Reformed denominations taught the Bible intensively, requiring students to memorize large amounts of Scriptural verse. Quaker and Mennonite schools used the Bible and Pastorious's New Primer, which was drawn mostly from Scripture.[6]

Most plantation owners of the southern colonies were of the Anglican faith. The 1606 charter of the Virginia Company specified "service of God and Christian faith [are] to be preached, planted, and used...."[7] In the mid-1700s, Virginia imposed a tax on all citizens to support the Anglican Church. From 1768 to 1774 Baptists were sentenced by courts to be whipped, jailed, and fined.[8] A 1776 Virginia law indicated that Unitarians and freethinkers were to be deprived of custody of their children.[9]

During most of the 1700's, the *New England Primer* was widely used throughout the colonies, and found in most homes, bookstores, and schools.[10] Religious messages were presented throughout the *Primer* to teach basic reading skills. In a typical edition, after a few pages that introduced the alphabet and syllables, there were rhymes to reinforce each letter of the alphabet. Those in one edition were as follows (with colonial spelling modernized):

A:In ADAM's Fall
We sinned all
B:Heaven to find,
The Bible Mind
C: Christ crucified
For sinners died[11]

There were also "Lessons for Youth" that reinforced the alphabet with religious doctrine. For "L" the lesson was "Liars shall have their Part in the Lake which burns with Fire and Brimstone" and for "U" the lesson was "Upon the Wicked, God shall rain an Horrible Tempest."[12] Interspersed throughout were short readings further underscoring moral lessons. One titled "Good Children Must" stated

Fear God all day,   Love Christ always,
Parents obey,   In secret pray,
No false thing say,   Mind little play,
By no sin stray,   Make no delay[13]

The Primer's final section was "The Westminster Assembly's Shorter Catechism" with 107 questions and answers about the Protestant faith that students were expected to memorize. Some versions replaced that catechism with a shorter one titled, "Spiritual Milk for American Babes."[14]

By the early 1700s the insular New England theocracies were weakening as the population moved westward and as commerce grew.[15] Arithmetic was added to the original 3 Rs of reading, writing, and religion. By the early 1800s, geography and history were added in response to nationalistic pride, English grammar was added, and arithmetic was given more attention.[16] The teaching of religion, however, had not disappeared from the schools. Noah Webster's "American Spelling Book" was reputedly the best-selling mid-century book in the world except for the Bible. The 1831 version includes both spelling instruction and short reading assignments with strong moral lessons. At the end there is a "Moral Catechism" which begins with:

Question: WHAT is moral virtue?
Answer: It is an honest, upright conduct in all our dealings with men.
Q: What rules have we to direct us in our moral conduct?
A: God's word, contained in the bible, has furnished all necessary rules to direct our conduct.[17]

The U. S. Constitution and first amendment prohibited most intertwining of federal government and religion but did not restrict states from such practices. As the Constitution was being ratified in 1788, six states had established state religions and five had limited office holding to Christians or more narrowly to Protestants. Only two (Rhode Island and Virginia) had official separation of church and state.[18] Delaware's constitution required profession of faith in Christianity and belief in the validity of the old and New Testaments, which precluded Jews from holding public office in the state. New Hampshire and North Carolina went farther, requiring all office holders to be Protestant. Georgia required the same of its state legislators.[19] New York's constitution made mention of "the spiritual aggression and intolerance" of "wicked priests."[20] Catholics were not allowed to vote or hold religious services except in Pennsylvania and Maryland.[21]

It had been common in colonial times for public funds to help support schools established and operated by churches. This practice continued for a few decades after ratification of the U.S. Constitution.[22] For example, when Connecticut sold its considerable Western Reserve in 1795, it put the proceeds in its school fund, stating it was to aid "schools and the gospel." [23]

CHANGING CONTEXTS THAT PUSHED SECULARIZATION OF PUBLIC EDUCATION

Several forces contributed to the secularization of public education during the 19th century. They were the nation's founding documents, increased religious diversity, the rise of science and technology, and the establishment of universal public education systems.

Secularism in the Founding Documents

A fundamental premise of the Declaration of Independence and the Constitution of the United States was that governance of the country would be guided by a large portion of the male population rather than the alliance of monarchs and church officials that had done so for centuries in Europe. That alliance had continued in Europe even after the Protestant Reformation, with John Calvin replacing Roman Catholic authorities in Geneva and the Anglican Church doing so in England.

The Declaration of Independence makes four references to God. In the opening paragraph it proclaims that independence is being declared by Americans in accordance "to which the laws of Nature and of Nature's God entitle them." The second paragraph explains that all men "are endowed by their Creator with certain unalienable rights, that among these are life, liberty and the pursuit of happiness." The closing paragraph states that the signatories of the document, "appealing to the Supreme Judge of the world for the rectitude of our intentions, do, in the name, and by the authority of the good people of these Colonies" declare independence. The very last sentence of the document is, "And for the support of this declaration, with a firm reliance on the protection of Divine Providence, we mutually pledge to each other our lives, our fortunes, and our sacred honor."

Clearly, the signatories were men of faith. They believed their right to independence was God-given. In addition, they appealed to God for guidance and assistance. It is telling, however, that each of Declaration's four references to a Divine Being expresses a dual appeal to both the secular and the sacred. Independence is declared under rights afforded by the laws of Nature as well as those of God. The unalienable rights endowed by the Creator include the pursuit of happiness, which a century earlier would have been denounced as satanic blasphemy by the Calvinists. While the Supreme Judge is looked to for moral guidance, the authority for the declaration comes from the people. Finally, support for independence is sought from both the Divine Being and the resources of the citizens.

When the founding fathers later drafted the U.S. Constitution, a document that guides the county's affairs far more than the Declaration, they inserted only two references to religion. Article VI states that high federal officials and members of state legislatures shall "be bound by Oath or Affirmation, to support this Constitution; but no religious Test shall ever be required as a Qualification...." The final paragraph indicates that representatives to the Constitutional Convention unanimously consented to the document in "the year of our Lord one thousand seven hundred and eighty-seven." As much by omission as by commission, the founding fathers created a federal government where there would be little intertwining of religion and governance.

It is clear that the Constitution provided no role for religion in the governance of the country. The first amendment, added four years later, established the converse principle—that the federal government would play little or no role in religion. It states, in part, "Congress shall make no law respecting an establishment of religion, or prohibiting the free exercise thereof." Thus the founding documents of the nation were a first step toward the secularization of public education.

Growing Religious Diversity

Immigration to America during the colonial period had been predominantly Protestant. Later, throughout the 1800s, a substantial portion of immigration was from Ireland and the Catholic regions of Germany. Between 1790 and 1900, the percentage of the U.S. population who were Roman Catholics rose from 1 to 13 percent.[24] The Irish immigrants tended to remain in New York City and Boston and became large portions of those cities' population. Many of the Germans were attracted to the growing midwestern cities. Immigration put the Catholics and Protestants elbow-to-elbow in the factories, city streets, and the evolving public school systems. It also gave Catholics political clout in several urban centers.

A fundamental contention of the Protestant Reformation in the 16th century had been that each individual must find God's will by reading the Bible, and that ecclesiastical officials—the Pope, bishops, and priests—do not have special access to Revelation. That belief created an incentive for the education of everyone. It also led rapidly to disagreements about what the Bible meant and what God wished of men and women. Schisms within the Protestant denominations were well under way before the colonization of America. They accelerated during an evangelical revival of the early 1800s, creating many uniquely American denominations. In 1890 the Census Bureau found 145 denominations of religious belief in the country.[25] Most of those denominations used the King James Bible, but there were strong-felt differences over scriptural interpretation, particularly concerning how one could achieve salvation.

While the Protestants argued intensely among themselves, most viewed Catholics with suspicion, distain, or trepidation. During the medieval period in Western Europe, the Pope and bishops had not only ruled religious practice, but had often exercised power over civil matters: thus the Catholic Church was perceived as a threat to democracy. In addition, the Catholic Church had not taken kindly to the Protestant Reformation. It denied that men and women had the right to choose their religious faith, condemned Protestant leaders as heretics, and urged European monarchs to suppress Protestantism. In the 1500s Catholics and Protestant Huguenots in France had crossed swords in a civil war that consumed the latter half of the century, and that slaughter was repeated over a wider stretch of Europe in the Thirty Years War of the following century. Protestants perceived Catholics as primitives who were unable or unwilling to find God's Revelation from their own reading of the Bible, a naïve people who clung to the superstition that the Pope, bishops, and priests could convey the message of God to them. Catholics viewed Protestants as doomed to damnation.

Small numbers of Jews had come to America in colonial times and immigration continued throughout the 1800s. During the mid- and late-1800s there was also substantial immigration from southern Europe, China, Japan, Turkey and south Asia, bringing people of many faiths, including Eastern Orthodox, Buddhism, Shinto, and Islam. There was no one holy book that could be acceptable to the diverse children of America.

Rise of Science and Technology

The historian William McNeill has argued that a diversity of ideas, as found in centers of trade and in areas with heavy immigration, stimulates innovation and progress.[26] During the 1700s, Europe had become the center of world trade, and then during the 1800s the United States had become the immigration destination of choice.

Concomitantly, science and technology blossomed on both sides of the Atlantic. Through the 1800s, the fundamentals of physical chemistry were determined and half of all elements identified. In 1800, chlorination began to be used to purify water supplies. In 1824, Portland cement was patented. In 1829, the first reliable locomotive was built and reached speeds of 29 miles per hour. Between 1821 and 1861, several scientists discovered the basics of electro-magnetic forces, which led to electric generators, electric motors, and then telegraph, radio, and television. Wheatstone built a successful telegraph in 1831 and a few years later Morse patented an improved version. Between 1825 and 1831, several harvesting and threshing machines were introduced on farms. The first insecticides and fertilizers for farm use were developed in the 1840s. The 1846 invention of a rotary printing press substantially reduced the cost of newspapers and books. In 1876, Bell invented the telephone and a year later Edison invented the phonograph. Edison went on to demonstrate the first durable light bulb in 1879 and soon thereafter began installing electrification networks in cities. Then, in 1880 Pasteur proposed the germ theory of disease and the following year he produced the first successful vaccine.

The 1800s were a vindication of the Enlightenment's assertion that human reason could provide explanations for vast parts of the world without the aid of religion. The dramatic advances from the new sciences and technologies created the impression that they alone might guide human affairs. Whole new categories of professional experts appeared during the century—agronomists, mechanical and electrical engineers, and pharmaceutical researchers. Prayer was no longer the only hope when difficulties arose. Penny newspapers, the telegraph and then the radio allowed one to draw on the expertise of people located thousands of miles away. This made people less dependent on Scripture, ministers, and priests for guidance in daily matters.[27]

By the middle of the century, Charles Darwin's widely publicized theory of evolution was contradicting the Biblical story of Creation. Archeological investigations were raising questions about other accounts in the Bible. While many Americans stood fast in their faith, others sought to modify their beliefs to be consistent with these new findings. They often "took a more figurative approach to religion, focusing on the concepts rather than literal interpretations."[28] Still others professed Deism, retaining a faith in a God but no longer believing the Bible was the Revelation of God.

The schools were influenced by the secularizing trends in society. In addition, the dramatic explosion in knowledge placed pressure on the schools to expand the curriculum, leaving less time for the teaching of religion.

Universal Public Schooling

The development of universal public school systems in the mid-1800s and the growing religious diversity at that time raised questions about the religious instruction that had prevailed during the prior two centuries. The managers of the school systems soon found themselves in the crossfire between adherents of the dominant faith in their community, who wanted the schools to continue to teach their religion, and those of other faiths, who did not want their children proselytized in public schools. Something had to give.

THE CAMPAIGN TO SECULARIZE PUBLIC EDUCATION

Frictions that had simmered when very limited public funds had been used to subsidize religious schools began to boil over as large universal public school systems were created. The first response was a move toward non-sectarian education, but that eventually was replaced by a campaign to secularize public education.

Horace Mann's Compromise

Irish Catholics had flooded into Boston and the surrounding towns during the early 1800s. This was a period of Protestant evangelical revivals, the splintering off of new denominations, and hot debate between Protestant sects. Several Catholic leaders saw the confusion as an opportunity to reassert Roman Catholicism. They stepped up efforts to convert Protestants to the Catholic faith and had some success. A few bishops went further, publicly proclaiming that the democratic republic would only be safe when led by people who had the infallible guidance of the Catholic Church.[29] Both actions inflamed Protestants' old antipathies toward Catholics.

Before Mann became Secretary of the Massachusetts Board of Education, the legislature had passed laws in 1827 and 1835 that prohibited doctrinaire religious teaching in publicly funded schools. The 1827 statute mandated that school committees shall "never direct to be used or purchased in any of the town schools any school books which were calculated to favor the tenets of any particular sect of Christians."[30] When Mann tried to secure compliance with the Act, there was an angry reaction by some. The editor of an Episcopal Church paper accused Mann of "watering down" Christianity.[31] One anonymously published attack contended:

> The Bible—in the naked simplicity of its annunciations; the Bible—unwarped, undiluted by sectarian expositions; the Bible, insisting on the great facts of man's moral ruin, of his need of a Redeemer, ... should be daily and thoroughly taught in the schools.[32]

The King James Bible was used by most Protestant sects and was widely perceived as non-sectarian, a view that Mann shared. The aforementioned laws did not exclude it from the schools. The problem arose from the interpretations of this Bible that were being provided in many schools, for it was the interpretations of the same Bible that distinguished the many Protestant denominations. Mann proposed that public schools conduct readings of the King James Bible without supplemental comment by the teachers and that they should offer non-sectarian prayers. He wrote,

Our Public Schools are not Theological Seminaries.... But our system earnestly inculcates all Christian morals ... it welcomes the religion of the Bible; and in receiving the Bible, it allows it ... to speak for itself. But here it stops, not because it claims to have [en]compassed all truth; but because it disclaims to act as an umpire between hostile religious opinions.[33]

Mann saw this as a fair compromise between two important needs—that of instilling virtue in the young and that of having schools appeal to a large portion of citizens. Almost everyone at that time thought that virtue could only be instilled in the young by teaching religion.[34]

Reading of the Bible in churches was often accompanied by commentary delivered by the minister or church elders, and that practice had been adopted in colonial schools and continued into the early 1800s. At the same time, most other school instruction was by rote memorization, without commentary or discussion. Thus Mann's proposal was both a break with past religious practice and consistent with most instruction in the schools.

That was no consolation to several religious leaders in the state. For instance, Reverend Mathew Smith assailed the Massachusetts School Board, claiming that the entire Bible should be taught as the inspired word of God, and that mere reading of passages from it would "make the schools a counter-poise to religious instruction at home and in Sabbath schools."[35] The minister went on to claim that this policy of "Godless schools" had increased intemperance, crime, and juvenile depravity. He proposed that local districts should be free to make schools as religious as they wished.[36] Mann responded by stating that the Bible was invaluable for forming the character of children, that it should be read in public schools, but to teach one creed or doctrine in the public schools would undermine the new public school systems.[37]

Mann and the Board had a liability in defending against these attacks. Most Board members were of the newer and more liberal denominations. Mann, although raised a Calvinist, had abandoned that faith for Unitarian beliefs, which leaders of the conservative denominations often considered a halfway house on the road to atheism. Mann and the Board were fortunate that many Protestant ministers supported the proposal for non-sectarian prayers and Bible reading without comment. They did so partly out of recognition of the increased religious diversity in the state, partly because of weariness with a century of internecine disputes among the Protestant sects, partly out of a belief in the need for common public schools, and partly to provide a united front against Catholics.[38] To teach and instill the specifics of their faiths, many of these ministers began church-based religious Sunday schools.

While Mann's compromise was acceptable to a majority of Protestant leaders, it was not acceptable to many Catholic leaders. Catholics used the Douay Bible, which differs from the King James version in several ways that are important to Catholic belief and dogma. In addition, reading the Bible without comment provides a challenge to the faith of Catholics who believe men and women might not correctly interpret Scripture without the guidance of ecclesiastical representatives.

New York City School Wars

As in Massachusetts, the face of New York City's population changed rapidly throughout the 1800s. Irish immigrants streamed into the city and soon comprised a sizable percentage of the population. In 1801, St. Peter's Church had established a school for Roman Catholic children and St. Patrick's did so in 1815. Both schools received public funds, as did other denominational schools, until 1825, when the Common Council decided to limit the allocations to nondenominational schools. This imposed a financial hardship on the Catholic churches. The Clergy objected strenuously, noting funds continued to go to overtly Protestant schools that claimed to be nondenominational. Their objections were ignored.[39]

A decade later, Bishop John Dubois voiced a complaint to the New York Public School Society, a publicly funded private organization entrusted with running schools for the city's poor. He charged that its textbooks were obviously Protestant in bias and included many aspersions against Catholics. He asked the Society to confer with him so it could identify and remove such passages. The Society agreed but did not follow through.[40]

In 1840 Governor Seward, anticipating growing contention between Protestants and Catholics in New York's urban centers, urged the cities to establish public schools where the teachers would be of the same language and religion as the students. With that encouragement, John Hughes, now Bishop of New York City, lead an effort to secure public funding for his expanding Catholic school system.[41]

Hughes was distressed by the anti-Catholic and anti-Irish sentiments in the city, by political exploitation of the Irish, and by the practices in the city's schools. He was offended by textbooks that described Martin Luther as a great man and spoke of "deceitful Catholics" and declared that immigration could make America "the common sewer of Ireland."[42] He fumed about how the school officials had persuaded the Common Council of the city to enact decrees "depriving the parents, in time of need—even when cold and starvation have set in upon them—of public relief, unless the children were sent to … schools."[43] He railed against the taxation of the Irish to support public schools that he condemned variously as overtly Protestant, anti-Catholic, and even godless. He explained that even if the public schools were secular, that would not meet the needs of Irish children who needed to be inculcated in their Catholic faith. Hughes proposed a return to the prior practice in which the city had distributed public funds to all religious schools to educate the poor among their congregation.[44] He wanted a share of the public funds, proportional to the share of children being educated in Catholic schools.

The School Society rebutted Hughes' charges and rejected his request for funding, stating that allocating public funding for religious schools was illegal and that Catholics were motivated by their own anti-Protestant sentiments. The Society's textbook committee, however, did discover considerable anti-Catholicism in the textbook and began steps to excise it.[45]

Bishop Hughes soon again requested public support for Catholic schools, this time from the city's Board of Aldermen. The Aldermen decided to ask interested parties to address the proposal. Hughes and the Society espoused their positions, and several Protestant ministers weighed in with their objection to the Catholic proposal. After months of further investigation and consideration, the Board of Aldermen rejected the Catholic request by a vote of 15-1.[46]

Hughes then went to the state capital, knowing that the Governor was sympathetic. Governor Seward's lead advisor on educational matters was John Spencer. Spencer realized that a bill to give public money to Catholic schools would create an uproar. Instead he proposed giving public money to all schools in the city that educated poor children. He suggested that each ward in the city become a school district, with its own elected board of trustees and one elected Commissioner to a citywide board. This would allow Catholic neighborhoods, and all other neighborhoods, to exercise some control over their public schools. Political maneuvering by opponents delayed action on the bill until after the fall elections.[47]

Bishop Hughes saw the delay as a challenge to his hopes, but also perceived it as an opportunity. He urged the Irish to vote in mass for ten Democrats and three independent Catholic candidates whom he had selected. It was a strange ploy, since Hughes had often criticized democratic politicians in the city for soliciting the Irish vote and then not tending to their needs. Nevertheless, his flock did as he urged, and the Democrats won 10 of 13 city seats in the legislature. All ten were those who Hughes had singled out for support. Equally important, both chambers of the state legislature were won by Democrats. Hughes had demonstrated that Catholics held the balance of power in New York City politics. He immediately warned the Democrats if they failed to support his cause in Albany, they would not get Irish votes in the city elections the coming summer.[48]

The Democratic leadership in the Albany legislature wanted to placate the Irish, but they did not want to alienate their Protestant supporters, who were dead set against Catholic controlled public schools. They decided to attack the Public School Society as an undesirable monopoly and to urge that universal education should be provided in consideration for equal rights, tolerance, and liberty of conscience. They proposed dividing the city school system into ward-districts, much as the Spencer bill had. Their bill passed in the assembly. It faced resistance in the Senate, until amended to prohibit support of sectarian education. This bill created the first true public school system in New York City, but it was a relatively secular one. Bishop Hughes won the election battle and lost the war for public funding of Catholic schools.[49]

Catholic children in public schools continued to face teachers who sometimes tried to proselytize them. For instance, in the 1850's, a Catholic child was whipped and expelled from school in Oswego , New York for refusing to read passages of the King James Bible. Legal action was taken against the teacher but failed to provide relief.[50]

The 19th Century Spread of Secularism

In Connecticut, Reverend Horace Bushnell, a well-known liberal theologian and supporter of common schools, proposed an ecumenical compromise. He urged Catholics and Protestants to join in the public schools, and he proposed that both the King James and Douay versions of the Bible be used, that scriptural lessons acceptable to all Protestants and Catholics be compiled and taught, and an agreed upon catechism of Christian morality, rather than articles of faith, be taught to all. He noted that such common Christian public schools would be a means by which:

> We may be gradually melted into one homogeneous people.... A means of cementing the generations to come in a closer unity, and a more truly catholic peace; that ... youth ... may learn how also to be no more strangers and foreigners, but fellow-citizens with the saints and of the household of God.[51]

It was an intriguing proposal, obviously motivated by the teachings of Jesus, but the proposal was rejected.[52]

In Philadelphia, in 1842, Catholic Bishop Francis Kenrick sent a letter to the Controllers of Public Schools, making the modest request that Catholic children in public schools be allowed to read from the Douay Bible instead of the King James version. The Board agreed, but Protestant leaders and local newspapers lambasted the decision. Rioting ensued, destroying two Catholic churches and causing several deaths [53]

Throughout the mid-1800s, the conflicts in Massachusetts, New York, Connecticut, and Philadelphia were repeated in many of the nation's cities where the Catholic population was substantial. Catholics insisted that reading of the King James version of the Bible in public schools was sectarian and threatened their children's faith. Since they were forced, like everyone else, to pay taxes that supported public schools, and since their conscience dictated they could not use those schools, they felt entitled to have state and local public funds pay for instruction in Catholic schools.

The Protestants countered strongly, intent on thwarting the Catholics because of the historic antipathies and fears that the Pope might spread his civil authority to America.[54] Early court rulings usually favored the Protestants. For instance, in 1854, the supreme court of Maine declared in *Bonahoe v. Richards* that a school board had the right to expel a student from school for refusing to read the Bible used in the school, even though the child and parents felt doing so violated their religious principles.[55] This decision held for more than three decades until the Wisconsin Supreme Court ruled the contrary in a similar case of *Weiss v. City of Edgerton*, which then put the matter in doubt.[56]

American Catholic bishops convened in 1829 and recommended the establishment of parish-supported schools. In 1866, they met again, and noting the dangers in public schooling, now exhorted implementation of that prior recommendation. As the predominantly working class parishes struggled to respond, they renewed efforts to secure public support.

In 1876, responding to the now national conflict, President Grant asked Representative Blaine to introduce an amendment to the Constitution that specified no government funds should be used to support any school or other institution:

> ... under the control of any religious or anti-religious sect, organization or denomination, or wherein the particular creed or tenets of any religious or anti-religious sect, organization or denomination shall be taught.... This article shall not be construed to prohibit the reading of the Bible in any school or institution.[57]

The proposed amendment won in the House by an overwhelming majority, but fell short—by one vote—of the needed 2/3 majority in the Senate. The same year Congress did pass legislation that required all new states subsequently admitted to the Union to adopt irrevocable ordinances guaranteeing "establishment and maintenance of a system of public schools which shall be open to all the children of said state and free from sectarian control...."[58]

In 1884 the American bishops again met. This time they *ordered* parishes to establish schools within two years, if they had not already done so. They also ordered parents to send their children to parochial schools.[59]

They would have to do so without public funding. During the latter half of the 1800s, almost every state adopted constitutional amendments prohibiting the use of state funds in church controlled schools.[60]

Neither the failed federal amendment nor most of the successful state amendments were intended or interpreted as prohibiting Bible reading, without comment, in public schools. By now, however, opposition to Bible reading and other religious practices in public schools was growing. Jews had joined Catholics in the opposition to the practice, and a liberal movement with the support of several Protestant ministers also raised a voice in opposition.[61]

20th Century U.S. Supreme Court Decisions

The first amendment's provision that "Congress shall make no law respecting an establishment of religion, or prohibiting the free exercise thereof" applied only to the federal government, not to the states or local governments. Following the Civil War, a fourteenth amendment was ratified. It was aimed partly at curbing state abuses of human rights, most graphically manifest by slavery, stating in part:

No State shall make or enforce any law which shall abridge the privileges or immunities of citizens of the United States, nor shall any State deprive any person of life, liberty or property, without due process of law; nor deny to any person within its jurisdiction the equal protection of the laws.

For nearly a century, the amendment was not held to pertain to the separation of church and state. That changed dramatically with the landmark U.S. Supreme Court decisions of the 1960s.

In the 1950s the New York Board of Regents composed a prayer that it recommended be recited daily in the opening exercises of all New York public schools. The prayer was, "Almighty God, we acknowledge our dependence upon Thee, and we beg Thy blessings upon us, our parents, our teachers, and our country."[62] Most school districts required the recitation, but made provisions for individual students to be excused if the prayer conflicted with their conscience. A small group of parents comprised of believers of the Jewish faith, of the Society for Ethical Culture, of the Unitarian Church, and one atheist, with a total of ten children in the schools, brought legal action, claiming that the use of this official prayer was contrary to their religious beliefs or practices. The school district objected, claiming parents have the right to raise their children with religion or without it, as dictated by their conscience, and that the school practice allowed both. The school district went on to indicate that the prayer was non-sectarian and justified by the American spiritual heritage. Three lower courts had ruled that the prayer was legal as long as the school did not require any student to recite it against the objection of his or her parents. The attorney generals of twenty-two other states filed amice curiae briefs urging the Supreme Court to affirm the lower court decisions. In 1962, the Court issued a six to one decision (two justices were absent) in the *Engel v. Vitale* case, declaring:

> ...the state of New York has adopted a practice wholly inconsistent with the Establishment Clause.... daily classroom invocation of God's blessings as prescribed in the Regents' prayer is a religious activity.... The constitutional prohibition against laws respecting an establishment of religion must at least mean that, in this country, *it is no part of the business of government to compose official prayers* for any group of American people to recite...[63]

The court noted that the voluntary participation of students did not matter because "the indirect coercive pressure upon religious minorities ... is plain."[64] Justice Black addressed the heritage argument noting that the heritage of America includes the fact that the Pilgrim settlers and subsequent Puritan colonists left England in part to avoid government imposed prayers.

The decision created a public furor unlike any prior Supreme Court case.⁶⁵ Within 24 hours, ten Congressmen had introduced strong attacks on the decision in the *Congressional Record*.⁶⁶ Senator Tallmadge asserted, "the Supreme Court has set up atheism as a new religion ... put God and the devil on an equal plane." ⁶⁷ Senator Eastman held well-publicized hearings for two days, limiting the testimony to critics of the decision even though supporters had requested to testify. The Conference of American Governors urged a constitutional amendment to restore non-denominational prayer to the schools. A total of 49 proposed amendments were filed. Cardinal Spellman's amendment revived Bishop Hughes' cause and would have permitted federal support for religious schools. Responses to the Court's decision from the various Protestant churches ranged from condemnation to applause. Most Jewish leaders supported the decision. So did President Kennedy, the first Catholic president in American history.⁶⁸

While the editorials were still flying, the Supreme Court agreed to hear another case about religion in the schools, this time about Bible reading. At the time, eleven states had statutes requiring Bible reading in the public schools and six others had statutes permitting the practice. In another 19 states, Bible reading was condoned without any applicable statute, and in five of those, the states' supreme courts had ruled it legal.⁶⁹ This was so even though all states had long ago added provisions to their constitutions that were similar to the first amendment to the U.S. Constitution, calling for a separation of church and state. The widespread view was that Bible reading in public schools did not constitute government "establishment" of religion. In most cases the Bible read in public schools was the King James Version, although there are reports that the Douay Bible was used in the public schools of Louisiana, a state with a French Catholic heritage.⁷⁰ The Scripture was usually read without comment, in accordance with the practice espoused by Horace Mann more than a century earlier.

In 1959 the Pennsylvania legislature had passed legislation mandating that the opening exercises of public schools include the reading, without comment, of a minimum of ten verses of the Bible. A subsequent amendment permitted students to be excused with written permission of a parent. The Abington School District had ordered that the reading be followed by recitation of the Lord's Prayer. A Unitarian family with three children in that school district filed suit to stop both the Bible reading and prayer. They claimed that some doctrines conveyed in the readings were contrary to their own religious beliefs. They felt that a request to be excused would label their children as "odd," and perhaps atheist and communist. In addition, the excusals would mean their children might miss important announcements made immediately after the Bible reading. The school district claimed that the Bible reading aided in developing the minds and morals of the children. It noted that students took turns reading the

Bible over the public address system and could read from any Bible they chose, although the district conceded only the King James Bible was available in the school. Lower court decisions in this case were appealed all the way to the U.S. Supreme Court.

Meanwhile, in Baltimore, avowed atheist Madeline Murray challenged Maryland laws and practices that were similar to those in Pennsylvania. Her appeal of the lower court decisions reached the Supreme Court shortly after the Pennsylvania case.

In 1963, the Supreme Court ruled on both cases with one opinion. In *Abington Township v. Schempp* and in *Murray v. Curlett*, the court declared:

> The reading of the verses, even without comment, possesses a devotional and religious character and constitutes in effect a religious observance.... The fact that some pupils, or theoretically all pupils, might be excused from attendance at the exercises does not mitigate the obligatory nature of the ceremony for ... [the Pennsylvania statute] unequivocally requires the exercises to be held every school day in every school in the Commonwealth.... The record shows it was the intention of ... the Commonwealth ... to introduce a religious ceremony into the public schools.[71]

School districts' initial responses to the twin rulings against Bible reading and prayer in classrooms were mixed. For a few it was moot, usually because their state supreme courts had previously ruled such practices illegal. For most, after turmoil and conflict, compliance was ordered by the school board. In some cases, that was because, once tempers cooled, a majority on the board thought it was the right thing to do, and in other cases it was because the board members feared expensive legal suits if they did not comply.[72] Others ignored the rulings, allowing students who were uncomfortable to remain silent and hoping that their parents would not sue.[73]

Still others decided to probe for circumstances under which Bible reading and prayers might be constitutional in schools. A flurry of such cases was taken to the Supreme Court during the latter decades of the 20th century. Consistently the Court ruled that teachers and administrators, in their official capacities, may not foster such activities, except that courses on comparative religion or the history of religion can examine the holy books and prayers of several religions. The Court's decisions appeared to erect an iron wall between public schools and religion. Gradually, however, the Court distinguished between activities initiated by school officials and those initiated by students, and by the close of the century the rulings indicated that students may voluntarily initiate Bible study, prayer, and discussions of religious beliefs at school to the same extent that students may engage in other nonreligious activities and speech that are not disruptive of instruction and order in the schools. School officials may not encourage or discourage such activities.[74]

In 1995 President Clinton's Secretary of Education issued guidelines on "Religious Expression in Schools" indicating student rights in initiating prayer and Bible study in public schools.[75] In 2003, President Bush's Secretary of Education distributed similar guidelines, but added, pursuant to recent revisions in the Elementary and Secondary Education Act, that schools denying student-initiated religious activities could lose most of their federal funds.[76]

SUCCESS OF THE REFORM EFFORT

The purpose of the secularization reform was to eliminate direct and indirect religious instruction in the schools. The ultimate goal was to preclude public schools from instilling religious beliefs in students and from converting students from one religion to another.

Achievement of the Goals

There is no doubt that there has been dramatic secularization of America's public schools over the past 150 years. The publicly aided schools of the 1700s were largely operated by churches and heavily emphasized direct religious instruction. Textbooks contained catechisms. Bible reading and prayer were the norm. During the 1800s, publicly controlled school systems replaced church schools. By 1900, ninety-two percent of total elementary school enrollments were in public schools.[77] Overt religious instruction was largely eliminated, but Bible reading in the classes, usually without comment, was still common. A national survey in 1896 had found that 454 responding districts reported Bible reading in the classes of all of their schools, 295 reported Bible reading in the classes of some of its schools, and 197 reported no Bible reading.[78] Bible reading was most common in the northeast and least common in the west, particularly in the large cities.

By the 1960s Bible reading and prayers in classrooms had been declared illegal throughout the country as a result of the two U.S. Supreme Court decisions. Some southern schools have long continued the saying of grace in the cafeterias before lunch. In addition, vestiges of religion remain widespread in the schools, such as the observance of Christmas and Easter holidays. Nevertheless, secularism became the norm for formal school activities.

The secularization reform was a curious success on at least three counts. There was no broad campaign striving to secularize public schools, the success of the reform was and is contrary to the majority's will, and complete secularization in public K-12 schools is inconsistent with accepted practices at other levels of education and government that have traditionally permitted some commingling of church and state.

As we saw, Mann's compromise was not intended to secularize the public school classrooms, but rather to limit the role of religion in schools and to abolish overt proselytization in the schools. There is no reason to think the first amendment to the U.S. Constitution was intended to fully secularize public schools, and it is quite clear that as states adopted similar provisions in their constitutions, most intended to preempt public funding of Catholic schools rather than eliminate Bible reading and brief prayers from classrooms. This is clearly a reform that rolled farther than the first generation of advocates intended.

Probably no other reform success described in this book has aroused more public disapproval. That might suggest that the secularization of public schooling was undemocratic. Our forefathers, however, consciously sought to craft a form of government that would prevent the will of the majority from trampling the rights of a minority.

The extent of church-state separation in public schools is greater than that required in many other domains of public life. For a half century, there has been federal funding for the education of military veterans that can be used at church-operated colleges and even at seminaries. The same is true of federal Pell Grants to assist low-income students to attend postsecondary education. The military employs chaplains who conduct religious education and services for members of the armed forces. The U.S. Congress opens each session with a prayer voiced by a chaplain paid for with federal funds. The Supreme Court, itself, is opened with the cry, "God save the United States and this honorable court."

Why this apparent double standard? No reason is clearly stated in the landmark 1960s Supreme Court decisions, although Justice Douglas's concurrence in the *Engel v. Vitale* decision suggests he found all these federal government practices troubling. Perhaps it is partly due to the impressionable age of K-12 students, perhaps it is partly due to the fact that parents usually have little choice over the public schools their children attend (other than by moving to another neighborhood), and perhaps it is partly due to the long prior history of publicly supported proselytizing of schoolchildren. College students are more mature and they select where they will use their veterans' benefits or Pell Grants. Not providing chaplains for military men and women would deprive them of spiritual counsel when they might most need it. Congressional chaplains are not reputed to proselytize members of Congress—although that may be due to the long lines of lobbyists ahead of them.

Unlike most school reform efforts discussed in other chapters of this book, the secularization reform did not aspire to larger goals beyond its objectives of removing religious practices from public classrooms. Critics have occasionally alleged that the goal was to drive religion out of American life or to substitute atheism for belief. Although a few proponents may have hoped for such an outcome, most were people of deep religious conviction—Horace Mann, Bishop Hughes, and most of the plaintiffs in the court cases that were appealed to the Supreme Court. In addition, as religious practice was being removed from the public schools over the 1800s, the available evidence, albeit limited, suggests the religious adherence did not decline.[79]

Unintended Side Effects

Some have suggested that the removal of Bible reading and prayer from schools have caused adverse side effects—exacerbating immorality, delinquency, and crime. It would take an entire book to explore that contention carefully. While statistics suggest that delinquency and crime rates, and perhaps the extent of other immorality, have increased over the latter half of the 20th century, it is likely that there were several contributing causes.

WAS SECULARIZATION INEVITABLE?

Something had to give when substantial numbers of Protestants and Catholics, with historic antipathies, were drawn into the universal public school system. Several European countries addressed a similar problem by providing public subsidies for all schools, including those of every church. Could the U.S. have done the same? Probably not, for unlike those European countries, the U.S. had large streams of immigrants that it sought to "Americanize" and that was less likely to be achieved by homogeneous church schools. Yet, if it had not been for the religious chauvinism of Protestants in the 1800s, something like John Spencer's plan, which would have permitted a mix of central and neighborhood control of public schools, might have come to prevail. To long endure, such a plan would have to have allowed religious minorities within a neighborhood to transfer to other public schools consistent with their religious beliefs or to an optional school free of religious instruction. A provision that religious instruction would not be paid out of the public school funds would also have helped. Would such a system have withstood appeals to the U.S. Supreme Court in the 1960s? Perhaps, because the prior court decisions were for public school systems that offered no choice by which parents could avoid objectionable religious practices, other than to withdraw their child from public schools.

FUTURE OF THE REFORM

The secularization of public schooling has been widely and largely implemented, despite a few holdouts. The reform cannot proceed much further. Therefore, the most likely future is little change or modest movement backward.

One route backwards would be through a Constitutional amendment permitting some official religious instruction and practices. Given the fate of prior such efforts, and given that amendments to the Constitution have been coming more slowly as time goes on, with the last one more than three decades ago, this is not a likely prospect.

A second route, and one already under way with the more conservative Supreme Court appointments of the 1980s, is a series of decisions that do not negate *Engel v. Vitale* and *Abington v. Schempp*, but allow practices not specifically excluded by those decisions. As mentioned above, recent decisions have declared that students may voluntarily initiate Bible study and prayer in school facilities under certain circumstances, with school officials neither favoring nor discriminating against such activity. It is not clear whether subsequent decisions might extend these rights, perhaps allowing students to invite ministers or church elders in to the school to assist with voluntary religious services.

A third route, and one likely to be rigorously explored in the early 21st century, is related to the new voucher reform effort. Proponents are pushing for parents to have the option of receiving publicly funded vouchers to be used at nonpublic schools of their choice—including church operated schools. In 2002, the U.S. Supreme Court ruled in *Zelman v. Simmons-Harris* that a publicly funded voucher program in Cleveland for poor children was legal, even though more than 90 percent of participating families used the voucher to enroll their children in Catholic or other religious schools.[80] A majority of the justices argued that because the vouchers could be used for public school options and non-religious private school options, that the state had not directed the funds to religious schools and the parents were free to do so. The court, however, was deeply divided in a 4-5 decision, and thus subsequent cases with slightly different facts might result in an opposite decision. On the other hand, this could become a landmark decision applicable to a wide range of voucher proposals. Some of the justices did note that government funds have long been used to support religion in other domains and suggested this is acceptable as long as the government does not favor any one religion over the others. Justice Thomas went further, suggesting that the 14th amendment's assurance of equal protection under state law did not make the first amendment's prohibition against Congressional establishment of religion applicable to state and local government actions. If his view prevails in subsequent decisions, states would be free, after modification of their state constitutions, to declare an official state religion and fully fund its activities with mandatory taxes imposed on all citizens. That would turn the clock back two centuries.

---

[1] Adolphe E. Meyer, *An Educational History of the American People* (New York: McGraw Hill, 1957), 23.
[2] Paul A. Freund, "The Legal Issue," in *Religion and the Public Schools*, by Paul A Freund and Robert Ulich (Cambridge: Harvard University Press, 1965) 3.
[3] Ellwood P. Cubberley, *Public Education in the United States: A Study and Interpretation of American Educational History*, rev. and enl. ed. (Boston: Houghton Mifflin, 1934), 74.
[4] Sam Duker, *The Public Schools and Religion: The Legal Context* (New York: Harper & Row, 1966), 16.
[5] Sam Duker, *The Public Schools and Religion: The Legal Context* (New York: Harper & Row, 1966), 15.
[6] Donald E. Boles, *The Bible, Religion, and the Public Schools* (Ames, Iowa: Iowa State University Press, 1961), 8.
[7] Sam Duker, *The Public Schools and Religion: The Legal Context* (New York: Harper & Row, 1966), 15.
[8] Sam Duker, *The Public Schools and Religion: The Legal Context* (New York: Harper & Row, 1966), 16.
[9] Sam Duker, *The Public Schools and Religion: The Legal Context* (New York: Harper & Row, 1966), 16.
[10] Clifton Johnson, *Old-Time Schools and School-Books* (1904; reprinted New York: Dover Publications, 1904, reprinted, 1963), 72.
[11] Clifton Johnson, *Old-Time Schools and School-Books* (1904; reprinted New York: Dover, 1963), 78.
[12] Clifton Johnson, *Old-Time Schools and School-Books* (1904; reprinted New York: Dover, 1963), 82.
[13] Clifton Johnson, *Old-Time Schools and School-Books* (1904; reprinted New York: Dover, 1963), 91.
[14] Clifton Johnson, *Old-Time Schools and School-Books* (1904; reprinted New York: Dover, 1963), 96-97.
[15] Ellwood P. Cubberley, *Public Education in the United States: A Study and Interpretation of American Educational History*, rev. and enl. ed. (Boston: Houghton Mifflin, 1934), 59.
[16] Lawrence A. Cremin, *American Education: The National Experience: 1783-1876* (New York: Harper & Row, 1980), 392-395.
[17] Noah Weber, *American Spelling Book* (1831; reprinted New York: Bureau of Publications, Teachers College, Columbia University, 1962), 169-180.
[18] Paul A. Freund, "The Legal Issue," in *Religion and the Public Schools*, by Paul A. Freund and Robert Ulich (Cambridge: Harvard University Press, 1965), 3.
[19] Donald E. Boles, *The Bible, Religion, and the Public Schools* (Ames, Iowa: Iowa State University Press, 1961), 38-42.

[20] Quoted in Donald E. Boles, *The Bible, Religion, and the Public Schools* (Ames, Iowa: Iowa State University Press, 1961), 39-40.
[21] Ellwood P. Cubberley, *Public Education in the United States: A Study and Interpretation of American Educational History*, rev. and enl. ed. (Boston: Houghton Mifflin, 1934), 87.
[22] Adolphe E. Meyer, *An Educational History of the American People* (New York: McGraw Hill, 1957), 177.
[23] Quoted in Ellwood P. Cubberley, *Public Education in the United States: A Study and Interpretation of American Educational History*, rev. and enl. ed. (Boston: Houghton Mifflin, 1934), 230.
[24] The initial percentage is from David B. Tyack, *The One Best System: A History of American Urban Education* (Cambridge, MA: Harvard University Press, 1974), 86; the latter figure is computed from U.S. Department of Commerce, Bureau of the Census, *Historical Statistics of the United States, Colonial Times to 1957* (Washington, DC: Government Printing Office, 1961), 7 & 228.
[25] U.S. Department of Commerce, Bureau of the Census, *Historical Statistics of the United States, Colonial Times to 1957* (Washington, DC: U.S. Government Printing Office, 1961), 228.
[26] William H. McNeill, *The Rise of the West: A History of the Human Community* (Chicago: University of Chicago Press, 1963).
[27] This does not mean that people gave up a belief and God or affiliation with the Church. Despite the obvious fruits of reason, men and women still had only partial understanding of life or control over it, and much remained mysterious.
[28] Andra J. Williams, "The Secularization of Education: A Reaction to Diversity," (Unpublished paper, 1999, 8.
[29] R. Freeman Butts, *Public Education in the United States: From Revolution to Reform* (New York: Holt, Rinehart and Winston, 1978), 116.
[30] Quoted in Ellwood P. Cubberley, *Public Education in the United States: A Study and Interpretation of American Educational History*, rev. and enl. ed. (Boston: Houghton Mifflin, 1934), 233.
[31] Quoted in Harry G. Good, *A History of American Education*, 2nd ed. (Toronto: The Macmillan Company, 1962), 165.
[32] Quoted in Ellwood P. Cubberley, *Public Education in the United States: A Study and Interpretation of American Educational History*, rev. and enl. ed. (Boston: Houghton Mifflin, 1934), 234.
[33] Robert Ulich, "The Educational Issue," in *Religion and the Public Schools*, by Paul A Freund and Robert Ulich (Cambridge: Harvard University Press, 1965) 37.
[34] R. Freeman Butts, *Public Education in the United States: From Revolution to Reform* (New York: Holt, Rinehart and Winston, 1978), 117.
[35] Quoted in Ellwood P. Cubberley, *Public Education in the United States: A Study and Interpretation of American Educational History*, rev. and enl. ed. (Boston: Houghton Mifflin, 1934), 235.
[36] R. Freeman Butts, *The American Tradition in Religion and Education* (Boston: Beacon Press, 1950), 118.
[37] Ellwood P. Cubberley, *Public Education in the United States: A Study and Interpretation of American Educational History*, rev. and enl. ed. (Boston: Houghton Mifflin, 1934), 235.
[38] R. Freeman Butts, *Public Education in the United States: From Revolution to Reform* (New York: Holt, Rinehart and Winston, 1978), 118-119.

[39] Lawrence A. Cremin, *American Education: The National Experience, 1783-1876* (New York: Harper & Row, 1980), 166.
[40] R. Freeman Butts, *Public Education in the United States: From Revolution to Reform* (New York: Holt, Rinehart and Winston, 1978), 120-121.
[41] Ellwood P. Cubberley, *Public Education in the United States: A Study and Interpretation of American Educational History*, rev. and enl. ed. (Boston: Houghton Mifflin, 1934), 236-237.
[42] Quoted in David B. Tyack, *The One Best System: A History of American Urban Education* (Cambridge, MA: Harvard University Press, 1974), 84-85.
[43] Quoted in David B. Tyack, *The One Best System: A History of American Urban Education* (Cambridge, MA: Harvard University Press, 1974), 85.
[44] Diane Ravitch, *The Great School Wars: New York City: 1805-1973* (New York: Basic Books, 1974), 46-49.
[45] Diane Ravitch, *The Great School Wars: New York City: 1805-1973* (New York: Basic Books, 1974), 51-52.
[46] Diane Ravitch, *The Great School Wars: New York City: 1805-1973* (New York: Basic Books, 1974), 54-57.
[47] Diane Ravitch, *The Great School Wars: New York City: 1805-1973* (New York: Basic Books, 1974), 58-66.
[48] Diane Ravitch, *The Great School Wars: New York City: 1805-1973* (New York: Basic Books, 1974), 67-70.
[49] Diane Ravitch, *The Great School Wars: New York City: 1805-1973* (New York: Basic Books, 1974), 71-83.
[50] Karl F. Kaestle, *Pillars of the Republic: Common Schools and American Society, 1780-1860* (New York: Hill and Wang,1983), 171.
[51] Rush Welter, ed., *American Writings on Popular Education: The Nineteenth Century* (Indianapolis, IN: Bobbs-Merrill, 1971), 199.
[53] Harry G. Good, *A History of American Education*, 2nd ed. (Toronto: The Macmillan Company, 1962), 138.
[54] Elywn Smith, *Religious Liberty: The Development of Church and State Thought Since the Revolutionary Era* (Philadelphia: Fortress Press, 1972), 103.
[55] 38 Maine 376 (1854).
[56] 76 Wisc. 177 (1890).
[57] Quoted in R. Freeman Butts, *Public Education in the United States: From Revolution to Reform* (New York: Holt, Rinehart and Winston, 1978), 125.
[58] R. Freeman Butts, *Public Education in the United States: From Revolution to Reform* (New York: Holt, Rinehart and Winston, 1978), 125-126.
[59] Anthony S. Bryk, Valerie E. Lee, and Peter B. Holland, *Catholic Schools and the Common Good* (Cambridge: Harvard University Press, 1993), 25.
[60] Ellwood P. Cubberley, *Public Education in the United States: A Study and Interpretation of American Educational History*, rev. and enl. ed. (Boston: Houghton Mifflin, 1934), 239.
[61] Donald E. Boles, *The Bible, Religion, and the Public Schools* (Ames, Iowa: Iowa State University Press, 1961), 33.
[62] 370 U.S. 422 (1962).
[63] 370 U.S. 421, 425 (1962).
[64] 370 U.S. 431 (1962).

[65] Rodney K. Smith, *Public Prayer and the Constitution: A Case Study in Constitutional Interpretation* (Wilmington, DL: Scholarly Resources Inc.,1987), 175.

[66] Paul Blanshard, *Religion and the Schools: The Great Controversy* (Boston: Beacon Press, 1963), 52.

[67] Paul Blanshard, *Religion and the Schools: The Great Controversy* (Boston: Beacon Press, 1963), 54.

[68] Paul Blanshard, *Religion and the Schools: The Great Controversy* (Boston: Beacon Press, 1963), 57-71.

[69] Donald E. Boles, *The Bible, Religion, and the Public Schools* (Ames, Iowa: Iowa State University Press, 1961), 51-52.

[70] Donald E. Boles, *The Bible, Religion, and the Public Schools* (Ames, Iowa: Iowa State University Press, 1961), 56.

[71] 374 U.S. 211 (1963).

[72] For instance, see William K Muir, Jr., *Prayer in the Public Schools: Law and Attitude Change* (Chicago: University of Chicago Press, 1967).

[73] For instance, see Kenneth M. Dolbeare and Phillip E. Hammond, *The School Prayer Decisions: From Court Policy to Local Practice* (Chicago: University of Chicago Press, 1971).

[74] 393 U.S. 503, 506 (1969) [Tinker v. Des Moines Indep. Community Sch. Dist.]; 515 U.S. 753, 760 (1995) [Capitol Square Review & Advisory Bd. v. Pinette]; 530 U.S. 302, 313 (2000) [Santa Fe Indep. Sch. Dist. V. Doe].

[75] U.S. Department of Education, "Religious Expression in Public Schools" (Letter to all U.S. school superintendents, August 10, 1995) [retrieved 03/20/03 from www.ed.gov/MailingLists/EDInfo/Archive/msg00029.html].

[76] U.S. Department of Education, "Guidance on Constitutionally Protected Prayer in Public Elementary and Secondary Schools" (February 7, 2003) [retrieved 03/20/03 from www.ed.gov/inits/religionandschools/prayer_ guidance.html].

[77] U.S. Department of Education, National Center for Education Statistics, *Digest of Education Statistics: 2001* (Washington, DC: Government Printing Office, 2002), 12.

[78] R. Laurence Moore, "Bible Reading and Nonsectarian Schooling: The Failure of Religious Instruction in Nineteenth-Century Public Education," *The Journal of American History* 86 (March, 2000): 1586.

[79] Steve Bruce (ed.), *Religion and Modernization: Sociologists and Historians Debate the Secularization Thesis* (Oxford: Clarendon Press, 1992); U.S. Department of Commerce, Bureau of the Census, *Historical Statistics of the United States, Colonial Times to 1957* (Washington, DC: U.S. Government Printing Office, 1961), 7, 229.

[80] 536 U.S. 639 (2002).

4

Progressive Education

Gregg B. Jackson, Sean B. Kelly, and Maria Soledad MacKinnon

"Education has in America's whole history been the major hope for improving the individual and society." Gunnar Myrdal

Calvinists of the 1600s believed that children were the devil incarnate and that memorization of Scripture and frequent beatings were the most appropriate education. The progressive educators of the late 1800s believed that all children were beautiful and that skillful guidance of their curiosity about the world around them was the best preparation for adulthood. That was a Copernican revolution in educational theory and practice.

There were three main streams of the progressive education movement. One focused on child-oriented pedagogy, the second emphasized broad preparation of students for adult life, and a third sought to prepare students to reconstruct a better American society.

INITIAL CONDITIONS

By the close of the 19th century, universal public elementary education had spread throughout the country. Enrollment in public schools doubled nation-wide in the 30 years ending with 1900, and it tripled in urban areas.[1] School attendance did not ensure a quality education. Educational leaders were increasingly concerned that schools were not teaching what was needed for adult lives. Most students were learning to read, but few were given much guidance in thinking, solving problems, and practicing democracy.

The sheer numbers of students made teaching difficult. Many schools were filled beyond capacity. The nation's average pupil-teacher ratio had risen to 36.6 and in several cities there were class sizes averaging 60.[2] The majority of schools were still one-room schoolhouses, with one teacher addressing the needs of students ranging in age from five to fifteen.

Curriculum and pedagogy were often of low caliber. Barbara Finklestein examined 1,000 descriptions of elementary classrooms that had been written between 1820 and 1880, finding two common patterns of teaching. The "intellectual overseers" spent most of the class time ordering memorization, orally examining students individually, and punishing errors. The "drillmasters" spent most of the class time leading students in unison recitations of the content to be memorized and conducting spelling bees and other contests. Writing still emphasized penmanship rather than communication. The common patterns of instruction varied little by region of the country, between urban and rural schools, or over the examined 60-year period.[3]

In 1892, Joseph Meyer Rice, a pediatrician, undertook an independent assessment of the quality of education by visiting schools in 36 cities. After talking with 1,200 teachers, observing class sessions, attending school board meetings, and speaking with parents, Rice found far more than overcrowding. In city after city, with a few exceptions, he found corruption in the governance of schools, untrained teachers, and public apathy. Rote memorization and recitations were the main means of education.[4] Although some sought to rebut Rice's reports, they rarely had the breadth of data that he had collected.

Flora Cooke, the principal of a progressive school in Chicago, made the following observation:

> In a great school of New York, I watched children take out their books, open them, and begin to study at the count of "One, two, three." They lifted their slates, poured on water, erased their work, again to count; they marched to place, stood in line, took position, read, spelled, or repeated the multiplication table and returned to seats. All worked as smoothly as a high power machine and it was the proud boast of the supervisor that she could go into any schoolroom of a given grade at a given hour and find the children working upon exactly the same lesson, using the same methods.[5]

By the late 1800s, the frequent flogging of schoolchildren for inadequate learning and misbehavior, so common in the earlier periods, had slowed. Physical punishment was still common in the rural schools, but urban schools increasingly relied on a mix of public recognition and humiliation.[6]

CHANGING CONTEXTS THAT PUSHED PROGRESSIVE EDUCATION

Progressive education was part of a larger social-political reform often called the "progressive movement" that began in the late 19th century and flourished in the early 20th century. It was also inspired by new developments in philosophy, psychology, and pedagogy and was a response to challenges raised by newly imposed compulsory education laws.

Social Stratification and Political Progressivism

The industrialization that had begun in the mid-1800s shifted into second gear in the late 1800s and early 1900s. In 1860, fifty-nine percent of the workforce was in the agricultural sector, but twenty years later that had declined to 49 percent, another twenty years later it had dropped to 37 percent, and by 1920 it was down to 27 percent.[7] Over the same period, employment in manufacturing increased about nine-fold and accounted for one-fourth of all jobs by 1920.[8] In 1900 there were 443 companies with more than 1,000 employees.[9] This was accomplished with dramatic technological advances, the introduction of fertilizers and machinery on farms, the extraction of coal and petroleum fuels to power machinery, the development of large-scale industry, and the expansion of corporate capitalism.

Gross national product per capita (the value of all goods and services produced per capita) tripled between 1870 and 1920.[10] The benefits of this gain were not shared by all, and the inequities were exacerbated by swings in the business cycle, which created serious unemployment in 1873, in the early 1880s, and again in the mid-1890s. Average industrial wages rose substantially during the mid-1800s and then stagnated during the latter three decades of the century, although the cost of living declined roughly 15-30 percent.[11] Then, average industrial wages tripled between 1900 and 1920, but the cost of living rose almost as rapidly.[12]

The lower and middle classes were concerned about the great wealth and abusive power of "robber baron" industrialists. Men such as Andrew Carnegie and his steel making conglomerate, Cornelius Vanderbilt and Jay Gould with railroad empires, and John D. Rockefeller and his Standard Oil had made real contributions to the economic development of the country. They also extracted a heavy toll, squeezing the lowest rank employees into poverty, bankrupting many small businesses with illegal business practices, defrauding middle class investors with various misrepresentations, and compromising the integrity of local, state, and federal government with a flood of bribes.[13] On the 100th birthday of the United States, it appeared to some that the escape from European aristocracies might only land Americans in the jaws of voracious capitalists.

Spurred on by Marx and Engel's 1848 *Communist Manifesto* and the subsequent formation of socialist parties in most countries, including the United States, working class leaders believed that social stratification was not inevitable. Americans formed unions to counter the power of corporate capitalists. Union-and employee-led work stoppages quadrupled over the last two decades of the 1800s and doubled again by 1920.[14]

The titans of industry and business justified their success and power with social Darwinism. As Andrew Carnegie propounded:

> While the law [of competition] may be sometimes hard for the individual, it is best for the race, because it insures the survival of the fittest in every department. We accept and welcome, therefore ... great inequality of environment, the concentration of business ... in the hands of a few, and the law of competition between these, as being not only beneficial, but essential for the future of the human race.[15]

Political progressives decried the disparities between the rich and poor, condemned the dehumanizing effects of factory work, showed sympathy for immigrants in the face of rising nativist backlashes, and rallied against political corruption. Their concerns were widely publicized by muckraking journalists during a rapid expansion in newspaper and magazine circulations.[16] They sought a more populist democracy, proposing direct primaries, referendums, and recall mechanisms for political office holders. They attempted to eliminate the abuses of big city political bosses. They organized labor unions and urged government regulation to constrain abuses of laissez faire capitalism. They also championed women's suffrage. Maintaining that "the rescue of children is the key to the problem of city poverty," progressives lobbied for child labor laws, compulsory education laws where there were none, and enforcement of those that existed.[17] They also sought changes in schools that would better prepare all youth, regardless of social class, to share in the fruits of American life.

New Philosophies, Psychology, and Pedagogy

The Enlightenment begot not only democracy but also humanism, which perceived beauty and hope in human nature, not original sin and damnation. Progressive educators hoped to advance American democracy and humanity by making the children of the elite more humane and less exploitive in their adulthood, and by helping the children of the poor to access leadership, occupational success, and status.

John Locke, the British political philosopher, whose 1690 "Two Treatises on Government" provided the DNA for the American Revolution and similar democratic uprisings through much of Europe, also set his mind to determining the optimum education for young gentlemen. In his "Essay Concerning Human Understanding," and his "Some Thoughts Concerning

Education," Locke urged that education be gentle and pleasurable, as this would instill a love of learning that would last through life. In addition, he argued, "the fittest time for children to learn anything is when their minds are in tune and well disposed to it."[18] He downplayed the extensive memorization required by the schools of his day, claiming, "Strength of memory is owing to a happy situation and not by any habitual improvement got by exercise."[19] He directed the teacher to strengthen reason as a tool for daily affairs and to work the student "into a love and imitation of what is excellent and praiseworthy; and in the prosecution of it, to give him vigor, activity, and industry."[20] Locke had different ideas about the education of commoners' children, but later thinkers argued his prescription for young gentlemen was the best prescription for all children.

While Locke hoped to socialize youth gently, the Swiss-French Enlightenment philosopher Jean Jacques Rousseau challenged conventional western premises, claiming that a child is an "innocent of nature" who is corrupted by society. Rousseau admonished that children are best educated by learning directly from experience, explaining "Let him know nothing because you have told him, but because he has learnt it for himself," and "You have not got to teach him truths so much as to show him how to set about discovering them for himself."[21]

In the late 1700s Johann Pestalozzi, partly inspired by Rousseau, created a school for impoverished children that was intended to help them realize their full potential. He believed that cooperation and sympathy could produce discipline in a homelike atmosphere. He developed a pedagogical approach based on three principles: (a) all education must be based on the nature of the learner; (b) education is essentially individual development and not something imposed upon the child from without; and (c) the method of teaching is to be sought empirically rather than constructed blindly or dogmatically.[22] Pestalozzi believed that students learned best by guided observation and inference rather than by reading, memorization, and recitation. He would have the teacher place an object before children and ask them to state what they observed. Intermittently the teacher would pose a question about the object that would set students to noting other characteristics. Specially made charts and arrayed beans were used for students to learn the nature of numbers and to master mental arithmetic. A window with two columns of five panes might be used to help students understand decimals. This was called "object teaching."

In the United States, the philosopher William James, who lectured on physiology and psychology at Harvard, helped chart new pedagogical territory. In 1890 he authored *Principles of Psychology*, which became a landmark in the field. In another publication intended for educators, he urged teachers to view children as having active minds designed to adapt to life. James urged that interests should be awakened and broadened, and the will should be strengthened, and the child's attention should be directed toward productive thought. The child should not merely accept ideas but test them out. According to James, the central task of education is inculcation of good and useful habits.[23]

G. Stanley Hall, a student of James, is credited with having conducted the first scientific research on child development and having inspired many others to do similar research. Noting that Western education had previously sought to fit the child to the school, with mixed results, Hall argued that the appropriate ideal for a republic would be to fit the school to the child. He advised: "The guardians of the young ... should strive first of all to keep out of nature's way, and to prevent harm, and should merit the proud title of defenders of the happiness and rights of children...."[24] Hall's massive text, *Adolescence*, published in 1904, shifted the focus of education from curriculum to the nature of adolescents. It also shifted the burden of responsibility. Traditionally, students' failure to learn was due to their own inadequacies. Now, Hall asserted, if children do not learn, it is the fault of the curriculum and teaching. This perspective would gain adherents throughout the 20th century and become the bedrock of a new education reform that will be discussed in Chapter 10.

Edward Thorndike, like Hall, had studied under James. Of the three, he was the most modern empirical scientist and made numerous contributions to research methods in psychology and education. His doctoral dissertation on the conditioned learning of animals remains a landmark contribution. He found that rewards over repeated sessions will speed learning and punishments over repeated sessions will slow learning. This finding was contrary to the widely held view that "practice makes perfect," without regard to the extent of failure, annoyance, or punishment that might be incurred during the process. Thorndike encouraged teachers to find ways to allow children to succeed, rather than suffer repeated failure. His research also found that learning did not transfer readily, contradicting the "mind stretching" that was alleged to accrue from the study of ancient languages and classical cultures. Because of that, he endorsed the teaching of utilitarian content and skills that students would actually use in adult life.

These new philosophies, psychologies, and pedagogies mainly contributed to the child-oriented stream of progressive education, refocusing attention from the subjects taught to the learner's developmental needs. Child-oriented education, to varying degrees, linked learning to the interests of student, gave the child some choices in what to learn and how to learn it, and replaced rote memorization with experiential and inferential learning. To a lesser extent, these philosophies and psychologies also informed the life-preparation stream of progressive education that sought to prepare youth for a range of occupations, family life, and civic responsibilities.

Compulsory Universal Education

The progressive education movement was partly a response to issues that arose from the universal education movement. As noted in Chapter 2, universal schooling was in place long before universal attendance. The reasons for non-attendance varied, including the need for children to contribute to the family income, parents who did not see the value of education, and children who found schooling boring or humiliating.[25] Compulsory education laws were first adopted by Massachusetts in 1852 and last adopted by Mississippi in 1918.[26] While the laws initially had little effect, they set a clear target: bring all children into school and keep them from dropping out. Educators concerned about the poor and working class youth, who disproportionately dropped out, felt they had to win those youth over to education by making school more enjoyable and useful in their lives.

That challenge was ratcheted up considerably as public high schools were expanded rapidly in the early 1900s. Many thought it inappropriate for those schools to mimic the Latin grammar schools that had prepared adolescents for college because, at that time, only about five percent of adolescents went on to college.[27] While critics argued that high school was unnecessary for those not going on to college, advocates argued it was needed to prepare non-college bound youth for the occupations and adult roles in a rapidly modernizing world.

CAMPAIGN FOR PROGRESSIVE EDUCATION

The campaign for progressive education was waged by many people on several fronts. The intellectual leaders, mostly university professors, developed the ideas and spread them through their writings and teaching. The directors of demonstration schools and those who first implemented progressive education in public school districts provided important examples for others.

Francis Parker's Quincy Schools

Francis Parker, sometimes considered the grandfather of progressive education, was troubled by the common practices of his day. He had served as a colonel during the civil war and then as a country schoolmaster for several years. With inspiration from the example of Horace Mann, he traveled to Europe to study the new philosophies and pedagogies that were developing there and returned to America hoping to put them into practice.

In 1873, the Quincy, Massachusetts' school board, sensing problems in the schools, decided to conduct a first-hand assessment. School board members conducted the annual examinations of students and were appalled by the results. Students could read from their textbooks but not from similar unfamiliar materials. They knew the rules of grammar but could not write a letter. The board sought a new superintendent and hired the charismatic Parker, giving him wide latitude to remake the schools.[28]

Parker emphasized conceptual understanding—classification, comparison, inference, and generalization. He involved students in observing, describing, and understanding phenomena. Many lessons began by examining an object. Textbooks were replaced with newspapers, magazines, and reading materials prepared by the teachers. Instead of studying grammar, students were to make frequent oral and written reports in response to their various lessons. Arithmetic was taught inductively, with students manipulating objects and inferring arithmetic rules. Students often worked in groups, learning from each other. Parker believed that all forms of expression, including artistic ones, clarified thinking. A humane man, he relaxed discipline.[29]

The approach appeared to be a great success. Enrollments doubled, truancy was reduced, and a Massachusetts State Board of Education assessment found the children excelled at reading, writing, and spelling, and were fourth in arithmetic. The Quincy schools earned national acclaim and drew hundreds of visiting teachers, school superintendents, and reporters.

Parker's activities also raised criticism and opposition. The school board had a running battle about whether to retain the changes. Parents were split, with some thinking that the fundamentals of education had been subverted. In professional circles, there were charges that Parker's approach was not original, was based on false principles, and had been subject to extravagant claims. A decade later, when Joseph Rice visited Quincy as part of his national assessment, he observed the school system's biggest problem was that other districts were luring away its teachers.[30]

Parker survived the controversy for seven years and then accepted an offer to become a school supervisor for the Boston school system. There he met fierce resistance from the old guard schoolmasters, as Horace Mann had previously, and Parker soon left.

In 1883, he became the head of the Cook County Normal School that prepared teachers for Chicago's schools. There he further developed his educational theories, testing them in an affiliated elementary school and conveying them to the next generation of teachers. Parker thought that school should be a model home and an embryonic democratic community.[31] He emphasized that the child, rather than content, should be the starting point for education and that several subjects should be inter-related to enhance their meaning to the child. Each school day would begin in an assembly hall with informal sharing and self-expression by teachers and students. In the classrooms, reading and writing were taught by having students write stories that were then duplicated for reading by their peers. This combined the learning of spelling, penmanship, grammar, composition, and reading. Drill was used as a supplement and in the context of student interests. Music, drama, drawing, painting, and modeling clay were important modes of self-expression. Science learning began with field trips in which students were to describe their observations with drawings and in writing. The fieldwork was sometimes followed with laboratory experiments in the classroom. Mathematics was often introduced during these experiments as well as in the manual training rooms where students were introduced to household and vocational skills.[32]

Parker was a creative innovator and a skilled administrator. His contributions were to the child-centered and life-preparation streams of the progressive education movement. Under his leadership, the normal school and affiliated elementary school drew much attention. G. Stanley Hall claimed to visit the elementary school annually "to set my educational watch." When John Dewey and his wife moved to Chicago, they enrolled their children in the school, and Dewey later acknowledged that he had been influenced by Parker's work. On the other hand, the Chicago politicians, who funded the normal school, were often skeptical or hostile and eventually cut his appropriations. Mrs. Emmons Blaine, a major philanthropist in the city, offered a million dollars for Parker to establish a private normal school where he could work unimpeded by the politicians. He accepted and began the work but died as the school was about to open.

John Dewey: Democracy and Education

John Dewey, a philosopher and educator, grew up in rural Vermont, the son of a shopkeeper. After completing college, Dewey taught for two years in Oil City, Pennsylvania and then went to Johns Hopkins University where he took a few courses from G. Stanley Hall while earning a doctorate in philosophy. In 1889, at the unusually young age of 30, he was well on his way to becoming a major American philosopher and was hired as Chair of the Department of Philosophy at the University of Minnesota. At the age of 35, he was lured away to chair the Departments of Philosophy, Psychology, and Pedagogy at the University of Chicago.

The Chicago to which Dewey moved was a microcosm of urban America—brimming with proud achievements and swelling with tensions and divisions. By 1890 nearly 80 percent of Chicago's population was foreign born.[33] In the closing decade of the century, crime was rampant, the mayor was assassinated, and strong union protests shook the city. Between 1885 and 1890, the Chicago population doubled and classrooms were commonly packed with 60-70 students.[34] Joseph Rice's 1892 study of 36 large school systems had identified Chicago as the worst of those systems.[35]

Dewey welcomed science and technology and industrialism but was deeply disturbed by the poverty amidst riches, discrimination against immigrants, and apparent hardening of social stratification. His thinking about education had been provoked by Pestalozzi and James. He was intrigued by the new science of psychology and impressed by the work of several American education innovations, including Jane Addams' settlement house and Francis Parker's schools. A bookish man, Dewey probably was also influenced by his marriage to Alice Chipman, an active feminist.

Unlike most philosophers, Dewey devoted considerable attention to education, thinking that philosophy and education rendered a reciprocal service. "The problem of philosophy is to clarify men's ideas as to the social and moral strifes of their own day."[36] Education, he thought, should promote those ideas. Dewey claimed,

> The ultimate aim of education is nothing other than the creation of human beings in the fullness of their capacities. Through the making of human beings, of men and women generous in aspiration, liberal in thought, cultivated in taste, and equipped with knowledge and competent method, society itself is constantly remade, and with this remaking the world itself is recreated.[37]

In 1897, Dewey wrote a short article titled, "My Educational Creed," laying out many of the premises that he would develop in numerous subsequent writings about education. He wrote,

> I believe that the active side precedes the passive in the development of the child nature; that expression comes before conscious impression; that the muscular development precedes the sensory.... Much of the time and attention now given to the preparation and presentation of lessons might be more wisely and profitably expended in training the child's power of imagery and in seeing to it that he was continually forming definite, vivid, and growing images of the various subjects with which he comes in contact in his experience

> All education proceeds by the participation of the individual in the social consciousness of the [human] race.... The only true education comes through the stimulation of the child's powers by the demands of the social situations in which he finds himself.... Through these demands he is stimulated to ... emerge from his original narrowness of action and feeling and to conceive of himself from the standpoint of the welfare of the group to which he belongs.

> School as an institution should simplify existing social life ... to an embryonic form. Existing life is so complex that the child cannot be brought into contact with it without either confusion or distraction....

> The teacher is not in the school to impose certain ideas or to form certain habits in the child, but is there as a member of the community to select the influences which shall affect the child and to assist him in properly responding to these influences....[38]

To demonstrate his ideas, in 1896, Dewey and his wife founded the University Elementary School (also known as the "Laboratory School") at the University of Chicago. Dewey was the director and his wife was the principal. Dewey used the school as much to test his ideas about philosophy and culture as those about pedagogy.[39] Formal subjects were not taught directly to the younger children. The task of the teachers was to use students' interests, either those brought to school or those elicited there, to engage them in individual and group problem solving, from which the students were to infer knowledge and skills. The problems were meant to challenge the students' creativity and inventiveness but not be overwhelming. Students were to learn to read, write, and spell as they explored literature and history. Similarly they were expected to learn arithmetic as they needed it when cooking, sewing, and woodworking.[40] One description of several learning activities indicated:

> Group IV, aged seven and a half to eight, poured melted lead pipe into sand molds to make weights for scales, estimating the amount of lead to be melted for each weight. They also constructed thermometers. Group V, aged eight to ten, looked at raw wool through a microscope, compared wool fibers with cotton fibers, carded wool by hand, and made a set of quilting frames.... Group X, aged thirteen, took observations of the sun's altitude and used their findings to determine the latitude of Chicago.[41]

Josephine Crane, a former student, remembered:

> First as to the sciences, no matter how young we were—too young to understand very much—we were given a chance to use our eyes, to observe the facts of nature more closely.... Secondly the activities—carpentry, cooking, weaving, sewing, art—all trained our hands and fingers to be useful.... I was trained to observe and given a chance to use what I observed in what I did."[42]

Grace Fulmer, who taught in the school for two years, recalled:

> It was Mr. Dewey's idea that each child should be free to develop his own powers to some ultimate purpose through the guidance of one whose experience was richer. Such also was his own relation to the teachers in his school. I know there were things in my own work, of which he did not approve and yet I always felt free to work on my own.[43]

From the beginning, the Laboratory School attracted attention and criticism. The University of Chicago's president, William Harper, was unsure whether the school was a jewel or embarrassment for his institution. It did not help that many of the faculty thought Dewey was a snob and resented his exhortations on how they should teach.[44] Although Dewey strove to have students practice democracy and community within the Laboratory School, many teachers and parents repeatedly complained that the school was run autocratically. After eight years of controversy, Dewey departed Chicago, took the family on a European holiday and then settled at Columbia University, where he continued to write prolifically and steadfastly refrained from running another school.

There is little evidence about how well the pedagogical methods of the Laboratory School worked. Dewey did not believe in testing and was less interested in academic knowledge and skills than in the general mental, physical, and emotional development of the children. It is known that critics voiced doubt that children would actually learn to read and write and do arithmetic in his school, but it is also known that two and a half years after the school's opening, enrollment had risen from 12 to 95, with most children from the Hyde Park neighborhood that housed successful professionals and university faculty members.[45]

In 1916, Dewey published *Democracy and Education*. It became his most influential book on education, although Dewey felt many of those inspired by the book had not fully understood it. The book addresses both the objectives and means of education:

Progressive communities....endeavor to shape the experiences of the young so that instead of reproducing current habits, better habits shall be formed, and thus the future adult society be an improvement on their own....

Science marks the emancipation of the mind from devotion to customary purposes and makes possible the systematic pursuit of new ends.... Without initiation into the scientific spirit one is not in possession of the best tools which humanity has so far devised for effectively directed reflection.... Pupils [in traditional schools] learn a 'science' instead of learning the scientific way of treating the familiar material of ordinary experience....

Direct observation is naturally more vivid and vital. But it has its limitations; and in any case it is a necessary part of education that one should acquire the ability to supplement the narrowness of his immediately personal experiences by utilizing the experiences of others....

A complex civilization is too complex to be assimilated in *toto*....
School is to provide a simplified environment. It selects the features
which are fairly fundamental and capable of being responded to by the
young. Then it establishes a progressive order, using the factor first
acquired as means of gaining insight into what is more complicated....

The sole direct path to enduring improvement in the methods of
instruction and learning consists in centering upon the conditions which
exact, promote, and test thinking. Thinking *is* the method of intelligent
learning....[46]

Several of Dewey's 30 books and hundreds of articles were widely read.
During the 20th century, no one has been given more credit and more blame
for progressive education than John Dewey.

Ella Flagg Young

Ella Flagg Young provided an important link between Dewey's small
Laboratory School and American public education. Born in 1845 into a
middle class family, she did not follow her older siblings to school,
apparently because her mother thought her too frail. At the age of eight or
nine, she taught herself to read from her mother's reading of books to her.
At the age of eleven she was enrolled in the local public school, where she
quickly exhibited a talent for mathematics. She was soon assigned to help
teach mental arithmetic and she relished the role.[47] Young rose through the
Chicago public school system, first as a dynamic teacher, then principal of
what came to be known as one of the best elementary schools in Chicago,
and then as an assistant superintendent of the system. From about 1890, she
also served on the Illinois State Board of Education, a position she held for
about 20 years. Young tirelessly campaigned to replace rote memorization
with learning based on experience and reflection. She was committed to
teacher development, and urged teachers to explore and reflect upon
various modes of teaching to find the ways that worked best for them and
their students, noting, "No one can work in another's harness."[48]

Well into her career, she decided to take a seminar from John Dewey
and quickly became one of his favorite students because of her keen mind
and willingness to express her own opinions. President Harper of the
University of Chicago eagerly recruited her as a doctoral student and
instructor in the Department of Pedagogy, thinking that having her on the
faculty would attract Chicago teachers to take courses at the University. At
Dewey's request, she also became the director of instruction for the
Laboratory School. Young strengthened the school's shaky administration,
clarified the teaching goals, and improved communication with the parents.
Dewey also credited her with clarifying his own thinking, noting, "More
times than I could well say I didn't see the meaning or force of some

favorite conception of my own till Mrs. Young had given it back to me," and "I would come to her with these abstract ideas of mine, and she would tell me what they meant."[49] Her dissertation, titled "Isolation in the Schools," described how American school systems had imposed deadening bureaucracy on students and teachers. She recommended that both be given more power in the schools so they could tap their intelligence and humanity. She added that unless teachers were allowed more initiative, most talented young adults would avoid teaching careers.[50]

After the Laboratory School, Young became the director of the Cook County Normal School, previously headed by Parker. Subsequently she was selected as superintendent of the Chicago public school system, the first woman to head a large city school system. During her six-year tenure, she helped principals focus on improving instruction in their schools, enhanced teacher preparation, established teachers' councils to advise school administrators, adapted the curriculum to students' interests, and expanded the teaching of industrial arts.[51] She also promoted democracy at all levels of the system, from the classroom through the superintendent's office. Dewey's Laboratory School had a peak enrollment of about 140; Young's Chicago public school system had more than 100,000 students.

In 1910 Young was elected the first woman president of the National Education Association. In that national forum and others she promoted the child-oriented and life-preparation streams of progressive education, and also advocated teacher involvement in school administration.

John D. Runkle: Manual Training

Even before Dewey, progressive education received an important push from John Runkle, who saw the need to apply education to the real world. As President of the Massachusetts Institute of Technology, Runkle became concerned that the graduates of his esteemed engineering programs were well prepared in the theory but had no skill with the tools used by practicing engineers. In 1876 he convinced the university trustees to establish shop courses in which students would be instructed in the use of these tools and have a chance to practice with them.[52]

Runkle thought similar training would have wide application at lower levels of education. He sent reports to the Massachusetts Board of Education and then addressed the National Education Association, proposing that shops be introduced in public schools. A few people thought it was an intriguing idea, but many strongly disagreed. In a subsequent debate at the NEA, one school superintendent claimed:

> The schools we have to conduct are to train boys and girls in those directions that are common to everybody, and one of the things that the

boys and girls ought to learn ... is how to get information from books. There is no information stored up in the plow or hoe.[53]

Despite opposition, several others took up Runckle's cause, and during the 1880s, at least 36 cities introduced manual and homemaking training in high schools or created separate manual schools.[54] A few labor unions welcomed this and others feared it was a plot by industry to recruit skilled non-union labor.[55] In 1904 the Association of American Agricultural Colleges and Experiment Stations weighed in, urging that agriculture be taught in rural schools.[56] By 1910, twenty-nine states had made provision for manual, agricultural, or homemaking education in existing schools or new special schools.

That year the National Education Association endorsed vocational training as "the central and dominant factor" in the education of students headed for industry.[57] Eight years later, it issued *Cardinal Principles of Secondary Education*, recommending the main objectives of high school education should be health, command of the academic fundamentals, worthy home membership for both boys and girls, vocation, citizenship, worthy use of leisure, and ethical character.[58]

Advocates of vocational preparation thought the state-by-state responses would be slow and inadequate. In 1906 an unusual coalition of educators, the National Association of Manufacturers, and the American Federation of Labor joined in establishing the National Society for the Promotion of Industrial Education to lobby for federal legislation supporting public vocational education. Employers saw vocational education as a way to increase productivity and competitiveness in international markets. Labor leaders saw it as a way to delay adolescents' entry into the labor markets. Educators saw it as a way of extending the preparation of students not inclined to attend college. Several of the Society's bills, introduced in Congress over a ten-year period, failed due to concerns about federal interference with education, the anticipated costs, and disputes about whether vocational preparation was a proper role of public schools. In the midst of World War I, with the country hard-pressed for skilled labor and fearful of Germany's industrial prowess, Congress passed the Smith-Hughes Act providing substantial aid for the creation of statewide vocational high school systems.[59]

George Counts

George Counts was a leader of the social reconstruction stream of progressive education. Marxist analysis has declared that the only hope of ridding the country of capitalist oppression was a proletarian revolution. Counts urged teachers to indoctrinate students in the evils of capitalism and the merits of socialism but otherwise offered few specifics about how schools should prepare students for reconstruction.⁶⁰ He belittled both the child-centered and life-preparation approaches, charging that the Progressive Education Association had failed to formulate a theory of social welfare, "unless it be that of anarchy or extreme individualism." He blamed that failure on what he called the "romantic sentimentalist" middle class leadership of the Association.⁶¹

School District Implementation

In the early 1900s, William Wirt converted the Gary, Indiana schools to Deweyan inspired learning communities. Students spent half the day in classrooms and half the day engaged in other learning activities in the school auditorium, library, shops, and playgrounds. This practice was widely duplicated elsewhere. An independent assessment of the Gary schools revealed advantages and disadvantages. Science was being taught inductively but sometimes not well. Most of the other subjects appeared to be taught conventionally. There was lively activity outside of the classrooms, but some was perfunctory or ill guided, and judged not likely to be very educative. Even after that mixed assessment, several other districts adopted the Gary Plan because it required half the number of classrooms as conventional schools.⁶²

In the 1920s, Carleton Washburne led affluent Winnetka, Illinois, in a two-pronged innovation. Instruction was individualized in reading, writing, mathematics, science and the social sciences. This allowed students to work through self-study materials (apparently the same materials for all students) at their own pace, repeating small units that they had not mastered. Students also engaged in self-expression activities and group projects involving the community life of the school—assemblies, dramatics, and student government. An evaluation showed improvements in reading, language, and arithmetic and a decline in spelling, with no increase in operating costs. Winnetka retained the system for two decades and several other districts adopted parts of it.⁶³

In the same decade, Jesse Newlon led the Denver Experiment, organizing 37 committees of teachers, each assisted by progressive education experts, to revise the curriculum so that it would connect with students' experiences and be relevant to their lives.⁶⁴ Newlon believed "no program of studies will operate that has not evolved to some extent out of the thinking of the teachers who are to apply it."⁶⁵ Each of the Denver Experiment committees was assigned to one subject area or course. A committee's first task was to review the professional literature in the field. Then it prepared objectives, selected content, designed instructional methods, suggested projects and materials that instructors might use, and developed tests to assess student progress. Teachers then tested and revised the materials.⁶⁶ After a few years, each committee rotated in new teachers and again undertook revision of its assigned course. The teachers found that the new courses worked well for the superior students but had disappointing results for less able students. Newlon and his successor, however, considered the effort an overall success because it boosted teacher skill, enthusiasm, and morale.[67] By the late 1920s, the Denver curriculum revision effort gained national attention and the praise of experts. Several large cities copied the process. With less able guidance, however, the committees sometimes bogged down in endless discussions.[68] Denver retained the process into the 1950s when national criticism of progressive education led to its demise.[69]

Support and Opposition

All three approaches of progressive education—child-oriented pedagogy, life preparation, and social reconstruction, had staunch supporters and critics. Few people, however, supported all three approaches. Support and opposition to the first two approaches began in the very late 1800s and continue as this book is being written. Support for the social reconstruction approach rose during the Great Depression of the 1930s and waned by World War II.

The child-oriented approach drew most of its support from intellectuals and upper-middle class parents who wanted their children schooled in a humane and affirming environment and were eager to replace rote memorization with the exercise of reason. Most of the demonstration schools were private ones, and most public school systems that pioneered progressive education served primarily middle class families.[70] Working class parents often opposed the child-oriented approach, believing it to be too soft in both content and discipline. Perhaps the former were confident in their ability to teach their children whatever basic skills they did not pick up in school, whereas the latter did not have that confidence or time to do so.

Business leaders, several labor leaders, ethnic group leaders, and some parents supported the life-preparation approach to progressive education. They wanted a curriculum that was more practical than the traditional 3Rs and prepared students better for later life responsibilities. They often supported the addition of courses in health, domestic science, and vocational training. Ethnic group leaders wanted history to represent the contributions of various ethnic groups, not just the descendents of colonists. Many also pushed hard to have their native language taught in the schools, sometimes urging that it be the language of instruction.[71] A portion of intellectuals and parents opposed the life preparation approach, arguing that formal education should focus on traditional academic subjects and that more specific preparation for adult responsibilities should come later. Several union leaders opposed vocational education as a means of reinforcing social distinctions and a plot to drive down workers' wages by expanding the labor pool.[72]

Radical reformists, socialists, and communists often supported the social reconstruction approach of progressive education. They wanted the schools to prepare the next generation of Americans to forge a socialist or communist state. Traditional American ideals and educators' middle class values resisted the social reconstruction approach. The child-oriented stream of progressive education strongly opposed the indoctrination proposed by George Counts. The dictatorial practices of Lenin, the relatively backward economy of Russia under communism, the subsequent purges of Stalin, and the rise of the Cold War between communist and democratic countries also fueled opposition to the reconstruction approach.

Traditionalists opposed all three approaches to progressive education, asserting that public schools should prepare boys and girls for adult responsibility through systematic training in reading, writing, arithmetic, history, and English, and through discipline and obedience. William Bagley, a professor of Education at the University of Illinois and editor of *School and Society,* insisted on a common core curriculum, one that was to be "the nucleus of a common culture for the children of the nation." He believed that maturity "means the capacity to sustain and control effort even if the effort is not pleasurable."[73] He accused public education of being weak and ineffective, conducive to appalling records of murder, assault, and other crimes.[74]

William Torrey Harris, a one-time U.S. Commissioner of Education, believed the role of education was to improve the intelligence of individuals through the study of the accumulated wisdom of the human race. He contended that discipline and development of good habits were necessary to teach children to think. He thought, "a system which proposes to let the individual work out his education entirely by himself ... is the greatest possible mistake."[75]

Even Dewey was a vocal critic of the extreme child-centered approach. In a 1949 address before the Progressive Education Association, Dewey explained:

Progressive schools set store by individuality, and sometimes it seems to be thought that orderly organization of subject matter is hostile to the needs of students in their individual character. But individuality is something developing and to be continuously attained, not something given all at once and ready-made.[76]

> In another statement, Dewey was blunter about extreme child-centered pedagogy: "Such an approach is really stupid. For it attempts the impossible ... and it misconceives the conditions of independent thinking."[77]

Robert M. Hutchins, who became President of the University of Chicago after Dewey left, was a proponent of a "Great Books" education and repeatedly denounced Dewey. Hutchins claimed,

> The essence of Mr. Dewey's position is that only science is knowledge; everything else is superstition. Only science is modern; everything else is out of date. History, philosophy, theology, religion, art and literature—almost everything, in short, that makes life worth living—are irrelevant and have no place in modern education.[78]

In the decade following World War II, historian Arthur Bestor, himself a graduate of a well-known progressive school, claimed, "Progressive education became regressive education ... because instead of advancing, it began to undermine the great traditions of liberal education and substitute for them lesser aims, confused aims, or no aims at all."[79] Bestor founded the Council for Basic Education to promote traditional discipline-based education for all students. In the mid-1950s two former school board members weighed in with indictments: Albert Lynd's was titled *Quackery in the Public Schools* and Mortimer Smith's was *Diminished Mind*. In 1959, eighteen months after the Soviets had launched the Sputnik satellite, *Life* magazine published a letter from President Eisenhower blaming Dewey for America's allegedly inferior educational system.[80]

Attacks on progressive education in the 1950s were most often rooted in political conservatism. By the 1960s and 1970s, liberal voices joined the criticism. Revisionist historians argued that progressive education aimed to perpetuate existing social order that oppressed the lower classes and did not address the needs of racial and ethnic minorities. Joel Spring even accused the progressives of promoting "education for social control."[81]

SUCCESS OF THE REFORM

Lawrence Cremin, the noted historian of America education, states that progressive education raised much hope through the country:

> To study the literature of the Progressive era is to be overwhelmed by the extent to which political reform is conceived essentially in educational terms. Negroes sought to achieve equality of citizenship by gaining access to popular schooling. Farmers and workingmen attempted to retain their share of the national income by promoting programs of vocational education. Humanitarians attacked the problem of poverty by establishing curricula in civics, hygiene, and domestic science. And businessmen reached for industrial supremacy by extending the scope of technical training.[82]

Progressive education changed the face of American education between the two World Wars. By 1940, discussions of education commonly included phrases like "recognizing individual differences," "personality development," "the whole child," "social and emotional growth," "creative self-expression," "the needs of learners," "real life experiences," and "teacher-student relationship."[83] Diane Ravitch, a historian and policy analyst, has criticized progressive education but acknowledges it was so widely accepted by the 1940s that it had come to be referred to as "modern education."[84] Further evidence of progressive education's pervasive influence in America is provided by the criticism that it continues to draw even today.

Nevertheless, advocates of progressive education do have reason for disappointment. Their ideas modified education but did not revolutionize it. Larry Cuban's history of American teaching over the past century reviewed numerous observational studies, surveys, pictures of schools, and other data. The data indicate that about 10-30 percent of instruction had become student-centered, another 20-40 percent was a mix of teacher-centered and student-centered, and the most prevalent pedagogy remained teacher-centered instruction.[85] Parker's and Dewey's calls for learning from experience and social interactions within schools did not become the main pedagogical approach in most schools, but since the 1950s most teachers have made some use of discussions, field trips, group projects, dramas, and science laboratories, all of which were popularized by progressive educators. Most students are assigned to write papers based on library research (now Internet research), a practice that was rare in elementary schools until the progressive era. Dewey's call for the practice of democracy has resulted in students electing class officers and school-wide student governments. Cuban concluded that many teachers have come to embrace a hybrid of student-centered and teacher-centered pedagogy.[86]

Progressives' proposals to jettisoning traditional subjects did not prevail, except in respect to classical languages, but traditional subjects have been supplemented by courses in the arts, health, physical education, and typing or microcomputer usage. Many high schools offer career exploration and guidance, and a substantial number offer vocational preparation courses, although these have been declining for the past two decades. Except for the latter, when schools have lacked these subjects, it is less the result of a deliberate policy decision than a shortage of resources.

The social reconstruction orientation of progressive education has been adopted only in a very weak form. Civics courses and student government offer introductions to the democratic governance of the country. Textbooks are more likely now to indicate some historical shortcomings of American society—slavery, discrimination, government corruption, notable abuses by business, and the problems of poverty. Critics, however, argue that these references are perfunctory and seldom challenge students to think about fundamental restructuring of America.

Some historians, both friends and foes of progressive education, claim this reform died in the 1950s.[87] Their eulogies are premature. New strains of progressive education continue to arise, although rarely under the label of "progressive education." In the 1960s, James Herndon, John Holt, Herbert Kohl, and Jonathan Kozol wrote best-selling books condemning the state of inner city schools and suggesting improvements that fell largely within the progressive education paradigm. Since the 1980s, cognitive scientists have developed new understandings about complex learning that were anticipated, in part, by the founding fathers of child-oriented pedagogy. Howard Gardner's popular writings on multiple intelligences provided a new perspective on child-oriented pedagogy. The American Association for the Advancement of Sciences' influential 1993 *Benchmarks for Science Literacy* advocates teaching fewer facts and more concepts, and its criteria for judging the pedagogy of textbooks specify that instruction should motivate student interest, take into account students' prior ideas about the topics, build on student curiosity, reward creativity, and provide opportunities to use new knowledge—a clear legacy of progressive education.[88]

E. D. Hirsch, Jr., a professor of English, has been highly critical of late 20th century schools for the failure to focus on the core knowledge, which he asserts all students must learn in order to be culturally literate. He has charged, "Political liberals really ought to oppose progressive educational ideas because they had led to practical failure and greater social inequity."[89] Nevertheless, the several hundred "Core Knowledge" schools that he inspired do not rely solely on rote memory but instead have students engaged in cooperative work groups, the creation of dioramas, and the staging plays—instructional practices drawn directly from progressive education.[90]

Achievement of Goals

Advocates and critics of progressive education had long argued about its effectiveness, mostly using anecdotal impressions. By the 1930s research methods in education had advanced considerably. What did the research results indicate about the merits and shortcomings of progressive education?

In 1930, J. Wayne Wrightstone made one of the first scientific appraisals of progressive education's effects. He concluded that students in progressive and traditional schools performed similarly. After taking into account the home backgrounds and intelligence scores of students, progressive schools did better on reading and spelling, and about the same on arithmetic. In assessments of the personal and social habits of students, there were no notable differences.[91]

J. Cayce Morrison conducted a study in New York City Schools between 1935 and 1941. The study compared students in 70 schools with progressive "activity classes" with students in traditional classes. Observations in classrooms found the activity classes spent somewhat less time on traditional subjects and somewhat more on arts and crafts than did the traditional classes. Teachers of the activity classes broke students into small work groups about twice as often—but only 16 percent of the total time. The data on students showed that those in the activity classes were superior in their interest in school, their self-assurance and self-reliance, their cooperative capabilities, their understanding of social relations, and their civic attitudes. There was no indication that they lacked a respect for authority. They were slightly stronger in reading and about equal on the other basic skills.[92]

"The Eight-Year Study," conducted between 1932 and 1941, was the most ambitious assessment of progressive education at the high school level. Thirty high schools, both public and private, were invited to participate in the demonstration. These schools were told to ignore college requirements and reconstruct their curriculum according to progressive principles so that they tapped the imagination of students and staff. More than 300 colleges agreed to waive their normal admissions requirements for recommended graduates of these high school programs. The objectives were to enhance: (1) mastery in learning, (2) continuity of learning, (3) the creative energies of students, (4) understanding of the problems of contemporary civilization, and (5) the individual guidance of students.[93] Each school revised its curriculum and instructional approach as it saw fit.

A team of measurement experts followed graduates of these schools through their college years and compared them with other college students of similar background and ability. They matched 1,475 graduates of progressive schools with those of other high schools on gender, age, race, scholastic aptitude scores, family background, and career and personal interests. They found that graduates of the thirty progressive schools received slightly higher grades and more honors in college; seemed to possess more intellectual curiosity and drive; seemed to be more precise, systematic and objective in their thinking; demonstrated more resourcefulness in meeting new challenges; had better orientation toward their choice of vocation; and demonstrated more concern about national and world affairs.[94] The differences, however, were generally small. Evaluators attributed this to the fact that the high schools had to gear up quickly for the demonstration, did little to learn from each other, and had no time to refine their educational approaches. With more time, testing, and feedback, the modest effects presumably would have been increased, but by the time the study was reported, the nation was headed into World War II and school reform was not a priority.

Taken together, these evaluation results do not demonstrate the dramatic positive effects that progressive education proponents had expected. They also do not support the condemnation that foes have voiced.

There is little evidence that progressive education reduced social stratification by narrowing the achievement gaps between lower class and upper class students, by reducing the dropout rates of lower class students, by increasing the college-going rates of lower class students, or by any other means. As mentioned earlier, there are indications that working class families tended to be less comfortable with child-centered pedagogy than middle and upper class families. The Eight-Year Study involved college-prep high schools at a time when only eight percent of 23-year-olds earned bachelor's degrees, making it doubtful that any of those schools served substantial portions of working class or poor youth.[95] The social deconstructionists" hope of using the schools to kindle a socialist revolution never received widespread support.

Unintended Side Effects

Critics of the child-oriented pedagogy of progressive education have often charged that it had negative side effects, contributing to the rise of self-indulgence, immorality, delinquency and crime in America. As we saw in Chapter 2, universal public education was proposed in the mid-1800s partly to combat just those problems, which had grown throughout the first half of that century. Then, in Chapter 3, we saw that the critics of the secularization of public education claimed that reform had exacerbated those ills in the latter part of the 1800s. In the 20th century progressive education drew the blame for the same enduring problems.

Critics of progressive education's expansion of the curriculum often charge that the new "life-preparation" courses displaced the academic fundamentals. This intuitive argument fails to recognize that from 1890 to 1940, as progressive education reforms were being implemented, the average number of days attended by students increased by 75 percent. That was partly because the school year was lengthened and partly because attendance rates increased substantially.[96] This made it possible to teach new subjects without reducing the time spent teaching traditional ones. At the high school level, over this period, there were declines in the percentages of students taking Latin, physics, algebra, and geometry, but there were similar increases in the percentages of students taking English, French, and biology, as well as increases in those taking physical education, home economics, and vocational courses.[97] In addition, those changes occurred during a period in which high school enrollments increased 30-fold.[98] Progressive educators had argued that making the curriculum more practical was necessary to attract and hold a large portion of adolescents in high school. They surely exalted in the high school enrollment trend. Although other factors undoubtedly influenced high school enrollments, the more engaging and practical curriculum probably did play a role.

While many middle class progressive educators dreamed of obliterating ethnic and class schisms in America, Marxist critics have observed that the provision of vocational education to attract and hold poor and working class youth in high school "reflected an implicit assumption of the immutability of the class structure."[99] The criticism ignores that progressives also encouraged middle class students to take non-academic subjects. On the other hand, enrollment data do show that lower class students more often enroll in the vocational track of high school and middle class students more often enroll in the college-prep track of high school.[100]

WAS PROGRESSIVE EDUCATION INEVITABLE?

A country with roots in the Enlightenment, born of a revolution, and suckled by science and technology, is unlikely to be long content with conducting its education in the manner of yore. Progress was a core value of late 19th and 20th century America. Given the social and economic changes of the late 1800s and early 1900s, given the expansion of compulsory education, and given the rise of the new science of psychology, education was almost certain to change.

That education had to change in the manner it did is more questionable. The advocacy of extreme child-centered education, urging that children should learn from whatever interests them whenever they are inclined, found in the writings of Rousseau, Locke, and Hall, appears to be more a rebellion against the rote memorization and harsh discipline of the past than a thoughtful prescription for an improved pedagogy. Indeed, if one accepts the thinking of those writers, it is not clear that formal schooling is desirable, a point that only Rousseau explicated. Dewey took a more moderate position, urging teachers to guide children's interests to increasingly challenging problems and projects from which the students would infer knowledge and skills, but his prolific writings were so unclear about instructional procedures that he inadvertently fueled the rebellion rather than quieting it. If psychology had been allowed to advance a few more decades before its application to education, more powerful pedagogies might have been developed and gained favor under the progressive education banner.

That the curriculum would expand in the 20th century seems almost inevitable. As we have already seen, expansion of the curriculum began in the 19th century long before progressive education was implemented in this country. During the early 20th century, compulsory universal education and then the Great Depression were forcing increasing percentages of students into high schools while the secondary curriculum inherited from the 1800s had been designed to prepare upper-middle class males for college. In the early 1900s, industrialization was generating substantial demand for mechanics and electricians, and expanding corporate and government offices boosted the demand for people with clerical skills. The high schools responded by providing preparation for a variety of adult roles, not just for college. Germany had met the challenge by developing a dual system of secondary education—one for academic education and one for vocational training. That required formal class distinctions, not unlike when the U.S. had charity schools in the 1700s and early 1800s. The alternative was to mix academic and vocational courses within each high school. The current attacks on occupational courses in high school are not intended to eliminate all such preparation but rather to move it to community colleges and postsecondary training centers. That is feasible today, but in the early 1900s there were very few community colleges, and many families could barely afford to delay their children's entrance into the workforce by the four years required of high school.

FUTURE OF THE REFORM

Mortimer Adler, one of the most learned and energetic advocates of traditional education, explained its merit with the following syllogism:
Major premise: Good habits (virtues) are the same for all men.
Minor premise: Education should aim at the formation of good habits.
Conclusion: Education should aim at the same objectives for all men.[101]
Even if one accepts the major and minor premise, that syllogism is not logical justification of traditional education. More than one instructional approach could develop those virtues, and indeed some approaches might do so better than traditional education.

There has been feverish criticism of American education throughout the latter half of the 20th century, but hardly anyone has suggested the country should return to considering children as the devil incarnate needing to be beaten into submission, that it should design curriculum and instruction with no effort to make school engaging to students, that it should replace all projects and papers with recitations of memorized materials, that it should eliminate science laboratories from the schools, that it should remove nurses and all health services from schools, and that it should abolish all extra-curricular activities. Given the lack of opposition to these practices, the legacy of progressive education on American education is likely to endure for many decades.

Progressive education is currently sustaining a counterattack that seeks to refocus the curriculum on basic academic skills and traditional subjects, eliminating the broad life preparation curriculum that was introduced widely over the first half of the 20th century. This effort has had moderate success. In addition, the new state and federal accountability reform efforts, if they are sustained, will further narrow the curriculum toward whatever is included in the high stakes tests, perhaps squeezing out art, music, and foreign languages. This could make the curriculum as narrowly focused as it was in the mid-1800s. The accountability reform effort will be analyzed in Chapter 10.

In one sense, a return to academic basics may not now be an abandonment of life preparation. The 20th century has seen a marked shift from an agricultural and industrial economy to a service and information economy, which has been accompanied by a dramatic narrowing of the skills valued in the workplace. In the early part of the century there was considerable demand for physically strong workers, for those with manual dexterity, and for those with well-developed intellectual skills. Over the succeeding decades, however, the demand for physical strength and dexterity has declined markedly. Most well-paying jobs in the current economy and in the foreseeable future require advanced cognitive skills that most people do not acquire without many years of formal schooling. Ironically, in the first half of the century reformers were trying to make school more like the workplace, and in the second half of the century the workplace has become more like school.

Yet, life involves more than employment. Youth of today need to be prepared to exercise civic responsibilities and leadership within their communities and within our increasingly diverse nation. They also need to be prepared for citizenship in an inter-dependent and dangerous global village, where products, services, cultures, terrorists, and industrial waste flow freely across the widest oceans and over the highest mountain ranges. One impetus for progressive education in the late 1800s was that homes, churches, and traditional academic instruction in school did not prepare youth well for their social and political responsibilities. There is no reason to think a simple return to academics will be any more effective for these purposes than it was formerly.

Generation after generation of aspiring liberal reformers of schools keep reinventing the three main approaches of progressive education—child-oriented education, education for life, and education for social reform—usually ignorant of their predecessors' attempts and results. While each of these, in thoughtful formulations, has made contributions to the advancement of education, none has achieved its full promise. If progressive education is to accomplish more, it will have to progress further, avoiding past shortcomings and building new strengths.

[1] U.S. Department of Education, National Center for Education Statistics, *120 Years of American Education* (Washington DC: Government Printing Office), 36; U.S. Department of Commerce, Bureau of the Census, *Historical Statistics of the United States: Colonial Times to 1957* (Washington DC: U.S. Government Printing Office, 1961), 9.

[2] U.S. Department of Education, National Center for Education Statistics, *120 Years of American Education* (Washington DC: Government Printing Office), 46; U.S. Department of Commerce, Bureau of the Census, *Historical Statistics of the United States: Colonial Times to 1957* (Washington DC: U.S. Government Printing Office, 1961), 46; Lawrence A. Cremin, *The Transformation of the American School: Progressivism in American Education* (New York: Alfred Knopf, 1961), 21.

[3] Barbara Finklestein, *Governing the Young: Teacher Behavior in Popular Primary Schools in Nineteenth-Century United States* (New York: Falmer Press, 1989), 44-45, 67-71, 136-137.

[4] Lawrence A. Cremin, *The Transformation of the American School: Progressivism in American Education* (New York: Alfred Knopf, 1961), 4-8.

[5] Quoted in Ida DePencier, *The History of the Laboratory Schools* (undated). Retrieved on 02/21/03 from www.ucls.uchicago.edu/About/history/ chapter2.html.

[6] Barbara Finklestein, *Governing the Young: Teacher Behavior in Popular Primary Schools in Nineteenth-Century United States* (New York: Falmer Press, 1989), 95-107.

[7] U.S. Department of Commerce, Bureau of the Census, *Historical Statistics of the United States: Colonial Times to 1957* (Washington DC: Government Printing Office, 1961), 74.

[8] U.S. Department of Commerce, Bureau of the Census, *Historical Statistics of the United States: Colonial Times to 1957* (Washington DC: Government Printing Office, 1961), 74.

[9] Robert Heilbroner & Aaron Singer, *The Economic Transformation of America: 1600 to the Present,* 3rd ed. (Fort Worth, TX: Harcourt Brace, 1994), 229.

[10] U.S. Department of Commerce, Bureau of the Census, *Historical Statistics of the United States: Colonial Times to 1957* (Washington DC: Government Printing Office, 1961), 139.

[11] U.S. Department of Commerce, Bureau of the Census, *Historical Statistics of the United States: Colonial Times to 1957* (Washington DC: Government Printing Office, 1961), 90, 91-92, 127.

[12] U.S. Department of Commerce, Bureau of the Census, *Historical Statistics of the United States: Colonial Times to 1957* (Washington DC: Government Printing Office, 1961), 91, 126, 127.

[13] Robert Heilbroner & Aaron Singer, *The Economic Transformation of America: 1600 to the Present,* 3rd ed. (Fort Worth, TX: Harcourt Brace, 1994), 156-161, 203-208.

[14] U.S. Department of Commerce, Bureau of the Census, *Historical Statistics of the United States: Colonial Times to 1957* (Washington DC: Government Printing Office, 1961), 99.

[15] Quoted in Robert Heilbroner & Aaron Singer, *The Economic Transformation of America: 1600 to the Present,* 3rd ed. (Fort Worth, TX: Harcourt Brace, 1994), 162.

[16] Maurice R. Berube, *American School Reform: Progressive, Equity and Excellence Movement, 1883-1993* (Westport, CT: Praegar, 1994), 1-9.

[17] Quoted in Maurice R. Berube, *American School Reform: Progressive, Equity and Excellence Movement, 1883-1993* (Westport, CT: Praegar, 1994), 4.

[18] Quoted in Adolphe E. Meyer, *Grandmasters of Educational Thought* (New York: McGraw-Hill, 1975), 134.

[19] Quoted in Adolphe E. Meyer, *Grandmasters of Educational Thought* (New York: McGraw-Hill, 1975), 133.

[20] Quoted in Frederick Mayer, *A History of Educational Thought* (Columbus, OH: Charles E. Merrill, 1960), 227.

[21] Quoted in Robert Rusk, *Doctrines of Great Educators*, 5th ed. (New York: St. Martin's Press, 1979), 122.

[22] Quoted in Adolphe E. Meyer, *The Development of Education in the Twentieth Century*, 2nd ed. (New York: Prentice Hall, 1949), 17.

[23] William James, *Talks to Teachers on Psychology: and to Students on Some of Life's Ideals* (New York: Dover, 1899), 54, 109.

[24] Quoted in Lawrence A. Cremin, *The Transformation of the American School: Progressivism in American Education* (New York: Alfred Knopf, 1961), 103.

[25] Stephen J. Provasnik, "Compulsory Schooling, From Idea to Institution: A Case Study of the Development of Compulsory Attendance in Illinois, 1857-1907" (Ph.D. diss., University of Chicago, 1999), 32-66, 148-182; David B. Tyack, "Ways of Seeing: An Essay on the History of Compulsory Schooling," in *History, Education, and Public Policy*, ed. Donald R. Warren (Berkeley, CA: McCutchan, 1978), 55-89.

[26] Lawrence A. Cremin, *The Transformation of the American School: Progressivism in American Education* (New York: Alfred Knopf, 1961), 127.

[27] Estimated for 1910 from: U.S. Department of Education, National Center for Education Statistics, *120 Years of American Education* (Washington DC: Government Printing Office), 34, 75.

[28] Lawrence A. Cremin, *The Transformation of the American School: Progressivism in American Education* (New York: Alfred Knopf, 1961), 129-130.

[29] Lawrence A. Cremin, *The Transformation of the American School: Progressivism in American Education* (New York: Alfred Knopf, 1961), 130-131; Harry G. Good, *A History of American Education*, 2nd ed. (Toronto, Ontario: MacMillan Company, 1962), 220-221); Samuel Chester Parker, *The History of Modern Elementary Education*, (1912; reprinted Towata, NJ: Littlefield, Adams & Co., 1970), 471-473.

[30] Lawrence A. Cremin, *The Transformation of the American School: Progressivism in American Education* (New York: Alfred Knopf, 1961), 130-131.

[31] [Lost Reference]

[32] See, Lawrence A. Cremin, *The Transformation of the American School: Progressivism in American Education* (New York: Alfred Knopf, 1961), 132-134; Adolphe E. Meyer, *The Development of Education in the Twentieth Century*, 2nd ed. (New York: Prentice Hall, 1949), 34.

[33] Joan K. Smith, *Ella Flag Young: Portrait of a Leader* (Ames, IA: Educational Studies Press), 1976), 40.

[34] Joan K. Smith, *Ella Flag Young: Portrait of a Leader* (Ames, IA: Educational Studies Press), 1976), 40, 43.

[35] Joan K. Smith, *Ella Flag Young: Portrait of a Leader* (Ames, IA: Educational Studies Press), 1976), 44.

[36] Adolphe E. Meyer, *The Development of Education in the Twentieth Century*, 2nd ed. (New York: Prentice Hall, 1949), 42-45.

[37] Quoted in Douglas J. Simpson & Michael J. B. Jackson, *Educational Reform: A Deweyan Perspective* (New York: Garland Publishing, 1997), 43.
[38] John Dewey, "My Pedagogical Creed," *The School Journal* 54 (January 16, 1897): 77-80.
[39] Adolphe E. Meyer, *An Educational History of the American People* (New York: McGraw-Hill, 1957), 252.
[40] Ida DePencier, *The History of the Laboratory Schools* (undated). Retrieved on 02/21/03 from www.ucls.uchicago.edu/About/history/ chapterone.html [about pages 5-6 of 7].
[41] Quoted in Ida DePencier, *The History of the Laboratory Schools* (undated). Retrieved on 02/21/03 from www.ucls.uchicago.edu/About/history/ chapter2.html [about pages 2-3 of 6].
[42] Quoted in Larry Cuban, *How Teachers Taught: Constancy and Change in American Classrooms: 1880-1990*, 2nd ed. (New York: Teachers College Press, 1993), 43.
[43] Quoted in Larry Cuban, *How Teachers Taught: Constancy and Change in American Classrooms: 1880-1990*, 2nd ed. (New York: Teachers College Press, 1993), 43-44.
[44] Joan K. Smith, *Ella Flag Young: Portrait of a Leader* (Ames, IA: Educational Studies Press, 1976), 68.
[45] Ida DePencier, *The History of the Laboratory Schools* (undated). Retrieved on 02/21/03 from www.ucls.uchicago.edu/About/history/ chapterone.html [about page 7 of 7], and www.ucls.uchicago.edu/About/ history/chapter2.html [about page 1 of 6].
[46] John Dewey, *Democracy and Education: An Introduction to the Philosophy of Education* (New York: The Free Press, 1916; reprinted 1944), 20, 79, 153, 157, 175, 189, 220, 223.
[47] Joan K. Smith, *Ella Flagg Young: Portrait of a Leader* (Ames, IA: Educational Studies Press, 1976), 4-7.
[48] David Tyack & Elisabeth Hansot, *Managers of Virtue: Public School Leadership in America, 1820-1980* (New York: Basic Books, 1982), 199.
[49] Quote in Joan K. Smith, *Ella Flag Young: Portrait of a Leader* (Ames, IA: Educational Studies Press, 1976), 63 and 64.
[50] Jackie M. Blount, "Ella Flagg Young and the Chicago Schools" in *Founding Mothers and Others: Women Educational Leaders During the Progressive Era*, eds. Alan R. Sadovnik and Susan F. Semel (New York: Palgrave, 2002), 164-176.
[51] Jackie M. Blount, "Ella Flagg Young and the Chicago Schools" in *Founding Mothers and Others: Women Educational Leaders During the Progressive Era*, eds. Alan R. Sadovnik and Susan F. Semel (New York: Palgrave, 2002), 164-176.
[52] Melvin L. Barlow, *History of Industrial Education in the United States* (Peoria, IL: Chas. A. Bennett Co., 1967).
[53] Quoted in Lawrence A. Cremin, *The Transformation of the American School: Progressivism in American Education* (New York: Alfred Knopf, 1961), 30.
[54] Lawrence A. Cremin, *The Transformation of the American School: Progressivism in American Education* (New York: Alfred Knopf, 1961), 32-33.
[55] Lawrence A. Cremin, *The Transformation of the American School: Progressivism in American Education* (New York: Alfred Knopf, 1961), 36.
[56] Lawrence A. Cremin, *The Transformation of the American School: Progressivism in American Education* (New York: Alfred Knopf, 1961), 48-49.
[57] Quoted in Lawrence A. Cremin, *The Transformation of the American School: Progressivism in American Education* (New York: Alfred Knopf, 1961), 50.
[58] National Education Association, Commission on the Reorganization of Secondary Education, *Cardinal Principles of Secondary Education* (Washington DC: Government Printing Office, 1918), 10-15.

[59] Larry Cuban, "Enduring Resiliency: Enacting and Implementing Federal Vocational Education Legislation" in *Work, Youth, and Schooling: Historical Perspectives on Vocationalism in American Education,* eds. Harvey Kantor & David B. Tyack (Stanford, CA: Stanford University Press, 1982), 45-50; Joseph F. Kett, "From Useful Knowledge to Vocational Education: 1860-1930" Conference paper #11 (New York: Institute on Education and the Economy, Teachers College, Columbia University, 1990), 34-37.

[60] C. A. Bowers, *The Progressive Educator and the Depression: The Radical Years* (New York: Random House, 1969), 15, 44, 139-140.

[61] Quoted in C. A. Bowers, *The Progressive Educator and the Depression: The Radical Years* (New York: Random House, 1969), 14-15.

[62] Lawrence A. Cremin, *The Transformation of the American School: Progressivism in American Education* (New York: Alfred Knopf, 1961), 154-160.

[63] Lawrence A. Cremin, *The Transformation of the American School: Progressivism in American Education* (New York: Alfred Knopf, 1961), 296-298.

[64] Lawrence A. Cremin, *The Transformation of the American School: Progressivism in American Education* (New York: Alfred Knopf, 1961), 299-301.

[65] Quoted in Lawrence A. Cremin, *The Transformation of the American School: Progressivism in American Education* (New York: Alfred Knopf, 1961), 299.

[66] Lawrence A. Cremin, *The Transformation of the American School: Progressivism in American Education* (New York: Alfred Knopf, 1961), 299-301; Larry Cuban, *How Teachers Taught: Constancy and Change in American Classroom: 1880-1990,* 2nd ed. (New York: Teachers College Press, 1993), 81.

[67] Lawrence A. Cremin, *The Transformation of the American School: Progressivism in American Education* (New York: Alfred Knopf, 1961), 301-302.

[68] Lawrence A. Cremin, *The Transformation of the American School: Progressivism in American Education* (New York: Alfred Knopf, 1961), 302-303.

[69] Larry Cuban, How Teachers Taught: Constancy and Change in American Classrooms: 1880-1990, 2nd ed. (New York: Teachers College Press, 1993), 90.

[70] See: Lawrence A. Cremin, *The Genius of American Education* (New York: Vintage Books, 1965), 204, 278-279; .Harry G. Good and James D. Teller, *A History of American Education,* 3rd ed. (New York:Macmillan, 1973), 381; Diane Ravitch, *Left Back: A Century of Battles Over School Reform* (New York: Simon and Schuster, 2000), 174-175.

[71] Jonathan Zimmerman, "Storm Over the Schoolhouse: Exploring Popular Influences Upon the American Curriculum," *Teacher College Record* 100 (Spring 1999): 602-626.

[72] Lawrence A. Cremin, *The Transformation of the American School: Progressivism in American Education* (New York: Alfred Knopf, 1961), 36-37.

[73] Quoted in Adolphe E. Meyer, *The Development of Education in the Twentieth Century,* 2nd ed. (New York: Prentice Hall, 1949), 152 & 155.

[74] Adolphe E. Meyer, *The Development of Education in the Twentieth Century,* 2nd ed. (New York: Prentice Hall, 1949), 151.

[75] Diane Ravitch, *Left Back: A Century of Battles Over School Reform* (New York: Simon and Schuster, 2000), 34.

[76] Quoted in Lawrence A. Cremin, *The Transformation of the American School: Progressivism in American Education* (New York: Alfred Knopf, 1961), 234-235.

[77] Quoted in Lawrence A. Cremin, *The Transformation of the American School: Progressivism in American Education* (New York: Alfred Knopf, 1961), 234.

[78] Robert M. Hutchins, *Education for Freedom* (Baton Rouge, LA: Louisiana State University Press, 1943), 35-36.
[79] Quoted in *Lessons of a Century*, Bethesda, MD: Editorial Projects in Education, 2000), 98.
[80] Maurice R. Berube, *American School Reform: Progressive, Equity and Excellence Movement, 1883-1993* (Westwood, CT: Praegar, 1994), 39.
[81] Quoted in Maurice R. Berube, *American School Reform: Progressive, Equity and Excellence Movement, 1883-1993* (Westwood, CT: Praegar, 1994), 27.
[82] Lawrence A. Cremin, *The Genius of American Education* (New York: Vintage Books, 1965), 10.
[83] Lawrence A. Cremin, *The Transformation of the School: Progressivism in American Education, 1876-1957* (New York: Alfred A Knopf, 1961), 328.
[84] Diane Ravitch, *The Troubled Crusade: American Education, 1945-1980* (New York: Basic Books, 1983), 43.
[85] Larry Cuban, *How Teachers Taught: Constancy and Change in American Classroom: 1880-1990*, 2nd ed. (New York: Teachers College Press, 1993), 98-146.
[86] Larry Cuban, *How Teachers Taught: Constancy and Change in American Classroom: 1880-1990*, 2nd ed. (New York: Teachers College Press, 1993), 6-8, 145-146.
[87] Lawrence A. Cremin, *The Transformation of the American School: Progressivism in American Education* (New York: Alfred Knopf, 1961), 347; Diane Ravitch, *The Troubled Crusade: American Education, 1945-1980* (New York: Basic Books, 1983), 78.
[88] See the American Association for the Advancement of Sciences' "AAAS Project 2061 Middle Grades Science Textbook Evaluation:Criteria for Evaluating the Quality of Instructional Support" (Washington DC: author, n.d.), retrieved 03/05/03 from www.project2061.org/newsinfo/research/ textbook/mgsci/criteria.htm.
[89] Quoted in *Lessons of a Century* (Bethesda, MD: Editorial Projects in Education, 2000), 100.
[90] *Lessons of a Century*, Bethesda, MD: Editorial Projects in Education, 2000), 101.
[91] Adolphe E. Meyer, *The Development of Education in the Twentieth Century* (New York: Prentice Hall, 1952), 158-159.
[92] Adolph E. Meyer, *Development of Education in the Twentieth Century*, 2nd ed. (New York, Prentice Hall, 1949), 160-161.
[93] Lawrence A. Cremin, *The Transformation of the American School: Progressivism in American Education* (New York: Alfred Knopf, 1961), 252.
[94] Dean Chamberlain et al: *Did they succeed in college?* Pp. 207-208; cited in *The Transformation of the American School: Progressivism in American Education*, Lawrence A. Cremin (New York: Alfred Knopf, 1961), 255-256.
[95] U.S. Department of Education, National Center for Education Statistics, *120 Years of American Education: A Statistical Portrait* (Washington DC: Government Printing Office, 1993), 68.
[96] U.S. Department of Education, National Center for Education Statistics, *120 Years of American Education: A Statistical Portrait* (Washington DC: Government Printing Office, 1993), 34.
[97] U.S. Department of Education, National Center for Education Statistics, *120 Years of American Education: A Statistical Portrait* (Washington DC: Government Printing Office, 1993), 50.

[98] U.S. Department of Education, National Center for Education Statistics, *120 Years of American Education: A Statistical Portrait* (Washington DC: Government Printing Office, 1993), 34.

[99] Samuel Bowles, "Unequal Education and the Reproduction of the Social Division of Labor," in *The Socially Disadvantaged*, ed. Earl J. Ogletree (New York: MSS Information Corporation, 1973), 36-64. pg 44

[100] Patricia C. Sexton, *Education and Income: Inequalities of Opportunity in Our Public Schools* (New York: Viking Press, 1961), 171-180.

[101] Mortimer Adler, "In Defense of a Philosophy of Education" in *Forty-First Yearbook: National Society for the Study of Education, Part I,* ed. Nelson B. Henry (Bloomington, Illinois: Public School Publishing Company, 1942), 239.

5

Professionalization of Teaching

Gregg B. Jackson

In colonial times, impoverished Europeans sometimes gained free transit to America by agreeing to be "redemptioners" with a subsequent four or five years of indentured servitude. One observer noted,

> Not a ship arrives with either redemptioners or convicts, in which schoolmasters are not as regularly advertised for sale, as weavers, tailors, or any other trade, with little other difference, that I can hear of, excepting perhaps that the former do not usually fetch so good a price as the latter.[1]

Definitions of professionalism vary but usually include the following cluster of five characteristics: 1) intensive specialized intellectual training that results in esoteric knowledge and skills, 2) challenging credentialing or licensure requirements, 3) considerable autonomy over the means by which the professional undertakes work responsibilities, subject primarily to professional standards, 4) professional associations that exercise substantial control over the training, certification, and standards of work, and 5) high respect or earnings. Occupational groups that have four or five of those characteristics are usually considered professionals.

INITIAL CONDITIONS

In colonial America, most schooling was at the elementary level (grades 1-8). As Chapter 2 explained, there were a few private Latin grammar (secondary) schools attended by sons of the upper classes preparing for college. By the mid-1700s, a number of private academies had also been established, providing middle class adolescents with a few years of academic or vocational training beyond the elementary level. Most adolescents, however, engaged in full-time work from about the age of 15.

Elementary School Teachers

As noted in Chapter 4, instruction in the colonial period focused on the four R's of reading, writing, arithmetic, and religion. The prevailing pedagogy of those times did not make heavy demands on a teacher. Teachers spent most of their time assigning materials to be memorized, having students recite the materials, and whacking those who made mistakes.[2] During this period the only qualifications for becoming an elementary school teacher were to profess Christianity (sometimes the specific denomination of the local community), adhere to moral propriety, have knowledge of the basic subjects to be taught, and be capable of disciplining a group of youngsters.[3]

By the mid-colonial period, applicants for teaching positions would first have their handwriting checked and then would be asked to read a passage aloud and solve simple arithmetic computations, but sometimes the committee members did not know the correct answers.[4] There are many reports of school committees being derelict in examining prospective teachers and of hiring decisions based on nepotism and patronage.[5]

By the early 1800s, most districts sought teachers who had completed the full eight years of elementary schooling, but many of these had not mastered the academic skills expected of such graduates and only a few had any additional preparation for teaching.[6] The first popular book on teaching, *Lectures on School-Keeping* by Reverend Samuel Hall, did not appear until 1829. It dealt with curriculum, teaching methods, and approaches to discipline.[7]

New teachers were assigned to isolated one-room schools, which precluded the opportunity for guidance from experienced teachers. One report indicated that the only way for new teachers to learn about instructional techniques and classroom management was to experiment on the job with the effect that: "The time, capacities, and opportunities of thousands of the children are now sacrificed winter after winter to the preparation of teachers, who.... are, notwithstanding, often very wretchedly prepared."[8]

Male teachers had initially been preferred because they could strong-arm the older boys when they became physically rebellious. By the later colonial period, women came into favor because they tended to be "better bred" than the males who gravitated toward teaching in rural schools, and because their presumed nurturing qualities were thought better suited for dealing with children, particularly the younger ones. Reformers saw middle class women teachers as more likely to instill genteel American values in their students.⁹ Another advantage of women was that they were given about half the salary of their male counterparts.

Elementary teachers had varying degrees of autonomy over their work. The school committee was supposed to supervise the school and monitor the teacher's work, but committee members often lived at a distance and were preoccupied with scraping a living from the soil. By the late colonial period, there are several reports of school committees selecting the texts to be used and mandating certain modes of instruction, but most reports suggest this was largely left to the teachers' discretion. School committees apparently provided more guidance about women teachers' personal lives than about their school responsibilities. Contracts often forbade card-playing, smoking, going out alone in the evening, socializing with men, and marriage.¹⁰ Parents and relatives occasionally expressed strong opinions about how the school should be conducted and occasionally complained about a teacher, usually for not disciplining students enough, or in a few cases, for disciplining them too harshly.¹¹

Work conditions were difficult. The one-room schoolhouses usually had students ranging in age from 5-15. The schools generally did not provide the textbooks and students often brought whichever texts their parents had acquired. School was commonly held in two semesters—a two- or three-month semester in winter and a shorter 5-6 week semester in the middle of summer, permitting the older children to be available to help on the farms during the busy spring planting and fall harvesting seasons. The schoolhouses were cold in the winter, even when equipped with a fireplace or wood-burning stove, and they could be stifling hot in the middle of summer. The teacher's title of "school keeper" included firing up the stove and janitorial services.

There are very few reports of teachers being fired for incompetence but many reports of firings for moral offenses and political differences, even unsubstantiated ones.¹² In addition, the older boys would occasionally "turn out" disdained teachers, by beating them off.¹³ Horace Mann reported that, in the late 1830s, three or four hundred school rebellions occurred each year in Massachusetts, closing one-tenth of all schools before the end of the term.¹⁴

Elementary school teachers were paid out of town taxes or fees charged to the parents. In early colonial times, the average salary was about one-fourth that of ministers, who were usually the highest paid town officials.¹⁵ As late as 1840, the weekly wages for male teachers in Massachusetts were about the same as for farm hands.¹⁶ Women, on average, earned about 40 percent of male teachers' pay in urban areas and 60 percent in rural areas.¹⁷

Teachers occasionally had difficulty collecting their wages.¹⁸ Many poor rural communities tried to compensate for the low pay by "boarding around," in which the teacher would spend a few days or a week living at each student's home—sometimes in the one room shared by the whole family. While this helped teachers to know their students and facilitated communication with parents, many of the teachers wearied of it quickly, and it was suspected to contribute to rapid turnover of teachers.

No one could make a living as a teacher because the wages were barely above subsistence and only paid when school was in session during the winter and again for a short period during the summer. Most teachers also worked at other trades.

From the mid-1700s, young women increasingly engaged in teaching as a respectable adventure before marrying. Most taught for only a semester or two.

Academies, Grammar Schools, and High Schools

Benjamin Franklin founded an academy in 1751 to teach practical arts beyond the elementary school level. One of the proclaimed purposes was "that others of lesser sort might be trained as teachers."[19]

The academies, which provided further academic and vocational training at the equivalent of today's high school level, were often taught by people who themselves had only completed academy schooling or perhaps a year or two of college. The few Latin grammar schools preparing young men for college were usually taught by ministers who had a college education or by young men who had just completed college. While they were well prepared in the subjects taught, these instructors had no preparation in teaching, classroom management, or motivation and discipline. The working conditions and pay of grammar schools were considerably better than those of elementary schools. Despite that, most of these young men went on to other careers, often in law or the ministry, although a few remained teachers and gained the respect of their communities.

CHANGING CONTEXTS THAT PUSHED THE PROFESSIONALIZATION OF TEACHING

There were at least four changing contexts that pushed efforts to professionalize teaching. They were the growing prosperity of the country, the expansion of universal education, the rise of new pedagogies, and expanding professionalism in America's occupational structure.

Growing Prosperity in America

The meager preparation of colonial elementary teachers, the short school year, and the low wages of teachers were all partly a result of a predominantly rural subsistence economy. Few families could afford to have their adolescent children to continue schooling beyond the elementary level because that would require paying tuition and forgoing the youths' labor on the farms.

As indicated in the earlier chapters, through most of the 1800s the country prospered. Many farmers and wage earners improved their lot substantially. In addition, a small number of people gained considerable wealth and cities began taxing to support public services. That permitted expanded expenditures for education but also made citizens demand more from schools. School leaders responded by arranging for better education of teachers, establishing credentialing systems, and improving teachers' working conditions in hopes of attracting and retaining more able people.

Expansion of Universal Education

By the late 1700s, the elementary school curriculum had expanded from the 4Rs to include history and geography. The "R" of writing had evolved from penmanship to composition. This new content added to the demands made on teachers' knowledge and skills.

Chapter 2 discussed the dramatic extension of universal public elementary education throughout the 1800s. Then in the first half of the 1900s, there was marked expansion of high schools, with the percentage of 14- to 17-year-olds enrolled rising from about ten percent in 1900 to 70 percent in 1950. That created a large demand for high school teachers, who obviously needed higher levels of subject matter mastery. Less obviously, but equally important, they needed to learn ways of motivating and disciplining older students, many of whom where not keen on being cooped up in school for several more years.

Rise of New Pedagogies

Chapter 4 noted how new developments in philosophy and pedagogy influenced progressive education. The historian Lawrence Cremin noted:

> From the beginning, progressivism cast the teacher in an almost impossible role: he was to be an artist of consummate skill, properly knowledgeable in his field, meticulously trained in the science of pedagogy, and thoroughly imbued with a burning zeal for social improvement.[20]

Progressive educator's advocacy of Pestalozzi's "object teaching," from which students learned by observing objects, required teachers to decide what objects to use, how the object experiences should be sequenced to reinforce prior learning and optimize new learning, and what questions should be asked of the students to prompt further observation and thought about the object.[21] In an ill-prepared teacher's hands, Pestalozzi's approach degenerated into the memorization of adjectives describing a given object.[22]

In the late 1800s, the pedagogical ideas of the German philosophy professor Johann Friedrich Herbart were considered the most advanced pedagogy of the day. He urged that every unit of instruction should include five steps: preparation (raising interest and linking to existing knowledge), presentation of new material, association (comparing new and prior knowledge), generalization (providing rules for use of the new material), and application (giving examples of practical use).

The use of Pestalozzian, Herbartian, and other progressive education pedagogies required far more preparation of teachers and far more complex decision-making on their part than did the colonial pedagogy of recitation and punishment. We saw in Chapter 4 that many teachers did not fully adopt progressive pedagogy but rather hybrids of progressive and traditional pedagogy. To do that well, teachers needed to acquire even a broader range of skills and the virtuosity to switch among them to optimize results. Indeed to rely on one method for all purposes and circumstances is contrary to professional practice in any field.

Growing Professionalism in America

In the 1600s, clergymen in the American colonies often carried out more than ministry functions. They acted as physicians, as legal advisors, and as teachers. Toward the end of that century and the beginning of the next, as the population increased and society became more complex, there was growing specialization in intellectual occupations. By the mid-1700s, medicine and law were generally full-time occupations and the practitioners were showing group consciousness. Apprenticeships were used to prepare the next generation and several physicians established proprietary schools, where for fees, they would lecture students.

By the early 1800s, doctors and lawyers had convinced most states to establish licensing laws to raise standards--and the income--of practitioners. Usually a liberal arts college education and subsequent apprenticeship were required for licensure. Then in the mid-1800s, with the rise of Jacksonian populism, laissez faire entrepreneurialism and a rapidly expanding western frontier, licensing statutes were repealed by several eastern states and eschewed by the new states joining the union.[23] Indiana's constitution declared, "every person of good moral character who is a voter is entitled to practice law in any courts of the state."[24] At the 1829 opening ceremonies at the University of Nashville, the University's President Lindsley observed that it was easier to qualify to practice law or medicine than to build a dray or shoe a horse.[25] Many proprietary schools of questionable merit sprung up to train the masses for the professions.[26]

State-level professional licensure did not make a comeback until the 1880s, when the excesses of robber-baron capitalists had wilted the bloom of laissez faire, when cities and states had pioneered the use of government to mitigate social problems, and when science brought new theory and technology to medicine and spawned an engineering profession.

In 1847, the American Medical Association was created "To initiate reforms to correct the deplorable condition of medical education which then prevailed."[27] It apparently was not successful at that task because, in 1910, the Carnegie Foundation for the Advancement of Teaching issued a searing indictment of medical education. Now commonly referred to as the "Flexner Report," it found medical school faculty "consisted of busy practitioners with no time for teaching and no thought of research."[28] Half of all medical schools closed as a result of the report and most of the others were substantially upgraded.[29]

Harvard's law school, established in 1817, required applicants to have a college degree or equivalent, but Columbia's law school, opened several decades later, required applicants only to prove good character.[30] The American Bar Association was established in 1878 by 100 lawyers in 21 states "for the advancement of the science of jurisprudence, the promotion of the administration of justice and a uniformity of legislation throughout the country...."[31] As late as 1954 several states required only two years of college and three years of law school before sitting for the Bar examinations.[32]

Rensselaer Polytechnic Institute was founded in 1824 to train engineers, in an age when most university faculties considered the humanities to be the only appropriate college curriculum and were refusing to permit the teaching of science and technology.[33] About a quarter-century later, Columbia, Harvard, Yale, and Dartmouth finally opened schools of engineering.[34] The mid-1800s had been a period of rapid technological advance and in response Congress enacted the Morrill Act of 1862 to encourage states to establish colleges of agriculture and mechanical arts. Within a decade the number of engineering colleges increased from six to 70.[35] The first professional association of engineers was established in 1852 and many associations followed as engineering became highly specialized. State licensing for engineers was introduced in 1907 by Wyoming and adopted by all other states over the following four decades.[36]

CAMPAIGN FOR THE
PROFESSIONALIZATION OF TEACHING

The campaigns to professionalize teaching were undertaken as a means of enhancing the quality of education and improving teachers' work lives. Some campaigns focused on all five of the commonly identified components of professionalism: specialized intellectual training, credentialing or licensure, autonomy subject to established standards, professional associations, and high respect or earnings. Other campaigns focused on just one or two of those.

Henry Barnard: The Preparation of Teachers

Henry Barnard was a contemporary of Horace Mann (see Chapter 2) with a similar career in Connecticut and Rhode Island. During the mid-1830s Barnard traveled to Europe to examine educational practices there and was impressed by what he saw in Pestalozzi's school and in the Prussian schools that used Pestalozzi's methods. Barnard served in the Connecticut General Assembly and was chairman of its Select Committee on Education. In 1838 the Assembly created a Board of Commissioners of Common Schools with a secretary who was to "devote his whole time to ascertain the conditions, increase the interest, and promote the usefulness of the common schools."[37] Barnard was selected for the position.

He collected information on the operation of Connecticut's public schools, organized friends of education in every county, made speeches throughout the state, distributed a pamphlet on Pestalozzi's methods to all teachers, and founded and edited the *Connecticut Common School Journal*. In his first annual report, he noted a host of problems in securing and retaining good teachers:

> Most of the teachers employed the past winter, have not taught the same schools two successive seasons. Out of 1,292 teachers returned, but 341 have taught the same school before.... nearly one month of the school is practically lost in the time consumed by the teacher in getting acquainted with the temper, wants, dispositions, and previous progress of his various pupils.... By the time the school is in good progress, the scholars begin to drop away, the school money is exhausted, and the school is dismissed. After a vacation of unnecessary length, as far as the recreation and relief of the children are concerned, the summer school commences with reduced numbers, under a less vigilant supervision, with a poorly compensated teacher, to go though the same course as before.[38]

In the 1820's and 1830s, a few private individuals had created "seminaries" for training of elementary school teachers. In 1839 Barnard asked the Connecticut General Assembly to establish a "normal school" for that purpose. It would have an attached elementary school that would provide trainees with an opportunity for guided practice and also serve as a model school that could be visited by school committee members from throughout the state.[39]

The Assembly failed to pass the needed legislation. Several similar proposals over the next few years also failed. The opposition thought there was no need for better prepared elementary school teachers. The costs to taxpayers were a concern. Owners of the private seminaries and academies that had developed programs to train teachers resented competition from a state institution. People doubted that one normal school could improve the state's whole educational system. There were impassioned objections from some who argued that the idea of teacher training had served as an instrument of Prussian despotism and thus it was unfit for a democratic nation. Advocates of local rights opposed the proposed normal school because it would give the State more control over local education. Part of the opposition assumed a pragmatic position and urged delaying a decision until other states had tried normal schools.[40]

Barnard was disappointed but undaunted by the rejection of his proposal. Believing that initiatives to improve teachers' skills were critical, he used his own funds and contributions from a few Hartford citizens to conduct a six-week teachers' institute to:

> show the practicability of making some provisions for the better qualifications of common school teachers, by giving them an opportunity to revise and extend their knowledge of the studies usually pursued in district schools, and of the best methods of school arrangements, instruction, and government, under the recitations and lectures of experienced and well-known teachers and educators.[41]

Twenty-six men attended the first institute. The following year Barnard conducted a second institute, this time for women teachers. Barnard hoped that these short institutes would help persuade the Assembly to support the more extensive preparation that could be provided by a normal school.

Barnard also tried to raise the wages of teachers as a means of recruiting more able people to teach and of retaining them for several years. He noted:

> All admit that there is far from being a competent supply of such [qualified] teachers.... Unquestionably, if increased pecuniary inducements, equal to what is now present to young men of character and talents in other pursuits, were offered them as teachers of schools, we should soon find numbers taking the necessary step to fit themselves thoroughly for the occupation. The same would be true with regard to young women.[42]

Barnard outlined several alternative strategies by which Connecticut could boost the wages of teachers. He indicated that the state could mandate minimum wages to be paid teachers; it could pay a percentage of the teachers' wages; or it could distribute funds in proportion to the local funds raised per capita relative to the taxable property, which would provide extra help to those districts with a low tax bases.[43]

Increased wages probably would have solved the problems districts were having in recruiting teachers. Barnard, however, had an additional agenda; he presumed that if communities had to pay teachers more, they would also expect more from them, which would raise the quality of education. One respected supporter of his proposals, Thomas Gallaudet, founder and principal of the American Asylum for the Deaf and Dumb at Hartford, argued that properly prepared teachers would be capable of teaching the entire elementary school curriculum in five years rather than the standard eight years.[44]

In 1842, Barnard suffered a major setback. The Democrats won the governorship and gained control of the Assembly from the Whigs, and Barnard was removed from his post. He had gained national attention for his work in Connecticut and was soon invited to Rhode Island to help that state create a public education system. He accepted that offer and pursued it with his typical vigor.

Meanwhile, Connecticut citizens interested in public education organized a five-day convention of teachers with lectures and discussions, and more than 250 teachers attended.[45] Clearly, teachers were hungry to improve their knowledge and skills. The Connecticut General Assembly promptly authorized the holding of two institutes in each of the state's eight counties. They were to demonstrate the best instructional and discipline methods, improve teachers' "cultural background," motivate teachers, and enhance the public's interest in public education.[46] The new superintendent of Common Schools in Connecticut reported that the institutes had been a great success, based on attendance of more than 1,000, the enthusiasm of participants, and the new methods conveyed to the teachers.[47]

In 1849, ten years after Barnard had first urged the Connecticut General Assembly to create a normal school, and several years after Massachusetts, New York and Philadelphia had subsequently created such schools, the Connecticut Assembly finally authorized such an institution. It was to have a capacity up to 220 students. Each local district was entitled to enroll at least one student. Applicants were to declare in writing their intention to teach in the common schools of the state and were to be admitted on the basis of "age, character, talents, and attainments." Training would focus on the best methods for "instructing and governing common schools of this state." The Assembly provided funding for operating expenses but required that the building and fixtures had to be provided by the city or town in which the school was established.[48]

Barnard was invited back to Connecticut, to establish the normal school, serve as its principal, and also serve as state superintendent of the common schools. He accepted on the condition that he could appoint an associate principal to handle the day-to-day affairs of the school. In the first year, he not only opened the normal school but also conducted fourteen institutes throughout the state, establishing the pattern of using normal schools for "pre-service" preparation of teachers and institutes for "in-service" professional growth of practicing teachers.[49]

The earlier opponents of a normal school soon attacked the new normal school and urged the Assembly to terminate its funding. They argued that admissions standards were low and that many students left before completing the planned studies. Both criticisms were correct. Most applicants had not mastered the elementary school subject matter that they would soon be teaching—as was known to be true for many of those already in teaching positions. The school responded by examining students' subject matter knowledge and starting them in one of three levels of the program. Because so many schools were eager to hire teachers regardless of their preparation, a large portion of the students left before completion. The school responded by setting a requirement that students must complete at least one session of training. Despite problems, and partly because of the responses to them, the graduates quickly acquired a reputation for being superior teachers. In 1853 the Connecticut General Assembly authorized four more years of funding with a 60 percent increase in the budget.[50]

Because of failing health, Barnard resigned his position in 1855. He established the *American Journal of Education,* which reported educational reform efforts throughout the country. He later recovered his health and in 1867 was appointed as the first commissioner of the newly established U.S. Department of Education. When appropriations for its operations were not forthcoming and when the Department was downgraded to a bureau, Barnard quit. He continued to manage the journal for 25 years. On the brink of poverty, after devoting most of his modest wealth to school reform efforts and his beloved journal, he died in 1890. He had earlier written Horace Mann saying, "I am ambitious of being remembered ... because of some service, however small, done in the cause of humanity."[51]

Barnard established a framework for teacher preparation in Connecticut that has been adopted by most other states and has endured until the present with modest evolution. As public high school enrollments expanded, the training came to include the preparation of high school teachers. As high school and college educational opportunities expanded for the masses, aspiring teachers were expected to receive more extensive preparation. Partly at the urging of the National Education Association, that preparation was gradually transferred from normal schools to state and private colleges in the early 1900s and then later to public and private universities. The focus simultaneously shifted from narrow occupational training to a combination of liberal arts education and occupational preparation. Model schools attached to teacher training institutions were gradually replaced by collaborations with surrounding public schools that provided sites for supervised practice teaching. Teacher certification or licensure requirements were imposed by most states. The "teacher institutes" that Barnard had established would gradually be replaced with in-service workshops sponsored by school districts and by summer or evening classes offered by universities, allowing certified teachers to extend their knowledge and work toward advanced degrees.

By the late 1800s, the course of study for preparing teachers commonly involved the subject matter to be taught, the history and philosophy of education, the organization and administration of schools, child and adolescent development, instructional methods, classroom management techniques, and supervised practice teaching. That too has endured for more than a century although it is now integrated with, or follows, several years of liberal arts college study.

Another evolution of Barnard's framework would indirectly affect teachers. In the early 1900s, universities began to train school administrators and researchers. Those administrators would go on to staff a hierarchical bureaucratic structure that would leave teachers at the bottom tier.

The Teacher Associations

The American Institute of Instruction was established in 1830. For many years the membership was comprised mostly of educational statesmen and leading scholars, but gradually school principals and others interested in education were allowed to join. During the mid-1800s, "Teachers Associations" were established in many of the eastern and mid-western states. A number were created and controlled by teachers but others were controlled by educational statesmen. In 1857, ten state teacher associations created a National Teachers Association, dedicated to insuring teachers "the dignity, respectability, and usefulness of their calling."[52]

The National Teachers Association became the first national forum for the exchange of ideas about education, although a relatively small one with only about 300 members. In 1870 it absorbed the American Normal School Association, the National Association of School Superintendents, and the Central College Association as departments, and changed its name to the National Educational Association, which was later modified to the National Education Association (NEA). By the end of the century it had about 2,000 members.[53]

The NEA served partly as an umbrella organization for these organizations and several others that were established later. It also became a greatly expanded national forum for education leaders and reformers, with meetings attended by college presidents, state superintendents of education, large city and county superintendents of education, and later by professors of education and teachers. It was the educational leaders, however, who dominated its agenda, even though teachers accounted for the largest percentage of the membership. There were many speeches on education as a profession during the first few decades of the association but few on promoting better working conditions, wages, and pensions for teachers.[54]

The leaders of the NEA gave precedence to building robust education systems and an education profession, presuming that once that was accomplished, teachers would achieve status, security, and good wages.[55] Several teachers were not content to wait. In Chicago, in 1897, elementary teachers (who at the time comprised 94 percent of all teachers and were overwhelmingly women) created the Chicago Teacher's Federation (CTF), which quickly assumed an activist role. It petitioned the school board for a raise, won a promise for one, only to have the board renege, claiming inadequate funding. In response, the CTF hired two of it own, Margaret Haley and Catherine Goggin, to pursue its interests on a full-time basis. They discovered several of the largest corporations and the public utilities in the city were not paying their taxes to the city, sued for payment of the taxes, and won. The Chicago school board gladly accepted the extra $250,000 in revenue but still refused to honor the promised wage increase. That prompted the CTF to sue the Board, and they won again.[56] When William Harper, President of the University of Chicago, recommended bold changes to improve Chicago's public schools, including preferential hiring, wages, and promotion for male teachers who he believed were superior teachers, the CTF organized opposition and defeated his bill.[57] Those examples of "teacher power" drew considerable attention. By the turn of the century the CTF had more members in Chicago than the NEA had throughout the country. Haley and Goggin spread their influence by assisting teachers to organize federations in Baltimore, Philadelphia, Boston, and St. Paul. Several of these joined together in a National Teacher Federation, and then in 1916 the American Federation of Teachers. Within four years, the organization had chartered 174 locals.[58]

At the 1899 annual convention of the NEA, Haley sought to get the NEA to address the low pay of teachers and to admit women into its leadership ranks, but she failed. During the 1901 convention, William T. Harris, the U.S. Commissioner of Education, gave a speech claiming that public education was flourishing. Haley arose from the audience, perhaps the first woman in NEA history to do so, and rebutted that claim, stating that education could not flourish when teachers were grossly underpaid. Applause followed her brief comments. Harris replied, "Pay no attention to what that teacher down there has said, for I take that she is a grade teacher ... tired, and hysterical."[59]

Haley was undeterred. By the 1903 NEA convention, she succeeded in getting women on the nominating committee, gained a promise from the NEA president to study teacher wages, pensions, and tenure, and secured an invitation to be a speaker at the next NEA annual meeting.[60] She used her NEA speech to advocate for democracy within the education establishment, for professionalism of teachers, and for equal pay and rights for women teachers. She warned that "factorizing education" had made teachers automatons "whose duty it is to carry out mechanically and unquestioningly the ideas and orders of those clothed with the authority of position, and who may or may not know the needs of the children."[61] She also charged that salaries of teachers were "wholly inadequate," that teachers worked with no job security and no provisions for their old age, and that they faced "overwork in overcrowded schoolrooms."[62]

By the early 1900s, there were growing power struggles in the large cities between teachers (about 75 percent female), who increasingly perceived themselves as professional educators, and school administrators (overwhelmingly male), who had already come to perceive themselves as professional educators. They fought over who should make various decisions, over secret performance ratings for teachers, and over salaries.[63]

One superintendent who tried to bridge the two groups was Ella Flagg Young, a long-time Chicago educator, an associate of John Dewey (see Chapter 4), and then superintendent of Chicago schools. In her latter role, she tried to limit patronage in the hiring of teachers, fought for higher wages, and created teacher councils to provide advice to the school and district administrators.[64] In 1911 Young became the first female president of the NEA.

During the last decades of the 1800s, the NEA's influence was largely through its small membership of prominent educational leaders, which had included Horace Mann and Henry Barnard. In 1892 it achieved a new source of influence when its Committee of Ten, headed by Charles Eliot, the president of Harvard, recommended that the emerging, and still not well defined public high schools should teach a classical liberal arts curriculum, just as did the private grammar schools that prepared adolescents for college. The report proposed curriculum standards for high school educators throughout the country. While the NEA did not have formal authority over local educators, it was the most influential education organization at the time and that helped the report gain widespread attention, including rebuttals by those who wanted high schools to serve less elitist goals.

Those critics would be gratified two decades later. The 1916 NEA report, "Social Studies in Secondary Education," recommended that high schools teach a course in the problems of democracy. This was probably the first time that a major organization had recommended the study of contemporary issues rather than formalized subjects such as history and literature.⁶⁵ Two years later, the NEA released the "Cardinal Principles of Secondary Education" recommending that high schools should prepare students for the practical affairs of adult life. In these two reports, the NEA joined the leading edge of the life-preparation stream of progressive education. These reports received widespread attention, provoked considerable discussion, and are reputed to have had substantial influence on public schooling. The NEA's *Journal* and its research bulletins and technical publications continued to highlight the best practices in progressive education for several decades thereafter.

In 1935, the NEA established an Educational Policies Commission to research and recommend policies to states and local school districts. The Commission's early reports, particularly those on teaching students democracy, received considerable favorable attention.

At mid-century, the NEA began to assume direct and visible roles in representing the interests of teachers. In the early 1940s an Oklahoma teacher was fired after exposing financial irregularities in her district. The NEA mounted a rigorous defense and succeeded in having her reinstated. In 1944 the NEA publicly rebuked New York mayor La Guardia for illegally interfering with the city's board of education. That year it also expelled the Chicago superintendent of schools from the NEA, declaring that city's schools "the worst ... in the United States."⁶⁶ Teachers across the country began to view the NEA as a powerful force representing their interests. Membership climbed quickly from 272,000 in 1944 to 659,000 in 1956.

Between 1950 and 1970, the number of public school teachers more than doubled,⁶⁷ bringing large numbers of young adults into the teaching force, many of whom had been impressed by the non-violent civil disobedience of the civil rights movement and by the college protests against the Vietnam War. In 1961 the United Federation of Teachers in New York City, affiliated with the American Federation of Teachers and assisted by Walter Reuther's Industrial Union Department of the Congress of Industrial Organizations, won an election against the NEA affiliate to represent teachers in collective bargaining. A one-day strike soon followed, and it won concessions from the Board of Education. That victory received considerable national press coverage.⁶⁸ The American Federation of Teachers capitalized on the publicity to triple its membership in one decade and set the norms for a unionist approach.

With the lost election in New York City, the NEA immediately recognized it had a problem. Several of its large city affiliates had previously complained that the NEA had not been helping them enough. The mood of the country had become more confrontational. At the same time, the Industrial Union Department, which had previously had cordial relations with the NEA, had been losing blue-collar members and now appeared intent on replacing them with white-collar members from NEA's fold.[69] In the 1962 NEA meeting, the secretary-treasurer of the Industrial Union Department, James Carey, was invited to speak. His speech was on the need for journalists, teachers and other professionals to organize so that they could counterbalance the power of large employers. He concluded by observing:

> If I sound shocked because the charwomen [cleaning women] in some high schools get a higher rate of pay than the high school teachers, understand it comes from the heart. And if the charwomen ... have more tenure on their jobs and more security than the high school teachers, to me it is shocking.... Or if the charwomen of the schools have enough sense to band together and organize and negotiate contracts, and teachers do not, I wonder sometimes who should have the degrees.[70]

The NEA had a complication not shared by the United Federation of Teachers or the Industrial Union Department. It had long been an association of not only teachers but also education managers—school principals and district administrators. The NEA members who were principals or district administrators were generally opposed to collective bargaining. On the other hand, the NEA teachers were increasingly eager to give it a try. In the mid-1960s, with NEA guidelines and training, affiliates began collective bargaining style negotiations on salaries, benefits, and working conditions.[71] By the end of that decade, 15 states had adopted statutes permitting collective bargaining by teachers.[72] Although the NEA hoped to avoid teacher strikes, which were illegal at the time in every state, strikes did occur. There were 105 in the year 1967. Over the following years, the American Association of School Administrators, the Association of Elementary School Principals, and several other national associations of specialists and administrators broke their relationships with the NEA and moved out of its headquarters building. By 1980, thirty-one states had laws authorizing various forms of collective bargaining by teachers.[73]

SUCCESS OF THE REFORM

The professionalization of teaching was aimed at providing professional status and prerogatives for teachers and at improving the quality of education for students. It will be judged in respect to each of those.

Achievement of Professional Stature

Have K-12 teachers become professionals? Do teachers receive intensive specialized intellectual training that results in esoteric knowledge and skills? Are they required to earn demanding credentials or licensure?

Are they granted considerable autonomy over their work? Are there associations that exercise substantial control over teachers' training, certification, and standards for work? Have teachers garnered high respect or earnings? While the perception of professionalism is a subjective judgment, it is usually based substantially on these characteristics.

Extensive Special Training in Esoteric Knowledge and Skills

Progress in advancing the education and training of teachers has been slow but dramatic over the past two centuries. In the early 1800s, only an elementary school education was required to teach elementary school. By 1935, ten percent of elementary school teachers possessed bachelor's degrees, as did 56 percent of junior high teachers and 85 percent of high school teachers.[74] Today virtually all teachers have at least a bachelor's degree.

Despite the limited education of teachers in the 18th and 19th centuries, those teachers were generally better educated than most of the population, as they are at the opening of the 21st century when only 24 percent of the adult population has earned a bachelor's or higher degree.[75] Nevertheless, most teachers have not achieved esoteric knowledge and skills. There are two domains of knowledge needed by teachers, knowledge of the subject matter to be taught and knowledge of education. Teachers rarely have unusual levels of subject matter knowledge. It would be almost impossible for elementary school teachers to have advanced subject matter preparation in the several different subjects normally taught, including literature, mathematics, history, and science. Secondary school teachers are expected to teach in only one subject area, but at the dawn of the 21st century no state requires more than an undergraduate major in the subject taught (about 30 credit hours of the 120 semester credits required for a bachelor's degree) and several permit less than that.[76] Of the several well recognized professions mentioned at the beginning of this chapter, only two require just a bachelor's degree: certified public accountants and engineers. Both those majors commonly require more than 30 credits in their respective fields. In addition, engineers often must take the equivalent of minors (about 15 credits) in both mathematics and physical sciences. Thus most teachers have substantially less subject matter knowledge than other recognized professionals.

Teachers also need knowledge about the purposes of education, child and adolescent development, teaching strategies, motivation and discipline, classroom management, the organization and operation of school systems, and the laws applicable to schooling. Most high school teachers have received about a year of college course work in education and supervised practice teaching. Elementary teachers often have received about 1.5 years of such preparation. Some contend that this provides the unique expertise that qualifies teachers as professionals. Others contest that claim.

Some critics argue that many of the people who go into K-12 teaching are not top-flight intellectually, and thus not likely to master the complex intellectual functioning expected of true professionals. Education majors do have moderately lower scores on tests of academic aptitude than students in most other majors.[77]

Several critics assert that the intellectual rigor of teacher preparation courses is low. There are anecdotal reports—including from students in teacher preparation courses—that these courses at some colleges and universities are "mickey mouse."[78] Linda Darling-Hammond, a leading scholar of teacher preparation, and one who is sympathetic to the plight of teachers, claims that for most of the 20th century, the common training of teachers has presumed that they are "a form of semiskilled labor requiring little more than the ability to 'get through the book' with the aid of a few simple routines and tricks of the trade."[79]

Other critics contend that anyone who knows the subject matter can teach well without special preparation. This is commonly asserted by university arts and science faculty members, who offer themselves as living proof, noting that they and their colleagues have never taken a course in education but are fine teachers. The argument is disingenuous but contains a kernel of truth. Liberal arts professors are not uniformly good instructors, as attested to by student opinion on almost every campus in the land, by reports of professional associations, and by a joint project of the Council of Graduate Schools and the American Association of Colleges and Universities aimed at improving the preparation of doctoral students for college teaching and service responsibilities.[80] Indeed surveys of doctoral students find that about half feel that they have not been adequately prepared for faculty teaching responsibilities.[81] On the other hand, it is true that some professors become excellent instructors without any formal preparation for teaching. Furthermore, teaching is a generic skill, widely undertaken by parents, work supervisors, and others, usually without any formal training, and a portion of these people exercise the skill very well.

Hardly anyone can do the full scope of work done by accountants, dentists, engineers, lawyers, or physicians, without the extensive training that members of those professions undergo, but a moderate portion of these professionals and of the general population can teach well in the areas of their substantive knowledge without formal preparation to do so. That does not suggest that courses in education are useless. Indeed, given how widely teaching skills are applied and given that only a modest portion of people seems to be "born teachers," it could be suggested that all undergraduates should take at least one course in teaching. Nevertheless, the fact that good teaching skills come to some people naturally or are easily acquired by them undermines teachers' ability to claim unique expertise in instruction.

Certification and Licensure

By 1911, fifteen states controlled the certification of teachers and another 18 produced exams and regulations that local districts were responsible for administering.[82] Gradually states have raised the standards and differentiated certificates for elementary education and each of the subjects taught at the secondary level. At the dawn of the 21st century, 32 states require high school teachers to have an undergraduate major in the subject taught, 38 require at least ten weeks of supervised student teaching, 40 states require a basic skills test for certification, 34 require a subject knowledge test, 23 require a written test of pedagogical knowledge, and 13 require a performance assessment of teaching skills.[83]

State certification standards have long been criticized. Part of the criticism is directed at relatively easy certification exams. Part of the criticism is leveled at the barrier that the certification requirements pose to people who would like to secure high school teaching positions and have excellent content knowledge—sometimes at the masters or even doctoral level—but lack the required coursework in education and supervised teaching experience necessary to qualify for certification. Some critics allege that certification requirements exist only to protect the vested interests of the education professors and the teachers' unions.[84] Many states now have alternative certification routes, usually for those possessing at least a bachelor's degree in subjects with shortages of teachers. They usually require a short period of intensive preparation in education before commencing teaching and then a year or two of mentoring on the job.[85]

At the close of the 20th century, almost half of all secondary schools in the country reported difficulties in finding qualified teachers in one or more subject areas,[86] which often resulted in circumvention of the certification requirements. Many states grant "temporary," "emergency," or "provisional" certification to teachers who do not yet qualify for full certification, requiring little more than an earned bachelor's degree, regardless of major. In 1991, only 73 percent of the nation's K-12 public school teachers had full certification,[87] and in many urban school systems the percentage was substantially less. In addition, many secondary school instructors are teaching courses outside of the subjects for which they have been certified. In 1993-94 an average of 34 percent of core academic classes in high schools were taught by teachers who had neither a major nor minor in the subject. The highest rates were 53 percent of history classes and 57 percent of physical sciences classes (physics, chemistry, space science, and geology).[88] A portion of the out-of-subject teaching is due to unexpected changes in the workforce caused by illnesses, deaths, and mid-year resignations and a portion is due to failures in recruiting teachers for hard-to-fill subjects.

While most people would agree that it is desirable to staff our schools with highly qualified teachers, the reality is that schools cannot be as selective as the medical and legal professions. The civilian workforce employs only 719,000 physicians and 926,000 lawyers and judges, whereas it employs 3.5 million teachers.[89]

Autonomy within Professional Standards

Teachers have lost autonomy over the past two centuries due to the increasing bureaucratization of public schools. In colonial times the school committee provided nominal oversight but little regular supervision. As states built universal public school systems in the mid 1800s, they structured them initially as four-level bureaucracies with the state board of education assuming top-level authority, district boards and their superintendents having the next two levels of authority over several one-room school houses, and teachers being the front-line workers. By the late 1800s, multi-room graded schools were gaining favor in the cities, and a principal was put in charge of each such school, bumping teachers down to the fifth level of the bureaucracies. In the mid-1900s, federal courts became increasingly active in ruling on educational matters and the federal government increasingly established legislation and regulations affecting schools. Now teachers were at the bottom of a seven-rung bureaucracy. In addition, the same confrontational culture of the 1960s and 1970s that nudged teachers towards collective bargaining also encouraged parents to challenge the school system, often starting with the lowest rung.

Other changes, however, partially compensated for the autonomy that teachers lost to the mushrooming bureaucracy. Teachers gained protections against the whimsical terminations that were allowed in colonial times. Some of the protection came with the bureaucracy, which tended to replace administrative discretion with procedural rules. In addition, at the behest of the NEA and AFT in the mid-1900s, most states adopted statutes providing "tenure" or "continuing contracts" for teachers who satisfactorily complete certain requirements. These contracts do not allow terminations except for specified reasons and with due process.[90]

U.S. Supreme Court decisions over the latter half of the 20th century have ruled that all citizens, including teachers, have more rights under the U.S. Constitution than had been previously acknowledged. Women can no longer be fired for marrying. The private lives of teachers, except for criminal activity and blatant disregard of community moral standards, are not legal grounds for dismissal. The courts have established that teachers are generally free to select their teaching approaches within limits set by the school board; they may use controversial materials in a balanced way that are directly related to the course content, suitable for students' ages, and not explicitly prohibited by the school board; and they may criticize school board decisions if they do so without serious misrepresentations.[91]

At the beginning of the 21st century, states and school districts generally control the curriculum and the main texts for required courses. Teachers generally have moderate autonomy on how to teach the courses, although district mandates, traditions, and parental complaints do constrain them. In addition, the fact that teachers work mostly behind closed doors allows those so inclined to exercise more initiative than the bureaucracy may wish.

Professional Associations with Influence

The National Education Association (NEA) is the largest and most influential association of teachers. In 2001, almost 60 percent of all public K-12 school teachers in the country were members.[92] For a century it has advocated upgrading teacher education and certification requirements. Critics of the NEA point to times when its positions, and those of its state affiliates, have obstructed progress on teacher education and certification matters. Similar charges, however, have been made against virtually every professional association of other occupations.

The NEA's influence on professional standards for teaching practice is debatable. For almost a century, its conferences were the most important forum for the exchange of ideas among educators, but the Association did not devote much effort to forging consensus about professional standards. Only in 1946, with the establishment of its National Commission on Teacher Education and Professional Standards, did it establish sustained influence over these matters, but by that time the states had assumed the regulation of teaching.[93] Six years later the NEA finally adopted a first code of ethics.[94]

There are unusual circumstances that have hindered the NEA from achieving wide recognition as a professional association. For more than half its existence, the NEA sought to be the professional association of both teachers and of their bureaucratic superiors, and then for the last half-century it has sought to be partly a professional association and partly a union, a combination not found in any other recognized profession in this country. In addition, teachers are overwhelmingly employed by democratically controlled public school districts, and no widely recognized profession has a membership that is employed predominantly by the public sector. Partly because of that, the NEA has long been actively involved in advocating for increased teacher wages and benefits, whereas most associations of other professionals have left members to set their fees or negotiate their wages on their own.

The NEA is not the only association of teachers. The American Federation of Teachers is the other major organization of teachers and has been active in a number of education reform efforts. There is an International Reading Association, a National Council of Social Studies, a National Council of Teachers of Mathematics, and associations for most other subjects. There are also associations that focus on other matters, such as the Council for Exceptional Children. All serve at least partly as professional associations and all have modest influence, but none has had the extent of influence over the training, certification, and professional standards as do the American Medical Association and the American Bar Association.

High Earnings and Respect

Since the efforts to professionalize teaching in the mid-1800s, salaries of teachers have increased considerably. Between 1870 and 1900, the mean annual salary of K-12 instructional staff, after controlling for inflation, more than doubled.[95] In 1890 the average wages of teachers were only 58 percent of the average annual earnings in all sectors of the economy, but that percentage rose to 75 percent in 1900.[96] Teachers' relative wages continued to rise gradually, with a few temporary dips, throughout most of the 20th century, peaking at 123 percent in 1990, and then dropping to 107 percent by the year 2005. In that latter year, the average teacher earned $49,109 per year.[97] This average obscures the considerable variations within and between states—the lowest state average was $29,360 in South Dakota and the highest was $51,210 in California.[98]

Teacher pay lags behind that of other professions requiring similar levels of education. For instance, in the year 2006, the $49,109 average salary for teachers compared with $54,630 for accountants, $68,600 for civil engineers and $75,930 for electrical engineers. There were even greater gaps in starting salaries. The average starting salary of teachers with a bachelor's degree was about $33,000, whereas it was about $46,718 for accountants, $48,590 for civil engineers, and $55,292 for electrical engineers, for those with only a bachelor's degree.[99] It should be noted that part of these salary differences can be accounted for by the fact that most teachers are paid for 10-month periods with two weeks of paid breaks, whereas other professionals are usually paid for 12-month periods with 3-4 weeks of paid vacation.

National public opinion surveys show low to moderate regard for the teaching profession. When a 1950 survey asked what profession you would suggest for a young man who was qualified for all professions, 29 percent said physician, 16 percent said engineers/builder, eight percent said lawyer, seven percent said clergy, and only five percent said professor/teacher. In 1991 when asked what kind of job you would most want your son or daughter to have, only two percent selected professor/teacher for their sons and only five percent selected that for their daughters. Then in 2000, when asked which of all occupations is most respected, ten percent indicated teachers (compared to 24 percent indicating physicians, one percent indicating lawyers, and 28 percent indicating clergy).[100] The data suggest teachers do garner modest respect but most people do not consider teaching to be a desirable occupation.

Overall Progress in the Professionalization of Teaching

The effort to professionalize teaching has had only partial success. Teachers are far better educated and far better paid than formerly, and that progress is substantially a result of the efforts by their professional associations. On the other hand, teachers do not have a monopoly on any esoteric knowledge and skills, their entry certification is widely perceived as lax, their autonomy is limited, their professional associations have not established widely accepted standards for teaching practice, and the prestige and pay of teachers is well below that of many other widely recognized professions. Most of these factors interact as a vicious circle, each exacerbating the others.[101]

Unintended Side Effects on Teachers

The first efforts to enhance the training of teachers in the mid-1800s did not notably reduce the rapid turnover of rural teachers, as had been hoped, but did hastened the drain of talent from rural to urban areas as it provided rural young men and women with education and skills that were in demand in the cities.[102] To the extent that teacher preparation courses were perceived by college students to be less demanding than liberal arts courses, such a perception probably served to attract less able or less ambitious students to teaching careers and at the same time probably discouraged a portion of the most able students from pursuing such careers.

Jurgen Herbst has argued, with considerable evidence, that the emphasis given to professionalizing education actually succeeded in making the predominantly male school *administrators* professionals, and their success undermined predominantly female teachers' efforts to achieve professional stature. He notes that leading universities preferred to focus on preparing education specialists, administrators, and researchers, leaving teacher training mostly to the lower status institutions—first the normal schools and later the state colleges. In addition, the lack of a career ladder within teaching meant that the most ambitious and able teachers had no option but to move into school administration or leave education.[103]

We have seen that the new pedagogies advocated by progressive educators required more complex teaching strategies than the traditional didactic instruction, memorization, and recitation. The increased complexity should have enhanced the professional stature of teaching, but progressive education also replaced the traditional authoritarian roles for teachers with nurturing and facilitative roles, which may have appeared less authoritative and thus served to counter professional status.

Teachers' success in minimizing capricious firings, achieved through union contracts that provide tenure after a few years of satisfactory teaching, has also inadvertently created a challenge to professional status. The tenure provisions have made it difficult for school districts to fire incompetent teachers and thus teachers who have been the subject of many complaints generally remain in the ranks, often just reassigned from one school to another.[104] Although every profession undoubtedly has some incompetents, most members of the other established professions, except college professors, work without tenure protections.

Achievement of Goals

For school reformers, the main purpose of professionalizing teaching was to improve the quality of instruction in public schools. Over the past century, teachers have been instructing dramatically larger percentages of our youth at the high school level and it is clear that it would not have been possible without substantial increases in the educational levels of teachers. That, in turn, would not have been possible without raising the wages of teachers considerably above that of farm hands. Thus the partial success of efforts to make teachers professionals have almost surely made for a higher quality of education than otherwise would have been possible.

It is more questionable whether the quality of education at a given grade level has improved, and if so, is that a result of modest progress in the professionalization of teachers. There have been many allegations that student learning has actually declined over the past half century. SAT scores have declined since the 1960s, but simultaneously larger percentages of high school students have been taking the test. The National Assessment of Education Progress Long-Term Trends, based on nationally representative samples designed to monitor change across time, has been administered only for three decades. Over that period, there have been modest gains in reading and mathematics by 9-year-old students and virtually no change among 17-year-olds.[105] While the available evidence suggests little decline in the effectiveness of public education, it also indicates little gain in effectiveness. This will be discussed further in Chapter 10.

WERE PROFESSIONALIZATION EFFORTS INEVITABLE?

Efforts to expand the training and wages of teachers well above those of farmhands were inevitable if the nation was to extend universal public education to high school, teach the new subjects of mathematics and science, and move pedagogy beyond recitation and corporal punishment. When better training and wages for teachers were becoming essential for supporting other changes in public education, several other occupations (those of physicians, lawyers, and engineers) were successfully establishing professional status, making professionalism attractive to education reformers. It was not, however, the only model that could have been pursued. Reformers might have sought to advance teachers as technicians, who are expected to have highly specialized training in a narrow domain, limited autonomy within narrow boundaries, and only moderate earnings and respect. Teachers could have been conceived as public servants, most of whom are expected to have moderate training, take direction from the electorate through a bureaucratic hierarchy, and have moderate earnings and respect. Teachers might also have been envisioned as entrepreneurial managers, who are expected to have moderate training, substantial autonomy with few established standards, and earnings based on how well they achieve the business objectives. Indeed, each of these models has had influence on teachers. Some teacher training approaches, such as microteaching exercises, intended to develop very specific instructional techniques, reflect the technician model. Taxpayers and parents often consider teachers to be public servants who should be responsive to the public will. And the current accountability reform effort, discussed in Chapter 10, would sometimes link teacher pay to their students' levels of learning.

FUTURE OF THE REFORM

The most notable movement toward professionalization of teaching at the opening of the 21st century was the National Board for Professional Teaching Standards (NBPTS), created a decade earlier. The Board has worked to codify the knowledge and skills of highly effective teachers, assess volunteer teachers' levels of the knowledge and skills, and award NBPTS certification to those who demonstrate mastery. By 2001, the Board had developed assessments in 26 fields defined by the age of students and the content taught. Teachers' expertise is assessed in six 30-minute content and pedagogy assessments at secure assessment centers and by expert review of a portfolio of work, including video tapes of teaching sessions, in response to given assignments.[106] Almost all states offer incentives for teachers to achieve NBPTS certification, and 23,904 teachers had earned certification by 2002.[107]

The next step was to conduct validity assessments to determine whether the Board certified teachers actually advance students' learning more than other teachers. Early results suggest they do advance learning, as measured by standardized achievement tests, but only by a small amount—about 2-4 weeks per academic year.[108]

Five decades of research focused on identifying characteristics of effective teachers has produced inconsistent or small results.[109] That might change if superior pedagogies are developed that markedly accelerate student learning on widely valued learning objectives, but the quest for that has been going on in the western world since the days of Socrates, with many claims of success that later have disappointed. In addition, these superior pedagogies will have to be difficult to master without specialized and lengthy training, and they will have to be mastered by most people allowed to teach at the K-12 level. Short of that, teachers will have a noble calling, but remain widely perceived as semi-professional public employees, several tiers down in a bureaucratic hierarchy.

There are also clouds on the horizon that could result in teaching becoming less professional than it is today. There are serious shortages of teachers in several parts of the country that may force states to lower credentialing standards or to tolerate more circumvention of the standards. Several of the relatively comprehensive school reform models that will be discussed in Chapter 10 are very prescriptive, leaving little room for teacher discretion. In addition, the new accountability reform effort, which will also be discussed in Chapter 10, could actually constrain teacher autonomy further, as school districts and states tighten the reins in an effort to meet high-stakes learning goals. That reform also proposes to identify and root out ineffective teachers, but unless it can attract other teachers to take their places, schools may have to retain those it has publicized as ineffective.

---

[1] Merle Curti, *The Growth of American Thought*, 2nd ed. (New York: Harper & Brothers, 1951), 32.

[2] Carl E. Kaestle, *Pillars of the Republic: Common Schools and American Society, 1780-1860* (New York: Hill and Wang, 1983), 18-19.

[3] See: Richard N. Pratte, "A History of Teacher Education in Connecticut from 1639 to 1939" (Ph.D diss., University of Connecticut, 1967), 2; Ellwood P. Cubberley, *Public Education in the United States: A study and Interpretation of American Educational History,* rev. and enlg. ed. (Boston, MA: Houghton Mifflin, 1934), 55.

[4] Willard S. Elsbree, *The American Teachers: Evolution of a Profession in a Democracy* (New York: American Book Company, 1939), 184.

[5] Larry Cuban, *How Teachers Taught: Constancy and Change in American Classrooms, 1880-1990, 2nd ed.* (New York: Teachers College Press, 1993), 31.

[6] Carl E. Kaestle, *Pillars of the Republic: Common Schools and American Society, 1780-1860* (New York: Hill and Wang, 1983), 20-21.

[7] Harry G. Good, *A History of American Education, 2nd ed.* (Toronto: Macmillan Company, 1971), 193.

[8] *American Journal of Education,* 16 (March, 1866): 93-96, quoted in *And Sadly Teach: Teacher Education and Professionalization in American Culture,* Jurgen Herbst (Madison, WI: University of Wisconsin Press, 1989), 59.

[9] Jurgen Herbst, *And Sadly Teach: Teacher Education and Professionalization in American Culture* (Madison, WI: University of Wisconsin Press, 1989), 27, 28.

[10] Staff of *Education Week*, *Lessons of a Century: A Nation's Schools Come of Age* (Bethesda, MD: Editorial Projects in Education, 2000), 183; and Adolphe E. Meyer, *The Development of Education in the Twentieth Century*, 2nd ed. (New York: Prentice Hall, 1949), 412-413.

[11] See: R. Freeman Butts and Lawrence A. Cremin, *A History of Education in American Culture* (New York: Holt, Rinehart and Winston, 1953), 233; and Carl F. Kaestle, *Pillars of the Republic: Common Schools and American Society, 1780-1860* (New York: Hill and Wang, 1983), 160-161.

[12] Alonzo F. Myers and Clarence O. William, *Education in a Democracy: An Introduction to the Study of Education—With Revisions* (New York: Prentice Hall, 1947), 285; Ellwood P. Cubberley, *Public Education in the United States: A study and Interpretation of American Educational History*, rev. and enlg. ed. (Boston, MA: Houghton Mifflin, 1934), 56.

[13] Ellwood P. Cubberley, *Public Education in the United States: A Study and Interpretation of American Educational History*, rev. and enlg. ed. (Boston, MA: Houghton Mifflin, 1934), 328.

[14] Harry G. Good, *A History of American Education*, 2nd ed., (Toronto, Ontario: Macmillan, 1962), 159.

[15] Richard N. Pratte, "A History of Teacher Education in Connecticut from 1639 to 1939" (Ph.D diss., University of Connecticut, 1967), 30.

[16] Harry G. Good, *A History of American Education*, 2nd ed. (Toronto: Macmillan Company, 1971), 159-160.

[17] Jurgen Herbst, *And Sadly Teach: Teacher Education and Professionalization in American Culture* (Madison, WI: University of Wisconsin Press, 1989), 27.

[18] Ellwood P. Cubberley, *Public Education in the United States: A study and Interpretation of American Educational History*, rev. and enlg. ed. (Boston, MA: Houghton Mifflin, 1934), 53.

[19] Ellwood P. Cubberley, *Public Education in the United States: A study and Interpretation of American Educational History*, rev. and enlg. ed. (Boston, MA: Houghton Mifflin, 1934), 372.

[20] Lawrence A. Cremin, *The Transformation of the School: Progressivism in American Education, 1876-1957* (New York: Alfred A. Knopf, 1961), 168.

[21] Samuel C. Parker, *The History of Modern Elementary Education* (Totowa, NJ: Littlefield, Adams & Company, 1912 (reprinted 1970), 327-328.

[22] Samuel C. Parker, *The History of Modern Elementary Education* (Totowa, NJ: Littlefield, Adams & Company, 1912 (reprinted 1970), 359.

[23] Samuel Haber, "The Professions and Higher Education in America: A Historical View," in *Higher Education and the Labor Market*, ed. Margaret S. Gordon (New York: McGraw-Hill,1974), 237-277. pg. 244-247

[24] Samuel Haber, "The Professions and Higher Education in America: A Historical View," in *Higher Education and the Labor Market*, ed. Margaret S. Gordon (New York: McGraw-Hill,1974), 237-277. pg. 250

[25] John S. Brubacher, "The Evolution of Professional Education," in *Education for the Professions: The Sixty-first Yearbook of the National Society for the Study of Education, Part II*, ed. Nelson B. Henry (Chicago, IL: The University of Chicago Press), 47-67. pg 61

[26] Samuel Haber, "The Professions and Higher Education in America: A Historical View," in *Higher Education and the Labor Market,* ed. Margaret S. Gordon (New York: McGraw-Hill,1974), 237-277. pg. 251

[27] Quoted in James H. Means "Homo Medicus Americanus" in *The Professions in America,* ed. Kenneth S Lynn and the Editors of Daedalus (Boston, MA: Houghton Mifflin, 1965), 50.

[28] Quoted in James H. Means "Homo Medicus Americanus" in *The Professions in America,* ed. Kenneth S Lynn and the Editors of Daedalus (Boston, MA: Houghton Mifflin, 1965), 56.

[29] George E. Miller, "Medicine," in *Education for the Professions: The Sixty-first Yearbook of the National Society for the Study of Education, Part II,* ed. Nelson B. Henry (Chicago, IL: The University of Chicago Press), 103-119. pg. 104

[30] John S. Brubacher, "The Evolution of Professional Education," in *Education for the Professions: The Sixty-first Yearbook of the National Society for the Study of Education, Part II,* ed. Nelson B. Henry (Chicago, IL: The University of Chicago Press), 47-67. pg. 62

[31] American Bar Association, "ABA History." Retrieved 02/21/03 from www.abanet.org/media/overview/phistory.html

[32] Joseph A. McClain, "Legal Education," in *Education for the Professions,* ed. Lloyd E. Blauch, (Washington DC: U.S. Government Printing Office, 1955), 109-120. pg 110-111

[33] See: John S. Brubacher, "The Evolution of Professional Education," in *Education for the Professions: The Sixty-first Yearbook of the National Society for the Study of Education, Part II,* ed. Nelson B. Henry (Chicago, IL: The University of Chicago Press), 47-67. pg 65; Frederick Rudolph, *The American College and University-A History,* (New York: Vintage Books, 1962), 130-135, 218-220.

[34] Henry H. Armsby, "Engineering Education," in *Education for the Professions,* ed. Lloyd E. Blauch, (Washington DC: U.S. Government Printing Office, 1955), 69-80. pg 71

[35] John S. Brubacher, "The Evolution of Professional Education," in *Education for the Professions: The Sixty-first Yearbook of the National Society for the Study of Education, Part II,* ed. Nelson B. Henry (Chicago, IL: The University of Chicago Press), 120-139. pg. 121

[36] Henry H. Armsby, "Engineering Education," in *Education for the Professions,* ed. Lloyd E. Blauch, (Washington DC: U.S. Government Printing Office, 1955), 69-80. pg 70-71

[37] Quoted in "A History of Teacher Education in Connecticut from 1639 to 1939" Richard N. Pratte (Ph.D diss., University of Connecticut, 1967), 107.

[38] Quoted in following two sources: John S. Brubacher, ed., *Henry Barnard on Education* (New York: McGraw-Hill, 1931), 168; Jurgen Herbst, *And Sadly Teach: Teacher Education and Professionalization in American Culture* (Madison, WI: University of Wisconsin Press, 1989), 24.

[39] John S. Brubacher, ed., *Henry Barnard on Education* (New York: McGraw-Hill, 1931), 174-75.

[40] Richard N. Pratte, "A History of Teacher Education in Connecticut from 1639 to 1939" (Ph.D diss., University of Connecticut, 1967), 111-112, 122, 144.

[41] Quoted in Richard N. Pratte, "A History of Teacher Education in Connecticut from 1639 to 1939" (Ph.D diss., University of Connecticut, 1967), 92-93.

[42] Quoted in John S. Brubacher, ed., *Henry Barnard on Education* (New York: McGraw-Hill, 1931), 171.
[43] John S. Brubacher, ed., *Henry Barnard on Education* (New York: McGraw-Hill, 1931), 171-172.
[44] Jurgen Herbst, *And Sadly Teach: Teacher Education and Professionalization in American Culture* (Madison, WI: University of Wisconsin Press, 1989), 31.
[45] Richard N. Pratte, "A History of Teacher Education in Connecticut from 1639 to 1939" (Ph.D diss., University of Connecticut, 1967), 93.
[46] Richard N. Pratte, "A History of Teacher Education in Connecticut from 1639 to 1939" (Ph.D diss., University of Connecticut, 1967), 94-96.
[47] Richard N. Pratte, "A History of Teacher Education in Connecticut from 1639 to 1939." (Ph.D diss., University of Connecticut, 1967), 96-97.
[48] Richard N. Pratte, "A History of Teacher Education in Connecticut from 1639 to 1939" (Ph.D diss., University of Connecticut, 1967), 372-375.
[49] Richard N. Pratte, "A History of Teacher Education in Connecticut from 1639 to 1939" (Ph.D diss., University of Connecticut, 1967), 118, 140, 147.
[50] Richard N. Pratte, "A History of Teacher Education in Connecticut from 1639 to 1939" (Ph.D diss., University of Connecticut, 1967), 169-173.
[51] Quoted in Adolphe E Meyer: An Educational History of the American People New York: McGraw Hill 1957 p. 166.
[52] Quoted in Robert H. Beck, *A Social History of Education* (Englewood Cliffs, NJ: Prentice-Hall, 1965), 118.
[53] David B. Tyack, *The One Best System: A History of American Urban Education* (Cambridge, MA: Harvard University Press, 1974), 260.
[54] Edgar B. Wesley, *NEA: The First Hundred Years: The Building of the Teaching Profession* (New York: Harper Brothers, 1957), 368-369.
[55] Edgar B. Wesley, *NEA: The First Hundred Years: The Building of the Teaching Profession* (New York: Harper Brothers, 1957), 280.
[56] See: Robert L. Reid, ed., *Battleground: The Autobiography of Margaret A. Haley* (Urbana, IL: University of Illinois Press, 1982), 42-85; Kate Rousmaniere, "Margaret Haley: Progressive Education and the Teacher," in *Founding Mothers and Others: Women Educational Leaders During the Progressive Era*, ed. Alan R. Sadovnik and Susan F. Semel (New York: Palgrave, 2002), 147-162; David B. Tyack, *The One Best System: A History of American Urban Education* (Cambridge, MA: Harvard University Press, 1974), 259-261.
[57] Gerald Grant and Christine E. Murray, *Teaching in America: The Slow Revolution* (Cambridge, MA: Harvard University Press, 1999), 98.
[58] *History (of AFT)* (Washington DC: American Federation of Teachers, undated). Retrieved January 10, 2005 from www.aft.org/about/history/ index.htm.
[59] Robert L. Reid, ed., *Battleground: The Autobiography of Margaret A. Haley* (Urbana, IL: University of Illinois Press, 1982), 131-133.
[60] Gerald Grant and Christine E. Murray, *Teaching in America: The Slow Revolution* (Cambridge, MA: Harvard University Press, 1999), 101.
[61] David B. Tyack, *The One Best System: A History of American Urban Education* (Cambridge, MA: Harvard University Press, 1974), 257.
[62] Quoted in *Lessons of a Century: A Nation's Schools Come of Age* by the staff of *Education Week* (Bethesda, MD: Editorial Projects in Education, 2000), 182.
[63] Paul E. Peterson, *The Politics of School Reform: 1870-1940* (Chicago: University of Chicago Press, 1985), 167.

[64] Paul E. Peterson, *The Politics of School Reform: 1870-1940* (Chicago: University of Chicago Press, 1985), 165.
[65] Edgar B. Wesley, *NEA: The First Hundred Years: The Building of the Teaching Profession* (New York: Harper Brothers, 1957), 298-299.
[66] Edgar B. Wesley, *NEA: The First Hundred Years: The Building of the Teaching Profession* (New York: Harper Brothers, 1957), 310.
[67] U.S. Department of Education, National Center for Education Statistics, *Digest of Education Statistics: 2001* (Washington, DC: U.S. Government Printing Office, 2002), 91.
[68] Allan M. West, *The National Education Association: The Power Base for Education* (New York: The Free Press, 1980), 51-56.
[69] Allan M. West, *The National Education Association: The Power Base for Education* (New York: The Free Press, 1980), 56-62.
[70] National Education Association, *Addresses and Proceeding of the One-Hundredth Annual Meeting,* (Washington DC: author, 1962), 52.
[71] Allan M. West, *The National Education Association: The Power Base for Education* (New York: The Free Press, 1980), 67-73.
[72] Allan M. West, *The National Education Association: The Power Base for Education* (New York: The Free Press, 1980), 264-265.
[73] Allan M. West, *The National Education Association: The Power Base for Education* (New York: The Free Press, 1980), 84, 81.
[74] Michael Sedlak and Steven Schlossman, *Who Will Teach? Historical Perspectives on the Changing Appeal of Teaching as a Profession* (Santa Monica, CA: RAND, 1986), 36.
[75] U.S. Department of Education, National Center for Education Statistics, *Digest of Education Statistics: 2001* (Washington, DC: U.S. Government Printing Office, 2002), 17.
[76] *Education Week: Quality Counts 2003, 22* (January 9, 2003): 91.
[77] Erling E. Boe and Dorothy M. Gilford, *Teacher Supply, Demand, and Quality: Policy Issues, Models, and Data Bases* (Washington DC: National Academy Press, 1992), 14-15.
[78] James Bryant Conant, *The Education of American Teachers,* (New York: McGraw-Hill, 1963), 12.
[79] Darling-Hammond, Linda, "Educating Teachers: The Academy's Greatest Failure or Its Most Important Future?" *Academe,* 85 (January-February, 1999): 28.
[80] See: Association of American Colleges, *Integrity in the College Curriculum: A Report to the Academic Community—The Findings and Recommendations of the Project on Redefining the Meaning and Purpose of Baccalaureate Degrees* (Washington, D.C.: Association of American Colleges, 1985); the Preparing Future Faculty Program website at www.preparing-faculty.org.
[81] See: National Association of Graduate-Professional Students, *32,000 Graduate Students Grade Their Doctoral Programs: Poor Report Cards in Career Guidance, Preparation for Teaching* (Washington DC: author, 2001), retrieved 04/07/03 from www.nagps.org; Cris M. Golde and Timothy M. Doer, *At Cross Purposes: What the Experiences of Doctoral Students Reveal About Doctoral Education,* a report prepared for The Pew Charitable Trusts, Philadelphia, PA, January, 2001, retrieved 04/07/03 from www.phd-survey.org/report.htm.
[82] Staff of Education Week, *Lessons of a Century: A Nation's Schools Come of Age* (Bethesda, MD: Editorial Projects in Education, 2000), 184.

[83] *Education Week: Quality Counts 2003, 22* (January 9, 2003): 90-92.
[84] James Bryant Conant, *The Education of American Teachers*, (New York: McGraw-Hill, 1963), 8, 11, 12 & 15.
[85] *Education Week: Quality Counts 2003, 22* (January 9, 2003): 66-67.
[86] Richard M. Ingersoll, *Teacher Turnover, Teacher Shortages, and the Organization of Schools*, (Seattle, WA: Center for the Study of Teaching and Policy, 2001), 14.
[87] National Commission on Teaching & America's Future, *What Matters Most: Teaching for America's Future, Summary Report* (New York: author, 1996), 10.
[88] Richard Ingersoll, *Out-of-Field Teaching, Educational Inequality, and the Organization of Schools: An Exploratory Analysis* (Seattle, WA: Center for the Study of Teaching and Policy, University of Washington, 2002), 18.
[89] U.S. Department of Commerce, Bureau of the Census, *Statistical Abstract of the United States: 2001*, (Austin, TX: Hoover's Business Press, 2001), 380.
[90] Staff of *Education Week, Lessons of a Century: A Nation's Schools Come of Age* (Bethesda, MD: Editorial Projects in Education, 2000), 186; M. Chester Nolte, *Nolte's School Law Desk Book* (West Nyack, NY: Parker Publishing, 1980), 139-141; Robert J. Shoop & Dennis R. Dunklee, *School Law for the Principal: A Handbook for Practitioners* (Boston, MA: Allyn and Bacon, 1992), 47-49,65.
[91] See: Robert C. O'Reilly and Edward T. Green, *School Law for the 1990s* (Westport, CN: Greenwood Press, 1992), 87-91; M. Chester Nolte, *Nolte's School Law Desk Book* (West Nyack, NY: Parker Publishing, 1980), 115, 123
[92] Calculated from Kathleen Lyons, NEA Public Relations Office, e-mail to Gregg Jackson, August 16, 2003, indicating that about 1.9 million of the NEA's members are K-12 public school teachers; the total number K-12 public school teachers in 2001 was 3.2 million according to: U.S. Department of Education, National Center for Education Statistics, *Digest of Education Statistics: 2001* (Washington DC: U.S. Government Printing Office, 2002), 13.
[93] Allan M. West, *The National Education Association: The Power Base for Education* (New York: The Free Press, 1980), 211-212.
[94] Edgar B. Wesley, *NEA: The First Hundred Years: The Building of the Teaching Profession* (New York: Harper Brothers, 1957), 338.
[95] Calculated from Michael Sedlak and Steven Schlossman, *Who Will Teach? Historical Perspectives on the Changing Appeal of Teaching as a Profession* (Santa Monica, CA: RAND, 1986), 6.
[96] Calculated from U.S. Department of Commerce, Bureau of the Census, *Historical Statistics of the United States: Colonial Times to 1957* (Washington DC: U.S. Government Printing Office, 1961), 91-92.
[97] U.S. Department of Education, National Center for Education Statistics, *Digest of Education Statistics: 2007* (Washington DC: U.S. Government Printing Office, 2008), 109.
[98] U.S. Department of Education, National Center for Education Statistics, *Digest of Education Statistics: 2007* (Washington DC: U.S. Government Printing Office, 2008), 107.
[99] U.S. Department of Labor, Bureau of Labor Statistics, *Occupational Outlook Handbook* (Washington, DC: U.S. Government Printing Office, 2007). Retrieved 06/07/08 from www.bls.gov/oco/ocos069.htm#earnings, www.bls.gov/oco/ocos001.htm#earnings , www.bls.gov/oco/ocos027.htm #earnings
[100] All survey results were retrieved through LexisNexis Academic from the Roper Center at University of Connecticut Public Opinion Online. Retrieved on 02/26/03

from proprietary website at http://80-web.lexis-nexis.com.proxygw.wrlc.org/universe/printdoc searching the terms "teacher" and "engineer." The source of the surveys and accession numbers are as follows: 1950: Gallup, #0033269; 1991: Great American TV Poll, #0236319 and 0236322; and 2000: Fox News Opinion Dynamic Poll, #0359633.

[101] Suzanne B. Ritter, *The Paradox of Professionalism: A History of Teacher Education in America* (unpublished paper, 2000), 41.

[102] Jurgen Herbst, *And Sadly Teach: Teacher Education and Professionalization in American Culture* (Madison, WI: University of Wisconsin Press, 1989), 84.

[103] Jurgen Herbst, *And Sadly Teach: Teacher Education and Professionalization in American Culture* (Madison, WI: University of Wisconsin Press, 1989), 1-11, 99.

[104] Myron Lieberman, *Beyond Public Education* (New York: Praeger, 1986), 80-100.

[105] U.S. Department of Education, National Center for Education Statistics, *Long-Term Trend Major Results*. Retrieved 06/06/08 from http://nces.ed.gov/nationsreportcard/ltt/results2004.

[106] Ann E. Harman, *National Board for Professional Teaching Standard's National Teaching Certification: ERIC Digest* (Washington DC: ERIC Clearinghouse on Teaching and Teacher Education, 2001), 2-5.

[107] *Education Week: Quality Counts 2003, 22* (January 9, 2003): 90.

[108] See: Linda Cavalluzzo, *Is National Board Certification An Effective Signal of Teacher Quality?* (Alexandria, VA: The CNA Corporation, 2004) 18-26; Leslie G. Vandevoort, Audrey Amrein-Beardsley, and David C. Berliner, "National Board Certified Teachers and Their Students' Achievement," *Education Policy Analysis Archives* 12 (September 8, 2004). Retrieved 06/06/08 from http://epaa.asu.edu/epaa/v12n46/v12n46.pdf

[109] See: Suzanne M. Wilson, Robert E Floden, and Joan Ferrini-Mundy, *Teacher Preparation Research: Current Knowledge, Gaps and Recommendations* (Seattle, WA: Center for the Study of Teaching and Policy, University of Washington), i-iii; Linda Darling-Hammond, *Teacher Quality and Student Achievement: A Review of State Policy Evidence* (Seattle, WA: Center for the Study of Teaching and Policy, University of Washington), 5-14.

6

Special Education

Gregg B. Jackson and John Y. Jones

At the time of the American Revolution, townspeople often dealt with abandoned mentally retarded and emotionally disturbed persons with a "warning out" (scaring them out of town) or a "passing on" (carting them off to another town).[1] As late as 1970, about one million children and adolescents with disabilities were excluded from public schooling.[2]

Special education provides special diagnoses, instruction, and related support services for students with disabilities. Disabilities include physical impairments, including blindness and deafness; mental retardation; speech and language impairments; emotional disturbances; and several specific learning disabilities affecting reading, writing, spelling, arithmetic, and organizational skills.

INITIAL CONDITIONS

In early colonial times, pleasure seeking, playfulness, and willfulness of children were widely perceived to be workings of the devil. If a child over 16 cursed a parent, such behavior constituted a capital offense in Massachusetts, although the maximum penalty was probably not exercised.[3] It was the parents' responsibility to guide or beat children out of such behavior. That usually was harder and took longer for children whose disabilities impaired their learning.

Throughout the colonial period, lifetime family care of children and adults with serious disabilities was the norm. When a family was unable or unwilling to provide the care, usually the town leaders sought to place the child with another family. Those who lacked care or violated social standards were warned out, passed on, or imprisoned.

Many causes of disabilities were postulated in the early 1800s. A few conditions were recognized as inherited. Intermarriage of close blood relatives was observed to increase the incidence of disabilities. Syphilis, tuberculosis, alcoholism, fright, and injury of the mother were also implicated. Cretinism—a thyroid inadequacy—was associated with dwarfism and mental retardation. Furthermore, scarlet fever, measles and mumps, meningitis, and other diseases were recognized to leave some children blind, deaf, and mentally enfeebled. Brain injuries had obvious effects. Proscribed sexual practices, especially masturbation, were also thought to cause disabilities.[4]

Disabilities, especially mental retardation and mental illness, were in turn thought to cause misconduct, immorality, intemperance, juvenile delinquency, crime, and impoverishment. The perception of a close connection between retardation and crime fueled calls for early detection and lifetime institutionalization as a means of preventing crime.

As cities grew in the early 1800s, almshouses were established to shelter and feed the indigent, who commonly suffered from disabilities. An inspection of New York State's facilities at mid-century found 1,307 children and 3,629 adults living in severely over-crowded facilities with such inadequate ventilation, heat, medical care, and supervision that 770 deaths had occurred in the prior year. The children were usually not given an education.[5]

Two other approaches were used in the early 1800s to provide orphaned and abandoned children with care. Kentucky, for instance, provided state aid to towns for placing out "idiots and lunatic" children with willing foster families. While many thought this an enlightened and humane approach, others worried that some foster families would abuse the children and that it would be difficult to monitor the quality of care. That concern led other states to build orphan asylums that could be more easily supervised. In these institutions, however, education was rare, discipline was usually strict and at times harsh, and placements soon exceeded capacity, causing overcrowding and deplorable conditions.

In the early 1840s, Dorothy Dix, a retired school-teacher, visited every jailhouse and almshouse in Massachusetts and then reported to the state legislature that she had found:

> More than 9,000 idiots, epileptics and insane in the United States, destitute of appropriate care and protection ... bound with galling chains, bowed beneath fetters and heavy iron balls attached to drag chains, lacerated with ropes, scourged with rods, and terrified beneath storms of cruel blows, ... abandoned to the most outrageous violations.[6]

That testimony was widely publicized and precipitated reforms in Massachusetts and other states.

CHANGING CONTEXTS THAT PUSHED SPECIAL EDUCATION REFORMS

Three changing contexts helped precipitate special education reform initiatives. In the early 1800s there was a religious awakening that disposed citizens to create benevolent institutions serving the less fortunate. In the early 1900s, the enforcement of compulsory education laws brought a larger portion of children into the public schools and kept them there longer, and some of the children had mild and moderate disabilities. A century later, the principles and tactics of the civil rights movement inspired the advocates of children with disabilities.

Second Great Awakening of Religiosity

The optimism of the American Revolution inspired changes in religious beliefs. The focus switched from original sin, the devil, and salvation, to building God's kingdom on the chosen land of America. Thomas Paine, whose *Common Sense* had rallied the revolution, came to think, "a revolution in the system of government would be followed by a revolution in the system of religion."[7] In his subsequent *The Age of Reason* he argued that only as men and women conformed their own lives and institutions to those of a benevolent God would the revolution's goals of equality, justice, and happiness be achieved. The first amendment to the U.S. Constitution prohibited the federal government from establishing a church, and soon after its adoption several eastern states began severing their former ties with organized religion. In addition, settlers pushing westward into the frontier were usually not accompanied by ministers. All this created a free market in religion that invited schisms and sparked a "Second Great Awakening" of religiosity as the new denominations aggressively sought to expand their membership and link religion to the American dream.[8]

The new theologies jettisoned the shackles of predestination and conceived of all men and women as having the spark of God within them. That made each human being, however wretched, deserving of love and dignity. The new theologies also hoped that the Kingdom of God would be planted in America, and that motivated the faithful to till the fields in preparation of that day, engaging in an unprecedented crusades for human advancement—abolition, women's rights, universal schooling, reformatories to save delinquent youth, and special education to assist children with disabilities.[9]

Compulsory Education Laws

As Chapter 2 described, universal public education systems were established in the mid- and late-1800s, compulsory education laws were adopted a few decades later, and the enforcement of those laws took awhile longer. Compulsory education initially exempted the ill and those with serious disabilities from mandatory attendance and sometimes explicitly excluded them. Even when those with disabilities were not excluded by law, school officials often rejected parents' pleas to enroll them.[10] Nevertheless, the enforcement of these laws brought into the schools substantial numbers of students who previously had not attended or had soon dropped out, including delinquent youth, rebellious youth who did not want to be in school, and children with an array of mild disabilities. The presence of such students forced the public schools to deal with "different" children, an experience that would prove helpful when children with more serious disabilities later began to enter the public schools.

Civil Rights Movement

When Kennedy campaigned in 1960 for the presidency, he pledged support for civil rights as well as a new frontier of economic opportunities. In turn, civil rights leaders and most of the African American community supported his candidacy. By 1962, eight years after the *Brown vs. Board of Education* decision ordering school desegregation, the border states had made substantial but incomplete progress toward desegregating K-12 schools while most southern states had made very spotty progress, with Mississippi, Alabama, and South Carolina having made virtually none.[11] Civil rights activists pressured Kennedy to pass federal legislation that would enforce the Court decision and their other Constitutional rights, but he stalled because of his slim electoral victory and the political backlash he knew such action would draw. Meanwhile some African Americans lost confidence in the 1950s civil rights strategies. Elijah Muhammad headed the Black Muslim faith, professing the superiority of black people and the inherent evil of whites, preaching black pride, separatism, and self-dependence. Malcolm X, who as a child had witnessed his family home in Michigan burned down by the Ku Klux Klan, joined the faith and became its most charismatic proponent, advocating the use of violence for self-protection. He rapidly gained adherents among young African Americans.

With the specter of a race war brewing, and with moderate civil rights leaders warning that their patience was not unlimited, in the spring of 1963, Kennedy sent a civil rights bill to Congress in 1963. It prohibited discrimination on the basis of race, color, or national origin in public accommodations; prohibited employment discrimination by federal contractors; and authorized the termination of federal funds to segregated schools. It also authorized the Justice Department to take an active role in enforcing civil rights. As the bill worked its way slowly through Congress, racial violence was escalating. In May of 1963, the Police Commissioner of Birmingham, Alabama turned fire hoses and attack dogs on African

American men, women, and children engaged in non-violent protest. In June, Medgar Evers, the NAACP state secretary of Mississippi, was murdered. In September, a Birmingham African American church was bombed, killing four children. Then, in November, Kennedy was assassinated. One century after the Civil War, it appeared that the country was again coming unglued.

National leaders, including those from the south, became eager to mend the expanding fissures. President Johnson, a southerner and grandmaster of Congressional maneuvering, succeeded in gaining passage of the broad Civil Rights Act of 1964 and the Voting Rights Act of 1965. The former forbid racial or ethnic discrimination in public facilities and services—including public schools, allowed the Justice Department to prosecute violations, and authorized the withholding of federal funds to communities that failed to comply. The latter legislation aimed to eradicate a slew of practices southern jurisdictions had invented to prevent African Americans from voting or to dilute the influence of those who did vote.

The 1950s-1960s civil rights movement left a legacy that influenced other groups, including the parents of children with disabilities. That legacy was to fight for rights denied—to bring group pressure to bear on officials, to seek court relief when the officials were unresponsive, and to secure state and federal legislation affirming rights and imposing sanctions on violators. During the 1970s, advocates of children with disabilities would move special education to a new level by following those precedents.

THE CAMPAIGNS FOR SPECIAL EDUCATION

Over the past two centuries there have been several campaigns for special education. We will describe early efforts to provide education to the deaf, the more complicated early and middle efforts to provide education for the mentally retarded, the initiation of special education in public day schools, and then the court and legislative initiatives that culminated in the landmark Education for All Handicapped Children Act, which revolutionized special education in the latter quarter of the 20th century.

Gallaudet's Education of the Deaf

Alice was a normal little girl until the age of four when spotted fever left her deaf. In 1814 the only available schools for deaf students were across the Atlantic. Her father, Dr. Mason Cogswell, could not bear to send Alice so far away, so he enlisted the support of two people to teach her to communicate with signs. One was a well-known poet and educator named Lydia Sigourney. The other was Cogswell's next-door neighbor, Thomas Gallaudet, a recent graduate of the Andover Seminary, an institution founded to train missionaries to serve the less fortunate in the western frontier and foreign countries. Both tried to teach Alice to communicate with signs but met with limited success.[12]

That motivated Cogswell to establish an American school for the deaf. He sent an inquiry to all Congregational clergymen in Connecticut asking about the number of deaf people in their communities. Based on the results, Cogswell estimated there were at least 80 in the state, 400 in New England, and 2,000 in the country, many of them of school age. He called together Hartford's social and financial leaders with the hope of inspiring private and public support for an American school for the deaf. The group's first action was to send Thomas Gallaudet to Europe to learn the methods of teaching deaf students that were being developed there.

Upon his arrival in England, Gallaudet was shocked to learn that the instruction of the deaf was conducted by one family, the Braidwoods. To train with them, Gallaudet would have to promise not to share what he learned with anyone for a period of seven years. As he considered his options, he happened upon an advertisement for a speech by Abbe Sicard, one of France's leaders in the education of the deaf. Gallaudet attended and found Sicard far more eager to share his ideas. When Sicard invited him back to Paris to study, Gallaudet gladly followed.[13]

Meanwhile, Mason Cogswell had received legislative permission to establish the Connecticut Asylum for the Education and Instruction of Deaf and Dumb Persons. The legislature appropriated $5,000 for the residential school and the governor issued a proclamation urging churches to take up a collection for the school, which Cogswell's group used to raise another $12,000.[14]

Gallaudet returned, and with Sicard's blessing, brought one of his top teachers, the deaf Laurent Clerc. They spent almost two years arranging facilities, finding and preparing teachers, and publicizing the school through the press and public addresses. At the opening in 1817, Gallaudet's speech noted,

> There is a sickness more dreadful than that of the body: there are *chains* more galling than those of the dungeon—*the immortal mind preying upon itself,* and so imprisoned as not to be able to unfold its intellectual and moral powers.... Such must often be the condition of the uninstructed deaf and dumb.[15]

This was the first school in North America dedicated to serving students with a disability. Students were taught sign language, basic academic skills, religion, and morality. They were also provided with vocational training to instill a work ethic and prepare them for adult employment. In recognition that it served more than Connecticut residents, the school's name was soon changed to American Asylum at Hartford for the Education and Instruction of the Deaf and Dumb.

The school was criticized by some as a "useless extravagance ... a quixotic undertaking.... and utterly impractical."[16] Its proponents responded with messianic fervor that God would approve of bringing these children more fully into the fold of humanity and that education would allow graduates to be self-supporting rather than a burden to their families and communities. The approach quickly gained a following. In 1818 New York City opened a similar facility to serve deaf children of the poor. Philadelphia, the state of Pennsylvania, and Kentucky soon did likewise. By 1867, fifty years after the establishment of the Connecticut Asylum, there were 24 schools for deaf children in 13 states.[17] Asylums to educate blind students soon followed, with the first established in Boston and New York City in 1832.

Gallaudet's youngest son, Edward, continued the family calling. At the mere age of 20, he took charge of the Columbia Institution for the Deaf and Dumb and Blind in Washington, D.C. By the 1850s, Edward and other leaders of education for the deaf were discussing the potential for establishing a college. Such an institution would not only provide advanced educational opportunities for deaf students but also dispel the myth of their intellectual inferiority. The 1862 Morrill Act, which provided federal funds for the establishment of land-grant colleges, appeared to offer an opportunity. With what Gallaudet would later describe as "monumental cheek," he had the directors of the Columbia Institution lobby Congress for degree-granting status and, to their surprise, they prevailed.[18] Thus was born the National Deaf Mute College, later renamed Gallaudet College (and then later, Gallaudet University), which was federally funded and served students from throughout the United States and its territories. It provided a liberal arts education and also prepared the deaf to become teachers of the deaf. A limited number of poor students could attend at no charge. Its graduates went on to provide much of the leadership in the organizations serving deaf people.

In 1867 the Clarke School for the Deaf was established in Massachusetts to teach the deaf by a different method than promoted by Gallaudet and Clerc. It was started by a few parents of deaf children who secured a state charter and a large private donation from John Clarke, a wealthy merchant who was suffering gradual hearing loss. This school eschewed sign language and instead taught lip-reading and speech. Alexander Graham Bell taught at the Clarke school for many years and invented the telephone when trying to develop a hearing aid. He advocated in behalf of the oral method, and because of his invention of the telephone, he had easy access to publicity.

Soon debate over the relative advantages of the manual and oral approach raged on both sides of the Atlantic. Manualists perceived deafness as a human difference and considered sign language as the natural mode of communication for the deaf. Oralists considered deafness a disability and perceived lip-reading and speech as the road to normality. Sign language was easier to learn; mastering speech was very difficult for students born deaf. On the other hand, sign language limited communication to those who knew the signs, whereas lip reading and speech allowed communication with everyone. Clerc perceived the oralists to be engaged in a plot to undermine the socializing, organizing, publishing, and marriage among the deaf that had been fostered in the early Asylums. Bell, whose mother had a moderate hearing impairment, argued that early acquisition of lip-reading and speech would allow the deaf to attend regular day schools and fully integrate in society. He also worried that if the deaf married the deaf, the rates of deafness would increase, a concern that reflected his support of the eugenics movement.[19] This debate over manual and oral communication continues to this day.

Bell also advocated offering special education for the deaf in local public schools. In his 1898 address to the National Education Association, he noted that about half of all deaf children in America were not attending school and proclaimed that children with disabilities had a right to a public education. He said they should be served in:

> ... an annex to the public school system, receiving special instruction from special teachers, who shall be able to give instruction to little children who are either deaf, blind, or mentally deficient, without sending them away from their homes or from the ordinary companions with whom they are associated. [20]

Bell noted that the per capita costs of asylums were more than twice those of public day schools. He suggested that deaf students, presumably after learning to read lips, could participate in regular classes for subjects such as writing and drawing.[21] He encouraged the NEA to support such efforts and it soon created a Department of Special Education. With Philip Gillett of Gallaudet College, Bell also helped to draft legislation for six states that would support day schools for the deaf. Those efforts often encountered opposition, including from directors of the asylums, their former students, and experienced teachers of the handicapped, who felt the needed expertise could not be provided in dispersed settings. Part of the deaf community despised Bell for his insistence that the deaf avoid their sign language and for his efforts to prevent the deaf from marrying the deaf. They complained that Bell's appeal was so strong that whoever "will get Dr. Bell to come out and appear before the legislature ... is going to have a day-school law, and it is going to be drawn just according to Dr. Bell's dictates."[22] Bell, however, did not always prevail with the legislatures, and where he did, the efforts soon crumbled because of a shortage of trained teachers, a paucity of materials, and the opposition of most school administrators and teachers.

Howe's and Sequin's Education for the Mentally Retarded

Samuel Howe was a tall physician with a fiery personality and a life-long commitment to helping the underdog. He fought with the Greeks in their war of liberation against the Turks, joined Polish revolutionaries, opened a school for refugees in Crete, and was an impassioned participant in many reform initiatives in Massachusetts. His most lasting contribution, however, was to the education of children with disabilities. He first gained renown as the founding superintendent of the Massachusetts Asylum for the Blind in 1832, which, within a few years, was serving students from several states, often with appropriations from their state legislatures. His charismatic personality, humane outlook, knack for promotion, and unrelenting advocacy quickly made him a leader in the field.

Moved by Dix's indictment of Massachusetts's treatment of "idiots" and the insane, and encouraged by his own early successes teaching a few blind students who were also mentally retarded, Howe turned his attention to children with mental retardation. Using the 1846 census, he estimated that there were 1,200 to 1,500 severely mentally retarded in the state of Massachusetts.[23] He persuaded George Sumner, a philanthropist and reformer, to travel to Europe to observe the methods being used there to educate the retarded, and Sumner reported astonishing progress made by some children who were thought not educable. Howe won a seat in the Massachusetts legislature and was appointed to chair a commission reporting on the problems of the mentally retarded. The commission estimated that one-third of the retarded could benefit from instruction and urged the creation of a school for them. Howe argued that society had a moral obligation to all of God's children and that education would develop habits of self-control, industry, and conscience.[24]

The legislature allocated funds to support the education of ten mentally retarded children for three years. Howe used the money to add a small wing in his school for the blind. Horace Mann recommended James Richards to head the wing, impressed by his success teaching young felons in the New York House of Refuge. Howe first sent Richards to Europe to learn more about the latest practices. Howe hoped to prove:

> ...that no idiot need be confined or restrained by force; that the young can be trained for industry, order, and self-respect; that they can be redeemed from odious and filthy habits, and there is not one of any age

who may not be made more of a man and less of a brute by patience and kindness directed by energy and skill.[25]

Only boys were admitted to Howe's institution. They were about eight years old and selected because they showed promise of benefiting from education. The intent was to return them to their parents after five-to-seven years of instruction. They were treated with respect but not coddled. Richards taught the students using a combination of physical activity, imitation, Pestalozzi's object teaching, repeated practice, monitoring of progress, and non-punitive obedience training.[26] Howe declared success after just three years, proclaiming the results showed that "many idiots are capable of improvement in their bodily habits, in their mental capabilities, and even in their spiritual natures; and almost all can be made less burdensome to their friends and the community."[27] In 1850 the legislature established the Massachusetts School for Idiotic and Feeble-Minded Children, which Howe oversaw for 25 years. Several other states did likewise during the mid-1800s.

Edouard Sequin had been a prominent theorist and leader of education for the mentally retarded in France before moving to the United States. He directed the Pennsylvania Training School for Idiots and joined Howe to assist in the establishment of similar institutions in three other states. Sequin emphasized development of muscular control, the nervous system, the five senses, general knowledge, abstract thinking, and moral principles.[28] He anticipated the basics of behavioral psychology, urging teachers to arrange learning to assure successes and then reinforce those successes. He used redeemable tickets as reinforcers. He also expected all the students to help with the work of the institution, partly because he thought idleness was bad for them and partly to learn practical skills. As a result, many of the asylums for the retarded engaged in commercial farming and light manufacturing to help pay their costs. Sequin's aims were broad—to harmoniously develop physical, intellectual, and moral capabilities.[29] He considered moral education to involve both the teachers' humane demeanor toward the students and the students' development of good personal and social behavior. He emphasized, "the idiot is endowed with a moral nature sensitive to the eulogy, reproach, command, menace, even to imaginary punishment" and "To make the child feel ... loved and ... eager to love in his turn, is the end of our teaching as it has been its beginning."[30] He had hoped to find a cure for mental retardation, and while he failed in that, he did prove that most mentally retarded children could learn basic life-coping skills and simple work skills.[31]

By 1860 there were eight asylum schools for the mentally retarded in six states, all led by physicians, several of whom had started small private facilities, often in their homes, and then advocated successfully for public support of larger facilities. Most of these asylums used the "colony model," establishing the facility in an isolated rural area that included supervised living quarters, a school, a vocational education shop, and a farm. There were at least three rationales for this model. The mentally retarded, more than the deaf and blind, seemed to come disproportionately from lower class families, and the remote location removed them from the perceived undesirable environment of their families and neighborhoods. Rural areas provided a spaciousness and natural environment that were thought to benefit the children. Finally, mentally retarded children were perceived to be inclined to anti-social, immoral, and criminal behavior, and the remote location protected others from them.

In 1876 the Association of Medical Officers of American Institutions for Idiots and Feeble-Minded Persons was formed, and later the Superintendents of the American Institutions for the Improvement of Idiots and Feeble Minded Children was established. By 1888 there were about 20 educational asylums for the mentally retarded with about 4,000 children.[32] As impressive as the growth was, educational asylums were then serving only about four percent of mentally retarded youth.[33]

As early as 1866, Howe had begun urging, "As much as may be, surround.... blind children with those who see; mute children with those who speak; and the like."[34] He suggested repeatedly that many children with disabilities could attend regular public schools. For those who could not be accommodated, he suggested establishing special day schools.

Elizabeth Farrell's "Ungraded" Day Classes

Elizabeth Farrell was the daughter of Irish and Welsh immigrants who had prospered in upstate New York. She completed two years of normal school preparation, taught in a rural one-room schoolhouse for a year, and then moved to New York City in the late 1890s.

By then the city had almost a half-million students, and the count would continue to increase rapidly because of an 1899 compulsory education law. This law also prohibited child labor by those aged 12-14 unless they also attended at least 80 days of school per year.[35] Students who never before passed through the school doors were now in attendance. Farrell was given a class of boys who had not been successful in regular classes. Included were children who were obviously mentally retarded, who were frequently truant, who were unruly and disruptive, or who had simply not learned in their regular classes. Although the city had a graded school system, Farrell's class ranged in age from 8-16, and thus it was called an "ungraded class," a confusing term since one-room school houses, with children of many ages, were still the norm outside of the cities.

When Joseph Rice (see Chapter 4) had made his national assessment of schools in the 1890s he noted:

The typical New York City primary school ... is nevertheless a hard, unsympathetic, mechanical-drudgery school, a school in which the light of science has not yet entered. Its characteristic features lie in the severity of discipline, a discipline of enforced silence, immobility, and mental passivity.[36]

With no preparation for her job, Farrell observed carefully and experimented. She strove to respond to the individual needs, capabilities, and goals of the students. She appealed to "the constructive, the acquisitive, the imitative instincts in the child" and made the classes "full of interesting activities to pursue, full of constructive activity."[37] Reading and writing were taught to those who could learn, and life-coping skills were taught to all.

The district superintendent was impressed and, in 1903, decided to establish ungraded classes in nine other schools, modeling them after Farrell's class. Farrell went to Europe for a month to study teaching methods for atypical children and returned to help guide the new classes. They appeared to be a success on at least three counts. First, the students were no longer disrupting the education of students in their former classrooms. Second, the ungraded classes held the students' interests and developed valuable skills and habits. Third, dropout also declined, which for such children was often thought to lead to criminal activity.

In 1906 the district superintendent decided to expand the ungraded classes and appointed Farrell as the Inspector of the Ungraded Class Department.[38] By 1911 she supervised 131 teachers assigned to ungraded classes in 95 of the city's schools, the largest special education program in the country at that time.[39] Farrell reported that for one group of 350 students who had gone through her program, only four percent were institutionalized; fifty-five percent were employed and nine percent of the unemployed were fit to work.[40]

Farrell's ungraded classes were threatened with elimination by the City's Board of Estimates and Apportionment. Repeatedly, the Board sought ways to rein in the mushrooming school budget and considered Farrell's classes an unnecessary frill. The superintendent held them off. Finally the Board hired Henry Goddard to evaluate the ungraded classes, knowing that he believed that intelligence was inherited and immutable. Goddard's findings were a surprise. He recommended expanding the program to serve seven times more children whom he estimated were in need of it. He concluded the assessment and placement of students in the program was unreliable and should be done on the basis of IQ tests. He noted that many of the teachers needed more training and he recommended a salary bonus for teachers of the ungraded classes. Farrell submitted a scathing rebuttal of Goddard's high estimate of the number of children needing ungraded classes and his recommendation that assessments be done by IQ tests, but she had previously sought, without success, resources for improved assessment, better teacher training, and incremental pay. As a result of Goddard's report and Farrell's rebuttal, the Board gave Farrell almost everything she wanted.

By now IQ tests were being promoted as a scientific and relatively inexpensive way of assessing a child's intellectual ability. One of the key developers, Alfred Binet, had expected such tests to be used only as a supplement to comprehensive observation, but practitioners in the United States quickly came to rely mainly, and often solely, on the test results. This was partly because several studies found the test results correlated fairly well with teachers' judgments of students' intellectual abilities, partly because the systematic nature of the testing and scoring seemed more scientific and more reliable than informal observations, and partly because it was quicker, cheaper, and easier to rely on one source of data than to make judgments based on multiple sources. Farrell used IQ tests but only in conjunction with other means. In 1913 Farrell convinced the school district to create a Psycho-Educational Clinic employing psychologists, physicians, social workers, and educators, who were to work jointly to assess students referred for ungraded classes. They made use of IQ tests, academic skill tests, family outreach, and their own clinical judgments.

By 1921 Farrell was overseeing 250 ungraded classes and a substantial staff in the Psycho-Educational Clinic. She spread her vision and expertise widely by teaching at New York University and then Teachers College of Columbia University. She founded the Ungraded Classroom Teachers' Association and edited its journal for several years. She served as vice-president and then president of the NEA's Department of Special Education. Then, in collaboration with several of her former students, she founded and served as the first president of the International Council for Exceptional Children, which is now called the Council for Exceptional Children.[41]

The first law requiring compulsory schooling of special needs children was passed in 1909, as the last states were passing compulsory education laws for normal children.[42] Between 1911 and 1920, New Jersey, New York, and Massachusetts passed legislation mandating that local school boards determine the number of children with disabilities in their district and provide special classes where ten or more were found. The first two of those states also provided a state subsidy for each special education child.[43] By 1929, 16 states had enacted legislation permitting or requiring the provision of special education in day schools. New York City limited class size to 18-25, depending on the homogeneity of the students, but other districts permitted as many as 70 in a class with one teacher.[44]

Some school districts responded to these new laws by establishing day schools exclusively devoted to children with disabilities, but most followed

Farrell's model, creating special classes in regular day schools. Several rationales were given for putting children with disabilities in special classes. Special classes allowed for specially prepared teachers to be assigned to these children, permitted the teachers to direct the instruction to the children's unique needs, protected the children with disabilities from disheartening competition and teasing that they were likely to experience in regular classes, allowed a faster pace of instruction for the normal children, and saved the regular teachers from distractions and frustrations that otherwise were caused by some of these students.

During the first half of the 20th century, a few people advocated that disabled children who could function well in regular classes should be placed in those classes. That probably occurred some by default but it was not the general policy.

The Depression and then World War II slowed progress in special education, but the war sparked new perceptions of people with disabilities by requiring every able-bodied man and woman to contribute, bringing the blind, deaf, and mildly mentally retarded into jobs. Their contributions in the workplace improved public opinion about their potential to contribute to society and to live independent adult lives.[45]

From Charity to Legal Rights

During the first half of the 1900s there was more exclusion than education of students with serious disabilities, and when special education was provided, it was considered public charity rather than a legal right. By 1900 only about half the states had special schools for deaf or blind students, and only a few states had legislation mandating the provision of education for children with disabilities.[46] By 1930, several states permitted special education but left provision of it up to the option of local school districts. Many state compulsory education laws still had provisions exempting ill and handicapped children, and some excluded children with serious disabilities. Students with disabilities who secured entry to public schools often were isolated and received minimal services.[47] Many sat idly in regular classrooms without any special assistance, waiting until they were old enough to drop out.

There had been many efforts to secure public education services for these students, but the parents of the children were a small minority with diverse needs, which made it difficult for them to marshal political clout. In 1948 an estimated 12 percent of children with disabilities were in special education. By 1968 the rate increased to 38 percent, but most of the rest were not even in school.[48]

Court decisions had repeatedly affirmed the right of public schools to exclude students with disabilities. In 1893 the Massachusetts Supreme Judicial Court ruled in *Watson v. City of Cambridge* that a child "weak in mind" who could not take care of himself could be expelled from public school. The 1919 case of *Beattie v. Board of Education* in Wisconsin had allowed school officials to remove a boy who had a condition that caused facial contortions and drooling, while, in 1934, Cuyahoga County Court of Appeals ruled that the mandate for compulsory attendance did not preclude officials from excluding certain students. As late as 1958, the Supreme Court of Illinois had ruled in *Department of Public Welfare v. Haas* that the state's compulsory attendance laws did not require a free education be made available to retarded children, or to any child who was incapable of benefiting from a good education.[49]

By the 1950s, there were more than 100 local groups of parents of mentally retarded children and they collaborated in founding the National Association for Retarded Citizens. They were no longer willing to accept "Nothing can be done for your child" responses by school and health officials, and they believed that the care of children with disabilities was partly a social responsibility. They lobbied state legislatures, often in uneasy alliance with special education professional groups, and experienced increasing success.[50] They sought improved residential facilities and better services for the mentally retarded in day schools. Many of the local groups became part of their local Community Chest or United Fund Agency as a way of raising supplemental funds.

The same advocates also lobbied the U.S. Congress for programs and financial assistance for special education. They had a powerful ally in President Kennedy, who had a retarded sister, and then President Johnson, who had sympathy for the underdogs of society and great belief in the power of government to alleviate their plight. Between 1956 and 1974, Congress passed 18 statutes or amendments that provided federal funding for research and resource centers, the training of special education teachers, preparation of special instructional materials such as captioned films, development of special education programs, and establishment of a model elementary and secondary school for the deaf at Gallaudet College. In addition, the Rehabilitation Act of 1973 prohibited discrimination in employment against people with disabilities, and after a 1974 amendment, also prohibited discrimination in educational services.[51]

Two decades after the *Brown v. Board of Education* decision had affirmed the right to equal opportunity in education, and with the example of the 1960's civil rights movement, the Pennsylvania Association of Retarded Citizens (PARC) decided to challenge in court the Commonwealth's failure to provide education for seriously retarded children. Although state statute provided a free public education for all children ages 6-21, the school codes and administrative interpretation of them excluded seriously mentally retarded children from special education classes in public schools, from the tuition reimbursement program for private schools available to children with other disabilities, and from publicly provided home education services. The Commonwealth claimed that seriously retarded children were "uneducable" and "untrainable." The plaintiffs argued that under the equal protection clause of the 14th Amendment, all retarded children were entitled to participate in publicly provided education and training. They provided extensive evidence that all mentally retarded children can, with appropriate instruction, learn at least a few self-care skills and that many are capable achieving self-sufficiency. The evidence also suggested that the earlier the instruction begins, the better the outcomes. The case of *Pennsylvania Association for Retarded Children v. Commonwealth of Pennsylvania* ended in a 1971 consent agreement specifying that all retarded children are entitled to a free public education, they are to be placed in the least restrictive environment from which they will benefit, their parents are to be provided with advanced notice of a child's evaluation, and their parents are to be allowed due process in appeals. [52] The same year, plaintiffs in the District of Columbia won a similar case. The *Mills v. Board of Education of the District of Columbia* decision extended the right of "suitable" special education to children with all types of disabilities. It also indicated that a school district's financial difficulties were not justification for excluding children with disabilities from public education.[53]

The *PARC* and *Mills* decisions triggered an avalanche of lawsuits around the county seeking public special education for all children with disabilities, better identification of handicaps, and more appropriate educational programs. Only a year later, 27 suits in 21 states were pending or had recently been completed, almost always with outcomes favoring the plaintiffs.[54]

The advocates of special education reform realized they had achieved only a partial victory. Litigation required considerable resources and there were many states with no pending cases. These lower court decisions could subsequently be overruled in appellate courts or the U.S. Supreme Court, which was becoming more conservative at that time. The costs of educating students with disabilities ran anywhere from two- to seven-times the normal costs of education, so school districts and states would either have to raise taxes or redistribute resources away from the other children—both of which would elicit political resistance. In addition, after a century and half of neglect, school bureaucracies could not be trusted to implement the court decisions, and judges were reluctant to micro-manage schools.[55]

The reform advocates decided to use the court decisions as a lever for state and federal legislation. For example, in Tennessee, a pending lawsuit was dropped after acceptable legislation was passed. As state and local officials became reconciled to providing special education to all who needed it, they began to look to the federal government for financial assistance. As a consequence, the advocates' former opponents became allies in the push for federal legislation.

As the reformers moved to the federal arena, they encountered serious hurdles. President Nixon was not interested in providing federal funding for special education and ordered the Bureau of Education for the Handicapped to provide only minimal technical information to Congress. Advocates, particularly the staff of the Council for Exceptional Children, found a few powerful members of Congress who were sympathetic with their cause and helped their staff to craft a bill addressing the historic discrimination against children with disabilities. They wanted a bill that clearly stated rights of handicapped students and their parents, mandated procedures to protect their interests, avoided prescribing the nature of the educational services, and provided federal financial assistance.[56]

Most major education associations—the National School Boards Association, American Association of School Administrators, National Education Association, American Federation of Teachers and others—favored federal legislation to support special education. So did many state and local officials eager for federal funds to share the costs of the court-mandated special education. In addition, because severe disabilities are distributed across all races and social classes of society, there was a wide base of public support for federal legislation.

Opponents decried the projected costs at a time of ballooning federal budget deficits and predicted considerable federal meddling with local education. Some undoubtedly thought education of children with disabilities was not a good investment for the country, although, by now, few would actually state that publicly. By the time Congress was seriously working on the legislation, both President Nixon and Vice President Agnew had resigned because of scandals, and Gerald Ford had assumed the Presidency.

In 1975 Congress passed the Education for All Handicapped Children Act with overwhelming votes of 87-7 in the Senate and 404-7 in the House. The Act partly consolidated prior federal statutes but also provided important new provisions. The Act mandated that a search be made for all children with disabilities who were excluded from public education, that all children with disabilities ages 3-24 have a right to a "free appropriate public education," and that careful assessment procedures should be applied. The Act required that school staff and the parents collaborate in developing an "individualized education program" (IEP) specifying needs, goals, and services; that the educational services take place in the "least restrictive environment," including regular classrooms "to the maximum extent appropriate;" and that procedural safeguards and due process be adopted, including informing parents of their rights, providing advanced notice of actions the school intends to take in respect to their child, and allowing due process hearings and the right to appeal. The act also specified that the federal government should conduct research, evaluation, and information dissemination, and that the federal government should pay a share of the additional costs of educating children ages 3-21 who have disabilities, with the cost-sharing percentage beginning at five percent in 1975 and plateauing at 40 percent by 1982.[57]

President Ford had grave concerns about this legislation and contemplated vetoing it. When that became known, the Council for Exceptional Children directed a barrage of phone calls to the White House.[58] Ford, wishing to set a conciliatory tone after the White House scandals that brought him to office, decided to sign the bill but issued a statement that included the following:

> Unfortunately, this bill promises more than the Federal Government can deliver, and its good intentions could be thwarted by the many unwise provisions it contains.... The funding levels proposed in this bill will simply not be possible if Federal expenditures are to be brought under control and a balanced budget achieved over the next few years.... [The bill] contains a vast array of detailed, complex, and costly administrative requirements which would unnecessarily assert Federal control over traditional State and local government functions.... [and] these requirements will remain in effect even though the Congress appropriates far less than the amounts contemplated.... Fortunately, since the provisions of this bill will not become fully effective until fiscal year 1978, there is time to revise the legislation and come up with a program that is effective and realistic.

SUCCESS OF THE REFORM EFFORT

Spectacular progress has been achieved in special education services, but heart-wrenching failure remains to this day.

In the mid-1800s, the creation of educational asylums with specialized services for the deaf, the blind, the mentally retarded, and the mentally ill, were a major advance. They met a pressing need and have continued to exist ever since. Nevertheless, they were an inadequate response. Such schools were complex and expensive institutions to run. Their capacities fell far short of the need. Their use required long separation of children from their parents and siblings. In addition, asylums were never intended to serve children with mild disabilities.

In the 1890s, day schools began providing special education, but by 1970 more than half of the children with disabilities who attended school were found not to be receiving appropriate educational services and about one million children with severe disabilities were receiving no educational service.[59]

The *PARC* and *Mills* court decisions and the federal Education for All Handicapped Children Act of 1975 dramatically changed that. Districts and states scrambled to achieve at least nominal compliance to avoid legal suits and to qualify for the new federal funds. Districts adopted assessment procedures to identify students with disabilities and prepared individualized education programs for those so classified. Parents had an opportunity for input into these activities. Students were placed in a variety of settings.[60] Over the first decade of the Act, 650,000 additional students were served in special education, even though total K-12 enrollments declined ten percent over the same period.[61] Most of the growth came from students with the most severe disabilities who previously had been excluded from public education and from students with the least severe disabilities, usually specific learning disabilities, whose special needs had often previously gone unnoticed.

At the close of the 20th century, 11 percent of all children were receiving special education.[62] Of those ages 6-21 receiving services, only 1.3 percent have hearing impairments, 0.5 percent have visual impairments, and 11 percent have mental retardation.[63] The high-incidence categories of disability are speech and language impairments (19.4 percent of the total) and specific learning disabilities (50.8 percent). Fifty years earlier, most children in the last category had been labeled lazy, inattentive, inept, or mildly mentally retarded.

Almost all special education services are now provided in regular day schools, with only 2.9 percent of students ages 6-21 served in separate day facilities, 0.7 percent in residential facilities, and 0.6 percent in homes and hospitals.[64] Those with hearing and visual impairments are in residential facilities about ten times as often as students with other disabilities. Within regular schools, almost half are served in regular classrooms for most of the school week. Other special education services are usually provided in classes devoted to special education children and in one-on-one sessions with an instructor or counselor.

The landmark federal legislation of 1975 has not only been sustained but has been extended and refined. In 1982 the Reagan administration proposed weakening the provisions of the original Act, but the public response was so overwhelmingly negative that the proposal was dropped. Then, during his second term, President Reagan signed into law the 1986 amendments that extended services to infants and toddlers with disabilities. The amendments of 1990 mandated inclusion of children with disabilities in regular classrooms when they would benefit from it, required children age14 and older to receive "transition services" to prepare them for adult life, and renamed the statute the Individuals with Disabilities Education Act

(IDEA). The amendments of 1997 required that children with disabilities be included in state and local achievement assessments when accommodations would make testing feasible, and that the assessment reports must report separately the data for special education students.

While the expansion of special education during the last quarter of the 20th century has been impressive, it has not been without serious problems and shortcomings. Special education has proven very expensive. The average per-pupil cost is almost three times that of regular students.[65] Federal funding increased from $100 million in fiscal year 1976 to $1.64 billion in fiscal year 1985, but that latter value was only about eight percent of the total additional costs of special education, far short of the 40 percent that was authorized in the legislation.[66] Indeed, the Federal share has not approached 40 percent in any of the 27 years since its passage. At the close of the century, the federal contribution was $2.6 billion, an estimated 17 percent of the total costs of special education.[67]

Assessment of disabilities, especially the milder and subtler disabilities, has proven problematic. There is still considerable disagreement among experts on how and when to diagnose specific learning disabilities. In actual practice, the assessment and classification of students with disabilities appears far from reliable.[68]

Staffing of special education has also been problematic. School systems across the country have struggled to recruit and retain special education teachers and support staff. In 1999 slightly more than nine percent of graduates with bachelor's and master's degrees in education had specialized in special education, as compared with the 11 percent of all school-age students who are identified as having disabilities.[69] The shortfall is far more severe than the two-percentage point gap suggests because special education usually requires half or a third the normal student/staff ratio. A 1999 survey suggested that 12,000 special education teaching positions nationwide were left vacant or filled by a substitute because a qualified candidate could not be found, and another 33,000 special education teachers were not fully certified for their main teaching responsibility.[70] At the high school level, special education teachers often have had little college course work in the multiple subjects that they teach.[71] A 1998 survey of regular and special education teachers found only 21 percent felt very well prepared to address the needs of students with disabilities and another 41 percent felt moderately well prepared.[72]

The original regulations accompanying the Education for All Handicapped Children Act were 149 pages long. A checklist of 814 requirements has been used in monitoring compliance. It is widely agreed that no state agency is in full compliance[73] and it is presumed that this is also the case for most of the 15,000 school districts in the country. The heavy mantle of regulations was established in response to the century of wanton disregard of handicapped children's rights and a history of state and local evasion of federal legislative intent. Nevertheless, it is clear that the paperwork burdens of the regulations are consuming considerable staff time that otherwise could be used for instruction and support services. A majority of special education teachers estimate that they spend the equivalent of a full day or more on paperwork each week.[74] Special education teachers who leave the field most often cite the paperwork and caseload work as the reasons. They report working an average of 53 hours per week, (versus 46 for all teachers) and indicate only half that time is spent in direct instruction.[75]

Achievement of Goals

The goals of special education are to help the students reach their full potential and live as independent and fulfilling lives as is feasible. There are plenty of examples of children who floundered until they received appropriate special education and then flourished academically, socially, and economically. General George Patton, Governor Nelson Rockefeller, and Bill Hewlett all achieved greatness despite dyslexia. Fifty-four percent of visually impaired students continue on to college and about 30 percent of hearing impaired students do so.[76]

That is the good news, but there is also disconcerting news. Achievement gaps between students with and without disabilities are large. In 2003, the percentage of 4th and 8th grade children with disabilities who exceeded the "basic score" on the National Assessment of Educational Progress (NAEP) reading and mathematics tests was half the percentage of other children, and only 6-13 percent of children with disabilities were above the "proficient" level on these tests.[77] The reality is worse than those numbers suggest because a moderate portion of children with disabilities are not tested, and they tend to be those with the most severe disabilities. The percentage of children with disabilities graduating with a standard high school diploma increased modestly over the 1990s, reaching 51 percent in the 2001-2002 school year, but the percentages ranged from 71 percent for those with visual impairments to 32 percent for those with serious emotional disturbances.[78]

These statistics are hard to interpret. Being able to read or do math at the basic level might be a major gain for one student after entering special education and no gain at all for another. Complex evaluations, which have not been done on large samples, would be needed to ascertain to what extent special education students have done better than they would have without special education services.

Unintended Side Effects

During the final decade of the 20th century, the number of youth age 6-21 increased ten percent while the number served under IDEA grew 30 percent.[79] That is partly the result of better compliance with the law, but it may also be the result of "perverse incentives." The availability of extra federal and state funds for students in special education has created an incentive for school districts to classify more children as having disabilities, thus bringing more funds to the district.[80] In addition Chapter 10 will discuss how state accountability systems, which had been pressing districts to raise achievement but did not hold special education students to the same standards, also created an incentive to classify more students as needing special education. Many critics of special education, and even some advocates of children with disabilities, think that all the special arrangements mandated for these children have lowered expectations for them and undermined their motivation. The very labeling of a child can affect the expectations of parents, teachers, classmates, and the children themselves.[81]

As school districts switched from exclusion of children with disabilities to providing education for all, there had been protests that minority children were being mislabeled as mentally retarded. The data clearly showed higher rates of such classification for minorities, but officials usually claimed that was an unfortunate reality. Then in the early 1970s, Jane Mercer brought careful research to bear on the matter. Following the practice urged by Alfred Binet but abandoned by American leaders of intelligence testing, she examined the results of both intelligence tests and adaptive behavior assessments. In a small California sample she found that all Anglos (non-Hispanic Whites) whose IQ was below 70 also failed an adaptive behavior test of personal care and social functioning expected of their age group, but 60 percent of Mexican Americans and 91 percent of African Americans with IQ scores below 70 passed the adaptive behavior test, and thus should not have been classified as mentally retarded.[82] That finding was used by plaintiffs in the *Larry P. v. Riles* court case to challenge the state's classification of African American children as mentally retarded at almost three times their percentage in the school population. The court decision enjoined California schools from using IQ tests to classify African American students as mentally retarded without prior demonstration to the court that the test and the testing procedures are valid for that purpose and not racially and culturally biased.[83]

At the end of the 20th century, some minority groups were still over-represented in special education. African Americans were 36 percent more likely to be in special education than expected from their portion of the population and twice as likely to be classified as mentally retarded. Similarly, Native Americans were 30 percent more likely to be in special education. On the other hand, Hispanics and Whites are slightly under-represented, and Asian/Pacific Islanders are substantially under-represented.[84]

Critics have charged that the disproportionate representation of some minorities in special education is the result of racist efforts to re-segregate minorities after the desegregation of school districts. California provided a prime example of this. In 1947 it repealed legislation that required racially segregated schools and in the same year passed legislation creating public school programs for the mentally retarded, which were soon filled disproportionately with Mexican Americans and other minorities.[85] Even today, the rates at which African American students are identified as mentally retarded and as seriously emotionally disturbed are noticeably higher in predominantly white districts than in predominantly minority districts.[86] Not all the evidence, however, supports the charge. For instance, Hispanics are not over-represented in special education nationally, even though their average academic achievement is substantially lower than that of non-Hispanic whites.

Another unfortunate side effect of the IDEA requirements has been some disruption of regular students' education. The regulations create difficulties in disciplining special education students, especially when the parents disagree with proposed discipline that involves a change in the student's placement (such as removal from a regular classroom). Discipline problems have been exacerbated by failures to provide needed services. For instance, a study in five large districts found 39 percent of children classified as emotionally disturbed had never seen a therapist, and another 22 percent had only one to four sessions.[87]

WAS SPECIAL EDUCATION INEVITABLE?

Children with special needs are found in every society. Societies differ only in how they respond. When states created universal public education systems and excluded children with moderate and severe disabilities, it was probably only a matter of time before the equal protection clause of the 14th Amendment would have forced a reversal of that exclusion.

It is far less clear whether the provision of special education was inevitable. It arose in the 1800s from humanitarian sentiments and proved to have social and economic benefits, but it remained quite limited until the 14th Amendment decisions in *PARC* and *Mills*. By then, the outrage of a century of illegal exclusion and the adroit political maneuvering of special education advocates won a strong federal mandate for special education. If the public school systems had not practiced exclusion, there might not be special education today; rather, there might only be open access to regular education, leaving students to benefit as best they could with little or no special assistance.

FUTURE OF THE REFORM

Special education is likely to endure, but there are two reasons to think it might contract in scope over the next several decades.

First, the best possible future is one where the need for special education will decline because new means are found to prevent or correct the underlying physical conditions that result in many disabilities. Genetic engineering, neural implants, and pharmaceutical advances hold promise of preventing or controlling some of these conditions.[88] It is also known that poor nutrition, drug and alcohol use, and smoking during pregnancy cause disabilities, and perhaps the country will become more successful at preventing these, although four decades of efforts have yielded only modest success on a national scale.

Second, the ratio of elderly people to children in the country is increasing rapidly and the care of the elderly will increasingly compete with schooling for public resources. Since the average cost of special education per capita is already far greater than for regular students, and since the vast majority of parents do not have children needing special education, special education will be vulnerable to budget cutbacks. Only if the national economy expands rapidly over the next three decades is this demographic force likely to be blunted.

The big push in special education at the turn of the century is for integration of students with disabilities into regular classrooms and all other aspects of school life, with accommodations and supports to make that work. This is an extension of the mandate to place students into the "least restrictive environment." It is inconceivable that all teachers can be prepared to deal expertly with a wide range of disabilities. Unless the teachers receive effective assistance and support, "mainstreaming" is more likely to reduce special education costs than it is to benefit students with serious disabilities.[89]

---

[1] Philip L. Safford and Elizabeth J. Safford, *A History of Childhood and Disability* (New York: Teachers College Press, 1996), 57.

[2] U.S. Department of Education, Office of Special Education Programs, *Twenty-second Annual Report to Congress on the Implementation of the Individuals with Disabilities Education Act* (Washington DC: author, 2000), v.

[3] Daniel Boorstin, *The Americans: The Colonial Experience* (New York: Random House, 1958), 28.

[4] Philip L. Safford and Elizabeth J. Safford, *A History of Childhood and Disability* (New York: Teachers College Press, 1996), 164-165.

[5] Henry W. Thurston, *The Dependent Child: A Story of Changing Aims and Methods in the Care of Dependent Children* (New York: Columbia University Press, 1930), 21-28.
[6] Quoted in Margaret A. Winzer, *The History of Special Education: From Isolation to Integration* (Washington DC: Gallaudet University Press, 1993), 111.
[7] Quoted in Lawrence Cremin, *American Education: The National Experience: 1783-1876* (New York: Harper & Row, 1980), 20.
[8] William L. Miller, *The First Liberty: Religion and the American Republic* (New York: Alfred A. Knopf, 1986), 250-254.
[9] See: Lawrence A. Cremin, *American Education: The National Experience: 1783-1876* (New York: Harper & Row, 1980), 32-43; William L. Miller, *The First Liberty: Religion and the American Republic* (New York: Alfred A. Knopf, 1985), 253-255.
[10] See: Jack Tweedie, "The Politics of Legalization in Special Education Reform," in *Special Education Policies: Their History, Implementation, and Finance*, ed. Jay G Chambers and William T. Hartman (Philadelphia, PA: Temple University Press, 1983), 48-73; (pg. 48-49); Margaret A. Winzer, *The History of Special Education: From Isolation to Integration* (Washington DC: Gallaudet University Press, 1993), 139.
[11] Lawrence A. Cremin, L., *American Education: The Metropolitan Experience* (New York: Harper and Row, 1988), 259-261.
[12] Margaret A. Winzer, *The History of Special Education: From Isolation to Integration* (Washington DC: Gallaudet University Press, 1993), 99.
[13] Margaret A. Winzer, *The History of Special Education: From Isolation to Integration* (Washington DC: Gallaudet University Press, 1993), 100.
[14] Margaret A. Winzer, *The History of Special Education: From Isolation to Integration* (Washington DC: Gallaudet University Press, 1993), 101.
[15] Quoted in Philip L. Safford & Elizabeth J. Safford, *A History of Childhood and Disability* (New York: Teacher's College Press, 1996), 62.
[16] Quoted in Margaret A. Winzer, *The History of Special Education: From Isolation to Integration* (Washington DC: Gallaudet University Press, 1993), 101.
[17] Margaret A. Winzer, *The History of Special Education: From Isolation to Integration* (Washington DC: Gallaudet University Press, 1993), 101-102.
[18] Quoted in Margaret A. Winzer, *The History of Special Education: From Isolation to Integration* (Washington DC: Gallaudet University Press, 1993), 124-25.
[19] Philip L. Safford & Elizabeth J. Safford, *A History of Childhood and Disability* (New York: Teacher's College Press, 1996), 92, 99, 105.
[20] B. R. Gearheart, "The Exceptional Child," in *Education of the Exceptional Child: History, Present Practices, and Trends*, ed. B. R. Gearheart (Scranton, PA: Intext Educational Publishers, 1972), 1-14. pg 1
[21] Margaret A. Winzer, *The History of Special Education: From Isolation to Integration* (Washington DC: Gallaudet University Press, 1993), 318-319.
[22] Quoted in Margaret A. Winzer, *The History of Special Education: From Isolation to Integration* (Washington DC: Gallaudet University Press, 1993), 319.
[23] Margaret A. Winzer, *The History of Special Education: From Isolation to Integration* (Washington DC: Gallaudet University Press, 1993), 112.
[24] Margaret A. Winzer, *The History of Special Education: From Isolation to Integration* (Washington DC: Gallaudet University Press, 1993), 112-113.
[25] Quoted in Leo Kanner, *History of the Care and Study of the Mentally Retarded* (Springfield, IL: 1964), 41-42.

[26] Philip L. Safford and Elizabeth J. Safford, *A History of Childhood and Disability* (New York: Teachers College Press, 1996), 162

[27] Quoted in Margaret A. Winzer, *The History of Special Education: From Isolation to Integration* (Washington DC: Gallaudet University Press, 1993), 113.

[28] Margaret A. Winzer, *The History of Special Education: From Isolation to Integration* (Washington DC: Gallaudet University Press, 1993), 212.

[29] See: Philip L. Safford and Elizabeth J. Safford, *A History of Childhood and Disability* (New York: Teachers College Press, 1996), 172-174; Margaret A. Winzer, *The History of Special Education: From Isolation to Integration* (Washington DC: Gallaudet University Press, 1993), 181, & 186.

[30] Quoted in Philip L. Safford and Elizabeth J. Safford, *A History of Childhood and Disability* (New York: Teachers College Press, 1996), 172 & 174.

[31] B. R. Gearheart, "The Trainable Mentally Retarded," in *Education of the Exceptional Child: History, Present Practices, and Trends,* ed. B. R. Gearheart (Scranton, PA: Intext Educational Publishers, 1972), 15-39. pg 17

[32] Philip L. Safford and Elizabeth J. Safford, *A History of Childhood and Disability* (New York: Teachers College Press, 1996), 160.

[33] Four percent is a rough estimate based on an estimated 10 million youth and a mental retardation rate of one percent. The number of youth is based on population data for 1888 and age distribution data for 1900 in U. S. Department of Commerce, Bureau of the Census, *Historical Statistics of the United States: Colonial Times to 1957* (Washington, DC: Government Printing Office), 7-8. The mental retardation rate is from Jack Hourcade, "Mental Retardation: Update 2002," ERIC Digest #E637 (November, 2002), retrieved 03/09/03 from http://ericec.org/digests/e637.html The rate of mental retardation may have been higher in those days of epidemic fevers, which sometimes caused brain damage.[33]

[34] Margaret A. Winzer, *The History of Special Education: From Isolation to Integration* (Washington DC: Gallaudet University Press, 1993), 317.

[35] Kimberly Kode, *Elizabeth Farrell and the History of Special Education* (Arlington, VA: Council for Exceptional Children, 2002), 23.

[36] Quoted in Kimberly Kode, *Elizabeth Farrell and the History of Special Education* (Arlington, VA: Council for Exceptional Children, 2002), 25.

[37] Quoted in Kimberly Kode, *Elizabeth Farrell and the History of Special Education* (Arlington, VA: Council for Exceptional Children, 2002), 27.

[38] Kimberly Kode, *Elizabeth Farrell and the History of Special Education* (Arlington, VA: Council for Exceptional Children, 2002), 39.

[39] Philip L. Safford and Elizabeth J. Safford, *A History of Childhood and Disability* (New York: Teachers College Press, 1996), 182.

[40] Philip L. Safford and Elizabeth J. Safford, *A History of Childhood and Disability* (New York: Teachers College Press, 1996), 183-184.

[41] Kimberly Kode, *Elizabeth Farrell and the History of Special Education* (Arlington, VA: Council for Exceptional Children, 2002), 75, 82-84, 87, 89; and Philip L. Safford and Elizabeth J. Safford, *A History of Childhood and Disability* (New York: Teachers College Press, 1996), 184.

[42] Margaret A. Winzer, *The History of Special Education: From Isolation to Integration* (Washington DC: Gallaudet University Press, 1993), 121.

[43] Marvin Lazerson, "The Origins of Special Education," in *Special Education Policies: Their History, Implementation, and Finance,* ed. Jay G Chambers and William T. Hartman (Philadelphia, PA: Temple University Press, 1983), 15-47. pg 27

[44] Philip L. Safford and Elizabeth J. Safford, *A History of Childhood and Disability* (New York: Teachers College Press, 1996), 184-185.

[45] Margaret A. Winzer, *The History of Special Education: From Isolation to Integration* (Washington DC: Gallaudet University Press, 1993), 372.

[46] Margaret A. Winzer, *The History of Special Education: From Isolation to Integration* (Washington DC: Gallaudet University Press, 1993), 102-103 & 323-324.

[47] Jack Tweedie, "The Politics of Legalization in Special Education Reform," in *Special Education Policies: Their History, Implementation, and Finance*, ed. Jay G Chambers and William T. Hartman (Philadelphia, PA: Temple University Press, 1983), 48-73. pg. 49

[48] Marvin Lazerson, "The Origins of Special Education," in *Special Education Policies: Their History, Implementation, and Finance*, ed. Jay G Chambers and William T. Hartman (Philadelphia, PA: Temple University Press, 1983), 15-47. pg 38

[49] Mitchell L. Yell, David Rogers, & Elizabeth L. Rogers, "The Legal History of Special Education: What a Long, Strange Trip It's Been!" *Remedial and Special Education* 19(4)(1998): 219-228.

[50] See: Marvin Lazerson, "The Origins of Special Education," in *Special Education Policies: Their History, Implementation, and Finance*, ed. Jay G Chambers and William T. Hartman (Philadelphia, PA: Temple University Press, 1983), 15-47; pg 38-39; Woodhull Hay, *Associations for Parents of Mental Retardates*, retrieved 03/29/03 from www.thearc.org/history/hay.htm; and Robert Segal, *The National Association for Retarded Citizens*, retrieved 03/29/03 from www.thearc.org/history/segal.htm .

[51] Scott B. Sigmon, *Radical Analysis of Special Education: Focus on Historical Development of Learning Disabilities* (Philadelphia, PA: Falmer Press, 1987), 24-26.

[52] 334 F.Supp. 1257 (PA 1971). [Retrieved 03/30/03 from http://tourolaw.edu/patch/Parc]

[53] 348 F.Supp. 866 (D.C. 1972).

[54] Jack Tweedie, "The Politics of Legalization in Special Education Reform," in *Special Education Policies: Their History, Implementation, and Finance*, ed. Jay G Chambers and William T. Hartman (Philadelphia, PA: Temple University Press, 1983), 48-73. pg.53

[55] Jack Tweedie, "The Politics of Legalization in Special Education Reform," in *Special Education Policies: Their History, Implementation, and Finance*, ed. Jay G Chambers and William T. Hartman (Philadelphia, PA: Temple University Press, 1983), 48-73. pg 54-56.

[56] Jack Tweedie, "The Politics of Legalization in Special Education Reform," in *Special Education Policies: Their History, Implementation, and Finance*, ed. Jay G Chambers and William T. Hartman (Philadelphia, PA: Temple University Press, 1983), 48-73. pg 55-60

[57] Public Law 94-142

[58] Roberta Weiner, *P.L. 94-142: Impact on the Schools* (Arlington, VA: Capitol Publications, 1985), 13-14.

[59] U.S. Department of Education, Office of Special Education Programs, *Twenty-second Annual Report to Congress on the Implementation of the Individuals with Disabilities Education Act* (Washington DC: author, 2000), v, vi.

[60] See: Alan Gartner and Dorothy K. Lipsky, "Beyond Special Education: Toward a Quality System for All Students," in *Special Education at the Century's End: Evolution of Theory and Practice Since 1970*, ed. Thomas Hehir and Thomas Latus, (Cambridge, MA: Harvard Education Review, 1992) 123-157, pg 128; Judith D.

Singer and John A. Butler, "The Education for All Handicapped Children Act: Schools as Agents of Social Reform," in *Special Education at the Century's End: Evaluation of Theory and Practice Since 1970*, ed. Thomas Hehir and Thomas Latus, (Cambridge, MA: Harvard Education Review, 1992), 159-190. pg. 160, 187-188.

[61] See: Alan Gartner and Dorothy K. Lipsky, "Beyond Special Education: Toward a Quality System for All Students," in *Special Education at the Century's End: Evolution of Theory and Practice Since 1970*, ed. Thomas Hehir and Thomas Latus, (Cambridge, MA: Harvard Education Review, 1992) 123-157, pg 128; and U.S. Department of Education, National Center for Education Statistics, *Digest of Education Statistics: 2001* (Washington DC: U. S. Government Printing Office, 2002), 12.

[62] U.S. Department of Education, Office of Special Education Programs, *Twenty-second Annual Report to Congress on the Implementation of the Individuals with Disabilities Education Act* (Washington DC: author, 2000), vii.

[63] U.S. Department of Education, Office of Special Education Programs, *Twenty-second Annual Report to Congress on the Implementation of the Individuals with Disabilities Education Act* (Washington DC: author, 2000), II-21.

[64] U.S. Department of Education, Office of Special Education Programs, *Twenty-second Annual Report to Congress on the Implementation of the Individuals with Disabilities Education Act* (Washington DC: author, 2000), III-4.

[65] Calculated from: President's Commission on Excellence in Special Education, *A New Era: Revitalizing Special Education for Children and Their Families* (Washington DC: U.S. Department of Education, Office of Special Education and Rehabilitation Services, 2002), 30.

[66] Alan Gartner and Dorothy K. Lipsky, "Beyond Special Education: Toward a Quality System for All Students," in *Special Education at the Century's End: Evolution of Theory and Practice Since 1970*, ed. Thomas Hehir and Thomas Latus, (Cambridge, MA: Harvard Education Review, 1992) 123-157, pg 128

[67] See: U.S. Department of Education, National Center for Education Statistics, *Digest of Education Statistics: 2001* (Washington DC: U. S. Government Printing Office, 2002), 97; and National Education Association, "Special Education and the Individuals with Disabilities Education Act," (Washington DC: author, undated), 1, retrieved 030803 from www.nea.org/specialed .

[68] Alan Gartner and Dorothy K. Lipsky, "Beyond Special Education: Toward a Quality System for All Students," in *Special Education at the Century's End: Evolution of Theory and Practice Since 1970*, ed. Thomas Hehir and Thomas Latus, (Cambridge, MA: Harvard Education Review, 1992) 123-157, pgs,128-137

[69] U.S. Department of Education, National Center for Education Statistics, *Digest of Education Statistics: 2001* (Washington DC: U. S. Government Printing Office, 2002), 306.

[70] Elaine Carlson, Marsha Brauen, Sheri Klein, Karen Schroll, and Sharon Willig, *SPeNSE: Study of Personnel Needs in Special Education: Key Findings,* Rockville, MD: Westat, 2002.

[71] James H. Lytle, "Is Special Education Serving Minority Students? A Response to Singer and Butler," in *Special Education at the Century's End: Evolution of Theory and Practice Since 1970*, ed. Thomas Hehir and Thomas Latus, (Cambridge, MA: Harvard Education Review, 1992), 191-197. pg. 193

[72] President's Commission on Excellence in Special Education, *A New Era: Revitalizing Special Education for Children and Their Families* (Washington DC: U.S.

Department of Education, Office of Special Education and Rehabilitation Services, 2002), 3.
[73] President's Commission on Excellence in Special Education, *A New Era: Revitalizing Special Education for Children and Their Families* (Washington DC: U.S. Department of Education, Office of Special Education and Rehabilitation Services, 2002), 12.
[74] Council for Exceptional Children, *IDEA Reauthorization Recommendations* (Arlington, VA: author, 2002), 18.
[75] "NEA Priorities of IDEA Reauthorization" Retrieved 03-08-03 from www.nea.org/specialed/ideareauthpriorities.html
[76] and U.S. Department of Education, National Center for Education Statistics, *Digest of Education Statistics: 2001* (Washington DC: U. S. Government Printing Office, 2002), 132.
[77] U.S. Department of Education, Office of Special Education Programs, *Twenty-sixth Annual Report to Congress on the Implementation of the Individuals with Disabilities Education Act 2004, Vol. I* (Washington, DC: Author, 2006), 65-66.
[78] U.S. Department of Education, Office of Special Education Programs, *Twenty-sixth Annual Report to Congress on the Implementation of the Individuals with Disabilities Education Act 2004, Vol. I* (Washington, DC: Author, 2006), 78.
[79] U.S. Department of Education, Office of Special Education Programs, *Twenty-second Annual Report to Congress on the Implementation of the Individuals with Disabilities Education Act* (Washington DC: author, 2000), II-19.
[80] Alan Gartner and Dorothy K. Lipsky, "Beyond Special Education: Toward a Quality System for All Students," in *Special Education at the Century's End: Evolution of Theory and Practice Since 1970*, ed. Thomas Hehir and Thomas Latus, (Cambridge, MA: Harvard Education Review, 1992) 123-157, pgs 132
[81] Alan Gartner and Dorothy K. Lipsky, "Beyond Special Education: Toward a Quality System for All Students," in *Special Education at the Century's End: Evolution of Theory and Practice Since 1970*, ed. Thomas Hehir and Thomas Latus, (Cambridge, MA: Harvard Education Review, 1992) 123-157, pgs,137-140, 147.
[82] Jane Mercer, *Labeling the Mentally Retarded: Clinical and Social System Perspectives on Mental Retardation* Berkeley, CA: University of California Press, 1973), 189.
[83] 343 F.Supp. 1306 (Cal. 1972).
[84] U.S. Department of Education, Office of Special Education Programs, *Twenty-second Annual Report to Congress on the Implementation of the Individuals with Disabilities Education Act* (Washington DC: author, 2000), II-25-27.
[85] Marvin Lazerson, "The Origins of Special Education," in *Special Education Policies: Their History, Implementation, and Finance*, ed. Jay G Chambers and William T. Hartman (Philadelphia, PA: Temple University Press, 1983), 15-47. pg. 40
[86] Donald P. Oswald, Martha J. Coutinho, and Al M. Best, "Community and School Predictors of Overrepresentation of Minority Children in Special Education" in *Racial Inequality In Special Education*, ed. Daniel J. Losen and Gary Orfield (Cambridge, MA: Harvard, 2002), 9-10.
[87] Judith D. Singer and John A. Butler, "Singer and Butler Reply to Lytle," in *Special Education at the Century's End: Evolution of Theory and Practice Since 1970*, ed. Thomas Hehir and Thomas Latus, (Cambridge, MA: Harvard Education Review, 1992), 197-201. pg. 198.
[88] For instance, see: BBC News, "Electronic Eye For Blind Man" (18 January 2000), retrieved 09/05/04 from http://news.bbc.co.uk/1/ hi/sci/tech/606938.stm; Marvin

Cetron and Owen Davies, *Probable Tomorrows: How Science and Technology Will Transform Our Lives in the Next Twenty Years* (New York: St. Martin's Press,1997); Miguel A. L. Nicolelis, "Actions From Thoughts," *Nature* 409 (18 January 2001), 403-407; Lee M Silver, *Remaking Eden: How Genetic Engineering and Cloning Will Transform the American Family* (New York: Perennial, 1998); and Joe Z. Tsien, "Building a Brainier Mouse," *Scientific American* 282 (April 2000), 62-68.

[89] Judith D. Singer and John A. Butler, "The Education for All Handicapped Children Act: Schools as Agents of Social Reform," in *Special Education at the Century's End: Evoluation of Theory and Practice Since 1970*, ed. Thomas Hehir and Thomas Latus, (Cambridge, MA: Harvard Education Review, 1992), 159-190. pg.169

7

Compensatory Education

Beth Antunez and Gregg B. Jackson

"If one class possesses all the wealth and the education, while the residue of society is ignorant and poor, it matters not by what name the relation between them be called; the latter ... will be the servile dependents, and subjects of the former.[1]" Horace Mann

During the colonial period, it was presumed that if students did not learn, they were to blame. Today it is presumed that schools have a responsibility for providing extra help to students who have not been well prepared for school. Compensatory education programs offer health services, nutrition, and early childhood education in preschool settings; special instruction or supplementary instruction in the elementary and secondary schools; and special orientations to postsecondary educational opportunities. Compensatory education differs from special education in that the latter is directed only to students with diagnosed disabilities.

INITIAL CONDITIONS

Throughout the history of universal public education, it had been recognized that many children of the impoverished families begin school less prepared than most middle and upper class children. They generally have higher incidences of uncorrected medical problems, higher rates of malnutrition, less developed English language skills, and less experience with children's books. Such children have often been referred to as "educationally deprived," or "disadvantaged." In school they have generally learned less, exhibited more discipline problems, and dropped out earlier.[2] In addition, because schools have been financed predominantly from local taxes in communities with widely varying wealth, children of the poor have tended to be enrolled in schools with less funding and fewer education resources.

While the public schools did not serve the children of the lower class as well as those of the middle class, minority children of color were often excluded entirely or forced into segregated schools with dilapidated facilities and meager resources.

Chapter 2 indicated that for long periods of their history in America, most slaves were denied education by their owners and then, in the mid-1800s, prohibited it by southern state laws. Even free African Americans in northern states were often denied education or relegated to segregated schools. Following the Civil War, African Americans in the south gained more access to schooling but in strictly segregated and usually inferior schools. As late as the 1920s, per capita expenditures for the education of African Americans in the south averaged one-third those for white students.[3]

After the U.S. conquest of southwestern lands, Mexican Americans were seldom denied public education, but they were sometimes discouraged from attending school and often required to enroll in inferior segregated schools. While some Mexican American families saw these schools as an opportunity for advancement of their children, others saw them as oppressive tools of conquest.

In the 1800s, Native American children did not fare better than African American children. White settlers, driven by "manifest destiny," believed that their conquest of America was the will of God. As a widely used high school textbook of the 1930s-1950s explained, "it was impossible that these few hundred thousand natives should stop the spread of the Europeans over the country. That would have been to condemn one of the fairest lands of the earth to the stagnation of barbarism."[4] As discussed in Chapter 2, the Naturalization Act of 1790 precluded Native Americans from U.S. citizenship, and then subsequent legislation and U.S. Army forces drove them from their lands into reservations, mostly west of the Mississippi River. In the 1880s, the Commissioner of Indian Affairs, noting it was "cheaper to educate Indians than to kill them," established a vast network of federally operated boarding schools to "Americanize" Indian children. Poor achievement became the norm for dispirited Indian children.

In 1897, after a long struggle with Spain, Puerto Rico became a semi-autonomous nation and quickly established a constitutional republic. Within weeks the United States invaded as part of its tactics in the Spanish-American War, and at the culmination of war, Spain gave Puerto Rico to the victor. The U.S. placed the island under the control of a military government operated by the War Department. U.S. representatives required Puerto Rican schools to teach U.S. history, pledge allegiance to the U.S. flag, and celebrate U.S. patriotic holidays. The second appointed commissioner of education wrote explaining his purpose, "Colonization carried forward by the armies of war is vastly more costly than that carried forward by the armies of peace, whose outpost and garrisons are the public schools of the advancing nation."[5]

Chinese first immigrated in substantial numbers to California to try their luck with the gold rush of the 1850s. When that fizzled, they took jobs building the transcontinental railroad. In the late 1800s and early 1900s, Japanese immigrated to Hawaii and California, often to work on plantations and farms. Filipinos followed, having become U.S. citizens as a result of the American conquest of the Philippine Islands. Asian immigrants, however, were greatly outnumbered by European immigrants and during that period never comprised more than two percent of the country's foreign born. The 1790 Naturalization Act had precluded Asian immigrants from citizenship, and that exclusion continued until WWII, but children of these immigrants who were born in the United States were automatically citizens under the 14th Amendment to the Constitution. California had provided universal public education only for "white children" until an 1885 legal challenge by a Chinese-American plaintiff. Two weeks after the court's decision for the plaintiff,[6] the California legislature authorized public education for Chinese students--in segregated schools. In 1906 San Francisco established a separate school for ethnic Japanese, Korean, and Chinese students, but the Japanese parents boycotted it and created such a political ruckus in Japan that President Theodore Roosevelt threatened San Francisco with federal action if it did not end the segregated system. San Francisco capitulated but much of the country continued the practice.[7] Nevertheless, a 1930s research study in California found that second-generation Japanese-American students had higher grades in school through the 8th grade than did their peers of European descent.[8]

CHANGING CONTEXTS THAT PUSHED COMPENSATORY EDUCATION

At least three contexts pushed the compensatory education reform. These contexts were the expansion of federal government activism, the push for school desegregation, and new research on poverty and education.

Expanding Federal Government Activism

A century after the successful founding of the new nation, Americans were becoming cautiously tolerant of a modest expansion of the federal government into education. The abuses of the British monarchs were a distant memory and there had been expanding federal action in other areas of social life that was widely perceived a success. In 1862 Congress passed the Morrill Act to provide aid for the establishment of colleges of agriculture and mechanical arts. A second Morrill Act of 1890 provided more aid for agriculture and engineering colleges and new aid for the establishment of colleges and normal schools to serve African Americans. Then, following a decade of legislative skirmishes, the Smith-Hughes Act of 1917 provided funding for vocational education in high schools.

The economy had grown substantially over the first three decades of the 1900s, with the gross national product per capita rising 73 percent (in constant dollars) by 1929. Then the stock market crashed and the country slid into a depression, losing most of the prior gains and leaving 24 percent of the workforce unemployed by 1932, a rate that would decline only slowly over the rest of that decade.[9] The calamity affected families from all spectrums in society—the wealthy, the middle class, and the poor. Franklin Roosevelt ran for President in that year promising a "New Deal" to mitigate the hardships and rebuild the economy. Within the first hundred days, Roosevelt had secured legislation creating the Federal Deposit Insurance Corporation to insure deposits in banks, the Securities and Exchange Commission to protect the public against fraudulent stock market practices, the Works Progress Administration to create jobs, the National Recovery Administration to regulate wages and assure workers collective bargaining rights, and the Agriculture Adjustment Administration to stabilize farm prices. Two years later Social Security was enacted and the Secretary of Agriculture was authorized to distribute food surpluses to the schools. These government programs did mitigate the hardships of the depression and proved so popular that most continue to this day.

As the country slowly climbed out of the depression, it was swept into World War II. Five years later, millions of homeward bound veterans were about to return to civilian status during a weak economy, raising the prospect of massive unemployment. That prompted Congress to pass the GI Bill, providing funding for tuition and living expense to those who chose to enroll in colleges, universities, and postsecondary job training programs. This too proved popular and similar programs for military personnel have continued ever since.

The Soviet Union's 1957 launch of Sputnik not only gave it leadership in the "space race," but also raised the specter that the Soviets would be able to strike America with nuclear weapons long before the United States would have a countervailing capability. Congress responded the following year by passing the National Defense Education Act, which was aimed at improving the teaching of science, engineering, mathematics, and foreign languages, particularly to the more able students. NDEA was generally well received, and thus helped to pave the way for more federal education legislation.

School Desegregation

Chapters 2 and 6 briefly described how civil rights activists in the 1950s and 1960s used political pressure, non-violent disobedience, litigation, and legislation to secure their Constitutional rights. Although the U.S. Supreme Court's decision against school segregation was initially met with considerable resistance, Federal enforcement initiatives during the early 1960s and the passage of the Civil Rights Act of 1964 made clear that state and local government induced school segregation would fade.

While that offered the promise of equal schooling for minorities, it also posed problems, since it was known that many African American children entered elementary school less ready than most other students and lagged behind them through their schooling. Compensatory education was expected to help all disadvantaged children—both minority and white—get off to a good start in their schooling. Many advocates hoped that school desegregation would eventually lead to integration within our society by "welding of pupils of diverse ethnic backgrounds into cohesive classroom groups in which common academic purposes are furthered in an atmosphere of mutual respect and cooperation."[10] Some other supporters thought, conversely, that compensatory education would placate civil rights activists without having to desegregate schools or society.

Research on Poverty and Education

After a decade-long depression and World War II, the U.S. economy began booming in the 1950s, increasing 37 percent (in constant dollars) by 1960, and then another 48 percent by 1970.[11] The good times were rolling and the middle class was better off than ever before. That affluence, however, illuminated large pockets of poverty. In 1963 there were nine million families with annual incomes below the equivalent of $17,000 in the year 2000 dollars.[12] Sixty percent were headed by a person with only a grade school education.[13] The President's Taskforce on Manpower Conservation found that half of the men called by the nation's draft boards were mentally or physically unfit for military service, mostly because of inadequate health care or education. Forty percent of those rejected had not made it into the 9th grade and another 40 percent had not graduated from high school.[14]

In 1961 Patricia Sexton's *Education and Income: Inequalities of Opportunity in Our Public Schools* detailed dramatic differences in education outcomes by social class in one large midwestern city. Poor children trailed others in achievement test scores, participation in "gifted" programs, subjects taken in high school, course grades earned, and college attendance rates. She noted that working class youth in Russia had twice the chance of going to college as did those in the United States. In the same year, James Conant, the former president of Harvard, released *Slums and Suburbs,* comparing schools and students in the suburbs with those in urban slums, warning that "social dynamite" was brewing in the latter. Michael Harrington's 1963 book, *The Other America,* shocked the country by estimating that nearly one-fourth of Americans lived in poverty, vividly portraying their deprivation and cultural isolation from mainstream America, noting that poverty was not limited to minorities—there were more impoverished whites. He illustrated how impoverished conditions perpetuated poverty. He argued that for the first time in history society had the material means of ending poverty, and he urged a massive program to do so.

At the same time, scholars began trying to identify educational approaches that would best meet the needs of impoverished and minority students. Frank Riesman's 1962 *The Culturally Deprived Child* stressed that disadvantaged children had a full range of talents, but their culture often was in conflict with the middle class culture of schools, and he suggested ways teachers could bridge the two cultures. J. McVickers Hunt's 1961 *Intelligence and Experience* marshaled evidence on the importance of mothering and other environmental experiences for determination of a child's intellectual capabilities. Benjamin Bloom published similar research and suggested intellectual abilities were most influenced by environmental factors during the first five years of life.[15] Kenneth Clark's 1965 *Dark Ghetto: Dilemmas of Social Power* explained how inner-city ghettos and "the stigma of racial inferiority" lead to many forms of self-destructive behavior. He also argued that teachers' low expectations for minority children were an important cause of their generally poor performance in school, and he called for imaginative and comprehensive new approaches to teaching poor minority children. James Coleman's 1966 *Equality of Educational Opportunity* massively documented wide disparities in school resources by race and ethnicity, and, surprisingly, he found that students' achievement was not much affected by variations in school facilities, equipment, and teacher characteristics. Instead, it was most associated with family socio-economic status (SES)—parents' family income and education levels. While a few, like Arthur Jensen, explained that was due to the primacy of inherited intelligence in learning,[16] others thought it was due to schools' disinterest or ineptitude in addressing the different learning needs and proclivities of poor and minority children. Coleman also found a modest peer group influence in schools—students of low SES did somewhat better when in predominantly middle class schools than in predominantly low SES schools, without adversely affecting the achievement of middle-SES students. That suggested desegregation could raise minority students' achievement.

In the above cited writings and others, at least six alternative hypotheses were advanced about why poor children and minority children often did poorly in school. One, the earliest, postulated that they were genetically inferior intellectually and nothing could be done to compensate for that. A second postulated that poor children were the victims of a capitalist and racist system, which was so stacked against their families and which so frequently discriminated against them that the children felt it was hopeless to strive for anything, even the overthrow of the system. A third hypothesis indicated that the capitalist and racist system had deprived these children of the pre-natal care, nutrition, health care, housing, and community facilities needed to develop physically, emotionally, and intellectually. A fourth postulated that poor children's home lives failed to give them the kinds of preparation needed for schooling that were commonly available in middle class homes—increasingly sophisticated conversation, an introduction to self-discipline, pleasant experiences looking at picture books and being read to by an adult, and the example of adults eagerly reading for their own gratification. A fifth hypothesis stated that most school administrators and teachers did not care about these students, thought they could not learn much, and simply did not try to educate them. A sixth postulated that the culture of minority and poor children, a different culture, not an inferior one, was in conflict with the middle class white culture of the school, posing a cultural chasm that the teachers and students seldom were able to bridge, even when they desired to do so. Compensatory education would be based mostly on the third, fourth, and fifth hypotheses, although a few programs would address all but the first.

In the early 1960s there had been a few demonstration programs that suggested extra educational services for poor children could boost their performance in school. In 1962 the mayor of New Haven, Connecticut declared war on the city's poverty. One of the city's initiatives was to establish a preschool for children ages three and four years old that involved their parents in the classroom activities.[17] It soon was drawing interested visitors from across the country. In Nashville, Tennessee, Susan Grey ran a three-year program that provided pre-school during the summer and weekly home visitations during the winter for poor African American children beginning at age three or four. She used conventional materials but in ways intended to promote achievement motivation, classification skills, and language development. After three years, the participants showed modest gains in IQ and verbal abilities, while a similar control group showed modest declines.[18]

In 1965, the U.S. Office of Education (USOE) sponsored a conference of the leading psychologists and sociologists who had been researching the education of disadvantaged children, asking them to synthesize knowledge on the topic and guidelines for best practice in the schools. The conference participants recommended that poor children be given access to nursery schools and kindergartens with well-prepared teachers. They urged elementary schools to assess incoming students' motivation and language skills and to offer several approaches to early instruction, assigning each student to whichever was most appropriate for him or her. Teachers should be specifically trained in developing basic academic skills and have specialists on whom they could call for advice and help. They believed that schools should switch the emphasis from memorization to developing higher mental processes and problem solving, focusing on basic ideas, the structure of knowledge, and methods of inquiry. The conference participants warned that school desegregation would not boost minority students' academic achievement unless the above changes were made. They also suggested several measures for improving high schools, but their clear preference was for early interventions that would bring disadvantaged students up to the level of their more advantaged peers, with the expectation that such leveling would be maintained through the rest of their schooling.[19]

THE CAMPAIGNS FOR COMPENSATORY EDUCATION

In the early 1800s, as the northeastern states were establishing universal public school systems, there were a few efforts by charitable organizations to create infant schools for poor children ages 3-5, with the hope that these schools would compensate for the deprivations of impoverished homes and help the children get off to a good start in life. Advocates of infant schools often argued that they would reduce adult crime and poverty.[20] Some infant schools were based on the gentle and nurturing educational practices of the European reformer Johann Pestalozzi (see Chapter 4), and others were modeled on the common educational practices of elementary schools, which emphasized basic skills development, memorization, and frequent corporal punishment for students who made mistakes during recitations. Amariah Brigham, a prominent Connecticut physician, published warnings that making impossible demands of young children might be injurious to their health—even causing later insanity.[21] By the mid-1800s infant schools lost popularity, so much so that there is little historical record of them.[22]

At the same time, kindergartens, which served children of about five years age, which was usually the year before they entered elementary school, gained popularity first with the affluent and then with charitable organizations hoping to prepare poor children for school. A few early kindergartens serving poor families also invited the mothers into the school to learn nutrition and home keeping skills.[23] By the 1890s a few large public school systems began offering kindergarten, although usually without the parent education component. By this time it became apparent that nutritional assistance and health care would be needed if the children of the poor were to develop well. The settlement houses were the first to provide such services, and then large cities began to hire nurses for their schools. In 1908 New York City created the first municipal Division of Child Hygiene to work with poor mothers and soon the city's infant death rate dropped notably.[24]

During the depression of the 1930s, the Works Progress Administration had been charged with creating jobs that provided needed infrastructure and social services. It established thousands of nursery schools throughout the country to serve children of the poor and to create jobs for unemployed school administrators, teachers, nurses, and janitors. Each community that wanted such a school had to provide leadership, space, and supplies.[25] During World War II, the federal government provided funding for thousands of day-care centers serving the children of mothers employed in defense industries. Little education was provided in these facilities.[26] Federal funding for them ceased after the war ended and most were closed.

General Federal Aid for K-12 Education

Throughout the first half of the 20th century there were repeated efforts to secure general federal funding for K-12 education. The rationale for this aid was that the national welfare required adequate education of all children and that only the federal government could help equalize the widely varying levels of state and district funding for education. The intent was *not* to provide compensatory education services to students needing extra help. At the urging of major education associations, bills to provide federal funds to states based on the numbers of students and relative ability of states to pay for education were introduced in the 1920s and 1930s but always failed.[27] Similar bills were repeatedly introduced in the Congress between 1943 and 1957 but none passed, despite the fact that mid-century national opinion polls showed that 75 percent of citizens favored such federal assistance.[28]

In opposition were three formidable forces. Catholic Church officials and the National Catholic Welfare Conference insisted that the aid be made available to private and parochial schools, and many other people were against that, renewing the 19th century conflict described in Chapter 3. Adam Clayton Powell, an African American, who had risen after several terms in the House of Representatives to chair the Education and Labor Committee, insisted that the aid should not be given to segregated schools, but the southern members of Congress were adamant against such a restriction. In addition, state rights advocates and the U.S. Chamber of Commerce feared that federal funds would result in unconstitutional federal control over public education.[29]

John Kennedy campaigned for the presidency in 1960 promising a "New Frontier" in which the government would stimulate economic, educational, and social improvement, both domestically and abroad. He reduced federal income taxes in hopes of growing the domestic economy, pushed through the Manpower Development and Training Act to retrain displaced workers, created the Peace Corps, and took steps to stimulate international trade. Kennedy also proposed a federal grant of $15 per pupil for either school construction or teachers' salaries, with a penalty for any district that did not at least maintain its previous funding effort. Private and parochial schools would not receive such aid. The National Education Association was delighted, but Catholic Cardinal Spellman of New York City savaged the proposal:

> It is unthinkable that any American child be denied the Federal funds allotted to other children which are necessary for his mental development because his parents chose for him a God-centered education.... [It amounts to] economic compulsion to force parents to relinquish their rights to have religion taught to their children.[30]

The nation's first Catholic President held his ground publicly, but he privately sent signals to Congress that he would consent to federally guaranteed loans for construction of private and parochial school facilities under the Sputnik-inspired National Defense Education Act (NDEA). He also managed to have Adam Clayton Powell agree not to insist on a provision prohibiting the aid to schools that were still segregated. The Senate passed the bill, but the House Rules Committee balked with opposition from Republicans and Catholic Democrats, who felt there was too little for private and parochial schools. At the end of his first year, Kennedy's education agenda was widely declared a fiasco, and he observed, "everyone is for education but they're all for a different education bill.... So we will be back next year."[31] He did return to the issue the next year. All he gained was a second defeat.

In his third State of the Union address, Kennedy declared aid to education as one of his four priorities for federal action. He conceded that broad aid to public schools was dead on arrival and focused on a modest extension of the NDEA, which for five years had been providing funds to improve the teaching of mathematics, science, engineering, and foreign languages. That proposal was virtually assured of Congressional passage in November of 1963 when an assassin's bullet killed the President.[32]

As Johnson assumed the presidency he immediately had to plan a campaign for the following November presidential elections. He promised to continue the legacy of Kennedy, for whom there was great national sympathy. He gave priority to three legislative initiatives: a tax cut, a war on poverty, and a civil rights bill. To take up the latter in an election year was a bold move because it was almost certain to cost Johnson southern votes. The unfinished priority of Kennedy that Johnson did not immediately champion was federal aid to K-12 education. Johnson had been a teacher and principal, and during the depression had been director of Texas' office of the National Youth Administration. He was sympathetic with the prior attempts, but he remembered how they had humbled his predecessor and did not want to risk that in an election year.[33]

Johnson achieved nearly all of his 1964 legislative agenda. Tax cuts were enacted. A strong Civil Rights Act was adopted after overcoming a 57-day filibuster in the Senate. Passage of the Economic Opportunity Act of 1964 initiated Johnson's war on poverty.

By this point in history, there were three primary models for eliminating poverty. The first was communism, which was widely disdained in this country. The second model was the social democracies of Europe—such as in Sweden, Germany, and England—where democratic governments bought and ran, or closely regulated, key industries, directing them to serve the social goals of full employment and comfortable wages. In addition, these countries provided income supports to the unemployed, usually for as long as they remained unemployed. That model was serving those countries fairly well at the time, although problems would later emerge, but it had limited appeal in the United States where the rugged individualism of the frontier was still valued and industrial capitalism had served most of the population very well since WWII. The third model was to use tax policy to stimulate economic growth and use government funded education and training programs to help the poor and temporarily unemployed prepare for the expected new jobs.

Johnson chose the third approach and compensatory education became part of a multi-pronged legislative program that included adult literacy programs, VISTA (a domestic service program), community action programs, an increased minimum wage, prohibitions against workplace discrimination, expanded federal assistance for low-income housing, and federally run health insurance for the elderly. While communism and the social democracies had leveled wealth downward to the poor, the Johnson administration hoped to level the poor upward.

Head Start

The Economic Opportunity Act of 1964 provided broad authorization for programs to eliminate poverty and its effects. A new Office of Economic Opportunity (OEO) was created to spearhead the War on Poverty. Creating a new agency for this purpose had two strategic advantages. Old bureaucracies are usually slow and often uncreative in carrying out new mandates, and a single agency could better coordinate diverse initiatives in education, training, and employment.

Johnson put Sargent Shriver, Kennedy's brother-in-law, in charge of OEO. Shriver had served for five years as President of the Board of Education in Chicago. Both he and his wife, Eunice, had been involved with the Joseph P. Kennedy foundation, which supported work on mental retardation. In that capacity he had learned of research showing that malnutrition can retard intellectual development and also learned of Susan Grey's educational enrichment program that had raised IQs and verbal abilities. Gradually the idea came to him that OEO should establish early childhood programs to combine nutrition and education as a way of boosting poor children's preparation for elementary school.[34] He realized, "In our society there is a bias against helping adults.... But there is a contrary bias in favor of helping children."[35] That thinking led to the creation of the Head Start preschool program. As Edward Zigler, a leading proponent of such programs, explained:

> Experts also believed in the supreme developmental significance of experiences during one magical period: the preschool years. Acceptance of that belief implied that intervention had to begin before the child reached age five in order to offset the effects of poverty on a child's intellectual and social development and fed the hope that preschool [with health and nutritional services] could eliminate the necessity for continuing services during childhood.... The child, they hinted, would be prepared to conquer the worlds of school and employment after preschool integrated him into the mainstream of American life.[36]

Several on the Head Start Planning Committee recognized that the knowledge base for designing such programs was limited and would have preferred to start with a series of demonstration programs so that lessons could be learned and program components refined before widespread implementation. Shriver, however, wanted to serve at least 10,000 participants in the first summer, and later, when applications flooded in, he funded 600,000. His rationale was that if the program gained high visibility and acquired a large constituency, Congress could not easily kill it.

The Planning Committee recommended that Head Start centers provide a comprehensive set of services aimed at fostering the physical, emotional, social, and intellectual development of the participating children. The intellectual development was focused on "Improving the child's mental processes and skills, with particular attention to conceptual and verbal skills."[37] Parents were to be involved in the direction of the program and the classrooms because they would have important perspectives on the children's needs and because participation would improve their parenting skills.[38] In May of 1965, with several of the Planning Committee members at his side, President Johnson announced the forthcoming eight-week summer programs in 2,000 centers throughout the country, stating,

Five- and six-year-old children are the inheritors of poverty's curse and not its creators. Unless we act these children will pass it on to the next generation, like a family birthmark. This program means that thirty million man years—the combined lifespan of these youngsters—will be spent productively and rewardingly, rather than wasted in tax-supported institutions or in welfare-supported lethargy.[39]

Several of the Planning Committee members did not expect so much from an eight-week intervention.

Head Start planners considered state and local government, including school districts, to be insensitive or hostile to racial/ethnic minorities and the poor, and thus sought to bypass them. Head Start programs were operated primarily by Community Action Agencies designated by OEO for a broad range of its economic and community development initiatives. Tribal Councils were also grantees. When such organizations were not available, awards were made to school districts.

Head Start centers were to provide health examinations and follow-up services, at least one nutritious hot meal a day and one snack, social and psychological services as needed, early childhood education that would lay the groundwork for subsequent education, parent participation in the direction and operation of the center, and parent education. Soon Head Start offered year-round services, with a portion of the children participating for two years. Not long after, the "Follow Through" program was authorized to continue support services for Head Start children during the early years of their elementary schooling.

Title I of the Elementary and Secondary Education Act

In the summer of 1964, Johnson assembled advisory taskforces on education, transportation, health, and several other topics. The education taskforce, chaired by John Gardner, reported back that the "foremost challenge facing American education today is to equalize educational opportunity for the disadvantaged segments of our population."[40] The taskforce also recommended the use of universities and cultural organizations to provide innovative supplemental services to disadvantaged students, creation of research and development centers to develop new educational approaches, the strengthening of state departments of education, and additional funds for poorer states and districts.[41]

Johnson won the 1964 election with a landslide victory over Republican Barry Goldwater. In addition, Democrats gained 38 seats in the House and two in the Senate, giving them overwhelming majorities in both chambers. Johnson was now well positioned to take up the cause of funding for K-12 education. Francis Keppel, Commissioner of Education, drafted legislation largely based on the Gardner taskforce recommendations. A key element of the bill was that funds would be allocated according to the number of children in poverty.

Outlines of the key provisions but not the details were discussed with the interest groups that had clashed over Kennedy's failed education bills—the National Education Association, the American Federation of Teachers, the National Catholic Welfare Conference, the Council of Chief State School Officers, and the American Council on Education. Keppel used the meetings to test out the ideas, receive input for possible refinements, build consensus, and remind the interest groups that without compromise on their part, this effort to provide federal aid for K-12 education would fail, as the previous ones had. Johnson and his close advisors revised Keppel's draft and in January the President announced the legislation in a special education message to Congress.

In March, Johnson invited two hundred local, state, and national school leaders to the White House, thanking them for their support of the bill and urging them to pressure Congress representatives for passage. He noted,

> Way back last summer I asked some of the most outstanding educational minds to ... find out how we can best invest each education dollar so it can do the most good.... We decided that our first job was to help the schools serving the children from the very lowest income groups.... We know that they cannot bear their share of the taxes to help pay for their education. And unless those children get a good education we know that they become dropouts and they become delinquents and they become tax eaters instead of tax payers.... We know that they will join the unemployed and that is why we put top priority on breaking the vicious cycle that today threatens the future of five million children in this great land of opportunity.[42]

With skillful shepherding, the bill rolled through Congress. The only substantial amendment was introduced by Robert Kennedy who, worrying that the local officials would not be responsive to the needs of poor children, added provisions to evaluate the effects of the funded programs. When the Commissioner of Education was asked if he wanted such evaluation, he replied privately,

> I want it, but I haven't got the nerve to do it on the executive side, because all the educators will scream bloody murder if anybody measures them. But if the *Congress* wants to put it on, that's my idea of how to deal with them.[43]

Just 87 days after introduction, the Elementary and Secondary Education Act (ESEA) was passed by Congress, with a vote of 263 to 153 in the House and 73 to 18 in the Senate. Johnson signed the bill in Stonewall, Texas, outside the one-room schoolhouse where he had begun his own schooling. Afterward he noted, "I will never do anything in my entire life, now or in the future, that excites me more, or benefits the Nation I serve more ... than what we have done with this education bill."[44]

What had begun as an effort to provide general federal aid to schools for teachers' salaries and the construction of facilities was transformed into a tool for civil rights and a war on poverty. Despairing of general aid, the Johnson administration precipitated the compensatory education reform effort that sought to give disadvantaged children a good start in school and in life.

Why was Johnson successful after Kennedy's repeated debacles and a half-century of prior failures? Johnson had spent 24 years in the House and Senate, becoming a masterful legislative strategist, and he made clear to all concerned his determination to get this bill passed. His landslide election over Goldwater swept more Democrats into the House Senate, giving them large majorities in both chambers. His impressive success with the Civil Rights Act in the face of heavy resistance probably intimidated or demoralized some potential opponents to ESEA. The Civil Rights Act mandated that federal funds be withheld for segregated schools and thus Adam Clayton Powell no longer insisted on amendments for that purpose. The new twist of focusing the funding on programs to enhance the education of impoverished children had wide appeal at a time when scholars and the two presidents had put the spotlight on poverty in an otherwise prospering economy. That poverty spanned all racial groups and all regions of the country contributed to the wide support. As school districts were being forced to desegregate by courts, federal agencies, and civil rights advocates, ESEA would provide schools with extra funds to help prepare African American children, almost half of whom were from families living in poverty, to get a good start in school. The old conflict between Catholics, who insisted that federal aid be available to parochial schools, and the Protestants and the NEA, who insisted it not be, was finessed by providing compensatory education aid for poor *students* who attended private schools, a compromise that was supported by both sides. The states' rights opposition was blunted by having the states administer most of the ESEA with explicit provisions barring the federal government from any control over the curriculum, instructional materials, methods, and personnel. Finally, after the interest groups watched general federal aid to K-12 schools slip away during three consecutive years of the Kennedy administration, they were more willing to compromise.

Many southerners had opposed the ESEA and a few civil rights leaders had been leery of it. The southerners feared it would give the federal government more leverage to desegregate southern schools. Civil rights advocates feared it would be used as a substitute for desegregation or to re-segregate minority children within desegregated schools. Both sets of concerns proved justified but not to the extent anticipated. Several districts did try to implement compensatory education in place of desegregation, but federal court rulings declared that insufficient. ESEA also fostered some re-segregation within desegregated schools, by the disproportionate assignment of minorities to compensatory education, although re-segregation within schools would have occurred anyway from the "tracking" of students by skill levels, a practice that was common in public schools prior to the legislation. In addition, white families had begun moving from the central cities to suburbs in the 1950s and the trend accelerated as large cities desegregated, leaving many African-American and Mexican-American children in predominantly minority schools.

The ESEA legislation specified its compensatory purpose, stating that the Act was intended to:

... provide financial assistance ... to local educational agencies serving areas with concentrations of children from low-income families to expand and improve their educational programs by various means (including preschool programs) which contribute particularly to meeting the special educational needs of educationally deprived children.[45]

The bulk of the ESEA funds were to go towards basic grants under Title I. Section 205 indicates that the grants were to be used for:

... programs and projects (including the acquisition of equipment and where necessary the construction of school facilities) (A) which are designed to meet the special educational needs of educationally deprived children in school attendance areas having high concentrations of children from low-income families and (B) which are of sufficient size, scope, and quality to give reasonable promise of substantial progress toward meeting those needs.[46]

The Title I legislation had few other specifics about the allowable uses for the funds. The broad latitude given to the school districts was partly to minimize federal control over local education and partly because there was little understanding at the time about how best to meet the needs of impoverished children.[47] The Act did have a provision stating "... appropriate objective measurements of educational achievement will be adopted for evaluating at least annually the effectiveness of the programs in meeting the special educational needs of educationally deprived children," suggesting that Congress was most intent on boosting the students' academic achievement.[48]

Title I has been subject to small modifications every few years since it was enacted. Amendments in 1968 required that parents be involved in program planning, operations, and evaluation. The reauthorization in 1988, during the last year of the Reagan Administration, made major changes, requiring states to specify the levels of educational achievement that Title I students should meet (they were free to set low or high standards), identify schools not making substantial progress toward those goals, and provide assistance to such schools. In addition, it specified that if at least 75 percent of students in a school are of low-income, the Title I funds can be used for all the students in the school, providing that the achievement of educationally deprived students in the school increases within three years. Early in his Presidency, Bill Clinton pushed successfully for the Goals 2000: Educate America Act that provided federal funding to help states that wished to develop academic standards for all students (not just Title I students) and tests for assessing students' mastery of those standards. In 1993 Clinton also proposed that the next Title I reauthorization require a five-year phase-in of such standards and testing, if the state wished to continue receiving Title I funds. That was a strong incentive since Title I is the largest source of federal funding for K-12 education. There was bi-partisan support for Clinton's proposal, but several Democrats sought to add provisions that would have also required states to establish and enforce "opportunity to learn" standards so that poor communities would be assured of resources needed to help their students meet the academic standards. Republicans and the President objected to these modifications, and the reauthorization was passed without them. That legislation also allowed schools with at least 50% low-income students to use the funds for school-wide interventions and provided relief from burdensome federal regulations. The rationale was that if all students—including poor children—were more academically challenged, most would learn more. The 1988 and 1994 reauthorizations of Title I also reflected a philosophical change, switching the focus from holding states accountable for program delivery to holding states accountable for student learning.[49] In 2002, more changes were made to Title I by President Bush's "No Child Left Behind" legislation. Those will be discussed in Chapter 10 under the "accountability" reform effort.

Although Head Start and Title I of ESEA became the centerpieces of compensatory education efforts in the United States and remained so into the dawn of the 21st century, they were accompanied by several other federal programs that had similar or complementary goals. Follow Through, initiated in 1967, was to provide continuing support services for former Head Start participants during their first three years of elementary schooling. The Bilingual Education Act of 1968 was intended to help non-English speaking and limited-English-speaking children (many but not all of whom were poor). Later, in 1988, the Even Start program combined early childhood education with adult literacy training and parenting skills training for the parents, in an effort to break a cycle of illiteracy. Job Corps Centers (1964) served low-income high school dropouts, providing academic instruction and job training at residential facilities that were intended to separate the adolescents from the bad influences of their home environments. Upward Bound (1964) aimed to prepare low-income high school students for admission to, and success in, college.

SUCCESS OF THE REFORM EFFORT

Head Start, ESEA Title I, and other compensatory education programs were widely implemented throughout the country within a few years. That was largely the result of the substantial federally legislated funding that was made available to states and local districts. Compliance with the accompanying regulations took longer.

In 1965, 600,000 children were served in Head Start programs, almost all in the summer program. By 1970, enrollment dropped to about 450,000, but more than half were in full-year programs. Federal funding began at the equivalent of $500 million in year 2000 dollars and two years later rose to the equivalent of $1.8 billion.[50]

The quick scale-up of Head Start made full compliance with the regulations initially unlikely. Appropriate facilities had to be found or prepared that complied with building codes, teachers had to be hired and neighborhood aides recruited, both had to be trained, and equipment and supplies had to be acquired (but could not be paid for with federal funds). Local control was part of the program design, inevitably creating a tension between the legislated goals and those the local people might desire. Funding per child was less than at high quality private day-care facilities, and providing day-care is far easier than providing the array of services intended for Head Start.

Various policy directives, procedural guidelines, training programs, technical assistance centers, and monitoring systems were adopted to improve the quality of services provided by the Head Start centers. The Program Performance Standards of 1975 specified that letters and numbers should be taught, that staff should make use of information of interest to the children such as their names and addresses, and that written language should be introduced through signs and labels.[51] These efforts were only partially successful, according to many scholars involved in Head Start.[52]

By the year 2000, Head Start had expanded to serve 858,000 young children and federal funding had risen to $5.3 billion.[53] Despite that, only 52 percent of children living in poverty participated in any kind of center-based early childhood development programs. African American children had the highest participation rate (73%) and Hispanic children had a markedly lower participation rate (44%).[54] In addition, children from non-impoverished families were even more likely to attend early childhood development programs than were children from poverty, although they seldom attended at Head Start centers.[55]

Title I was a larger program than Head Start, operated by school districts with many other priorities, and its service delivery had to be coordinated with regular schooling, all of which made its implementation more problematic. It has served 4.4 – 5.1 million children each year since 1965, at an annual federal funding equivalent to about $5.5 billion in year 2000 dollars.[56]

Initially there was widespread non-compliance and even instances of malfeasance, with districts and schools using the funds for general purposes rather than to assist educationally disadvantaged children. A 1969 report found that Title I funds had been used to "buy books and supplies for all schoolchildren in the system, to pay general overhead and operating expenses ... and to equip superintendent's offices with paneling, wall-to-wall carpeting, and color televisions."[57] Some districts that devoted the funds to educationally disadvantaged children had reduced the amount of their own funds devoted to these children, undermining the federal intent to provide extra help. Other districts were directing the resources appropriately but using them for activities that were of dubious benefit to the children.

The federal response was to amend the Title I legislation to tighten up the loopholes. For instance, provisions were inserted that required the district to maintain its former level of funding and use the federal funds to supplement the services that the disadvantaged child would have received if the Title I funds had not been provided. The USOE expanded its regulations and stepped up enforcement activities. Local districts and states sometimes complained about that enforcement to their congressional representatives, who threatened USOE with appropriation cuts. Title I, however, gradually created a constituency that lobbied at the local, state, and federal level for implementation in accordance with the legislative intent. The constituency included parents of educationally disadvantaged children, civil rights groups, child advocacy organizations, child welfare lawyers, and Title I program coordinators in the larger districts. With pressure from these groups, most of the Title I resources did gradually go to the targeted children.

It took about a decade before there was widespread compliance.[58] Why did that take so long? There are several reasons.

The objectives of Title I had been stated broadly. The legislation indicated little more than that the federal funds were to be used to meet the "special educational needs of educationally deprived children." Given the legislative history in which Title I was proposed, after several bills for general aid to schools had failed, some members of Congress thought the compensatory education was a political cover for funding that was intended to be used for general aid.[59] USOE's regulations were also ambiguous in several places. In addition, political power was sometimes wielded to allow non-compliance. For instance, when the Commissioner of Education tried to recover funds misspent by the Chicago school district, Mayor Daley complained forcefully to his congressional representatives and the White House, and the President told the Commissioner to back off.

The USOE was not prepared to administer ESEA and the equally complex Higher Education Act of 1965. USOE, a few Johnson advisors, and several members of Congress had urged slow growth in ESEA, but the education interest groups and members of Congress pushed for rapid expansion of eligibility, funding, and program components.[60] Between 1961 and 1966, the budget of the programs administered by USOE had increased six-fold, the number of programs had increased 2.5-fold, and the staff had not quite doubled. The office had disproportionately few high-level staff, and most were former educators without modern management training. Ninety-nine percent of the funds were spent in the field but only nine percent of the staff members were located outside Washington DC. Efforts were made to improve the managerial capabilities of the Office, but putting them in place while ramping up large new programs produced chaos and morale problems, which resulted in resignations and retirements. This in turn created many vacancies that had to be filled through the slow federal hiring process.[61]

State Education Agencies (SEAs) were often poorly organized and staffed to administer Title I. To gain broad congressional support, the legislation assured that almost all of the then 29,000 local school districts would be eligible to apply for Title I funds. They were to submit a plan explaining how they would use the Title I funds, and the SEA was required to review the plan and provide "assurance" to the USOE that the proposed uses were consistent with the federal legislation and the regulations. That required many of the SEAs (and a few territorial offices) to review and sign off on hundreds of proposals. If a proposal was not satisfactory, the SEAs had to provide feedback and then examine the revised proposals that might be submitted. In addition, during the 1960s, federal education programs proliferated from about 20 to 130, administered by a dozen federal departments and agencies, with minimal coordination, creating a bureaucratic nightmare for states and local districts that wished to take full advantage of the federal resources.[62]

Another hurdle to implementation was that the federal funding had to be divided among thousands of school districts and a much larger number of schools. That resulted in an average of about $1,100 per student served each year (in year 2000 dollars) until moderate funding increases were provided in the mid-1990s. Federal funds have always made up a very small portion of public school revenues. In 1960 all federal funding accounted for only 4.4 percent of the total K-12 funding, but in 1966 it was 7.9 percent and in 1980 it was 9.8 percent.[63] In 2000, Title I was funded at $8.3 billion and total K-12 public school expenditures were $375 billion.[64]

In the mid-1960s, there was little knowledge about what types of services would best help educationally disadvantaged students to benefit fully from their education and subsequent life opportunities. That initially forced local officials to choose service delivery without much guidance. Within a few years entrepreneurial scholars and businesses were offering a flurry of advice, products, and services, many of which had been hastily pulled together and would later prove ineffective.

Innovation in any bureaucracy is not easy. The principals of Title I schools were expected to undertake needs assessments, plan new services, hire extra staff, and prepare various reports. At a time when there was not yet the expectation that schools should provide special help to disadvantaged students, some school principals chose not to apply for funds and others chose to finesse implementation. At one large school district, during the late 1960s, many of the principles in designated Title I schools transferred out to non-Title I schools to avoid the extra burdens. That pattern ceased only when the district began providing year-round contracts, salary increments, and other incentives for principals in those schools.[65]

Despite serious problems in implementation, the compensatory education reform swept the country far faster that any prior one in history. Within 15 years of the initial Title I legislation, compensatory education was being provided in almost every school district in the country. At the close of the century, an estimated 54 percent of public schools received Title I funding.[66]

Achievement of Goals

Federal compensatory education programs have been subject to unprecedented evaluation. This is partly because they have been the largest federal K-12 education programs. It is partly because Robert Kennedy insisted that the original Title I legislation mandate evaluation. It is also partly because the social sciences had developed new tools in the 1950s and 1960s that could be used for such evaluations.

Both Head Start and Title I were legislative programs that set objectives and provided funding but allowed considerable discretion in the specific services that were provided to the children. Both programs could legitimately be interpreted as directed toward the academic, personal, social, and even physical development of the children. That multiplicity of objectives, however, would make it difficult to judge the success of the programs.

There has been considerable evaluation of Head Start since its founding in 1965. A major review of the national evaluations available by 1977 concluded that Head Start did have a broad range of immediate benefits on personal-social development (improved handling of frustration, persistence, task orientation, achievement orientation, and leadership) and on school readiness (IQ, knowledge of letters and numbers, and level of general information). Nevertheless, summer Head Start programs had little or no effects on early school achievement after the first grade of elementary school and the full year programs had only modest effects.[67] Even these modest effects tended to erode over the following few years of school and "the final levels of achievement ... are still not high enough to offer much encouragement for regarding Head Start as a powerful way to equalize educational achievement."[68]

A 1979 review of several models of early childhood education programs—models that might be used in Head Start programs—found generally less grade retention in the middle or late elementary school grades, about half the rate of special education placements (with the exception of one model), mixed results on reading test scores--with some models' participants reading better than the control group children and other models' participants reading about the same as the controls, and similarly mixed results on mathematics test scores.[69]

"Follow Through" services provided continuing support to a portion of Head Start participants through the first few years of elementary school. A national evaluation of selected models of Follow Through found little evidence that any of the models had substantial and sustained effects.[70]

A 1989 review of the evaluations of private model programs and Head Start programs concluded that several model programs had achieved substantial impacts on IQ scores, achievement, and socio-emotional development over the year of the program, and that Head Start programs, on average, had achieved moderate impacts. All those effects declined within a few years. The model programs did have long-term effects on reduced placement in special education, but Head Start programs did not. The model programs may have had modest enduring effects on teen pregnancy, delinquency, employment, and welfare dependency, but the Head Start programs did not.[71]

The evaluation results for Title I compensatory education have been similar to those for Head Start. An eminent researcher's 1982 summary of the extensive, conflicting, and contested evidence on Title I participants' learning gains was that overall there are modest short-term gains, but they varied across schools, grade levels, and subjects tested. Gains in arithmetic were sustained through elementary school, but those in reading dissipated after the third grade. This researcher went on to note, "These gains, if real, are modest in comparison with the original promise of Title I."[72]

A meta-analysis was conducted on 17 national evaluations of Title I that had been conducted between 1966 to 1993.[73] It statistically analyzed and synthesized the results of the individual studies. Title I was found to have slight effects in the 1960s and 1970s and modest effects thereafter. The authors of this analysis attribute that to many years of program improvement efforts and better implementation compliance. The effects were slightly greater when services were provided in the early years of schooling; they were modestly greater for mathematics than for reading; and the evidence suggests partial erosion of gains over the summer. The authors concluded, however, that Title I "has not fulfilled its original expectation: to close the achievement gap between at-risk students and their more advantaged peers."[74]

A national evaluation of Title I (renamed "Chapter I" at the time) that was released in 1997 affirmed the earlier results. It found the services were generally being provided to the students most needing extra academic assistance, but the services did little to close the achievement gap between advantaged and disadvantaged children.[75]

Another way to assess the impacts of compensatory education is to look at possible changes in national trends in achievement for disadvantaged students since compensatory education became widespread. This allows examining possible cumulative effects from several different programs. Of course these trends are likely to be influenced by other factors too, so they are an imperfect assessment. There was no national tracking of student achievement in the United States until the National Assessment of Educational Progress, which began in the early 1970s. While 1970 is five and six years after Head Start and Title I were introduced, we have seen that Title I and, to a lesser extent, Head Start were not widely implemented as intended until the mid-1970s. NAEP did not collect data on family income but does collect data on parental education levels. For students whose parents had not graduated from high school, the trends from the early- or mid-1970s to the mid-1980s were that students age 9 and 13 showed small increases in reading, mathematics, and science.[76] In addition, the gap between black and white students' average scores declined moderately from the early 1970s to the mid-1980s, declining anywhere from 8 to 22 points, and then it widened moderately over the subsequent years as white students showed greater gains. A similar but less pronounced pattern was exhibited for Hispanic students.[77] A sophisticated analysis relating NAEP score changes from the mid-1970s through 1990 to changes in family characteristics concluded that NAEP scores for African Americans and Hispanics increased more than would be expected from changing family characteristics, suggesting that schools made the difference.[78] The same study concluded that the smaller NAEP score gains of whites (non-Hispanics) were mostly the result of changing family characteristics.

What changed in the schools to cause the modest improvements in the NAEP scores of children from families with limited education and of African American and Hispanic children? Many schools with substantial numbers of low-income students had implemented compensatory education programs so that could be part of the answer. Another possibility is that the main educational approaches used in schools for all students became better adapted to the needs of low-income and minority students. If the latter is the case, it is conceivably because the widespread implementation of compensatory education throughout the country moved educators to make such modifications.

Some policy analysts have suggested that compensatory education was doomed to small effects because of the small funding devoted to it. In the early 1990s, the funding per participant averaged about 20 percent above the schools' normal level, not a large increase but not a trivial one.[79] The historical record indicates that the initial advocates of compensatory education thought that modest supplementary services, mostly in the early years of life, would compensate for initial disadvantages and allow recipient children to progress thereafter at the same pace as others, as is implicit in the name "Headstart." It is now clear that expectation has not been achieved and short-term gains from compensatory education erode over time. It is possible that new approaches to compensatory education will have more sustained effects, but it is also possible that sustained effects can only be achieved with sustained compensatory education services throughout elementary and secondary schooling—a far more expensive service than initially conceived.

At the end of the 20th century, the average 17-year-old from parents who did not graduate from high school read slightly less well than the average 13-year-old from a family with at least one parent having some post-secondary education. The differences were almost as large for science skills and smaller for mathematics.[80] The world's economies increasingly demand workers with complex information handling skills, and yet, over a three-decade period, average reading scores for all American 17-year-olds merely inched up from 285 to 288. The comparable gains in mathematics went from 304 to 308. The average science scores actually fell one point.[81]

Unintended Side Effects

There were at least three side effects of the federal compensatory education programs initiated in the 1960s. First, they called for parent advisory committees, and that gave poor parents legitimacy in communicating with public school officials. Previously, poor parents would either not try to communicate or tried and were ignored. Some poor parents parlayed their experience on parent advisory councils to advocacy in other venues, even electoral politics.[82]

Second, Head Start programs needed many aides to help staff the preschool rooms, and the regulations directed them to try to fill those positions with parents of the participating students. That was expected to create synergies, reducing the poverty that was strongly associated with educational disadvantage and also improving the parenting practices of poor families, which was thought to contribute to educational disadvantage. By 1966, Head Start employed about 45,000 poor people.[83] Title I also created 67,000 full-time equivalent teaching aide positions,[84] and they were often were filled with parents. A portion of these aides, inspired by their experiences, sought further education, earned certification as teachers, and returned to the classrooms in higher paid positions.[85]

It has been said that the War on Poverty helped the poor only modestly but that it substantially benefited lower-middle class African Americans and Hispanics who worked their way up in the administrative structure of the programs. This progress did not go unnoticed by the Ku Klux Klan, which burned crosses in front of several Head Start centers in Mississippi, Alabama, and Florida.[86]

Head Start and Title I also changed the consciousness of the nation toward disadvantaged students. Prior to the widespread adoption of these federal initiatives, most Americans and most educators felt that the blame for educational failure, except in cases of severe disabilities, belonged to the child and his or her parents. Head Start and Title I transferred the locus of responsibility from the child and parents to the schools. Within two decades, most of the nation and most educators came to assume that those students who entered school not well prepared deserved extra help. By the early 1990s, twenty-eight states provided special funding for compensatory education.[87] By 2001, forty-seven states provided additional funding for their Head Start programs or for other early childhood education programs.[88] This expanding perception of school responsibility became one foundation of the accountability reform movement that will be described in Chapter 10.

WAS COMPENSATORY EDUCATION INEVITABLE?

Efforts to assist students who come to school ill-prepared and soon lag behind was probably inevitable, given the nation's gradual expansion of the franchise to all adults, given initial hopes for universal public education, and given the national guilt that arose during the mid-20th century from the country's long legacy of racism. Compensatory education, however, was not the only feasible response. In 1829 the New York City socialist journal *Free Enquirer* proposed an alternate vision of universal public schools comprised of a national system of boarding schools for all children age two to 16, with the belief that only such a system would obliterate the unequal advantages that accrued to children from widely varying family resources.[89] In the 1970s, Marxist-oriented scholars such as Colin Greer and Michael Katz laughed at the folly of thinking government controlled schools would eliminate capitalist induced socio-economic stratification and suggested that only the replacement of capitalism with democratic socialism would eliminate an underclass in America. Both of these alternatives were rejected because they contradicted strongly held American values about childrearing and economic freedom.

FUTURE OF THE REFORM

The compensatory education reformers were moved by the same sentiments as some universal public education reformers—that the happenstance of a child's family circumstances should not preclude opportunity to develop his or her talents. The sentiment has so long been widespread in American society that it is not likely to disappear soon. Although the country has become more conservative politically, and that may continue with the aging of the population, only the hardest of hearts would deny extra help to children who start at a disadvantage through no fault of their own. In addition, despite the disappointing results of Title I, it has been reauthorized continually since its establishment in 1965. Compensatory education will probably be around for at least several more decades, even if the name of the programs and administrative mechanisms change.

What is harder to predict is the future focus of compensatory education, the favored intervention approaches, the age levels that will be targeted, and the institutional arrangements that will be used to manage the compensatory education. A plethora of proposals has been offered for policymakers' consideration. Many experts have argued that more money is needed or that the given funds should be targeted more narrowly on high poverty schools. Some assert that physical, emotional and behavioral problems have to be corrected first, others say the emphasis should be on academics, and still others say it should be on higher-order intellectual skills. Several experts have suggested that early childhood enrichment services should start at age one and be delivered in the home, some have suggested that preschools start at the age of three, many have suggested that there should be multiple years of early intervention. Some recommend better curriculum materials and teacher preparation. Others suggest that pullout remedial education is inherently flawed and recommend that comprehensive school reform be used to boost all students' learning. President Bush's "No Child Left Behind" legislation, enacted in January 2002, allows the districts more discretion on the use of the federal funds while holding them more accountable for the academic progress of the students, and it stipulates that when progress is not achieved, the parents can choose to use the Title I funds for private tutoring. These changes will be discussed further in Chapter 10.

---

[1] Quoted in James L. Jarrett. (1971). "The Meanings of Equality," in *The Conditions for Educational Equality*, ed. Sterling McMurrin (Washington, DC: Committee for Economic Development, 1971), 15.

[2] Michael B. Katz, *The Irony of Early School Reform* (Boston, MA: Beacon Press, 1968).

[3] Caroline Hendrie, "Years of Entrenched Inequality," *Education Week*, 18 March 1999 [accessed August 17 2003 from www.edweek.org searching the "Archives" by title].

[4] This is a quote from and unspecified widely used textbook by David Muzzey, cited in Gary B. Nash, "American History Reconsidered: Asking New Questions About the Past" in *Learning From the Past: What History Teaches Us About School Reform*, ed. Diane Ravitch and Maris A.Vinovskis (Baltimore, MD: Johns Hopkins Press), 135-163. pg. 138

[5] Aida Negron De Montilla, *Americanization in Puerto Rico and the Public-School System 1900-1930* (Rio Piedras, PR: Editorial Edil, 1971, 62.

[6] Tape v. Hurley, 66 Cal. 473.

[7] Joel Spring, *Deculturalization and the Struggle for Equality: A Brief History of the Education of Dominated Cultures in the United States* (Boston: McGraw Hill, 2001), 55-65

[8] Joel Spring, *Deculturalization and the Struggle for Equality: A Brief History of the Education of Dominated Cultures in the United States* (Boston: McGraw Hill, 2001), 66.

[9] U.S. Department of Commerce, Bureau of the Census, *Historical Statistics of the United States: Colonial Times to 1970, Part 1* (Washington, DC: U. S. Government Printing Office, 1975), 139 and 73.

[10] Doxey A. Wilkerson, "School Integration, Compensatory Education and the Civil Rights Movement in the North," *Journal of Negro Education* 34 (Summer 1965): 300-309 pg. 306

[11] U.S. Department of Commerce, Bureau of the Census, *Historical Statistics of the United States: Colonial Times to 1970, Part 1* (Washington, DC: U. S. Government Printing Office, 1975), 224.

[12] U.S. Department of Commerce, Bureau of the Census, *Historical Statistics of the United States: Colonial Times to 1970, Part 1* (Washington, DC: U. S. Government Printing Office, 1975), 289. Note: the $3,000 income level of 1961 was inflated to year 2000 dollars using the purchasing power index in U.S. Department of Commerce, Census Bureau, *Statistical Abstract of the United States: 2001* (Austin, TX: Hoover's Business Press, 2001), 451.

[13] Edward Zigler and Karen Anderson, "An Idea Whose Time Had Come: The Intellectual and Political Climate for Head Start," in *Project Head Start: A Legacy of the War on Poverty*, Edward Zigler and Jeanette Valentine, eds. (New York: The Free Press, 1979), 3-20. pg 5

[14] Edward Zigler and Karen Anderson, "An Idea Whose Time Had Come: The Intellectual and Political Climate for Head Start," in *Project Head Start: A Legacy of the War on Poverty*, Edward Zigler and Jeanette Valentine, eds. (New York: The Free Press, 1979), 3-20. pg 5

[15] The best overview of this early research is: Benjamin Bloom, *Stability and Change in Human Characteristics* (New York: John Wiley, 1964).

[16] Arthur Jensen, "How much can we boost IQ and scholastic achievement?" *Harvard Educational Review* 39: 1-123.

[17] Josh Kagan, "Empowerment and Education: Civil Rights, Expert-Advocates, and Parent Politics in Head Start, 1964-1980," *Teachers College Record* 104 (April 2002), 516-562. pg 524

[18] Edward Zigler and Karen Anderson, "An Idea Whose Time Had Come: The Intellectual and Political Climate for Head Start," in *Project Head Start: A Legacy of the War on Poverty,* Edward Zigler and Jeanette Valentine, eds. (New York: The Free Press, 1979), 3-20. pg 10-11

[19] Benjamin S. Bloom, Allison Davis, and Robert Hess, eds., *Compensatory Education for Cultural Deprivation* (New York: Holt, Rinehart and Winston, 1965) 1-3, 8-40.

[20] Maris A. Vinovskis, *History and Educational Policymaking* (New Haven, CT: Yale University Press, 1999), 70.

[21] Maris A. Vinovskis, *History and Educational Policymaking* (New Haven, CT: Yale University Press, 1999), 71.

[22] Maris A. Vinovskis, *History and Educational Policymaking* (New Haven, CT: Yale University Press, 1999), 72

[23] Catherine J. Ross, "Early Skirmishes with Poverty: The Historical Roots of Head Start," in *Project Head Start: A Legacy of the War on Poverty,* Edward Zigler and Jeanette Valentine, eds. (New York: The Free Press, 1979), 21-42. pg 29

[24] Catherine J. Ross, "Early Skirmishes with Poverty: The Historical Roots of Head Start," in *Project Head Start: A Legacy of the War on Poverty,* Edward Zigler and Jeanette Valentine, eds. (New York: The Free Press, 1979), 21-42. pg 30-31

[25] Catherine J. Ross, "Early Skirmishes with Poverty: The Historical Roots of Head Start," in *Project Head Start: A Legacy of the War on Poverty,* Edward Zigler and Jeanette Valentine, eds. (New York: The Free Press, 1979), 21-42. pg 34

[26] Catherine J. Ross, "Early Skirmishes with Poverty: The Historical Roots of Head Start," in *Project Head Start: A Legacy of the War on Poverty,* Edward Zigler and Jeanette Valentine, eds. (New York: The Free Press, 1979), 21-42. pg 34-35

[27] Allan M. West, *The National Education Association: The Power Base for Education* (New York: Free Press, 1980), 163-164.

[28] Allan M. West, *The National Education Association: The Power Base for Education* (New York: Free Press, 1980), 174-175.

[29] Allan M. West, *The National Education Association: The Power Base for Education* (New York: Free Press, 1980), 166.

[30] Quoted in Hugh D. Graham, *The Uncertain Triumph* (Chapel Hill, NC: University of North Carolina Press, 1984), 13.

[31] Quoted in Hugh D. Graham, *The Uncertain Triumph* (Chapel Hill, NC: University of North Carolina Press, 1984), 25.

[32] Hugh D. Graham, *The Uncertain Triumph* (Chapel Hill, NC: University of North Carolina Press, 1984), 44-50.

[33] Hugh D. Graham, *The Uncertain Triumph* (Chapel Hill, NC: University of North Carolina Press, 1984), 53-55.

[34] Edward Zigler and Karen Anderson, "An Idea Whose Time Had Come: The Intellectual and Political Climate for Head Start," in *Project Head Start: A Legacy of the War on Poverty,* Edward Zigler and Jeanette Valentine, eds. (New York: The Free Press, 1979), 3-20. pg 12-13

[35] Sargent Shriver, "*The Origins of Head Start,*" in *Project Head Start: A Legacy of the War on Poverty,* Edward Zigler and Jeanette Valentine, eds. (New York: The Free Press, 1979), 52.

[36] Jeanette Valentine, Catherine J. Ross and Edward Zigler, "Epilogue," in *Project Head Start: A Legacy of the War on Poverty,* eds. Edward Zigler and Jeanette Valentine (New York: Free Press, 1979), 509-510.

[37] Julius B. Richmond, Deborah J. Stipek, and Edward Zigler, "A Decade of Head Start," in *Project Head Start: A Legacy of the War on Poverty,* Edward Zigler and Jeanette Valentine, eds. (New York: The Free Press, 1979), 135-152. pg. 137

[38] Edward Zigler and Karen Anderson, "An Idea Whose Time Had Come: The Intellectual and Political Climate for Head Start," in *Project Head Start: A Legacy of the War on Poverty,* Edward Zigler and Jeanette Valentine, eds. (New York: The Free Press, 1979), 3-20. pg 14-15

[39] Lyndon B. Johnson, "Remarks on Project Head Start, May 18, 1965," in *Project Head Start: A Legacy of the War on Poverty,* Edward Zigler and Jeanette Valentine, eds. (New York: The Free Press, 1979), 67-72 pg 68

[40] Quoted in Hugh D. Graham, *The Uncertain Triumph* (Chapel Hill, NC: University of North Carolina Press, 1984), 66.

[41] Christopher T. Cross, *Political Education: National Policy Comes of Age* (New York: Teachers College Press, 2004), 24-26.

[42] Quoted in Allan M. West, *The National Education Association: The Power Base for Education* (New York: Free Press, 1980), 178.

[43] Quoted in Hugh D. Graham, *The Uncertain Triumph* (Chapel Hill, NC: University of North Carolina Press, 1984), 79.

[44] Quoted in John F. Jennings, "Title I: Its Legislative History and Its Promise" in *Title I: Compensatory Education at the Crossroads,* ed. Geoffrey D. Borman, Samuel C. Stringfield, and Robert E. Slavin (Mahwah, NJ: Lawrence Erlbaum Associates, 2001), 1-24. pg 4

[45] Public Law 89-10, Section 201, April 11, 1965.

[46] Public Law 89-10, Section 205 (1), April 11, 1965.

[47] John F. Jennings, "Title I: Its Legislative History and Its Promise" in *Title I: Compensatory Education at the Crossroads,* ed. Geoffrey D. Borman, Samuel C. Stringfield, and Robert E. Slavin (Mahwah, NJ: Lawrence Erlbaum Associates, 2001), 1-24. pg 7-9

[48] Public Law 89-10, Section 205 (5), April 11, 1965.

[49] John F. Jennings, "Title I: Its Legislative History and Its Promise" in *Title I: Compensatory Education at the Crossroads,* ed. Geoffrey D. Borman, Samuel C. Stringfield, and Robert E. Slavin (Mahwah, NJ: Lawrence Erlbaum Associates, 2001), 1-24. pg 14-20

[50] Enrollment and funding levels are from: Julius B. Richmond, Deborah J. Stipek, and Edward Zigler, "A Decade of Head Start," in *Project Head Start: A Legacy of the War on Poverty,* Edward Zigler and Jeanette Valentine, eds. (New York: The Free Press, 1979), 135-152. pg. 142; funding levels were re-stated in year 2000 dollars applying the purchasing power index in U.S. Department of Commerce, Census Bureau, *Statistical Abstract of the United States: 2001* (Austin, TX: Hoover's Business Press, 2001), 451.

[51] Barbara Biber, "Introduction [to 'The Preschool-Education Component of Head Start'],"in *Project Head Start: A Legacy of the War on Poverty,* Edward Zigler and Jeanette Valentine, eds. (New York: The Free Press, 1979), 155-161. pg. 156-157.

[52] This point is made in several of the articles in Edward Zigler and Jeanette Valentine, eds., *Project Head Start: A Legacy of the War on Poverty*, (New York: The Free Press, 1979).

[53] U.S. Department of Commerce, Census Bureau, *Statistical Abstract of the United States: 2001* (Austin, TX: Hoover's Business Press, 2001), 357.

[54] U.S. Department of Education, National Center for Education Statistics, *The Condition of Education: 2001* (Washington DC: U.S. Government Printing Office, 2001), 6.

[55] Federal Interagency Forum on Child and Family Statistics, *America's Children: Key National Indicators of Well-Being: 2003* (Washington DC: U.S. Government Printing Office, 2003), 49. [available online at http://childstats.gov]

[56] Iris C. Rotberg and James J. Harvey, *Federal Policy Options for Improving the Education of Low-Income Students: Volume I: Findings and Recommendations* (Santa Monica, CA: RAND, 1993), 2, 11; funding levels are expressed in 2000 dollars using the purchasing power index in U.S. Department of Commerce, Census Bureau, *Statistical Abstract of the United States: 2001* (Austin, TX: Hoover's Business Press, 2001), 451.

[57] Quoted in John F. Jennings, "Title I: Its Legislative History and Its Promise" in *Title I: Compensatory Education at the Crossroads*, ed. Geoffrey D. Borman, Samuel C. Stringfield, and Robert E. Slavin (Mahwah, NJ: Lawrence Erlbaum Associates, 2001), 1-24. pg 9

[58] James J. Vanecko, Nancy L. Ames, and Francis X Archambault, Jr., *Who Benefits from Federal Education Dollars? The Development of ESEA Title I Allocation Policy* (Cambridge, MA: Abt Books, 1980), 67-68.

[59] Milbrey Wallin McLaughlin, "Implementation of ESEA Title I: A Problem of Compliance," *Teachers College Record* 77 (February 1976), 397-415. pg 402.

[60] Hugh D. Graham, *The Uncertain Triumph* (Chapel Hill, NC: University of North Carolina Press, 1984), 114-130.

[61] Hugh D. Graham, *The Uncertain Triumph* (Chapel Hill, NC: University of North Carolina Press, 1984), 95-99.

[62] Hugh D. Graham, *The Uncertain Triumph* (Chapel Hill, NC: University of North Carolina Press, 1984), xix.

[63] U.S. Department of Education, National Center for Education Statistics, *Digest of Education Statistics: 2001* (Washington DC: U.S. Government Printing Office, 2002), 178.

[64] U.S. Department of Education, National Center for Education Statistics, *Digest of Education Statistics: 2001* (Washington DC: U.S. Government Printing Office, 2002), 34, 434.

[65] Milbrey Wallin McLaughlin, "Implementation of ESEA Title I: A Problem of Compliance," *Teachers College Record* 77 (February 1976), 397-415. pg 411

[66] U.S. General Accounting Office, *Title I Program: Stronger Accountability Needed for Performance of Disadvantaged Students* (Washington DC: author, 2000), 6.

[67] Lois-ellin Datta, "Another Spring and Other Hopes: Some Findings from National Evaluations of Project Head Start" in *Project Head Start: A Legacy of the War on Poverty*, eds. Edward Zigler and Jeanette Valentine (New York: Free Press, 1979), 405-432. pgs 410-419

[68] Lois-ellin Datta, "Another Spring and Other Hopes: Some Findings from National Evaluations of Project Head Start," in *Project Head Start: A Legacy of the War on Poverty*, eds. Edward Zigler and Jeanette Valentine (New York: Free Press, 1979), 405-432. pg407.

[69] Francis H. Palmer and Lucille Woolis Andersen, "Long-Term Gains from Early Intervention: Findings from Longitudinal Studies," in *Project Head Start: A Legacy of the War on Poverty,* eds. Edward Zigler and Jeanette Valentine (New York: Free Press, 1979), 433-466.

[70] Linda B. Stebbins, Robert G. St. Pierre, Elizabeth C. Proper, Richard B. Anderson, and Thomas R. Cerva, *Education as Experimentation: A Planned Variation Model, Vol. IV-A* (Cambridge, MA: Abt Associates, 1977).

[71] Ron Haskins, "Beyond Metaphor: The Efficiency of Early Childhood Education," *American Psychologist* 44, (February 1989): 274-282.

[72] Marshall Smith undoubtedly made this summary in the following co-authored article: Carl F. Kaestle and Marshall S. Smith, "The Federal Role in Elementary and Secondary Education, 1940-1980," *Harvard Educational Review* 52 (November, 1982): 384-408. pg 398.

[73] Geoffrey B. Borman and Jerome V. D'Agostino, "Title I and Student Achievement: A Meta-Analysis of Federal Evaluation Results," *Educational Evaluation and Policy Analysis* 18 (Winter 1996): 309-26.

[74] Geoffrey B. Borman and Jerome V. D'Agostino, "Title I and Student Achievement: A Meta-Analysis of Federal Evaluation Results," *Educational Evaluation and Policy Analysis* 18 (Winter 1996): 309-26. pg 324

[75] Michael J. Puma, Nancy Karweit, Cristofer Price, Anne Ricciuti, William Thompson, and Michael Vaden-Kiernan, *Prospects: Final Report on Student Outcomes* (Cambridge, MA: Abt Associates, 1997), iv-v.

[76] U.S. Department of Education, National Center for Educational Statistics, *NAEP 1999 Trends in Academic Progress: Three Decades of Student Performance* (Washington DC: author, 2000), 46,-51.

[77] U.S. Department of Education, National Center for Educational Statistics, *NAEP 1999 Trends in Academic Progress: Three Decades of Student Performance* (Washington DC: author, 2000), 39-40.

[78] David W. Grissmer, Sheila Nataraj Kirby, Mark Berends, Stephanie Williamson, *Student Achievement and the Changing American Family* (Santa Monica, CA: RAND, 1994), xxx-xxxi.

[79] Iris C. Rotberg and James J. Harvey, *Federal Policy Options for Improving the Education of Low-Income Students: Volume I: Findings and Recommendations* (Santa Monica, CA: RAND, 1993), xii, 33.

[80] U.S. Department of Education, National Center for Educational Statistics, *NAEP 1999 Trends in Academic Progress: Three Decades of Student Performance* (Washington DC: author, 2000), 46-51.

[81] U.S. Department of Education, National Center for Educational Statistics, *NAEP 1999 Trends in Academic Progress: Three Decades of Student Performance* (Washington DC: author, 2000), 9.

[82] See: Lois-ellin Datta, "Another Spring and Other Hopes: Some Findings from National Evaluations of Project Head Start," in *Project Head Start: A Legacy of the War on Poverty,* eds. Edward Zigler and Jeanette Valentine (New York: Free Press, 1979), 405-432; pg 407-409 and Jeanette Valentine, Catherine J. Ross and Edward Zigler, "Epilogue," in *Project Head Start: A Legacy of the War on Poverty,* eds. Edward Zigler and Jeanette Valentine (New York: Free Press, 1979), 405-432; pg 511.

[83] Joel Spring, *The Sorting Machine: National Educational Policy Since 1945* (New York: David McKay, 1976), 223-224.

[84] Iris C. Rotberg and James J. Harvey, *Federal Policy Options for Improving the Education of Low-Income Students: Volume I: Findings and Recommendations* (Santa Monica, CA: RAND, 1993), 2.

[85] See: Lois-ellin Datta, "Another Spring and Other Hopes: Some Findings from National Evaluations of Project Head Start," in *Project Head Start: A Legacy of the War on Poverty*, eds. Edward Zigler and Jeanette Valentine (New York: Free Press, 1979), 405-432; pg 407-409 and Jeanette Valentine, Catherine J. Ross and Edward Zigler, "Epilogue," in *Project Head Start: A Legacy of the War on Poverty*, eds. Edward Zigler and Jeanette Valentine (New York: Free Press, 1979), 405-432; pg 511.

[86] Josh Kagan, "Empowerment and Education: Civil Rights, Expert-Advocates, and Parent Politics in Head Start, 1964-1980," *Teachers College Record* 104 (April 2002), 516-562. Pgs 531-532.

[87] Steven D. Gold, David M. Smith, & Stephen B. Lawton, *Public School Finance Programs of the United States and Canada, 1993-1994* (Albany, NY: State University of New York, 1995).

[88] "Quality Counts: 2002," *Education Week* XXI (17) (January 10, 2002), 60.

[89] Carl F. Kaestle, *Pillars of the Republic: Common Schools and American Society, 1780-1860* (New York: Hill and Wang 83) 144.

8

Multicultural Education

Daniel C. Padolsky

"Our History is being distorted and polluted and our children thereby deAmericanized.... The achievements of the many different races—Irish, German Italian, French, Scandinavian, Slavic, Polish, Spanish, etc. ... are treated with contempt to the glory of England.[1]"

So wrote the Knights of Columbus, the largest Catholic organization in the United States, during the 1920s. Similar appeals by a wide range of nationalities and ethnic groups in America have been common since the establishment of universal public education systems in the mid-1800s.

The multicultural education reform movement sought to infuse the various cultural heritages of Americans into the public schools—into the curricula, textbooks, literary canon, language courses, teaching strategies, school decorations, and school celebrations. The objectives included: creation of a welcoming environment for students of different ethnic backgrounds, increasing the motivation of minority students, adapting instruction to meet the needs of these students, preserving and extending the ethnic heritages of these students, and preparing Anglo-Americans to live with tolerance and appreciation of the various cultural heritages of the nation.

INITIAL CONDITIONS

Chapter 3 described 19th century schools' efforts to protestantize Catholic children. Chapters 2 and 7 briefly described the schools' efforts to exclude or segregate, Native Americans, African Americans, Mexican Americans, and Asian Americans—efforts that often continued through the middle of the 20th century.

Catholics and people of color were not the only targets of these efforts. During mid-colonial times, the Dutch felt threatened by the majority English culture and founded their own schools with curricula based on their traditions, language, and religion. In 1727, fear of the German culture led to the passing of a law "requiring all male German immigrants in America to swear an oath of allegiance to the British Crown."[2] At that time, proposals were made to prohibit German printers and German books from entering the colonies. In the mid-1700s German immigrants often desired that their children be schooled in the German language, but nativist Anglo-Americans, fearing an expansion of German culture in the United States, sought to require instruction in English.[3] Benjamin Franklin, one of the most cosmopolitan of the founding fathers, advocated that school instruction be solely in English, a stand that provoked Germans to help vote him out of the colonial assembly. Franklin, always quick to learn from his mistakes, later established one of the first German language newspapers in the country.[4]

During the 19th century, Poles, Czechs, Germans, Lithuanians, Russians, Irish, Scandinavians, and Jews immigrated to America in large numbers, settled in ethnic communities, and formed their own parochial and private schools that taught in their respective native languages.[5] Catholics built a large parochial school system in the late 1800s. In 1922 the Oregon legislature tried to eliminate religiously based schools by outlawing all private schools in the state. In just one year, the Supreme Court declared that unconstitutional in *Pierce v. Society of Sisters*, indicating that the statute unreasonably interfered with the freedom of parents to direct the education of their children.[6]

As indicated in Chapter 2, universal public school systems were created partly to Americanize immigrant children. Fueling that effort were opinions that "the immigrant, fresh from his undemocratic soil, was considered incapable of understanding and appreciating America's free institutions."[7] There was also the desire to forge core values and a common language during the nation building of the 19th century. Calvin Stowe, an educator in Ohio, warned in 1835 that "it is altogether essential to our national strength and peace, if not even to our national existence, that the foreigners who settle on our soil, should cease to be Europeans and become Americans."[8] Although parents might reject assimilation, he continued, their offspring might persuade them otherwise.

The public school textbooks of the 1800s and early 1900s often celebrated the historical figures of Anglo-Saxon descent while demonizing other groups.[9] Examples of this were cited in Chapter 3 when discussing Bishop Hughes' complaints about New York City textbooks' portrayals of Irish Catholics. Textbooks usually described Native Americans as warlike, emphasizing their scalping of white heroes, with little or no explanation of the white peoples' provocations. African Americans were commonly portrayed as childlike, simple, scared, and superstitious. Especially offensive were historical accounts of African Americans during Reconstruction, which often described them as raping and pillaging the white South.[10]

Racial and ethnic minority leaders pointed out and called for elimination of the "historical neglect" and "base untruths" in American textbooks. If successful, a few of their heroes and contributions were inserted into the textbooks; however, even with the new faces, the general story often remained one of simplistic, straightforward glorification of Anglo-America supremacy.[11] When a few textbook authors tried to provide a more balanced portrayal, they often found their books subject to scathing attack and boycotts. After doctoring a book to suit critical citizen groups, one harried author wrote, "I have this moment finished the first draft of the 'Book of Lies' otherwise known as Channing's 'Elements of United States History.'"[12] In New Jersey, legislators discussed enacting a law that would ban certain history textbooks considered "treasonous" because the authors appeared to have decreased the importance of the Founding Fathers.[13]

Ethnic and racial minorities sometimes eagerly embraced the schools' efforts to Americanize their children, sometimes uncomfortably tolerated the denial and denigration of their cultural heritages as the price to be paid for American citizenship, and other times challenged and resisted these efforts. While some resistors desired to create native enclaves in America, many hoped that their children would be bi-cultural—that they would be German-Americans and Mexican-Americans rather than so thoroughly acculturated that they became Anglo-Americans.

Germans were particularly adept at using political pressure to maintain their identity in cities throughout the Midwest, such as St. Louis, Chicago, and Cincinnati, where they had substantial numbers. In 1840 Germans in Cincinnati were instrumental in passage of a law mandating that whenever 75 freeholders requested in writing for German to be taught in elementary schools, the schools were to be bilingual, teaching children both German and English, before they moved on to other subjects, such as math and science, which were to be taught in English. In the early 1850s, German parents received permission to transfer their children out of the district to a German language school when no such school existed near them. By 1899, 17,584 students were studying the German language in Cincinnati, most of them in elementary schools. For the first four years of their schooling, pupils divided their time equally between an English speaking teacher and a German-speaking teacher. This bilingual instruction helped to preserve the German culture and gave employment to nearly 200 German teachers.[14]

In areas where other immigrants flocked in large numbers, they also were able to exert political pressure to have their cultures and foreign languages introduced into the public elementary schools. Usually taught as a separate subject, the languages included Dutch, French, Czech, Polish, Italian, Norwegian, and Spanish. In 1915 Milwaukee had 811 children studying Italian, 3,102 studying Polish, and 30,368 studying German. In San Francisco in 1917, two elementary schools taught Spanish, four taught French, six taught Italian, and eight taught German.[15]

Mainstream American fear of Germans continued into the 20th century. With the onset of World War I, many states passed laws limiting German culture in public schools. Only a few years later, the U.S. Supreme Court, in *Meyer v. Nebraska,* declared these laws unconstitutional under the equal protection clause of the Fourteenth Amendment.[16]

European immigration dropped dramatically during World War I, revived briefly afterwards, and then was cut back dramatically by legislation.[17] White ethnic identities blurred as successive generations were born and raised in the United States without the infusion of many new arrivals from the homelands.

Despite the challenges to the language and culture of European immigrant groups, they generally fared better in the schools than did minority groups of color. In the 1880s, the Commissioner of Indian Affairs established a vast network of federally operated boarding schools for Indian children. The schools were often located far from the children's homes, even off the reservation. They were run in a para-military manner, requiring European clothing, teaching only in English, punishing the use of native languages, compelling Christian religious practices, requiring substantial hours of labor on the school grounds or nearby private farms, and occasionally forbidding students to return home even during the summer vacation.[18] Children as young as six were sent to the boarding schools, often against their parents' wishes but occasionally with their parents' desperate hope that the schooling would allow their children to escape the poverty of the reservations. By the early 1900s, investigations of these boarding schools found cases of overcrowding, poor nutrition, half-day sessions, forced labor, severe punishment, and epidemics of tuberculosis and trachoma. In 1926 the Secretary of the Interior commissioned a report of Indian education, popularly known as the Meriam report, which concluded that the past policies had undermined Indian culture and destroyed initiative. It recommended establishment of day schools within the Indian communities that would keep children united with their parents, integration of education with reservation life, and rebuilding the cultural life of American Indians.[19]

Many of the schools in the southwestern United Stated deliberately sought to Anglicize the Mexican-American children, providing instruction only in English, forbidding the speaking of Spanish on school grounds, teaching little—if anything—about the history of Mexican Americans, and often belittling their culture. In 1855 the California Bureau of Instruction mandated that all public school instruction be in English, and in 1870 the Texas legislature adopted the same provision. In 1918, Texas made it a criminal offense for school staff to instruct in any language other than English.[20] Several jurisdictions ignored the mandate either because of the local community's wishes or the practical need to communicate with whole classrooms of children who came to school not understanding English. In California, bilingual education was offered by some parochial schools and by private schools created by the Mexican American community.[21] These practices continued well into the 20th century.[22]

In Hawaii during the first decades of the 20th century, Japanese had created private Japanese language schools, operating after regular school hours, to preserve their language and culture. The state passed a law to close those schools. The Japanese challenged it and in 1927 the U.S. Supreme Court ruled the law unconstitutional.[23]

CHANGING CONTEXTS THAT PUSHED MULTICULTURAL EDUCATION

There are at least three changing contexts that led to the establishment of a nationwide multicultural education reform movement. They were changing interpretations of the Fourteenth and Fifteenth Amendments, changes in the objectives of the Civil Rights movement, and the large influx of non-English speaking immigrants into the United States during the latter half of the twentieth century.

Fourteenth and Fifteenth Amendments

While the Civil War formally emancipated millions of slaves, southerners quickly invented "Black Codes" and other means to continue the subjugation of African Americans. To counter those efforts, Congress passed the Fourteenth and Fifteenth Amendments to the U.S. Constitution. The first section of the Fourteenth Amendment specifies that the basic guarantees of the Bill of Rights cannot be subverted by state or local governments:

> No State shall make or enforce any law which shall abridge the privileges or immunities of citizens of the United States; nor shall any State deprive any person of life, liberty, or property, without due process of law; nor deny to any person within its jurisdiction the equal protection of the laws.

The Fifteenth Amendment made explicit that the vote was not to be denied citizens "on account of race, color, or previous conditions of servitude."

Initially these amendments had little impact. Southern states passed "Jim Crow" laws that ordered public institutions and business owners to separate their white and African American clientele, punished consorting across racial lines, made racial intermarriage illegal, and undermined the franchise of African Americans by gerrymandering districts and imposing literacy tests and voting taxes. Only following the passage and enforcement of the Civil Rights Act of 1964 and the Voting Rights Act of 1965 would the overt vestiges of Jim Crow be widely stamped out.

As the vote became broadly available to African Americans and Mexican Americans, they began running for and winning election to a wide range of offices, including positions on school boards. That gave them power over the education of their children. Simultaneously, the Supreme Court began interpreting the Fourteenth Amendment in manner that made it a powerful tool in the quest for equal educational opportunities.

Civil Rights Movement

The Civil Rights movement of the 1950s and early 1960s had been dominated by a vision of equal *access* to education and other aspects of social, economic, and political life. Integration of schools and society was hoped to result in a "melting pot" where African American and Anglo-American cultures would blend together, enriching each other. By the mid-1960s two other visions of civil rights were gaining prominence. Both were partly born of the protracted delays in achieving equal access from the time of the Emancipation Proclamation in 1863 until a decade after the widely ignored 1954 Supreme Court decision in *Brown v. Board of Education.*

One of these visions focused on *equal results* rather than equal access. This vision insisted that minority children should achieve as well as white middle class children in school, minority youth should graduate from colleges at the same rates, minorities should hold a proportionate share of prestigious jobs, and minorities should have the same income distribution. The rationale for this vision was that whites had so long undermined efforts for equal access that they could not be trusted to provide it. The only convincing proof of equal access would be equal results. This vision urged compensatory education as well as affirmative action in college admissions and employment.

The other vision of civil rights that gained prominence during the 1960s was that of Elijah Muhammad and Malcolm X, the Black Panthers, the American Indian Movement, La Raza Unida Party, and other groups that advocated racial and ethnic pride, separatism, and power. They argued that self-determination over their livelihoods and schools was the only way their people could counteract the pervasive racism in American society. Abandoning the desire for success defined by white middle class standards, they sought to establish racial and ethnic solidarity, build their own institutions, and acquire countervailing power to prevent exploitation by whites. School desegregation was perceived as a waste of time and the establishment of Afro-centric and Chicano-centric schools was seen as the best hope for their people. This vision was too radical for most racial and ethnic minorities in the country, but it would influence multicultural education.

Immigration

The Emergency Quota Act of 1921 and the Immigration Act of 1924 had tightly limited immigration, but in 1964 Congress passed the Immigration and Nationality Act, which facilitated immigration for individuals with needed occupational skills and for those seeking to reunite with their families. Legal immigration increased at a rapid pace. Illegal entry into the country also rose dramatically. Between 1970 and 2000, the foreign-born population increased from 10 million to 28 million—with 15 million of those from Latin America and 7 million from Asia. In the year 2000, over 55 million people, or 20 percent of the total population, were either foreign-born or the first generation children of immigrants.[24]

Traditionally, when immigrants arrived in the United States, most settled in major cities such as New York, Los Angeles, or Chicago. Then succeeding generations fanned out to the suburbs. During the last 30 years, however, the pattern has changed, with substantial numbers of immigrants going directly to the suburbs. Edison, N.J., a town with a population of 89,000, went from a total of 900 East Indians in 1980 to 6,000 in 1990. Over the same decade, Westchester County, outside of New York City, had its Hispanic population almost double to 86,000.[25] This made the multicultural diversity of the United States directly visible to a far larger portion of the country than was previously the case.

CAMPAIGN FOR
MULTICULTURAL EDUCATION REFORM

Since the end of the Civil War, African American leaders and citizens have carefully deliberated on how best to educate their children. W.E.B. DuBois, a co-founder of the National Association for the Advancement of Colored People (NAACP) and editor of its *Crisis Magazine*, argued that the experience of slavery had eliminated the cultural consciousness of African Americans, creating a veil behind which they were forced to hide. Only an education based on the knowledge of these historical experiences would lead African Americans out from behind the veil and restore their consciousness and self-respect.[26] DuBois thought such an education would make blacks discontent enough with their social position in America to struggle against white oppression.

Carter G. Woodson, a writer and editor, and a peer of DuBois, criticized the education that was commonly available to African Americans in the decades after the Civil War. He believed that their historical experiences were undervalued or ignored, while the history and culture of Europe were overvalued. This he thought alienated African Americans by creating a chasm between them and their culture. With such an upbringing, they were likely to reject their own traditions and be doomed to the margins of European culture. He believed that this situation would result in the decline of African Americans, both culturally and psychologically. To avoid that, he proposed that African Americans should be taught the culture and history of Africa within their American heritage.[27] In 1915 he founded the Association for the Study of Negro Life and History (later renamed the Association for the Study of Afro-American Life and History), which published the *Negro History Bulletin*, providing elementary and secondary school teachers with lessons on African American history.

Malcolm X believed that for African Americans to find an equal place in white America, they would have to seek out a new pride in their identity, completely separate from the white community. To do this, he felt that African Americans had to recreate their cultural identity based on their African roots. He spoke of the need for a cultural, philosophical, and psychological migration to the motherland Africa, as a way of restoring ancestral bonds and providing "the spiritual strength and the incentive to strengthen our political and social and economic position right here in America."[28] That would allow African American people to cast off DuBois's "veil" of slavery and the identity imposed upon them by the white community.

The philosopher John Dewey, a white contemporary of DuBois and Woodson, was an advocate of cultural diversity and multicultural education. Dewey opposed enculturation for a "melting pot," stating,

> To maintain that all the constituent elements, geographical, racial and cultural in the United States should be put in the same pot and turned into a uniform and unchanging product is distasteful. The same feeling that leads us to recognize each other's individuality, to respect individuality between person and person, also leads us to respect those elements of diversification in cultural traits which differentiate our national life.... Where there are many sorts of independent vigorous life, one provides nationality for interchange, for give and take of culture.[29]

Dewey thought that a good society should be judged by its answers to the following questions: "How numerous and varied are the interests which are consciously shared? How full and free is the interplay with other forms of association?" He then argued that "Democracy is more than a form of government; it is primarily a mode of associated living, of conjoint communicated experience."[30]

Horace Kallan coined the term "cultural pluralism" in the early 1900s and devoted his life to promoting the concept. He argued that for America to be genuinely democratic, it should consist of a harmony of distinct and independent nationalities that were concerned with the welfare of the whole. These nationalities would have to understand that "democracy means self-realization through self-control, self-government, and that one is impossible without the other."[31] Kallan used Switzerland as proof that a country could live in such a manner.

The Ethnic Studies Movement

In 1968, with inspiration from DuBois, Woodson, Malcolm X, and other African American thinkers, black students at Merritt Junior College (in Oakland, California) protested the Euro-centric-bias of the school's curriculum. They pressured the college to provide a new course titled "Negro History." Then the Black Student Union at San Francisco State College agitated successfully for the establishment of a Black Studies Program with eleven courses. This was the first such curriculum in the country.[32] The following year, Merritt College established an Afro-American Studies program, despite opposition from several white college officials who argued that the previously established courses in African Civilization and Negro History were sufficient. The students prevailed, and the added courses included "Survey of Afro-American Art," "Afro-American Writers," "Contemporary Education of Afro-Americans," and "Black Psychology."[33] Between 1968 and 1975, over 500 academic programs or departments offering Black Studies courses were established in the 2,500 colleges and universities of the nation.[34] Courses and programs on Hispanics, Asian Americans, Native Americans, and women soon followed.

In 1971 Congress passed the Emergency School Aid and Quality Integrated Education Act, providing $500 million in 1972 and $1 billion in 1973 to local education agencies to help "overcome the adverse educational effects of minority group isolation."[35] In response to student and parent advocacy, a substantial number of elementary and secondary schools used these funds to implement ethnic study units or courses, allowing African American, Mexican American, and Puerto Rican students to study the history and culture of their ancestors. According to James Banks, a scholar and advocate of multicultural education, school districts sometimes responded with hastily conceived courses and employed individuals who were not well qualified to teach them. The majority of the study units and courses focused on a single ethnic group with Black Studies courses found in predominantly African American schools and Puerto Rican studies in schools that were predominantly Puerto Rican. It was generally assumed that each group only needed to learn about its own history and culture.[36]

In the early 1970s, many scholarly journals and popular media took notice of the ethnic pride and ethnic studies movements. Several journals devoted complete issues to ethnic matters—including *Phi Delta Kappan*, *Society*, *Antioch Review*, and *Instructional Technology*. Additionally, hundreds of magazines, newspapers, and journals featured articles on the growing ethnic studies movement. In 1971 the Ford Foundation announced that it would spend $100 million on minority and ethnic education, mainly at the university level. A portion of this money helped to stimulate the development of several grass-roots organizations and research groups, which then networked and became a driving force behind federal legislation providing financial support for ethnic studies.[37]

The National Ethnic Studies Assembly and other organizations lobbied for federal legislation that would provide more explicit and enduring support for ethnic studies than the Emergency Act mentioned above. A groundswell of support arose from ethnic and multicultural organizations around the country, and from some academics. Leading the opposition was a group calling itself The National Confederation of American Ethnic Groups, which argued that such a bill would increase divisiveness and revive historic hatreds.

The proponents managed to secure passage of the Ethnic Heritage Studies Act in 1972, which became Title IX of the Elementary and Secondary Education Act. It provided funding to communities and ethnic organizations for projects that would train educators and develop and disseminate curricular materials for ethnic heritage studies. Although the money distributed under the Act was always modest—just $2.3 million in the first year of funding—the Act was widely perceived as giving legitimacy to the contributions of minorities of color in the United States. It implied that the homogeneity of a "melting pot" approach to education was to be replaced with the diversity of a "salad bowl" approach. It also provided funding to multi-ethnic organizations, thereby laying the seeds for the subsequent development of multicultural education.[38]

At Mission High School in San Francisco, a tangential event sparked changes in the curriculum. In 1993 a school security guard who was popular among Hispanic students for establishing a Hispanic club and raising ethnic pride was suspended without pay for reasons that were never revealed. A crowd of over 200 students walked out of classes in protest and marched to the steps of the Board of Education. Once there, the protest became a boisterous rally for better education, with students demanding ethnic studies, more multicultural history, job training, and Spanish-speaking counselors. Using a megaphone, one student yelled, "We got messed up books in our school! We need more 'Raza' books!"[39] District officials stood by watching and listening from the edges of the crowd. Eleven students signed up to represent the protesters and meet with school administrators. A month later, students attended a school board meeting to comment on planned changes to the school curriculum that they had precipitated. The board announced Mission High would soon be offering new ethnic studies courses before and after school and more job-readiness and college-preparatory classes. Senior Ramon Gonzales told the board that he hoped the ethnic studies courses would be open to all students and not just students of certain ethnicities or races. Agreeing, a second senior explained, "If my peers become more culturally aware, they will become more tolerant of my culture." A third student urged that each culture's philosophical values be taught, "not just facts and figures," and the audience applauded. Following the meeting, the principal of Mission High told reporters, "The kids had legitimate complaints.... This was an attempt to respond."[40]

From Ethnic Studies to Multicultural Education

Several scholars and practitioners thought that ethnic studies were not sufficient to overcome the educational disadvantages of many low-income minority youth in K-12 schools. They urged the creation of a more explicit transitional bridge between minority ethnic heritages and the dominant culture. Geneva Gay, a scholar of multicultural education, indicates that most multicultural education proposals or programs have one or more of the following goals: the addition of formerly excluded histories and the correction of distorted ones, creation of a greater sense of self for those students who were formerly ignored, confrontation of prejudices and stereotypes that afflict society, the defusing of tensions among the various ethnic groups by teaching human relations skills, adaptation of curriculum content and pedagogies to the various cultural backgrounds of students so that all students have an equal chance to learn and succeed, and, ultimately, creation of a change process that influences changes in the rest of society and makes for a more equitable society.[41] A few advocates thought these goals could be accomplished within the school curriculum, but most thought that they would also require changes in the hiring and training of the teaching staff, arrangements for limited proficient English speakers, the décor of the school buildings, and the celebration of holidays.[42]

Project Reach

In the early 1970s, a young Gary Howard joined the Teacher Corps to make a contribution to the welfare of others. He had no prior training as a teacher but was given six weeks of "boot camp" preparation to get him started. During that training, two of his instructors were James A. Banks and Carl A. Grant, leading thinkers in the new multicultural education movement. Howard liked what they had to say. He was particularly impressed with Grant's recommendation that ethnic study courses focusing on one individual ethnic group be replaced with the study of all major racial and ethnic groups. Grant proposed that each group's history would be taught in the social studies and history courses, each group's literature would be taught in literature courses, and each group's contributions to the sciences and arts would be taught in those courses. Howard was also impressed with what Banks' called the "transformational" approach to multicultural education. As Howard understood it,

> This means that we work at undoing the power and privilege that have historically allowed the white (Eurocentric) perspective to dominate the construction of knowledge and the design of educational systems and practices.... This is when a 3rd grade teacher from Des Moines realizes that her approach to teaching about Thanksgiving has been entirely constructed from a white middle class perspective, and she goes back to transform her lesson using authentic information and perspectives she has now learned from Native American presenters. This is when a high school principal from Denver realizes that he has accepted as "normal" the fact that very few students of color are in the AP and Honors classes in his building. He goes back to his school excited to undo this de facto academic segregation.[43]

Howard thought multicultural education could reduce or eliminate racial and ethnic prejudice among whites in America. With funding from ESEA Title IVc (for innovative projects) and then from the Ethnic Heritage Studies Act, he developed Respecting Ethnic and Cultural Heritage (REACH), a school curriculum and teacher training program that reflected the ideas of Grant and Banks.

The REACH program focuses on developing awareness of one's own culture, multicultural awareness, and human relations skills. Materials and exercises have been developed for use from kindergarten through the twelfth grade. For instance, in kindergarten, students learn how a Native American baby is named and discuss the significance of various Native American names. Then the students are read a story about the naming of a child and afterwards draw a picture of the child's name. These exercises are intended to build not only listening, vocabulary, drawing skills, but to convey a respect and appreciation of various cultures.

Evaluation results showed REACH increased students' knowledge about various cultures and improved students' comfort when with students of different racial and ethnic groups.[44] The program was certified as effective by the U.S. Department of Education's National Diffusion Network, and it was implemented in a modest number of schools within each of the 50 states.

Project REACH faced one of its greatest challenges in the mid-1980s after Phyllis Schlafly published *Child Abuse in the Classroom*, a book highlighting the testimonies of parents and citizens at Department of Education hearings about proposed regulations under the Protection of Pupil Rights Amendment. This legislation required schools to seek written parental permission before schoolchildren could participate in any research that would acquire sensitive information, including critical appraisals of the students' family members. In this book, one person's testimony criticized the REACH program books, particularly the book on Native Americans, for it asked students "to go home and ask their parents about their beliefs about Indians, a definite violation of the.... Amendment."[45] After reading this, some parents from a school district in Washington State asked representatives from Schlafly's Eagle Forum to assist them in removing the REACH program from the district. In the following months, there were a series of community meetings and board reviews, after which the local School Board reaffirmed its support of the REACH program.[46]

The Sobol Task Force Report

Thomas Sobol's 1987 appointment as the New York State Commissioner of Education drew criticism from the state legislature's Black and Puerto Rican Caucus, which felt there were qualified minority candidates for the position who would have better addressed the state's weaknesses in educating minority students. In response to the criticism, Sobol appointed a Task Force on Minorities to assess how well the state curriculum, instructional materials, and school personnel policies reflected the pluralism of the state. Two years later, the task force released a report, "A Curriculum of Inclusion," which began with:

> African-Americans, Asian-Americans, Puerto Rican/Latinos and Native Americans have all been the victims of an intellectual and educational oppression that has characterized the culture and institutions of the United States and the European American world for centuries.[47]

The main findings of the task force were that the state's instructional materials bolstered respect and understanding of a multicultural society, but they still failed in "adequately and accurately reflecting the cultural experience in America." The report went on to recommend improvements in the state curriculum and staff development to increase the self-respect and self-esteem of minorities and to temper the "arrogant perspective" of children of European descent.[48]

The report drew a firestorm of criticism. Many considered it anti-white and inflammatory. Bill Honig, Superintendent of Education in California, said the report was "nothing but racism."[49] Some felt that the call for equally portraying the contributions of all racial and ethnic groups in American history would be distorting, since, however lamentable, most of "the major decisions have been made by white Christian men."[50]

Sobol asked Diane Ravitch, a historian and policy analyst, to comment on the report. She criticized the taskforce for viewing the curriculum only from the perspectives of racial and ethnic minorities, for incorrectly referring to all white people—whether they be Jewish or Russian or Italian—as Anglo-Saxons, and for "finding nothing in western history and white people but racism, greed, egoism, and intolerance." She challenged the claim that the Iroquois Indians' political system should be considered as having as much influence on the U.S. Constitution as the European Enlightenment. She also questioned whether a white-oriented curriculum accounts for African American and Hispanic minority students' often low achievement, asking, "If this is true, why do Asian American children outperform every other group in the population, including white children?"[51] Nevertheless, Ravitch thought that both cultural pluralism and a unifying "sense of an American community" should be provided in the education of all students.

Sobol pronounced the taskforce report to have been helpful. He asserted that the primary message was that "we should be more inclusive in teaching our history and culture," and he claimed that even most of the critics of the report agreed with that.[52]

California History Textbooks

In 1988 with Bill Honig as state superintendent of schools, California published a history and social science framework that was to guide curriculum, textbook adoption, and instruction in those subject areas.[53] The framework had 12 "strands" including "civic values," "economic literacy," "national identity," and "cultural literacy." A multicultural approach was reflected in the latter two strands.[54] While there had been the inevitable disagreements among the many experts involved, the *Framework* had not provoked major controversy during its development or after its publication. Then in 1990 as California tentatively decided to purchase social studies textbooks by Houghton-Mifflin, controversy erupted, with critics charging that the texts were not adequately multicultural. A few complained that the point of view of the narration implied that the readers were all descendents of immigrants, which was not true for those descended from Native Americans and most African Americans. African American critics insisted that the point of view of their enslaved ancestors be clearly distinguished from that of white ethnic groups. Stanford Professor Sylvia Wynter argued that the texts' treatment of African Americans would not foster a sense of empathy among students but rather one of "liberal pity" instead. One critic found a hand-drawn picture of an escaping slave with a whiplashed back that was supposed to evoke empathy but instead seemed, to her and her two teenage children, to be depicting the slave as an animal.[55] Other complaints were raised by several groups. Chinese Americans sought more coverage of their history. Muslims and Jews requested editorial revisions and corrections. Lesbians and gays sought inclusion.[56]

The adoption committee countered that the texts were a significant break from the past Euro-perspective, devoting much space to "world cultures, their history, achievements, and world view."[57] With few options to choose from and a general belief that the Houghton-Mifflin books were generally better than their predecessors, most school districts accepted them, but several did so with a qualifying statement they would have to supplement the books with other materials. The only districts to refuse the book were Ravenswood City and Oakland, both areas with large minority populations.[58]

The Literary Canon

The literary canon, the corpus of literature that scholars consider important for study by well-educated students, has long been debated. During the 1600s and 1700s, most American colleges taught only the Greek and Roman classics in the original languages, but by the early 1800s, despite impassioned resistance, English literature and then American literature gradually made their way into the college curriculums.[59] Since then, the debate has been about which works, whether classics or contemporary, are of such substantive and aesthetic merit that they should be read by all students.

The late 1960s and early 1970s saw the introduction of the first courses on African American literature and women's literature in universities and colleges. These courses suggested the literature of such authors was of merit. Subsequently, the major anthologies of literary works that were widely used in high school courses began adding material from a few black and women authors. For instance, Frederick Douglass's 1845 *Narrative of the Life of Frederick Douglas* and Kate Chopin's *The Awakening* were popular choices. Still, minorities of color and women remained marginally represented in the literary canon.[60]

Then, in 1982, Yale University undertook a project to examine the latest scholarship and its implications for the teaching of American literature. The resulting book, *Reconstructing American Literature*, presented a collection of syllabi for alternatives to the normal American literature courses.

According to the editor, Paul Lauter, the volume was supposed to serve as a tool "to change the teaching of American literature and, therefore, the definition of what we call American culture."[61] Lauter argues for "opening" the canon because the experiences students encounter in poems and books can influence their perception of life and thus their actions. He explains that if all one reads are works by white authors, the lives of people of color will remain marginalized while the lives of whites are central, and that the canonization process, by defining the "marginal" and "central" people, helps to decide who teaches, who studies, and "who has power in determining priorities in American colleges."[62]

Reconstructing American Literature was a prelude to the battle over opening the literary canon to minorities and women that would heat up in the mid-1980s. That battle was initially at the college level, advanced by professors who often had been involved in the fight for civil rights in the 1960s and 1970s and resisted by traditionalists. Later the battle moved to the high school and elementary school level.

In 1985 following considerable pressure from minority students, Stanford University modified a Eurocentric "Western Culture" course required of all students, changing it into a course on "Culture, Ideas, and Values" with more writings by authors of color. This was the first time that a prominent university *required* a multicultural course of all students.

One of the African American graduates of Stanford, Steve Phillips, later won election to the school board of the San Francisco Unified School District (SFUSD). The District required all high school students to read ten books that were chosen from a district reading list: *Romeo and Juliet, Canterbury Tales, Huckleberry Finn*, four chosen by their teacher, and three of their own choosing. At a March 1998 school board meeting, Phillips and another African American board member quietly proposed a plan to require seven of the ten books be by authors of color. There was no response in the meeting, but when the press reported the proposal there was strong public reaction. Well-known local authors had mixed opinions on the proposal.[63] One citizen's letter to the editor of a local paper called the proposal "the worst kind of Hitlerian racism." A second urged that the school board should be "discharged immediately as dangerous and illiterate fascists." A third charged the proposal was an effort "to push aside European-American children."[64] Many teachers opposed the proposal and took it as an affront to their professionalism. Reina Bautista, an English teacher in the district for 25 years, said that by making such a proposal, the board members were saying, "teachers are not good judges of what's worth teaching."[65] Several teachers also questioned the board's awareness of what books were being read in the classroom, with one explaining, "Students already spend their entire 10th-grade English class studying 'The Ethnic Experience in Literature'," which could include works such as Toni Morrison's *The Bluest Eye* or *Sula*, Richard Wright's *Black Boy*, and

Maxine Hong Kingston's *The Woman Warrior*, among others. Other teachers regarded selecting books for students based on the author's ethnicity a bad notion. Eugene Mattingly, a veteran English teacher, stated that "To pretend that kids have a problem with reading because they don't like the ethnicity of a book is either naïve or cynical."[66] Student reactions were mixed. Some students opposed the proposal because, they argued, by not reading the traditional European classics, they would be less competitive when seeking admission to college. Others, like Fatima Matuu, liked the idea of reading more books by authors of color because it would give students a broader perspective and helped them to identify with the tribulations of other cultures.[67]

Initially, most of the school board seemed to support the proposal. As controversy arose, Phillips and his colleagues reduced their proposal from the original seven books to four books. District superintendent Bill Rojas opposed that policy and a local newspaper poll found 94 percent said "no" to the question, "Should there be a diversity quota for high school books?"[68] Finally the board adopted a policy requiring that one of the ten books had to be by an author of color. SFUSD is thought to be the first school district in the nation to have established such a requirement.

Bilingual Education

Despite the long heritage of bilingual education in the United States, in 1855 the California Bureau of Instruction mandated that all classes be conducted in English. In 1870 the Texas legislature passed a law requiring the same, and then in 1918 passed another law making it a criminal offense to use any language of instruction other than English.[69]

The Immigration Act of 1965 reopened the doors to immigration that had been almost closed since World War I. Two years after passage, Senator Ralph Yarborough of Texas, aware of the strains on schools caused by the new influx of Spanish-speaking immigrants, introduced a bill to give federal assistance to school districts with limited English learners. The bill recommended, among other things, "the teaching of Spanish as a native language, the teaching of English as a second language, and programs designed to give these students an appreciation of their ancestral language and culture." [70] Even though this particular bill was limited to native Spanish speakers, another 37 bills followed it, addressing other children with limited English proficiency. All of these bills were consolidated into what became known as the Bilingual Education Act of 1968 (also known as Title VII of the Elementary and Secondary Act of 1968). The legislation recognized the unique needs faced by non-English speaking students and provided funds for innovative programs to meet those needs among economically disadvantaged students. It also reinforced the concept that language is an important component of multicultural education.[71]

The 1973 U.S. Supreme Court's decision in *Lau v. Nichols* gave a boost to bilingual education. The plaintiffs, a group of non-English speaking Chinese students, charged that the San Francisco Unified School District had violated their rights, failing to provide them with special language assistance needed to benefit from their education. Instead the district had merely placed them in classes taught in English, leaving them to learn the best they could in a language they did not understand—a practice often referred to as English immersion. The Supreme Court ruled that *identical* education for all does not constitute *equal* education under the Civil Rights Act of 1964 and that schools failing to provide non-English speaking students with a "meaningful opportunity" to participate in their education were in violation of the Act.[72]

Two different instructional approaches soon became widely used to provide the mandated services and continue to be used today. English as a Second Language (ESL) provided intensive instruction in speaking, reading, and writing English. The language is taught much as French or Spanish is taught to native English speaking children. Students are either placed in ESL classes for a year or two and then placed in regular classes, or they are immediately placed in regular classes and given ESL instruction simultaneously—before or after the regular school day or when pulled out of their regular class for an hour or so each day. In contrast, the other instructional approach, Bilingual Education, begins instruction in all subjects in the child's native language and simultaneously teaches English. As rudimentary English skills develop, both English and the native language are used for instruction. As proficiency in English is acquired, there are two options. One is to place the students in regular classrooms with the instruction given in English (this is called "transitional bilingual education"). The other is to keep the children in classes where both their native language and English are used for instruction, building more advanced skills in both languages (this is called "maintenance bilingual education").

Afro-Centrism

Some minority educators were not satisfied with multicultural education and advocated ethnocentric education, focusing primarily on their own ethnic heritage. Afro-centric education is the most common example but there have been examples by other ethnic groups.

Calls for Afro-centric education go back at least to Dubois and Woodson. According to Katrina Hazzard-Gordon, Afro-centrism is an "Africa-centered world view ... [that] seeks to include African contributions to the world alongside, and sometimes in place of, those of Europe. It challenges the Western historical perception of European pre-eminence in art, culture, science, mathematics, religion and philosophy."[73] Molefi Asante, echoing the words of Woodson, explains the purpose of

Afro-centric education is a repositioning of the centrality of the African experience in the lives of African Americans who have been dislocated both psychologically and physically by European domination of the curriculum. Malcolm X and the Black Panthers also encouraged similar approaches. In an Afro-centric school, students devote heavy attention to African and African American history, read mostly literature by African American authors, study Swahili or other African languages, learn about African American art and music, and participate in African and African American celebrations. Afro-centric schools sometimes draw on Cheikh Anta Diop's *The African Origin of Civilization: Myth and Reality*, which claims Egyptians were an Ethiopian tribe and thus Africans were at the center of world developments. Most archaeologists and historians think Egyptians were a mix of African and Middle Eastern peoples, and in any case, the culture of ancient Egypt differed markedly from those of the rest of Africa.[74] Afro-centric schools also sometimes make use of Asa Hilliard III's *African-American Baseline Essays*, a collection of essays about the African and African American contributions to the world in mathematics, language arts, art, science and technology, music, and social studies, which has come under criticism for historical inaccuracies. Gilbert T. Sewall, editor of the American Textbook Council Social Studies Review, charges that many of the claims in the *Essays* are unverifiable or false.[75] Despite the controversy, within three years of their publication, the city of Atlanta had adopted the *Essays* as a resource document, and Indianapolis, Washington, D.C., Prince George's County, Md., and Detroit (among other cities) were using it as a model to develop programs in their schools.[76]

While Afro-centric education is no more multicultural than the Anglo-centric education that predominated in the United States for three centuries until the 1960s, it has served as a counterpoise. It has allowed multicultural education to become a moderate compromise between the two extremes, which has wide appeal in principle, even if eliciting disputes over the details. The forgers of the compromise include minority scholars and educators as well as those of European descent.[77]

Opposition to Multicultural Education

Multicultural education has been hotly debated throughout much of the country. There are four main arguments raised against it: that it adds marginal figures to history and marginal works to the literary canon, that it presumes all cultures are good and glosses over their shortcomings, that it engages in therapy rather than intellectual discipline, and that it could disunite the country.

Alvin Schmidt's review of a wide variety of texts, including elementary and secondary textbooks, found that several minority figures have been added to the textbooks with little historical evidence that they existed or did what was described, and that several persons of importance to America's history have been displaced by the addition of persons of color and women of lesser historical significance.[78] Critics have suggested that a focus on lesser, or at least unconventional historical figures and literature could impair students' ability to compete for admission to selective colleges and success in college coursework.

Multicultural education has been criticized for "cultural relativism," the presumption that all cultures are of equal merit and deserve equal respect. Critics argue there are absolute standards of moral conduct and cultures that violate them are inferior, that industrial societies are more advanced than non-industrial ones, and that democracy is the only admirable form of governance. They insist students should be taught this and nothing contrary. Other less dogmatic critics are concerned that the cultural relativism creates pressures to present all cultures in only a good light, glossing over the undesirable features of each. Schmidt found that new history books tend to avoid discussion of the less admirable aspects of the heritages of minorities of color (such as the human sacrifices and cannibalism of some Indian tribes).

Multicultural education's aim to develop minority students' self-image and ethnic pride, with the expectation that it will help them achieve success academically, socially, and intellectually, is derided by several critics as educational therapy. Arthur Schlesinger, the historian, claims that in multicultural education, history and literature are no longer taught as "intellectual disciplines, but ... therapies whose function is to raise minority self-esteem."[79] Ravitch claims self-esteem does not come from studying heroic figures of one's cultural heritage but rather from hard work and success.[80] She also asserts that developing self-esteem has little to do with the school curriculum, and much to do with the influences of society, mass media, community, and family.

Perhaps the gravest concern about multicultural education is that it will exacerbate divisions within the country rather than heal them. Schlesinger's book *The Disuniting of America* applauds the addition to the curriculum of the "shamefully overdue recognition to the achievements of minorities"[81] but argues that a monocultural model is a crucial aspect of the American education system, for it cultivates unity among diverse citizens. He claims that when multiculturalism bolsters and celebrates ethnic identities and origins, the result is a separatism that cultivates prejudices, exaggerates differences, and roils antagonisms. If these "separatist tendencies go on unchecked," he continues, "the result can only be the fragmentation, resegregation, and tribalization of American life."[82] He suggests multicultural education could balkanize the United States much as Yugoslavia had been balkanized.

SUCCESS OF THE REFORM EFFORT

It is premature to judge the success of the multicultural education reform effort, which is younger than the other reform efforts discussed in the prior chapters. Nevertheless, multicultural education has established trends that are worth noting.

According to James A. Banks, the implementation of multicultural education requires that several "institutional changes must be made, including changes in the curriculum; the teaching materials; teaching and learning styles; the attitudes, perceptions, and behaviors of teachers and administrators; and the goals, norms, and culture of the school."[83] There is good evidence that significant changes have been widely implemented in the curriculum and teaching materials, in the accommodation of children's language differences, and in the preparation of teachers. All three will be discussed below.

As the ethnic studies movement gained strength in the 1970s, school districts established ethnic studies courses on the Native American, African, and Hispanic heritages in America.[84] Beginning in the mid-1980s, school boards around the country started adopting policies favoring multicultural curricula in schools. Districts in Washington, Alaska, Pennsylvania, Colorado, the District of Columbia, Maryland, California, Ohio, Minnesota, New York, Nebraska, and Massachusetts all instituted multicultural curricula.[85] By 1994, fourteen states were known to expect their schools to have multicultural curricula.[86] A 1992 study examining the curricula of the 28 largest school districts in the United States found that 20 of those districts had multicultural curricula. Fifteen were urban school districts and five were suburban ones. Half of the eight districts without multicultural curricula were planning to adopt them.[87]

One study of high school American history textbooks found that in the 1950s the coverage of African American figures was only 0.1 percent that of whites, but in the 1980s it was eight percent. Further, the coverage of women went from 3.8 percent that of men to 10.3 percent over the same time period. The nature of the portrayal of minorities of color and women also became more positive. In the 1980s, fifty-seven percent of the portrayals of black women were positive, as were 45 percent of black men, 45 percent of white women, and 33 percent of white men. The researchers concluded,

> American history textbook authors transformed the texts from scarcely mentioning blacks in the 1940s to containing a substantial multicultural (and feminist) component in the 1980s. The changes began during the 1960s, accelerated during the 1970s, and became the settled norm of the 1980s.[88]

The following is an example of the nature of the changes made in social studies textbooks.

My Country Fifth grade social studies text published in 1947 by the State of California	*United States and Its Neighbors* Fifth grade social studies text published in 1993 by Macmillan/McGraw-Hill
The Negroes were brought from Africa and sold to the people of our country in early times. After a while there came to be thousands and thousands of these Negro slaves. Most of them were found in the southern states. On the southern plantations, where tobacco and cotton and rice were grown, they were worked away quite cheerfully. In time many people came to think that it was wrong to own slaves. Some of them said that all the Negro slaves should be freed. Some of the people who owned slaves became angry at this. They said that the black people were better off as slaves in America than they would have been as wild savages in Africa. Perhaps this was true, as many of the slaves had snug cabins to live in, plenty to eat, and work that was not too hard for them to do. Most of the slaves seemed happy and contented. ------------------ Perhaps the most fun the little [white] masters and mistresses have comes when they are free to play with the little colored boys and girls. Back of the big house stand rows of small cabins. In these cabins live the families of Negro slaves. The older colored people work on the great farm or help about the plantation home. The small black boys and girls play about the small houses. They are pleased to have the white children come to play with them.[89]	After 1670 all Africans brought to Virginia were enslaved for life. Their children were also enslaved. This change came about because planters realized that they could make more money with slave labor than with indentured servants. Servants could leave after a few years. Planters could force enslaved people to work for life. ------------------ Enslaved Africans were treated as property. They had to work from the time they were six until old age. As one captive African put it, 'Slave young, slave long.' Owners also broke up enslaved families by selling a father, mother, or child. Despite their separation, parents often walked miles to visit their children. ------------------ Planters only wanted captives who worked hard and obeyed orders. Those who did not were punished. William Byrd's diary reveals that he whipped captives for such things as spilling water on a couch or 'doing nothing.' Enslaved Africans fought back at every chance. Field slaves did work called 'eye service'—working only when the overseer was watching. And in 1776 an enslaved woman in Maryland burned down the owner's big house, tobacco house, and other buildings. Still others broke their tools or worked very slowly. Some also tried to escape.[90]

Another review of textbooks also found multicultural changes in U.S. history, world history, science, and math texts. For example, *Concepts in Science*, a textbook from the 1960s, shows only one drawing of an adult

African American, several brown-skinned children, and no Asian Americans. Two decades later, the science textbook *Science* (1987), shows "many drawings and photographs of children and adult scientists with African American, Native American, Middle-Eastern and Far-East Asian features."[91]

Not all the studies of textbook changes have been favorable. After analyzing 41 texts used in elementary schools around the United States during the 1990s, the authors of one study concluded that most text changes were cosmetic, while the more substantial additions of diverse perspectives and experiences were lacking.[92]

In 1995-96, a national survey of 2,474 students in grades 7-12 found that 61 percent disagreed with the statement that their "school does not offer classes that teach students about the history and culture of people who came to the U.S. from different parts of the world, such as Asia, India, Africa or South America." African American students were only slightly less likely to disagree than white students. Forty-five percent of students said that schools offered "the right amount of emphasis" on multicultural education, while 28 percent said there was not enough, and 11 percent said there was too much. Seventy-one percent of students indicated they were "somewhat" or "very" interested in learning more about events and holidays celebrated around the world.[93]

Like the textbooks, the literary canon has been influenced by multiculturalism, although not as much as multicultural advocates would like and not without some criticism. The College Board, which has influence over high school curriculum because of its SAT tests, recommends 100 "great books" to be read. In 2003, twenty-seven are by minorities of color or by women.[94]

Arthur Applebee's 1991 survey of secondary schools throughout the United States, with 322 respondents, found that 16 percent of the most widely assigned literary works were by nonwhite authors and 21 percent were by women. Applebee wrote that although changes had been made in the canon, they were not "sufficient to reflect the multiculturalist heritage of the United States."[95] Others have suggested that the actual percentages are higher than Applebee found, because there is less consensus about which works of minority authors are of most importance, and thus those works are less likely to be among the most widely assigned even though they are used by a moderate portion of schools.[96] Seven years later, when Applebee was asked to give his opinion on the current status of the literary canon, he said there had been "modest" increases in diversity but extensive adoption of a multicultural canon had not happened yet. In addition, he said criticism of multicultural education had led "some teachers to self-censor and avoid changing the literature they use for fear of criticism."[97] In 2003, Applebee, referring to a few recent local and regional studies, concluded there had been further diversification of the literary canon but it was "relatively limited."[98]

There is disagreement on what constitutes equitable inclusion of minorities of color in textbooks and the literary canon. Some suggest that because 40 percent of America's students are minority, that is the percentage to aim for. Others point out that minorities of color comprised a considerably smaller percentage of the population through most of the history of the United States and a far smaller percentage of published authors, and thus 40 percent would misrepresent their contributions. Some retort that the gross under-representation of the past is best corrected by a period of over-representation. Still other people are seriously disturbed by any "quotas," saying the decisions should be made on the basis of the quality of the contributions.

In 1997, the number of American students with limited English proficiency was 3.5 million.[99] About 14 percent of students with limited English proficiency received bilingual education services under the federal legislation. In 1998, 11 states mandated bilingual education, three states prohibited it, and 27 states provided funding that could be used for bilingual education.[100]

The Bilingual Education Act of 1968 was reauthorized repeatedly but the emphasis changed some over the years. The 1978 reauthorization expanded eligibility from non English speakers to those with limited English proficiency, but it also required that the services focus on facilitating a "transition" to English proficiency, downplaying the development of literacy in the native language. Subsequently, the 1984 reauthorization again allowed for some native language "maintenance" activities. Federal funding for bilingual education was always modest, and reached only $448 million in 2001, an all-time high in constant dollars.[101]

In that same year, however, the Bilingual Education Act was replaced with the English Language Acquisition, Language Enhancement, and Academic Advancement Act, which was Title III of the No Child Left Behind Act. This essentially terminated overt federal support for Bilingual education, although some Title III money probably continued to be used by schools for such educational services.

Critics of bilingual education have asserted that efforts aimed at students with limited English proficiency should use the English as a Second Language (ESL) approach, teaching the students English proficiency as quickly as possible, so that they can then benefit from regular classes. Although ESL usually results in more rapid development of English skills than does bilingual education, it either delays the start of academic instruction (if the ESL is provided first), or it forces students of limited English proficiency into regular classes before they are fully capable of benefiting from these classes (while they simultaneously receive ESL outside of the classes). There has been some determined opposition against bilingual education, and in 1998 California passed "Proposition 227: English Language in Public Schools," which essentially mandated, with a few exceptions, ESL instruction for all students with limited English proficiency. The evaluation evidence suggests that bilingual education has not been substantially more effective than ESL in respect to boosting standardized achievement scores of limited English proficient students, but it also does not support the opposition's contention that ESL is more effective.[102] Bilingual education, on the other hand, also aims to develop native language skills, something that ESL ignores. Despite the opposition, bilingual education continues to be used in parts of the country.

Professional teacher education organizations have been strong supporters of the multicultural education movement for many years. In 1969 the American Association of Colleges for Teacher Education published "Teachers of the Real World," urging teachers to prepare themselves to teach diverse students. Three years later the Association issued a policy statement titled "No One Model American: A Statement on Multicultural Education."[103] That inspired the National Council for Accreditation of Teacher Education in 1978 to include a statement on multicultural education as part of its accreditation criteria for teacher education programs. In 1981 the statement became a standard: "The institution provides for multicultural education in its teacher education curricula, including both the general and professional studies components."[104]

In 1972 the National Council for Teachers of English passed a resolution advising testing organizations that "questions about American Literature should require the examinees to demonstrate knowledge of the literature of racial and ethnic minorities in America."[105] Three years later, the Council passed a resolution urging publishers of textbooks and other study materials to "accurately and sensitively depict Mexican American, Asian American, Afro-American, Native American, and other indigenous minority cultures and traditions...."[106] Then, in 1986, as a few publishers were moving to drop minority authors from their anthologies and publication lists for the school market, the Council issued another resolution urging publishers "to recognize that the English profession ... needs the continuing availability of materials of all cultures in order to expose students to the whole literary and language heritage of our society...."[107]

Efforts to prepare teachers for multicultural education have not been without problems and limitations. One scholar, after analyzing the multicultural education standards of National Council for the Accreditation of Teacher Education (NCATE) and the National Council for the Social Studies (NCSS), suggested that multicultural education is like "the tale of the four blind people being asked to describe the elephant. The response one receives will depend on which person is asked, and what part of the phenomenon has been experienced."[108] She notes there is considerable vagueness in the NCATE text on multicultural education and "it is obvious that multicultural education in teacher education is a hit-or-miss affair."[109] Donna Gollnick, senior vice-president of NCATE has acknowledged that the preservice preparation of teachers for multicultural education is often inadequate.[110] For instance, in 1997, a study at one midwestern university that had met NCATE standards, concluded "students in the study [had] not captured even the most basic tenets of what it means to be a multicultural educator," because of "a lack of articulation of issues of diversity throughout the teacher education program."[111]

The problems in teacher preparation have been caused by varying definitions of multicultural education, the tendency of college programs to present multicultural education in one course rather than infusing it throughout the preparation of teachers, and the large portion of aspiring teachers who come from white middle class backgrounds and with little exposure to multiculturalism.[112] Sonia Nieto and many other minority scholars believe that development of multicultural teachers requires the teachers to become multicultural people. She suggests one must not only acquire content knowledge of other cultures but also confront his or her personal biases and racism because these aspects of a person's personality are deeply rooted and affect one's teaching.[113]

The accumulated evidence is overwhelming that American public education is substantially more multicultural today than it was 40 years ago. Minorities are depicted more in the textbooks, their oppression and their contributions to the country are discussed more in the history courses, their literary works are more likely to be included in the canon to which students are exposed, bilingual education is now available for some students with limited English proficiency, and many aspiring teachers now receive an introduction to multicultural education. Despite the progress, many advocates of multicultural education feel the progress has been limited, slow, and inadequate, adopting bits and pieces of multiculturalism but not creating schools that are multicultural in purposes, organization, and processes. The greatest disappointment is on the part of those who desired a "reconstructionist" form of multiculturalism in which the schools, staff, students, and community would band together to forge social change.[114]

Achievement of Goals

Multicultural education has three broad goals—to preserve and pass down the ethnic heritage of the country's diverse students, boost the educational success of minorities of color, and foster racial and ethnic tolerance within the country.

Multicultural education has clearly contributed to the first goal by spurring scholarship on the history and cultural heritages of the many American peoples. For instance, the editor of the *Harvard Guide to Afro-American History* identified over 200 books and 1,200 articles dealing with African Americans during the period 1765-1830 that had been written in the three decades following 1965.[115] In addition, many public schools are now teaching part of the legacy of Native Americans, African Americans, Mexican Americans, and Asian Americans.

Assessing whether multicultural education has boosted the educational achievement of minority students of color is difficult. No national evaluations of the impacts of multicultural education have been conducted. A report of a study by the Council for Great City Schools, "Beating the Odds III," used state mandated achievement test data to examine achievement trends in urban school districts. It found that between 1994 and 2002 the achievement gaps of Hispanic and African American students when compared to white students had narrowed moderately in the 59 studied urban districts. The gap was found to have narrowed as a result of minority student achievement gains, not white student achievement declines.[116] That may have been partly due to multicultural education, because urban districts have large minority populations and many have implemented multicultural education. Nevertheless, as Chapter 7 indicated, at the close of the 20th century, average minority student achievement in reading, mathematics, and science was still substantially below that of white students nationally, and many worry whether even white achievement is up to the levels necessary for the future of the country.

On the other hand, it is clear that African American educational attainment has advanced substantially over the last three decades of the 20th century. The percentage of young adults who have completed high school rose from 58 percent in 1970 to 87 percent in 2000.[117] Between 1975 and 2000, the percentage of African Americans ages 18 to 24 who were enrolled in colleges and universities rose from 20 to 31 percent.[118] This might be because of multicultural education, but it could also be due to other factors such as compensatory education, changes in consciousness resulting from the Civil Rights movement, and higher education's efforts to attract a more diverse student body. Hispanics have not made similar advances in higher education. The data series do not report rates for Native Americans and Asian Americans.

Another goal of multicultural education is to improve students' racial and ethnic tolerance and respect. In 1986 Los Angeles implemented a "Multicultural Awareness" course. A few years later, racial violence erupted at several of the high schools. Responding to questions about the violence, several students noted that some of their classmates had mistaken lessons on ethnic pride for ethnic chauvinism.[119] One student in a school where Hispanic and black students fought the year before explained it this way: "They teach you that you have to identify with your own group.... Then they tell you to go out and mix."[120] Esther Taira, the designer of the course, has said that she would now develop the course differently—instead of emphasizing the similarities between cultural groups, she would have students identify and discuss their differences, to establish bridges between them.[121]

At Prospect Middle School in Pittsburgh, which reportedly had one of the most comprehensive adoptions of multicultural education in 1989, there was a dramatic drop in racial clashes during the first year.[122] A student survey asked if students agreed with the statement "Black and White students want to work together in this school." Eighty-five percent of sixth graders agreed during the first year of implementation, but that dropped to 79 and 54 percent in the following years, purportedly because of subsequent staffing problems.[123]

There is evidence that American society is becoming more tolerant and appreciative of various cultures, and that may be partly because of multicultural education. National surveys taken in 1987 and 1999 found the percentage of Americans agreeing with the statement "I don't have much in common with other races" declined from 23 percent to 12 percent.[124] The same survey found a 25 percentage point increase in the approval of interracial dating, with 73 percent approval in 1999. A 1980 Gallup poll found that only 17 percent of teenagers (not including Hispanics) had dated someone racially or ethnically different from them. In 1997, however, asking a slightly different question about having gone out with someone of a different race or ethnic group, the poll found that *57 percent* of those who have dated responded affirmatively.[125] On viewing these statistics, Elijah Anderson, a sociologist and ethnographer at the University of Pennsylvania, said, "For a lack of a better term, there is a kind of 'de-racialization' of American society hinted at in these statistics."[126] Analysis of data from the 2000 General Social Survey found that "the youngest cohort, those less than thirty years old, report the greatest acceptance of racial and ethnic minorities and the most contact with them, while the oldest cohort, those sixty-five and over, are the least tolerant and have the least contact."[127]

Unintended Side Effects

A few adverse side effects of multicultural education have been discussed above. In the effort to represent minorities in American history, errors have been introduced in some materials, and several historical figures of modest importance have displaced others of greater significance to the country's development. In addition, some early programs may have unintentionally exacerbated racial friction within schools. The fear that multicultural education would disunite America, however, has not been realized, judging by racial attitudes and inter-racial dating.

WAS MULTICULTURAL EDUCATION INEVITABLE?

Repeatedly, through America's history, white ethnic groups have aggressively sought inclusion of their cultures in the public schools. Then in the latter third of the 20th century minorities of color, having successfully broken the shackles of unconstitutional oppression, sought the same inclusion. Multicultural education is inevitable in a truly democratic country populated by long resident Native Americans and Mexicans Americans, by descendents of African slaves, and by immigrants from many nations.

FUTURE OF THE REFORM

Unless the 14th and 15th amendments are repealed, or immigration is curtailed and intermarriage becomes so common that racial and ethnic distinctions fade, moderate forms of multicultural education are likely to continue well into the future. Conflicts over multicultural education will also continue, as conflict is inherent in a diverse democratic society. For instance, soon after the September 11, 2001 terrorist attacks on America, several advocates urged expanded multicultural education with more emphasis on Islam and middle-eastern history, and critics derided that as absurd and instead urged more teaching of patriotism, civics, and American history.[128]

Advocates of multiculturalism fear that it has been losing support since the mid-1990s.[129] Elimination of the Bilingual Education Act in 2001 has had both symbolic and financial consequences.

The accountability reform movement that began in the mid 1980s is perceived to be a threat because it emphasizes the academic achievement that is measured on standardized achievement tests. Accountability will not be a barrier to the inclusion of minorities in textbooks and the literary canon, provided the tests include such content, but multicultural education's emphasis on building minority students' ethnic awareness and on improving inter-group relations is given no priority in the accountability movement, which will be discussed in Chapter 10.

The growing interest in school choice is also feared to be a threat to multicultural education. It need not be, for states have long exercised control over minimum standards for private education, and they could insist on textbooks that portray the various racial and ethnic groups of the country, on exposure to a multicultural literary canon, and on the teaching of inter-group respect and communication. Nevertheless, part of the rationale for choice is to allow families to self-select the educational approach that they desire. That could result in increased racial and ethnic isolation in schools and more ethno-centric schools—Anglo-centric ones, Afro-centric ones, and Islam-centric ones—rather than multicultural schools. The choice reform movement will be discussed in Chapter 10.

---

[1] Quoted in Jonathan Zimmerman, "Storm over the Schoolhouse: Exploring Popular Influences Upon the American Curriculum, 1890-1941," *Teachers College Record* 100 (Spring 1999): 605.

[2] Joel Spring, *The American School: 1642-1996*, 4th ed. (New York: McGraw-Hill, 1997), 16.

[3] Joel Spring, *The American School: 1642-1996*, 4th ed. (New York: McGraw-Hill, 1997), 16.

[4] James Crawford, *Bilingual Education: History, Politics, Theory and Practice*, 4th ed. (Los Angeles, CA: Bilingual Educational Services, 1999), 3-4.

[5] Lawrence P. Crouchett, "The Development of the Sentiment for Ethnic Studies in American Education" (Paper presented at the annual meeting of the Pacific Coast Regional Conference on English in the Two-Year College, Santa Cruz, CA, 9-10 November 1973).

[6] 268 U.S. 510 (1925).

[7] Richard Pratte, *The Public School Movement* (New York: David McKay Company, 1973), 64.

[8] David B. Tyack, ed. *Turning Points in American Educational History* (Waltham, MA: Blaisdell Publishing, 1967), 229.

[9] Jonathan Zimmerman, "Each 'Race' Could Have Its Heroes Sung: Ethnicity and the History Wars in the 1920s," *The Journal of American History* 87 (June 2000): 93-94.

[10] Jonathan Zimmerman, "Each 'Race' Could Have Its Heroes Sung: Ethnicity and the History Wars in the 1920s," *The Journal of American History* 87 (June 2000): 103-104.

[11] Jonathan Zimmerman, "Each 'Race' Could Have Its Heroes Sung: Ethnicity and the History Wars in the 1920s," *The Journal of American History* 87 (June 2000): 94, 103.

[12] Jonathan Zimmerman, "Storm over the Schoolhouse: Exploring Popular Influences Upon the American Curriculum, 1890-1941," *Teachers College Record* 100 (Spring 1999): 607.

[13] Jonathan Zimmerman, "Each 'Race' Could Have Its Heroes Sung: Ethnicity and the History Wars in the 1920s," *The Journal of American History* 87 (June 2000): 92.

[14] David B. Tyack, *The One Best System: A History of American Urban Education* (Cambridge, MA: Harvard University Press, 1974), 106-107.

[15] David B. Tyack, *The One Best System: A History of American Urban Education* (Cambridge, MA: Harvard University Press, 1974), 108-109.

[16] 262 U.S. 390 (1923).

[17] U.S. Department of Commerce, Census Bureau, *Historical Statistics of the United States: Colonial Times to 1957* (Washington DC: U.S. Government Printing Office, 1961), 56.

[18] See: Central Michigan University, Clarke Historical Library, "Indian Treaties: Their Ongoing Importance to Michigan Residents: Federal Education Policy & Off-Reservation Schools: 1870-1933," undated [accessed August 16, 2003 at www.lib.cmich.edu/clarke/indian/treaty education.htm]; Matt Kelly, "American Indian Boarding Schools: 'That Hurt Never Goes Away'," *CNEWS*, 28 April 1999, [accessed August 16, 2003 at www.canoe.ca/CNEWSFeatures9904/28_indians.html]; Jon Reyhner, "Changes in American Indian Education: A Historical Retrospective for Educators in the United States" *ERIC Digest* (April 1989), 1-2 [ERIC Document ED314228]; Joel Spring, *Deculturalization and the Struggle for Equality: A Brief History of the Education of Dominated Cultures in the United States* (Boston: McGraw Hill, 2001), 28-31.

[19] Joel Spring, *Deculturalization and the Struggle for Equity*, 3rd ed. (Boston: McGraw-Hill, 2001), 30-32.

[20] Guadalupe San Miguel, Jr, *"Let All of Them Take Heed": Mexican Americans and the Campaign for Educational Equality in Texas, 1910-1981* (Austin, TX: University of Texas Press, 1987) 33.

[21] See: Leonard Pitt, *The Decline of the Californios: A Social History of the Spanish-Speaking Californians: 1846-1890* (Berkeley, CA: University of California Press, 1966), 225-226; and Guadalupe San Miguel, Jr, *"Let All of Them Take Heed": Mexican Americans and the Campaign for Educational Equality in Texas, 1910-1981* (Austin, TX: University of Texas Press, 1987) 6-10.

[22] U.S. Commission on Civil Rights, *Toward Quality Education for Mexican Americans: Report VI: Mexican American Education Study* (Washington DC: author, 1974).

[23] Joel Spring, *Deculturalization and the Struggle for Equality: A Brief History of the Education of Dominated Cultures in the United States* (Boston: McGraw Hill, 2001), 65-66.

[24] U.S Department of Commerce, Census Bureau, *Current Population Reports, Series P-23-206, Profile of the Foreign-Born Population in the United States: 2000* (Washington DC: U.S. Government Printing Office, 2001), 2, 10 [available online: http://www.census.gov/prod/2002pubs/ p23-206.pdf].

[25] Lisa W. Foderaro, "The New Immigrants: Reshaping the Region," *The New York Times*, 7 December 1991, Section 1:1

[26] Bartley L. McSwine, "The Educational Philosophy of W.E.B DuBois," (Champaign, IL: Philosophy of Education Society, 1998. [available online: http://www.ed.uiuc.edu/EPS/PES-yearbook/1998/mcswine.html].

[27] Daniel Schugurensky, "In 'The Mis-education of the Negro', Carter Woodson Outlines the Basis for Afrocentric Education" in *History of Education: Selected Moments of the 20th Century* by Daniel Schugurensky (Toronto, Canada: Ontario Institute for Studies In Education, 2002), [Retrieved August 22, 2003 at http://fcis.oise.utoronto.ca/~daniel_schugurensky/assignment1/1933woodson.html]

[28] Lawrence H. Fuchs, *The American Kaleidoscope: Race, Ethnicity, and the Civic Culture* (Hanover, NH: The University Press of New England, 1990), 187.

[29] Quoted in Ronald Kronish, "Horace M. Kallen and John Dewey on Cultural Pluralism and Jewish Education," in *The Legacy of Horace M. Kallen*, ed. Milton R. Konvitz (Cranbury, NJ: Associated University Presses, 1987), 94-99, pg. 95.

[30] John Dewey, *Democracy and Education* (New York: Free Press, 1916), 83 and 87.

[31] Ronald Kronish, "Horace M. Kallen and John Dewey on Cultural Pluralism and Jewish Education," in *The Legacy of Horace M. Kallen*, ed. Milton R. Konvitz (Cranbury, NJ: Associated University Presses, 1987), 94-99. pg. 97.
[32] Claudine Michel and Jacqueline Bobo, eds., *Black Studies: Current Issues, Enduring Questions* (Dubuque, IA: Kendall/Hunt, 2001), 10.
[33] Sidney F. Walton, Jr. *The Black Curriculum: Developing a Program in Afro-American Studies* (East Palo Alto, CA: Black Liberation Publishers), 128-129, 131-132.
[34] See: Claudine Michel and Jacqueline Bobo, eds., *Black Studies: Current Issues, Enduring Questions* (Dubuque, IA: Kendall/Hunt, 2001), 10. U.S. Department of Education, National Center for Education Statistics, *Digest of Education Statistics: 2001* (Washington DC: U.S. Government Printing Office, 2002), 205.
[35] Raymond H. Giles, Jr., *Black Studies Programs in Public Schools* (New York: Praeger, 1974), 5.
[36] James Banks, *Multiethnic Education: Practices and Promise*, Fastback 87 (Bloomington, IN: Phi Delta Kappa Educational Foundation, 1977), 14.
[37] James M. Anderson, "Government Support of Ethnicity" (Ph.D. diss., University of Michigan, 1978), 101-103.
[38] James M. Anderson, "Government Support of Ethnicity" (Ph.D. diss., University of Michigan, 1978), 103-105, 9-10, 107, 133.
[39] Nanette Asimov, "Mission High Rallies for Suspended Guard: March on S.F. Board of Education Turns Into Demand,"*The San Francisco Chronicle*, 16 December 1993, A-24; and "The Need is Great," *The Sun Reporter* (27 April 1994), 7.
[40] Susan Herbert, "Mission High Gets New Ethnic Studies, Career Programs: District Responds to Students' Pleas for Needed Classes in Cultural Awareness," *The San Francisco Independent*, 1 February 1994, Section 1, p.9.
[41] Geneva Gay, *A Synthesis of Scholarship in Multicultural Education* (Oakbrook, IL: North Central Regional Educational Laboratory,1994), [accessed Aug 10, 2003 at http://www.ncrel.org/sdrs/areas/issues/ educatrs/leadrshp/le0gay.htm]
[42] Christine E. Sleeter and Carl A. Grant, "An Analysis of Multicultural Education in the United States," *Harvard Educational Review* 57, (November 1987): 422, 432, 434-435.
[43] Gary Howard, e-mail to Daniel Padolsky, May 19, 2003.
[44] *REACH Center Respecting Ethnic and Cultural Heritage* (Seattle, WA: REACH Center), 10-15.
[45] Phyllis Schlafly, ed., *Child Abuse In the Classroom*, (Alton, IL: Pere Marquette Press, 1984), 70.
[46] Email from Gary Howard to Dan Padolsky, 19 May 2003.
[47] Quoted in Diane S. Ravitch, "Multiculturalism in the Curriculum" (Paper presented at the Manhattan Institute, Manhattan, N.Y, November 27, 1989): 1. [ERIC document # ED329622].
[48] Quoted in Edward B. Fiske, "Lessons," *The New York Times*, 7 February 1990, B-5.
[49] Edward B. Fiske, "Lessons," *The New York Times*, 7 February 1990, B-5.
[50] Quoted in Joseph Berger, "Now the Regents Must Decide If History Will Be Recast," *New York Times*, 11 February 1990, Section 4, p. 5.
[51] Diane S. Ravitch, "Multiculturalism in the Curriculum" (Paper presented at the Manhattan Institute, Manhattan, N.Y, November 27, 1989): 6-8. [ERIC document # ED329622].
[52] Joseph Berger, "Now the Regents Must Decide If History Will Be Recast," *New York Times*, 11 February 1990, Section 4, p. 5.

[53] California Department of Education, *History-Social Science Framework for California Public Schools: Kindergarten through Grade 12* (Sacramento, CA: author, 1988).
[54] Catherine Cornbleth and Dexter Waugh, *The Great Speckled Bird* (New York: St. Martin's Press, 1995), 65.
[55] Catherine Cornbleth and Dexter Waugh, *The Great Speckled Bird* (New York: St. Martin's Press, 1995), 66-67.
[56] Robert Reinhold, "Class Struggle," *The New York Times*, 29 September 1991, Section 6, p. 26.
[57] Quoted in Catherine Cornbleth and Dexter Waugh, *The Great Speckled Bird* (New York: St. Martin's Press, 1995), 62.
[58] Robert Reinhold, "Class Struggle," *The New York Times*, 29 September 1991, Section 6, p. 26.
[59] Christopher J. Lucas, *American Higher Education: A History* (NY: St. Martin's Griffin, 1994), 131-137.
[60] Paul Lauter, ed., *Reconstructing American Literature: Courses, Syllabi, Issues* (Old Westbury, NY: The Feminist Press, 1983), xiii.
[61] Paul Lauter, ed., *Reconstructing American Literature: Courses, Syllabi, Issues* (Old Westbury, NY: The Feminist Press, 1983), xiv.
[62] Paul Lauter, *Cannons and Contexts* (New York: Oxford University Press, 1991), ix.
[63] Michael Dougan, "Authors Passionate In Book List Debate," *San Francisco Examiner*, 12 March 1998, A-1, A-20.
[64] "Must a Required Quota of Books Be By 'Authors of Color?'" *San Francisco Examiner*, 13 March 1998, A-22.
[65] Julian Guthrie, "Teachers Call Book Quotas Insulting: Works by Minorities Already Being Taught," *San Francisco Examiner*, 15 March 1998, D-1.
[66] Julian Guthrie, "Teachers Call Book Quotas Insulting: Works by Minorities Already Being Taught," *San Francisco Examiner*, 15 March 1998, D-2.
[67] Katherine Seligman, "Many Teens Welcome Change In Reading Lists: Say They Find It Tough Relating To Classic Literature," *San Francisco Examiner*, 13 March 1998, A-1, A-18.
[68] "Sound Off Results," *San Francisco Examiner*, 15 March 1998, D-2.
[69] Joel Spring, *The American School: 1642-2000* (Boston: McGraw-Hill, 2001), 199-201.
[70] Gloria Stewner-Manzanares, "The Bilingual Education Act: Twenty Years Later" *Focus: The National Clearinghouse for Bilingual Education*, (Fall 1988). [Available online: www.ncela.gwu.edu/ncbepubs/classics/focus/ 06bea.htm]
[71] Gloria Stewner-Manzanares, "The Bilingual Education Act: Twenty Years Later" *Focus: The National Clearinghouse for Bilingual Education*, (Fall 1988). [Available online: www.ncela.gwu.edu/ncbepubs/classics/focus/ 06bea.htm]
[72] 414 U.S. 56 (1974).
[73] Quoted in Phil Petrie, "Afrocentrism In a Multicultural Democracy, *American Visions* 6, (August 1991), p.20-26. pg. 21
[74] Gary B. Nash, "American History Reconsidered: Asking New Questions About the Past," in *Learning form the Past: What History Teaches Us About School Reform*, eds. Diane Ravitch and Maris A. Vinovskis (Baltimore, MD: Johns Hopkins University Press), 133-163. p 151
[75] Michele Marriott, "As A Discipline Advances, A Debate On Scholarship," *The New York Times*, 11 August, 1991, section 1, part 1, p.18.
[76] See: Mary A. Johnson, "Black Males Are Getting a Sense of Their History," *Chicago Sun-Times*, 20 January 1992, 1; Janita Poe, "A Global School of Thought" *St.*

Petersburg Times, 5 January 1992, B-1; John Leo, "A Fringe History of the World," *U.S. News & World Report*, November 12, 1990, 25.

[77] Gary B. Nash, "American History Reconsidered: Asking New Questions About the Past," in *Learning form the Past: What History Teaches Us About School Reform*, eds. Diane Ravitch and Maris A. Vinovskis (Baltimore, MD: Johns Hopkins University Press), 133-163. p 152-156

[78] Alvin J. Schmidt, *The Menace of Multiculturalism* (Westport, CT: Praeger, 1997), 12.

[79] Arthur M. Schlesinger, *The Disuniting of America, rev. and enlarged ed.* (New York: W.W. Norton, 1998), 22.

[80] Diane S. Ravitch, "Multiculturalism in the Curriculum" (Paper presented at the Manhattan Institute, Manhattan, N.Y, November 27, 1989) [ERIC document # ED329622], 8.

[81] Arthur M. Schlesinger, *The Disuniting of America, rev. and enlarged ed.* (New York: W.W. Norton, 1998), 20.

[82] Arthur M. Schlesinger, *The Disuniting of America, rev. and enlarged ed.* (New York: W.W. Norton, 1998), 23.

[83] James A Banks and Cherry A. M. Banks, *Handbook of Research on Multicultural Education* (New York: Macmillan Publishing, 1995), 3-4.

[84] M. Hussein Feresteh, "*Multicultural Education In the United S*tates: A Historical Review," *Multicultural Review*, 4 (1995): 38-45.

[85] Dick Lilly, "Students Rally For Multicultural Curriculum, *The Seattle Times*, 18 November 1995, A10; Scott Stephens, "Multiculturalism Guide Published," *Plain Dealer* (Cleveland, Ohio), 23 December 1994, 1B; Maureen M. Smith, "Superintendent Proposes More Teacher Evaluations," *Star Tribune* (Minneapolis, MN), 22 June 1994, Saint Paul Edition, 2B; Dennis Hevesi, "Cortines Moves to Devise New Multicultural Curriculum, *The New York Times*, 18 November 1993, B-3; Muriel Cohen, "School Days Begin for Boston: Harrison-Jones Unveiling A New Look for Academic Year," *The Boston Globe*, 5 September 1993, Learning-39; Patricia H. Partnow, *Curriculum Writers' Guide: Writing Alaska Studies Materials for Alaska Schools*, (AK: Alaska Native Education and Technical Assistance Center VI,1992), [ERIC document ED355080]; Linda Chavez, Diversity In the Schools: Are the Multicultural Experiments Working? Two Views, *The Washington Post*, 1 August 1993, R-1; Bill Scanlon, "Teaching Diversity: Suburban Schools Push Multiculturalism As Minority Student Enrollment Soars," *Rocky Mountain News* (Denver, CO), 16 February 1997, A.-42. Judith Nygren, "For All and About All: Norfolk Teacher Sees Need For Multicultural Education" *Omaha World-Herald*, 12 November 1995, E-1.

[86] Donna M. Gollnick, "National and State Initiatives for Multicultural Education," in *The Handbook of Research on Multicultural Education*, eds. James A. Banks and Cherry A. M. Banks (New York: MacMillan, 1995), 56.

[87] Zollie Stevenson, Jr. and Lillian Gonzalez, "Contemporary Practices in Multicultural Approaches to Education Among the Largest American School Districts," *Journal of Negro Education* 61, (Summer 1992), 359-360.

[88] Robert Lerner, Althea K. Nagai, and Stanley Rothman, *Molding the Good Citizen: The Politics of High School History Texts* (Westport, CT: Praeger, 1995), 70, 71, 84.

[89] Gary B. Nash, "American History Reconsidered: Asking New Questions About the Past," in *Learning from the Past: What History Teaches Us About School Reform*, eds. Diane Ravitch and Maris A. Vinovskis (Baltimore: Johns Hopkins University Press, 1995), 137.

[90] James A Banks et al., *United States and Its Neighbors* (New York: Macmillan/McGraw-Hill, 1993), 270-271.
[91] Janita Poe, "Textbooks: Then and Now," *St. Petersburg Times* (Florida), 5 January 1992, City Edition, B-4.
[92] Anita P. Bohn and Christine E. Sleeter, "Multicultural Education and the Standards Movement: A Report From the Field," *Phi Delta Kappan* 82 (October 2000):157.
[93] *The Metropolitan Life Survey of the American Teacher: Students Voice Their Opinions on: Learning About Multiculturalism,* Part IV, (New York: Metropolitan Life Insurance Company, 1996), 7,9, 12.
[94] "101 Greatest Books" Available online http://www.collegeboard.com/parents/article/ 0,3708,703-704-0-21276,00.html, retrieved July 30, 2003.
[95] Arthur N. Applebee, *Literature in the Secondary School: Studies of Curriculum and Instruction in the United States* (Urbana IL: National Council of Teachers of English: 1993) [ERIC document: ED357370], 193, 216.
[96] Peter Applebome, "Class Notes," *The New York Times*, 1 March 1995, B-8.
[97] Paul Van Slambrouck, "Mandating a Colorful Canon," *The Christian Science Monitor*, 17 March 1998, 1.
[98] Arthur N. Applebee, e-mail to Dan Padolsky, April 19, 2003.
[99] U.S. Congress, General Accounting Office, *Public Education: Title I Services Provided to Students With Limited English Proficiency* (Washington DC: author, 1999), 1.
[100] Anita Garcia and Cynthia Morgan, "A 50 State Survey of Requirements for the Education of Language Minority Children." Retrieved November 1997 from http://www.ceousa.org/50state.html
[101] U.S. Department of Education, National Center for Education Statistics, *Digest of Education Statistics: 2001* (Washington DC: U.S. Government Printing Office, 2002), 423.
[102] Rossell and Baker's 1996 review is often cited by advocates of ESL, but the review did *not* conclude that ESL is more effective than bilingual education in boosting achievement test scores of limited English proficient children, rather it shows there is little difference in the effectiveness of the two approaches. Green's subsequent reanalysis of the strongest studies that had been examined by Rossell and Baker concludes that bilingual education does have a modest advantage, but his analysis was based on only 11 evaluations. The National Academy of Science's recent report on preventing reading difficulties recommended that when children arrive in school with no proficiency in English, it is best to teach them first to read in their native language, if there are the appropriate staff and resources are available, and if not, it is best to teach those students to speak English. See: Catherine E. Snow, M. Susan Burns, and Peg Griffin, eds., *Preventing Reading Difficulties in Young Children* (Washington DC: National Academy Press, 1998); Jay P. Greene, *A Meta-Analysis of the Effectiveness of Bilingual Education* (Los Angeles CA: University of Southern California, Thomas Rivera Policy Institute, 1998); Christine H. Rossell and Keith Baker, The Educational Effectiveness of Bilingual Education," *Research in the Teaching of English,* 30 (1996): 7-74.
[103] Patricia L. Marshall, "Toward a Theoretical Framework," Paper presented at the Annual Meeting of the National Council for the Social Studies, (1992, November) [ERIC document #ED353246], 7.
[104] National Council for the Accreditation of Teacher Education, *NCATE Standards for the Accreditation of Teacher Education* (Washington, DC, author,1982), 14.

[105] "On Preparing Teachers with Knowledge of the Literature of Minorities," National Council of Teachers of Education, Annual Business Meeting, Minneapolis, MN, 1972, retrieved online August 3, 2003, at http://www.ncte.org/resolutions/minlit721972.shtml .

[106] "On Multicultural Curriculum Materials," National Council of Teachers of Education, Annual Business Meeting, San Diego, CA, 1975, retrieved online August 3, 2003, at http://www.ncte.org/resolutions/materials 751975.shtml.

[107] "On the Availability of Literature by Minority Writers," National Council of Teachers of English, Annual Business Meeting, San Antonio, TX, 1986, retrieved online August 3, 2003 at http://www.ncte.org/resolutions/ literature861986.shtml.

[108] Patricia L. Marshall, "Toward a Theoretical Framework," Paper presented at the Annual Meeting of the National Council for the Social Studies, (1992, November) [ERIC document #ED353246], 5.

[109] Patricia L. Marshall, "Toward a Theoretical Framework," Paper presented at the Annual Meeting of the National Council for the Social Studies, (1992, November) [ERIC document #ED353246], 9-11.

[110] Donna M. Gollnick, "National and State Initiatives for Multicultural Education," in *The Handbook of Research on Multicultural Education*, eds. James A. Banks and Cherry A. M. Banks (New York: MacMillan, 1995), 58-59.

[111] Renee S. Martin and Robyn S. Lock, "Assessing the Attitudes of Student Teachers Toward Issues of Diversity: A Dilemma for Teacher Educators," *Journal of Intergroup Relations* 24 (Spring 1997), 42.

[112] Renee S. Martin and Robyn S. Lock, "Assessing the Attitudes of Student Teachers Toward Issues of Diversity: A Dilemma for Teacher Educators," *Journal of Intergroup Relations* 24 (Spring 1997), 42. Robert Smith, "Challenging Privilege: White Middle-Class Opposition in the Multicultural Education Terrain," in *Speaking the Unpleasant: The Politics of (non) Engagement in the Multicultural Education Terrain*, eds. Rudolgo Chavez Chavez and James O'Donnell (Albany, NY: State University of New York Press, 1998), pg. 197-98. Lynne T. Diaz-Rico, "Toward a Just Society: Recalibrating Multicultural Teachers," in *Speaking the Unpleasant: The Politics of (non) Engagement in the Multicultural Education Terrain*, ed. Rudolgo Chavez Chavez and James O'Donnell (Albany, NY: State University of New York Press, 1998), pg. 71.

[113] Sonia Nieto, *Affirming Diversity: The Sociopolitical Context of Multicultural Education*, (New York: Longman, 1992), 275.

[114] S Christine E. Sleeter, "Multicultural Education As a Social Movement," *Theory Into Practice* 35 (Autumn 1996): 239-247.

[115] Gary B. Nash, "American History Reconsidered: Asking New Questions About the Past," in *Learning form the Past: What History Teaches Us About School Reform*, eds. Diane Ravitch and Maris A. Vinovskis (Baltimore, MD: Johns Hopkins University Press), 133-163. p 139

[116] *Beating the Odds: A City-By-City Analysis of Student Performance And Achievement Gaps on State Assessment Results from The 2001-2002 School Year* (Washington DC: Council of the Great City Schools, 2003) iii-vii.

[117] U.S. Department of Education, National Center for Education Statistics, *Digest of Education Statistics: 2001* (Washington DC: U. S. Government Printing Office, 2002), 17.

[118] U.S. Department of Education, National Center for Education Statistics, *Digest of Education Statistics: 2001* (Washington DC: U. S. Government Printing Office, 2002), 219, 221.

[119] Sharon Bernstein "Ethnic Study Notion Has Teachers Worried," *Chicago Sun-Times* (13 December1992): 37.

[120] Sharon Bernstein, "Multiculturalism Gets a Second Look," *The Houston Chronicle*, 6 December 1992, A-12.

[121] Sharon Bernstein "Ethnic Study Notion Has Teachers Worried," *Chicago Sun-Times*, 13 December1992, 37.

[122] Marco R. della Cava, "Raising Racial Respect: Harmony Is Part of School's Lesson Plan: Pride Is Up As Prejudice Goes Down," *USA Today*, 14 March 1990, D-1.

[123] Saundra Murray Nettles, Barbara McHugh, and Gary D. Gottfredson, *Meeting the Challenges of Multicultural Education: The Third Report from the Evaluation of Pittsburgh's Prospect Multicultural Education Center* (Pittsburgh, PA: Center for Social Organization of Schools and the Center for Research on Effective Schooling for Disadvantaged Students, Johns Hopkins University, 1994) [ERIC document ED430072], 36.

[124] Pew Research Center for the People & the Press, "Retro-Politics," 11 November 1996 (accessed Aug 10, 03 at http://people-press.org/ reports/print.php3?ReportID=50), about 1/6 down and 11/12 down web page.

[125] Karen S Peterson, "Interracial Dating For Today's Teens: Race 'Not an Issue Anymore'." *USA Today*, 3 November 1997, A-1.

[126] Karen S. Peterson, "Interracial Dating for Today's Teens, Race 'Not an Issue Anymore'," *USA Today*, 3 November 1997, A-1.

[127] Tom W. Smith. *Intergroup Relations in a Diverse America: Data from the 2000 General Social Survey* (New York: The American Jewish Committee, 2001), 18-19.

[128] See: Valerie Strauss "Sept. 11 Prompts Lesson Review: Educators Rethink Multiculturalism," *Washington Post* (1 October 2001): B-1; Richard Rothstein, "Terror, Excuses And Explanations," *The New York Times*, 17 October 2001, A-20; Celeste Katz, "Veep's Wife: Don't Blame U.S. Society for Terrorism," *Daily News* (New York), 6 October 2001, 26.

[129] Alberto Bursztyn, "The Path to Academic Disability: Javier's School Experience" in *Rethinking Multicultural Education: Case Studies in Cultural Transition*, eds. Carol Korn and Alberto Bursztyn (Westport, CT: Bergin & Garvey, 2002), 161.

9

Lessons from the Past

Gregg B. Jackson

The "good old days" of American public education were not so good. How many Americans, after reading Chapters 2-8, would choose to turn the clock back, taking on the whole of another age? Those who want religion infused in public education would have to return at least to the early 1800s when schooling usually ended with the 8th grade, and they would need to be of the Protestant faith or prepared to convert. Those who want to avoid all of progressive education would have to return to the mid-1800s when learning was largely by rote memorization without concern for conceptual understanding. Those who want to experience the zenith of high school academic rigor would probably have to return to 1910 when there were high rates of academic course-taking but only 15 percent of the age cohort enrolled in high schools, and most were from affluent white families.[1]

The Dramatic Changes in American Schooling

The historical record indicates that American public schools have changed dramatically over the past two centuries. There have been changes along five dimensions: the purpose of education, the organization of schools, the curriculum and pedagogy, the accommodation of individual student's needs, and the extent of schooling.

The main purpose of education shifted from the salvation of souls to the preparation for life in a differentiated economy and a pluralistic society. The latter purpose spans academic, social, physical, and occupational development.

Control of the schools has shifted from local school committees, each in charge of one schoolhouse, to joint local-state-federal control of school districts that have multiple schools. The structure of schools has gone from the one-room schoolhouse serving students ages 5-15, to a three-tier system of graded elementary, junior high, and high schools, with teachers at the top two tiers specializing in teaching one or two subject areas. The daily management has shifted from "school masters" who served as administrators-teachers-janitors to the current hierarchical bureaucratic organizations, run by a phalanx of professionals with varied specializations.

The curriculum that initially focused almost exclusively on reading, writing, and religion has dropped the latter and expanded to include mathematics, social studies, the physical and natural sciences, the arts, and practical skills like microcomputer use and vocational preparation. The exclusion of minorities from textbooks--or their demeaning representation--has generally been replaced with respectful depictions.

Pedagogy has evolved from individual memorization, recitation, and corporal punishment for errors, to a mix of lecturing, recitations, discussions, laboratory experiments, research and written essays. The intent now is not only to convey knowledge but also to develop understanding, problem solving, and creativity.

Until the mid 1800s, children with disabilities were considered the burden of their parents. The children with limited English proficiency had to fend for themselves in the schools. And children otherwise ill prepared for classrooms generally received no special assistance. Gradually over the 20th century, all children with disabilities have come to be afforded a public education, special provisions have been made for students with limited English proficiency, and compensatory education has become widely available.

For two centuries, children were expected to study a single curriculum taught in a common manner. It was not until late 1800s that progressive education allowed students some opportunity to pursue individual interests with electives courses that are now common in high school.

Public schooling was initially voluntary but now it is compulsory from the age of six to about 16. As a result of that, and the lengthening of the school year and expansion of public schooling to the high school level and then to the college level, the average youth today receives about five times as many hours of schooling as the average youth of the early 1800s.[2]

If a school committee of the early 1800s could visit today's schools, they would be astounded by the change. The major changes are summarized below.

Reform	1801	1901	2001
Universal Ed.	Not yet common, although northeastern states had high enrollment rates in the elementary schools.	Present throughout almost every state at elementary level but with very limited enrollment at the high school level.	Everywhere, with about **88 percent** completing high school; community or state colleges also available almost everywhere.
Secularization of Public Education	Religious instruction was one of the primary purposes of the schools.	The Bible was commonly read aloud without comment and pan-Protestant prayers were commonly said in many states.	Schools' staff members are prohibited from directing the reading of the Bible or saying of prayers, but students may voluntarily do.
Progressive Ed.	Curriculum: 4 Rs; Pedagogy: Rote memorization, recitation, and corporal punishment for errors.	Curriculum: Had deleted religion and added social studies; Pedagogy: Still heavily emphasizing memorization, but cities were replacing corporal punishment with public recognition and humiliation.	Curriculum: Includes sciences, arts, practical skills, and vocational skills. Pedagogy: Mix of lectures, recitation, discussions, laboratory sessions, and written projects.
Professionalization of Teachers	Elementary teachers needed only 8th grade education, and many had not mastered those skills. Pay was about same as farm hands.	Elementary teachers needed high school or "normal school" ed. Secondary teachers needed normal school or college study. Pay was 75% of Amer. Average.	All teachers needed college degree, with some coursework in ed. and supervised teaching experience. Pay was 116 % of American average earnings.

Special Ed.	Children with serious disabilities excluded from school; the rest have to do best they can without special help	Many states have ed. asylums for blind, deaf, and mentally retarded, or pay to send such students to facilities in other states.	All students with disabilities are to be provided with education tailored to their special needs.
Compensatory Ed.	Rarely provided.	Rarely provided.	Students in low-income schools who appear to need extra help do get some, but it has not raised their achievement substantially.
Multicultural Ed.	Schools consciously sought to deculturalize immigrants and minorities of color, imbuing them with the Anglo-American culture.	Same as in 1801 except large concentrations of European immigrants sometimes succeeded in lobbying for multicultural schools.	Most textbooks portray minorities of color respectfully. Many schools try to be respectful of the varying ethnic heritages of students while also helping immigrants learn to function in the dominant American culture.

Partial Success in Achieving Reform Objectives and Goals

While each of the above reforms has substantially changed public schooling, most have been only partially successful in achieving their objectives and goals.

Universal public schooling was initially aimed at inculcating morality, preparing white youngsters to be a wise electorate, "Americanizing" immigrant children, helping poor youngsters rise above poverty and crime, and preparing a workforce for a changing economy. There is evidence that it has contributed to these goals but not by as much as was expected by the reformers. Furthermore, for long periods, public education has actually worked at cross-purposes with some of these goals, particularly in perpetuating racial and ethnic discrimination in America.

The secularization of public education reform initially sought to limit religion to pan-Protestant prayers and reading of the Bible without comment, but later sought to eliminate even these practices from schools. Those efforts succeeded except in some small homogeneous communities that persist with adult led school prayers.

The progressive education reform has succeeded in making schooling more humane by the introduction of more varied modes of instruction and elimination of most corporal punishment, but school remains boring for many students and humiliating for some. Progressive education also strove to enhance conceptual understanding, problem solving, and creativity, but limited evidence suggests that progressive education has only marginally improved those outcomes except with the most academically able students.

Efforts to professionalize teaching have dramatically improved the training and pay of teachers, and that has surely attracted more able people and better prepared them than would otherwise have been the case. Nevertheless, teaching is not widely perceived as an attractive occupation for the intellectually talented.

Special education has helped millions of children acquire some academic skills. A few have gone on to prominence, but many make limited academic progress and lead adult lives of dependency.

Compensatory education was targeted at helping disadvantaged children benefit fully from their education and life opportunities. The extensive evaluations, although with varying and debated findings, generally show that compensatory education does modestly benefit participants' academic, personal, and social development, but the average gap with non-disadvantaged students is far from eliminated, and the benefits erode after the compensatory education services are terminated.

Multicultural education is intended to boost the academic success of minority students, assist in the preservation of their heritages, and facilitate racial and ethnic tolerance and respect throughout the nation. Since its introduction 35 years ago, minority academic achievement at the K-12 level has inched up some, enrollments in college have increased dramatically for African Americans but not for Hispanics, and national surveys show increased racial tolerance and interaction among young adults. Multicultural education probably has contributed to the progress but is unlikely to be the sole cause.

Despite some progress from these reforms, serious problems remain. In 1999, *eighteen percent* of high school seniors taking the National Assessment of Education Progress test could not read well enough to locate and organize information in lengthy passages, paraphrase it, make generalizations about the main ideas, and infer the author's purposes—

things that 16 percent of the nation's tested 9-year-olds have mastered.[3] The percentage of *all* 17-year-olds who have not mastered these mid-level reading skills is actually about *25 percent*, because a portion of students with the weakest skills drop out of school before their senior year and because six percent of students sampled for the NAEP testing were excluded after being judged unable to "meaningfully participate in the NAEP assessment" due to disabilities or limited English proficiency.

Although the percentages of students taking algebra and geometry increased substantially during the last two decades of the 20th century,[4] when seniors were asked, "Which is the best unit to use when measuring the growth of a plant every other day during a 2-week period? A) Centimeter, B) Meter, C) Kilometer, D) Foot, and E) Yard," *13 percent* answered incorrectly. When they were asked, "A certain machine produces 300 nails per minute. At this rate, how long will it take the machine to produce enough nails to fill 5 boxes of nails if each box will contain 250 nails?" *51 percent* of the students did not answer correctly. When students were told Town A's population increased from 5,000 to 8,000 over a decade and Town B's population increased from 6,000 to 9,000 over the same period, and that Brian claims both towns grew by the same amount but Darlene claims Town A grew more, only *three percent* of seniors could explain why both claims were justified.[5] Again, the failure rate for the nation's entire population of 17-year-olds is actually higher than what is reported here, for the same reasons as explained previously for the reading test results.

Why have the reforms been only partially successful in achieving their objectives and goals? There are several factors that probably have contributed to this. First, as explained above, several of the reforms have not been implemented as thoroughly as was intended and that probably has limited their effects. Second, the targeted objectives and goals of the reforms are affected by many factors over which the reforms have little or no control, including the incidence of disabilities, the rates of immigration, and the economic and social conditions in the communities from which the students come. Third, it is rare that any educational or other social intervention fully corrects the problems to which it is directed. Automobile design and highway engineering have reduced the probability and severity of automobile accidents but not eliminated them. Similarly, local building code standards and Underwriters Laboratory certification have reduced the probability and severity of home fires but not eliminated them.

Misperceptions That Schools Have Not Changed

During the past few decades of the 20th century, several historians, many politicians, and numerous pundits have claimed that American schools have not changed, that they are the least innovative sector of American economic and social life, and that they are fossilized relicts of a bygone age. Why are these claims so prevalent given our documented findings of dramatic changes in American education over the past two centuries? Let us examine the claims of a few of the scholars, who undoubtedly are more informed about the past than most others.

David Tyack and William Tobin claim that a "grammar" of bureaucratization was established in the mid-1800s during the rapid expansion of universal public education systems, and subsequent change efforts that challenged that grammar "typically ... have not lasted for long."[6] Bureaucratic structures from corporate industry were adopted to achieve efficiencies. The one-room schoolhouse was replaced with schools having graded classrooms allowing teachers to focus their teaching on students at about the same level of knowledge and skills. As high schools were introduced to provide instruction at more advanced levels, teachers specialized in teaching just one or two subjects, and students changed teachers every hour to study a different subject. While problems with this grammar have long been recognized—for instance not all students progress at the same rate and not all lessons fit within a 50-or 55-minute interval—it has prevailed for a century and a half despite many efforts to change it.[7] The authors cite a number of examples of change attempts that challenged the conventional grammar of schooling: the Dalton plan that used learning contracts and individualized study to replace most classroom instruction, the Eight-Year Study of progressive education mentioned in Chapter 4, and "open high schools" with inter-disciplinary courses and substantial free time to be used at the students' discretion. Tyack and Tobin report that each was implemented with considerable optimism in a small number of schools but was soon abandoned because of parental concerns, teachers' burnout from the additional work that was involved, and misuse of the unstructured time by those students who were lacking motivation.[8] Contrary to Tyack and Tobin's suggestion, none of these reasons for abandonment is a direct result of the long prevailing "grammar" of the schools. In addition, Chapters 3-8 of this book have documented several reforms that changed schooling even when operating within the established grammar. Thus the prevailing grammar of schools does not preclude substantial changes, although it may preclude certain kinds of changes.

Larry Cuban, a historian of education, asks, "How can it be, then, that so much school reform has taken place over the last century yet schooling appears to be pretty much the same as it has always been?"[9] He answers the question by distinguishing between first-order and second-order changes. First-order changes seek to improve the efficiency or effectiveness in achieving old objectives and goals, "without disturbing the basic organizational features, [and] without substantially altering the ways in which adults and children perform their roles."[10] Examples of such changes are adding new courses, revising textbooks, and raising teacher salaries. Second-order changes alter the fundamentals—"the goals, structures, and roles"—transforming the ways schools undertake their work.[11] He cites decentralized community control of schools, open classrooms, and child-centered instruction as examples. Cuban claims that most attempted reforms of the past century have been first-order ones and that they have had modest success. He also claims the few attempted second-order reforms "were either adapted to fit what already prevailed or sloughed off, allowing the system to remain essentially untouched."[12] Cuban's focus on only a single century is one reason why he finds little change while we found considerable change. The universal education reform and the secularization of public education, which dramatically changed the structure and purpose of public education, were well under way before the last century. Cuban considers progressive education's introduction of courses in the arts, sciences, and occupational skills as minor changes, whereas we consider them significant ones. He acknowledges the important expansion of opportunities for children with disabilities and minorities of color, and he asserts that special education, compensatory education, and bilingual education have "altered existing rules, modified practices, or led to the hiring of specialized staff members"—which would seem to qualify as "role" changes under his above quoted definition of second-order changes—but then he dismisses them as having "seldom dented existing organizational structures."[13] While Cuban, like Tyack and Tobin, is correct about the essentially unchanged structure of public schooling for 150 years, it is unclear why he chose structure as the sine qua non of change. If it is the only meaningful standard of change, then many long established corporations—with their bureaucratic structures and division of labor—have likewise remained unchanged for almost a century, as has New York City.

Cuban is also the author of the book *How Teachers Taught: Constancy and Change in American Classrooms*. This is the most thorough examination of the extent to which teachers adopted the child-oriented pedagogy advocated by many progressive education reformers. The first edition of the book was widely interpreted as indicating that teaching had not changed over a century. The second edition adds more evidence and explicitly states conclusions to avoid what the author thought were "exaggerated interpretations" of the first edition.[14] As we reported in Chapter 4, that evidence indicates that since the initiation of the progressive education reform movement in the early 1900s, about 10-30 percent of teachers' pedagogy has been student-centered, another 20-40 percent has been a mix of teacher-centered and student-centered, and the rest has been traditional teacher-centered instruction. Cuban concludes that most teachers have come to embrace a "hybrid" of "student-centered" and "teacher-centered" pedagogy.[15] Thus, in this book, Cuban acknowledges role changes despite the continuing bureaucratic structure of schools.

Michael Katz, another historian of education, claims that, "the basic structure of American education was fixed by about 1880 and that it has not altered fundamentally since that time."[16] He defines "basic structure" as "universal tax-supported, free, compulsory, bureaucratic, racist, and class-biased." He argues that structure is like a box, and things within it can be moved around and some can even be replaced with other things providing that they fit within the box, but the walls of the box remain fixed.[17] He acknowledges that a few changes have been adopted—such as kindergarten classes, vocational education, testing, and various new curricula—and they have made some difference but have not altered the stated structural features. The compulsory, free, and tax-supported characteristics that Katz decries as stubborn persistence of structure are what Chapter 2 described as long maintenance of the universal education reform. Katz apparently considers these characteristics undesirable because he thinks they have perpetuated a racist and class-biased educational system. Katz notes that universal public education was not the only way to structure American schools. He observes that there were three other structures in considerable use prior to the mid-1800s—"democratic localism" of rural America's one-room school houses controlled by local school committees, "paternalistic volunteerism" of the charity and pauper schools, and "corporate volunteerism" of the private tuition-charging academies and grammar schools,[18] all of which have been briefly described in Chapter 2. He implies that if universal public education had not largely supplanted those structures, education would have been less racist and class-biased during the past century. That is an ironic conclusion given that racial exclusion and class stratification of schools was the norm when these three other structures prevailed. Indeed, universal public education systems were advocated partly to counter the neglect of local school committees, to eliminate the stigma of charity and pauper schools, and later to provide access to secondary education that was previously available only to those who could afford the tuition of private grammar schools and academies. Racism and bias have not been eliminated by universal public education, and for long periods of history these systems reinforced both. Nevertheless, Chapters 2, 7, and 8 indicate that far more educational opportunities are now available to minorities of color and to the poor than were available 50, 100, or 200 years ago.

There is no doubt that many attempts to introduce change to American education have failed to gain widespread implementation or have soon thereafter disappeared. In addition to the examples cited above there are others: teacher control of schools, team teaching, the new math of the post-Sputnik era, educational radio and educational film, pass-fail grading, and others. Nevertheless, it is one thing to say many change efforts have failed and quite another to conclude schools have not changed over the past century or two.

There are several reasons why many people have reached the latter conclusion incorrectly. First, if one goes looking only for failure, he or she can easily find it. Second, short-term assessments of a reform's progress can provide a misleading view, for most of the reforms described in this book required at least a half-century to become widespread and several required a century. Third, the basic bureaucratic structure adopted by the universal public education reform during the late-1800s has not changed substantially since then, so focusing on changes that require structural changes will blind one to the other changes that have occurred. Fourth, unrealistic expectations for perfect implementation or complete achievement of targeted objectives are sure to be met with disappointment. A glass that is half full can legitimately be perceived as half empty, although describing it merely as "full" or as "empty" is misleading. Fifth, the described reforms have generally been more successful in changing the nature of American education than in achieving their objectives and goals, and that is a legitimate source of discontent. The hopes that education reforms would equalize power and status in American society have been largely unfulfilled, although many individuals have risen or fallen in the social order because of their education.

Those who are convinced of the overwhelming failure of educational change efforts also appear to be unaware of the high rate of failed innovation in other areas of human endeavor. Thomas Edison was the most prolific inventor in recorded history, but it took him 1,200 tries to produce a durable light bulb, he failed in attempts to create an undersea telegraph, and he lost most of his considerable wealth after repeated failed efforts to find a better way of extracting iron from ore.[19] Similarly, the pharmaceutical industry reports that only 1 of 5,000 drugs identified as promising for treating a given medical condition ever makes it to market.[20]

In addition, modern medicine, which has eradicated several diseases, has achieved only partial success in preventing or treating others, such as asthma and cancer, despite a half-century of concerted efforts. For instance, in 1930 cancer was the second cause of death in the United States and it remained so in 2002. During the last three decades of the 20th century, the federal government invested about $50 billion in cancer R&D and private industry made considerable additional investments. The results: Cancer incidence rates rose, particularly among the elderly; between the mid 1970s and late 1990s the five-year survival rate improved only from about 50 percent to 60 percent; and over the same period the age-adjusted death rate increased slightly from 199 per 100,000 to 203 per 100,000.[21] Indeed, education has made more progress in eliminating ignorance in America than modern medicine has made in eradicating the common cold.

On the other hand, education compares unfavorably with medicine and other technology in that it has no successes that have doubled learning rates for a sustained period or halved the incidence of learning difficulties, whereas medicine and technology can claim several large advances. There are several vaccines and medicines that work successfully in more than 90 percent of cases for which they are intended (smallpox vaccine, polio vaccines, streptomycin for treating tuberculosis—until recently, and penicillin for treating several bacterial infections). Examples of other technologies that have dramatically increased outputs include agricultural fertilizers and harvesting machinery, power looms for weaving textiles, the Bessemer process of steel making, rotary printing presses, internal combustion engines, optic fiber conductors, and micro-chip based computers). There are no reforms or innovation in education that have comparably boosted the rate or extent of learning.

Will and Ariel Durant's lifelong study of history, published in the 11 volumes of *The Story of Civilization*, led them to conclude that 99 percent of new ideas will probably be inferior to traditional ones. They observed:

> It is good that new ideas should be heard, for the sake of the few that can be used; but it is also good that new ideas should be compelled to go through the mill of objection, opposition, and contumely; this is the trial heat which innovations must survive before being allowed to enter the human race. It is good that the old should resist the young, and that the young should prod the old; out of this tension ... come a creative tensile strength, a stimulated development, a secret and basic unity and movement of the whole.[22]

It should be noted that not all accomplishments of the above investigated education reforms will be uniformly applauded as progress. The secularization reform largely succeeded in eliminating religious instruction and practices from public schools, but millions of Americans consider that undesirable. Multicultural education has been successful in having textbooks present the contributions of minorities to America, but it has also sometimes propagated historical errors and exacerbated racial and ethnic frictions. "Progress" can be judged only by the intersection of facts and values. We leave our readers to determine for themselves whether the reforms examined in this book constitute progress or regress for the country.

Lessons Learned from the Studied Reforms

If generalizations can be inferred about the causes of moderate success in several major reforms, that knowledge might be used to help assess the prospects of current reform efforts and to help guide the reforms toward success. Achieving such understanding, however, is not an easy task for several reasons.

Scientists look for three conditions when establishing causality. First, here must be an association or correlation between a suspected causal factor and the effect. Second, the causal factor must temporally precede the effect. Third, there must be controls that rule out other possible causal factors.

The first condition requires a substantial number of cases with varying levels of success. It is desirable to establish that an alleged cause of reform success was present in most of the relatively successful reforms and was absent in most of the relatively failed reforms, but that is not possible in our case. In Chapter 1, we distinguished "reforms" from less ambitious "innovations" and from "evolutionary changes." In this book we have examined seven reforms that have been at least moderately successful. Only five other education reforms are known to this writer and all achieved some level of success. The bureaucratization of schools (mentioned in Chapters 2, 4, and 5) achieved its purposes of standardization and economic efficiencies. Vocational education was a partial success in keeping academically disinterested adolescents in high school and providing them with some occupational preparation, although the research suggests it did not appreciably boost their earnings. Standardized achievement testing was widely adopted in the 20th century and has gained even more influence as part of the ongoing accountability reforms. School desegregation by court orders and voluntary compliance eliminated most government-induced school segregation, but the impact on minority student's achievement was modest and re-segregation has become widespread. The use of computers in instruction remains a limited innovation today but may evolve into a reform within another decade or two. There probably have been many failed reform efforts, but failures tend to slip from the grasp of history leaving only a few shards of their stories.

The second condition for establishing causality—temporal ordering—can usually be established in historical case studies.

The third condition for establishing causality—controls to rule out other possible causal elements—is often difficult to meet from historical case studies and policy analysis. Many factors might influence the success of a given reform effort and it is unlikely that all can be anticipated and analyzed for their impact. David Fisher, in his examination of the logic of historical inference, suggests that history's best approximation to the third condition is to establish "at least a presumptive agency which connects" the alleged cause and effect.[23] He also urges modesty, since a plausible explanation of how an alleged cause operates could be mistaken.

It should be noted that generalizations about the causes of successful education reforms can be of several types. There might be individual causes that are necessary but not sufficient by themselves. There may be interchangeable causes with any one or several being sufficient for success In addition, some causes may precipitate a reform, and later causes may sustain its momentum or redirect its course.

If there are principles guiding the success of education reform, they should be applicable to most reforms, although perhaps not to all, because the reasons explained immediately above. Of course, there may be superficial variations in the cause as it appears in the various reforms but there should be a common essence. On the other hand, it is important to avoid the reductive fallacy—claiming large differences are nothing but minor variations on the essence.

With the above strategies and caveats in mind, eight lessons appear justified from the prior chapters of this book.

Lesson 1: Successful reforms are stimulated and pushed along by several changing social, economic, and/or political contexts that pose problems or opportunities within society or the schools. All seven of the reforms detailed in this book had multiple changing contexts that helped precipitate the reform, inform it, and push it along. The universal education reform effort resulted partly from the establishment of a democratic nation, massive non-British immigration, rapid industrialization and urbanization, and expanding government action. Secularization of education followed secularization in the nation's Constitution, growing religious diversity, the rise of science and technology that challenged former religious beliefs, and the establishment of universal schooling for a diverse citizenry. Progressive education was prompted partly by political progressivism; by the rise of new philosophies, psychology, and pedagogies; and by the adoption of compulsory education laws, which eventually put substantial numbers of unwilling children in the schools. The professionalization of teaching followed growing prosperity in America that allowed greater educational expenditures, the expansion of universal education to high school, the rise of new and more complex pedagogies, and the expansion of professionalism in several other occupations. Special education was partly precipitated by the second great awakening of religiosity, which fueled many crusades for human advancement; by compulsory education laws, which brought modest numbers of special needs children into public schools even while excluding those with severe disabilities; and by the Civil Rights movement of the 1950s and 1960s. Compensatory education resulted largely from expanding federal government activism, the Civil Rights movement and the school desegregation struggle, and a growing body of research on the relationship between poverty and education. The multicultural education movement received support from the 14th and 15th amendments, guaranteeing equal protection and voting rights for racial and ethnic minorities—both of which were only belatedly enforced after the mid-1960s; from the Civil Rights movement; and from a 20th century wave of immigration from non-English speaking countries.

Four changing contexts influenced three or more of the studied reforms. The founding of a democratic nation, guided by the U.S. Constitution and subsequent amendments, pushed three of the reforms and had important influences on several others. Immigration and the resulting diversity affected three of the reforms. The Civil Rights movement helped precipitate two of the reforms and redirected the special education reform. Finally, the universal public education reform became a changing context that pushed three other reforms and influenced all the others. These four—democracy, immigration, universal public schooling, and the Civil Rights movement—might be considered the "great contexts" propelling American education reform over the past two centuries.

Most of the changing contexts occurred before the reforms were initiated. A few occurred at midstream and changed the character of a reform that was already under way, such as when compulsory education laws moved special education from the asylums to the public schools and when the Civil Rights movement changed special education from a public service to a legal right. A few of the changing contexts occurred at one point in time or over a short duration, but it is striking how many, like massive immigration, industrialization and urbanization, growing prosperity, and the Civil Rights movement continued for several decades, providing a sustained push for the reforms.

The changing contexts usually posed problems for society or the school system, and the reforms sought to mitigate the problems. For instance, the determination to have a democratic nation imposed a problem because most citizens had little preparation for their new civic responsibilities, and universal public education was undertaken partly to address that problem. When the nation finally committed to ending locally mandated school segregation, many impoverished minority children were not prepared to succeed in desegregated schools, and compensatory education was implemented partly to remedy that.

On the other hand, a few of the changing contexts created opportunities that facilitated responses to problems. That was the case with the urbanization that accompanied industrialization, which eased the establishment of universal public school; the growing prosperity in American, which provided the financial means of expanding teacher training and raising teacher pay; and the expanding role of the federal government, which established precedents for federal initiation of compensatory education programs.

It appears that the major education reforms of the past two centuries do not constitute "great men histories" but rather social histories in which events beyond public education had profound effects on the reforms. Will and Ariel Durant concluded that each person who becomes a great mover of history—whether in political, social, or scientific domains—"grows out of his [or her] time and land, and is the product and symbol of events as well as their agent and voice; without some situation requiring a new response his [or her] new ideas would be untimely and impracticable."[24]

Lesson 2: Ambitious changes, once initiated, are more likely to succeed than modest ones, although they take more effort and time. All the reforms detailed in this book were aimed at making pervasive changes in education. The universal public education reform sought to establish education as a right rather than a luxury and to make education available to all children—including those of immigrants, the working class, and the poor. The secularization reform redirected the purpose of education from spiritual salvation to secular prosperity. Progressive education sought to replace rote memorization with intellectual inquiry, to supplement academics with life preparation, and to counter social stratification. The professionalization of teaching sought to recast the role of the teacher from recitation leader and disciplinarian to diagnostician, motivator, and multifaceted instructor. Special education and compensatory education sought to bring effective education to substantial subpopulations that were either excluded from school or expected to fail. Multiculturalism sought to undo two centuries of racism.

Many educational innovations with smaller ambitions than our studied reforms failed. The Dalton plan mentioned by Tyack and Tobin claimed to have individualized instruction, but that was done primarily by having all students work their way alone through the identical instructional materials at whatever rate was comfortable for each—a minimal form of individualization. Team teaching, new math, and educational radio and film were all smaller change efforts than those described in this book, and all failed. Open schools and open classrooms, which allow students considerable discretion in their learning activities, were two forms of the child-centered education stream within progressive education, forms that failed while others partially succeeded. On the other hand, a few modest innovations, such as chalkboards and kindergartens, have achieved some success and endured for more than a century.

It should be noted that Lesson 2 does not deny that small evolutionary changes occur in schools. They obviously do, as curriculums, textbooks, and exams are modified, as teachers gradually revise instructional strategies, as graduation requirements change, and as the years of schooling completed creep upward. This book, however, is not about evolutionary changes but rather about deliberate change initiatives intended to make substantial and pervasive changes in the purposes or means of schooling.

Three of the reforms described in this book gained "legs," expanding their ambitions as they were achieving the initial ones, going far beyond what the early reformers had targeted. Universal public education began as an effort to make good elementary schooling available to all white children, but it went through four subsequent progressions: compulsory education, universal public high schooling, the inclusion of minorities of color and children with disabilities, and finally widely expanded public postsecondary education. The secularization of education reform aspired to limit religious instruction and practice in public schools to Bible reading without comment and non-sectarian prayers, but later went on to preclude teachers from leading either within schools. Special education aspired to establish residential educational asylums for the deaf and blind, and later expanded to address other disabilities and to provide services within public day schools, allowing students to live at home with their families.

Ambitious reforms are more likely to succeed because they excite the imagination and gain greater attention. At best, new math could be expected to make youth better at mathematical thinking, whereas progressive education was expected to make youth better in mathematics, science, the arts, civic responsibilities, and their occupational lives.

Ambitious changes are also harder to get started than small ones, and thus more effort is put behind those that are actually launched than more modest innovations, which are usually initiated by obscure groups with few contacts or resources to sustain the change effort. Chapter 2 described the prodigious efforts made by Horace Mann, but it also illustrated that the success of the universal public education reform was partly the result of his close contacts in the Massachusetts legislature and his cultivation of contacts with educational leaders throughout the United States. Of course, big changes are also likely to encounter more resistance from inertia and from opponents. Nevertheless, the historical record suggests that disadvantage is offset by the advantages of ambitious changes.

It is possible, even likely, that many individuals have tried to launch ambitious reforms that never budged from the boatsheds of their minds. It would be presumptuous to conclude that all educational reform initiatives will succeed. Rather, the case studies of this book and the overwhelming majority of modest innovations known to have failed suggest that ambitious changes that actually get a start are more likely to achieve at least partial success than are more modest ones. The case studies also prove conclusively that ambitious education reforms are indeed possible to implement and sustain nationwide.

Lesson 3: Successful reforms offer multiple appeals for various stakeholders, often with different appeals for parents, educators, business leaders, citizens, and politicians. All the reforms detailed in this book had multiple appeals, promising different benefits to different groups of stakeholders. Universal public education was promoted to immigrants as a means of preparing their children for the opportunities of America, to ministers as a means of bringing the irreligious to salvation, to politicians as a way of Americanizing immigrants, to businessmen as a means of preparing a more productive workforce, to nativists as a means of civilizing immigrants, and to the wealthy as a way of forestalling revolt by the poor. The secularization of education was presented to universal public education supporters as essential for the survival of that reform, to Protestants as enlightened pan-Protestantism, to Catholics and Jews as the suspension of Protestant proselytization in public schools, and to nativists as a means of forestalling the spread of papal civil authority in America. Progressive education was sold to the upper classes as humane and enlightened child development, to the working classes as a means to better prepare their children to compete with the upper-class children, to teachers as a way of engaging apathetic students, to school board members as a means to raise lagging achievement, to business leaders as a key to advancing American science and technology, and to political progressives and socialists as a means of nurturing converts to their cause. The professionalization of teaching was presented to the school boards and the public as a way of improving the quality of education and it was presented to teachers as a way of improving their training, instructional effectiveness, status, pay, and quality of work life. Special education was promoted to parents of children with disabilities as a means of surmounting those disabilities, to the public as a humane responsibility and later as a legal obligation, and to all as a means of minimizing adult dependency. Compensatory education was sold to the poor as a pathway to the Great Society, to frustrated civil rights activists as a new educational opportunity, to religious schools as a first opportunity to receive federal aid, to teachers as assistance with children who needed extra help, and to the education associations as an alternative to repeatedly thwarted federal financial aid for general education. Multicultural education was promoted to frustrated minorities as a means of regaining their pride and countering white racism, to immigrant communities as a helping hand for new arrivals, to liberals as a just representation of American society, and to those opposing school desegregation as an alternative that might pacify the African American community.

Reformers tailored their arguments to each audience, appealing to nobility, pragmatics, and fear. Oscar Ameringer observed, "Politics is the gentle art of getting votes from the poor and campaign funds from the rich, by promising to protect each from the other."[25] While some reform leaders probably cynically tried to manipulate support, most of the appeals cited above appear to have been at least partially fulfilled by the reforms.

The multiple appeals served to create broad support for the reform and also to defuse potential opposition. In only two of the reforms examined did the multiple appeals result in broad coalitions that campaigned for the reforms. That occurred when the Whig party pressed for universal public schooling. It occurred again later when a coalition of parents, disability professionals, and public school officials coordinated lobbying for legislation that culminated in the Education for All Handicapped Children Act of 1975. For the rest of the reforms the multiple appeals attracted several stakeholder groups that mostly worked independently for the reform or lent their support through elections, referendums, and school meetings.

Lesson 4: A large corps of reform leaders is needed for nationwide success, highlighting the problems or opportunities, proposing the reform, and managing implementation throughout the states, districts, and individual schools. Impassioned, charismatic, and energetic leadership usually must be exercised by several individuals to get a major reform started, but thousands of leaders over two or more generations are usually necessary to secure adoption and implementation throughout the country. As the reform spreads, leadership is needed at multiple levels, all the way down to the individual schools.

The case studies in the prior chapters contain little information about the subsequent generations of state and local reform leaders who have carried the torches of the reforms, except for a few who were identified as changing the course of the reform mid-stream. Although they are seldom credited in the history books, any reform that hopes to spread throughout 50 states, 15,000 school districts, and 92,000 schools is dependent on the determination and skill of many leaders.

The initial leaders of the studied reforms were mostly from the upper-middle-class but otherwise of diverse backgrounds. Their class status, whether by birth or their own upward mobility, gave them financial resources and access to the power elite. Thomas Jefferson was from a family with substantial land holdings, Horace Mann and Henry Barnard were lawyers, Francis Parker had served as a colonel during the Civil War, John Dewey was a professor, John Runkle was president of MIT, the teachers Ella Flagg Young and Elizabeth Farrell were from families that had prospered, Thomas Gallaudet had studied for the ministry, Samuel Howe was a physician, and Lyndon Johnson had long been a politician after a short career as a teacher and school administrator.

These leaders were driven by diverse motives. Most evinced strong humanitarian sympathies; many wished to make democracy a reality for a larger portion of the citizenry, and several clearly enjoyed the prestige of their leadership. Their power came not only from financial means but also from confidence in their ideas, from their persuasiveness, and in most cases, from strong organizational skills. Their tactics varied, but three were used repeatedly. Most leaders relied on research to examine and document the extent and nature of the problems that the reform addressed. Mann started this practice with his 500-mile horseback ride visiting schools throughout Massachusetts, followed by his elaborate annual reports. Most did not concoct the reform in their own minds but searched widely for promising means to address the identified problem, with 19th century leaders looking to Europe and 20th century leaders scouting domestically. In the 19th century, a common tactic for initiating a reform was to start a small privately funded demonstration and later seek state funding to expand the services. This was true of Mann who started a normal school with private funds, Barnard who started teachers' institutes with private funds, Cogswell and Gallaudet's establishment of the first asylum for the deaf, and Dewey's establishment of his Laboratory School. That tactic was less common in the 20th century, perhaps because by then citizens were accustomed to government playing an important role.

The Federal government played a small role in leading education reform until the mid-1900s. As will be seen in Chapter 10, the federal government is directly involved in all three of the major education reform initiatives being undertaken at the dawn of the 21st century. In the past half-century the federal government has become the alpha male of education reform, with bi-partisan support for its new assertiveness, although not without critics on both sides of the aisle.

Lesson 5: Federal or state mandates, incentives, and monitoring usually accelerate reforms. The federal Head Start Program and Title I of the Elementary and Secondary Education Act funds were critical to the swift spread of compensatory education throughout the land. Supplemental funding from several states further expanded the numbers of children served and the intensity of the services provided. Monitoring and enforcement also helped—as was illustrated with ESEA when gross abuses of Title I funds were largely eliminated in the second decade. U.S. Supreme Court decisions in 1971 and the Education for All Handicapped Act of 1975 jump-started the provision of public education services to severely disabled youth and substantially changed the quality of services offered within a single decade.

It is clear, however, that federal support does not assure success. For instance, the post-Sputnik "new math" innovation was developed and disseminated with considerable support from the National Science Foundation, but it failed to take hold.

It might appear that the federal effect is merely a reflection of preexisting widespread support for the reform. The facts indicate otherwise. The 1962 Supreme Court decision banning non-sectarian prayer in schools elicited widespread public furor, far exceeding any of the Court's prior decisions, but the decision largely achieved its objective. Compensatory education was limited to just a few demonstration programs and the imaginations of several social scientists until President Johnson put it on the national agenda. Federal mandates and incentives provide a reform with publicity and credibility, and usually offer financial resources for compliance or threaten sanctions for non-compliance.

Although the amount of money the federal government offers as incentives, even for its largest program, is never more than a small percentage of total public school expenditures, school systems have large fixed costs for their buildings and staff salaries, leaving them with small discretionary budgets that sometimes can be considerably expanded with federal funds. This is particularly true in poor districts, which receive a disproportionate share of federal compensatory education funding.

Horace Mann was quick to use state financial incentives to induce local school committees to improve their schools, and he also established reporting systems to monitor compliance. In the mid-1800s, states funded normal schools to prepare teachers and then latter required examinations for those who sought teaching certificates. By the late 1800s many states were funding residential schools for children with disabilities or had adopted provisions to pay the expenses when children were sent to other state's facilities. At about the same time, several state supreme courts ruled religious instruction and practices unconstitutional under their state constitutions. By the 1970s many states also provided funds to supplement the federal compensatory education funding.

Above it was observed that 19th century initiators of reforms often started small demonstrations with private funds and then sought state support to implement the reform more widely and that practice that fell from favor in the 20th century. In place of that strategy, policy entrepreneurs have sought to initiate legislated programs on a large scale so that the funding can be spread widely to many school districts, thereby quickly creating a large constituency that lobbies for continuation of the program. This latter strategy, however, risks implementing and maintaining programs that do not work well.

Lesson 6: High costs do not necessarily thwart reforms, although they may preclude adoption by certain districts at given points in time. Five of the seven studied reforms were expensive to implement. Universal public education was very expensive, first bringing additional students into elementary school for a longer school year, then bringing almost everyone in for another four years of high school, and more recently enrolling 63 percent of high school graduates in postsecondary education.[26] Progressive education required smaller classes, science laboratories, art supplies, musical instruments, vocational education shops, and much better trained teachers. The efforts to recruit more able and better prepared teachers have increased average teacher salaries from about that of farm hands to 116 percent of all full-time earnings in the year 2000.[27] The average costs for the 11 percent of students assigned to special education are almost three times those of regular education.[28] Compensatory education cost the federal government almost $15 billion dollars in 2001, and many states and several districts make additional expenditures for these services from their own funds.[29] Only the secularization reform and the multicultural education reform have added little to the cost of education.

American education reform has been dependent on a dramatically expanding national economy. Without rapid expansion in Gross Domestic Product per person, several of the studied reforms would have been stillborn.

Lesson 7: Reliable and favorable information about the reform helps, including information on the problem or opportunity being addressed, the resources needed for the reform, approaches that facilitate implementation, and the impacts of the reform. Horace Mann was perhaps the first to collect and disseminate data on problems of schools, and used that data to support the universal public education reform. Barnard reported on the inadequacies of teacher preparation, demonstrated teacher institutes as a means of improving teaching, and used the results of the institutes to lobby for state support of such institutes. Progressives used school surveys showing dismal student achievement to gain support for their new pedagogies and then use evaluations to assess the effects of progressive education. Cogswell surveyed Connecticut clergymen on the number of deaf persons in the state to help launch a school for deaf children and then used the school as a model for others. Social scientists' findings helped provoke the compensatory education reform and then their modern evaluation methods assessed its impacts. Textbook analyses documented the exclusion and derogatory representations of minorities of color from primary instructional materials. Of course, unfavorable information about a reform's implementation or effects can undermine the reform.

The development of a new reform inevitably involves unknowns, and pioneers understand that. School districts that are early adopters usually realize there may be unforeseen risks as well as benefits. Most of the 15,000 school districts in the country are not early adopters but are cautiously looking for proven solutions to their problems. Developers' enthusiasm for their reforms and innovations often creates the impression of a proven solution before that has been established, and occasionally the developers engage in deliberate false advertising.[30]

The United States has long maintained a Food and Drug Administration and a Federal Aviation Administration to assure effectiveness and safety in those domains, but the country has nothing comparable for education. In the 1970s, the U.S. Department of Education created a Joint Dissemination Review Panel (later named the Program Effectiveness Panel) to judge the effectiveness education innovations, but it did not visit implementation sites or monitor the evaluation work, and it required developers only to submit evidence of benefits, allowing them to withhold any other data indicating zero or negative effects.[31] In 2002 the federal government contracted for a What Works Clearinghouse to review and synthesize existing research and evaluations in an effort to determine what works in education.[32] That clearinghouse has articulated and applied guidelines for judging the adequacy of the evidence that it synthesizes but has no control over the research or evaluation upon which it must rely, other than to disregard those studies that it judges inadequate.

Lesson 8: Persistence is essential—often for 50 or 100 years, for difficulties and setbacks are inevitable. Most reforms have been phased in and spread nationally only with the passage of many decades. Universal elementary education spread through the growing country between 1840 and 1900, but universal high school education did not become common until the 1930s. Secularization of education began with Horace Mann's 1840s efforts to reduce the role of religion in public schools but was not achieved nationwide until after two Supreme Court decisions in the 1960s. Progressive education first gained notice in the 1870s but did not reach its heyday until the 1940s. Efforts to professionalize teaching extend back to the 1840s and are being continued today by the National Board for Professional Teaching Standards and other groups. The first American school for children with handicaps was opened in 1817, but special education was expanded and changed dramatically in the early 1900s with the introduction of "ungraded" classes for students with special needs and then changed dramatically again in the 1970s following the enactment of the Education for All Handicapped Children Act.

Only the compensatory education and multicultural education reforms spread rapidly. Compensatory education had spread through the country in less than a decade and has evolved only slowly since, although the test-based accountability reform, to be discussed in Chapter 10, was grafted onto it beginning in the 1980s. Multicultural education has antecedents that go as far back as the late colonial period but began as a reform movement in the 1960s and by the 1990s it had modified textbook treatment of minorities of color and the literary canon.

Many of the early reform leaders suffered daunting setbacks. Jefferson was a three-time loser before his first success at education reform. A few years after becoming the first Secretary to Massachusetts' Board of Education, Mann's position was almost eliminated when Democrats wrestled control of the state legislature from the Whigs. Barnard in Connecticut did lose his job to the same political transition and had most of his work undone, only to be invited back seven years later to piece it together again. Despite Francis Parker's innovations and apparent success in Quincy, he was driven out by his critics, was routed from Boston after a short stay, and then settled in as the head of Cook County Normal School, only to have Chicago politicians slash his budget. Dewey and his wife,

Alice Chipman, suffered the disdain of the University of Chicago president, had a string of quarrels with the parents and staff of their laboratory school, and left after just eight years. John Runkle, President of MIT, sought to have the NEA endorse vocational education as a supplement to academic coursework, but it took the association three decades to do so. Gallaudet almost failed in his European trip to learn methods for teaching the deaf. Farrell constantly had to wrangle for funds and answer to critics of her classes for children with disabilities, even though she had the strong support of her superintendent. President Johnson had to suppress temporarily the enforcement of ESEA regulations to keep a restive Congress from undoing the legislation.

Education reform is like hiking up a steep mountain during torrential rains—a strenuous trek on a slippery slope—for 50 or 100 years.

Resistance and conflict are inevitable in education reforms for several reasons. Public schools are democratically controlled institutions and democracy unveils conflict. Americans hold a strong belief in the importance of schooling for the development of youth and the progress of the nation. There are a wide range of goals to which education can be directed including: The development of basic academic skills, knowledge about the natural world and the human legacy, respect for authority, manners, self-discipline, competitive instincts, artistic sensitivities and expression, life-coping skills, occupational capabilities, responsible citizenship, interpersonal and social skills, social cohesion, initiative and leadership, critical thinking skills, an inquiring mind, logical thinking skills, the love of learning, individuality, creativity, understanding and appreciation of American culture, spirituality, and salvation. Selection among these goals is largely a matter of values, making disagreements inevitable. In addition, for any given goal, there can be great differences of opinion about the optimal means for achieving it, with each opinion based on varying mixes of facts, analysis, political ideology, and personal interests. Most American adults consider themselves experts on education, having studied its practices first hand for 12-20 years during their own schooling, and that tends to exacerbate the disputes. Finally, there are usually both winners and losers during major policy changes. Machiavelli noted the difficulty of reform five centuries ago:

> And it ought to be remembered that there is nothing more difficult to take in hand, more perilous to conduct, or more uncertain in its success, than to take the lead in the introduction of a new order of things. Because the innovator has for enemies all those who have done well under the old conditions, and lukewarm defenders in those who may do well under the new.[33]

Gibbon, in his *History of the Decline and Fall of the Roman Empire*, concludes even more darkly, observing that one of the verities of history is the human predilection for faction and strife that arises from differences in racial, cultural, and economic experience. Gibbon understated the problem, for even within a group of similar people, there will be substantial differences of opinion, as evidenced by family strife, church committee disputes, and professional association debates. Nevertheless, our case studies demonstrate that the persistent pursuit of a reform can prevail.

Comparisons with Findings from Prior Studies

Hundreds of scholars have sought to infer lessons about education innovation and reform success or failure from various sources of evidence. How do their findings agree, disagree, or complement the lessons inferred above? We cannot begin to cover all the scholars' work in this chapter but we will focus on several who provide a wide range of perspectives.

The historians David Tyack and Larry Cuban scanned the last century of public school reform in a book titled *Tinkering toward Utopia*. They concluded that the reforms that were relatively smoothly implemented and long enduring had the following characteristics: 1) they were add-ons that did not interfere with standard operating procedures of schools, 2) they were non-controversial, 3) they created influential constituents interested in seeing the changes continued, and 4) they often were required by law and easily monitored.[34] They observe that changes in schools have occurred gradually and in unforeseen ways—much like a slinky moves, and that reforms often are not adopted as initially intended but rather adapted and hybridized with former ways. They suggest that the encouragement of hybridization would be a good strategy for reformers—that "reform policies could be stated as principles, general aims, to be modified in the light of experience, and embodied in practices that vary by school or even by classroom."[35] They also note that "Change where it counts the most—in the daily interactions of teacher and students—is the hardest to achieve and most important."[36] Findings from the case studies in our book are only partly consistent with Tyack and Cuban's conclusions. Three of our studied reforms lacked at least two of the four characteristics that they identified as important—universal public schooling, the secularization of public education, and progressive education. The first and third of those were not add-ons, all three raised considerable controversy, and the third was not mandated by law. The secularization reform created only a very small constituency of supporters, leaving the majority and a large Catholic minority dissatisfied. On the other hand, our four most recent reforms—professionalization of teaching, special education, compensatory education, and multicultural education are consistent with Tyack and Cuban's findings: they could be considered add-ons, they did create large constituencies that supported them, and they were either required by law or partly supported by federal grant programs. Tyack and Cuban's other findings are about the micro level reform—where reforms play out in local districts and schools.

Paul Berman, Milbrey McLauglin, and colleagues, mostly policy researchers, examined 293 local education change projects undertaken in the mid-1970s with funding from four federal programs. They found that most local districts achieved general compliance with the federal guidelines, but many had difficulty fully implementing the intended changes, and only a few maintained them for long. These researchers identified a few predictors of success: ambitious projects were more likely to change teaching than modest, narrow ones, although those aspiring to system-wide change usually failed; active commitment of the school district leadership was important to implementation and maintenance; simple adoption of pre-packaged programs usually failed whereas efforts to adapt changes to the local school setting, with feedback and adjustments, were more likely to succeed. Opportunistic projects (usually undertaken mainly to win the grant funds offered) were less successful than those undertaken to address recognized needs. The widely publicized conclusion of Berman and McLaughlin's study was that policies made at high levels rarely change local schools.[37] McLaughlin revisited these findings a decade later, using another set of projects funded under a different federal program. She found that high-level policy mandates that were initially opposed at the local level sometimes gained local acceptance over time—suggesting, "Belief can follow practice."[38] She also concluded that skilled external change agents can be more effective than initially thought, bridging the gap between policy and the local staff who are asked to implement change. Nevertheless, she confirmed that implementation of school change is difficult, not likely to achieve quick fixes, and unlikely to affect classroom practices unless targeted there.[39] Some of these findings reinforce the lessons drawn from the case studies of this book. The observation that change is more often *adapted* by local districts than simply *adopted* by them, consistent with a conclusion of Tyack and Cuban, is at the micro level of reform, generally not examined by our case studies.

David Plank and William Boyd, education policy analysts, suggest that democratic decision-making is best for fostering educational reforms, because it requires marshaling broad support from parents, teachers, employers, and taxpayers, and such support is necessary for successful implementation and operation of reforms.[40] These writers contend that "antipolitical" arenas of decision-making—the courts and free markets—undermine the broad support needed to sustain reform. The case studies in our book suggest otherwise. Court decisions were the key to the second phase of the secularization of public education and to the expansion of special education in the 1970s. The effect of markets on public education decision-making has only recently been tested widely, with charter school options and a few limited voucher demonstrations, both of which will be discussed in the next chapter.

In the early 1990s, the National Academy of Sciences (NAS) was asked by the U.S. Department of Education to examine how the Department's research might contribute more to school reform. The NAS study committee, which included several people who had achieved eminence in research outside of education and the social sciences, identified "supply side" barriers and "demand side" barriers to the use of research in education reform.[41] Supply side problems include: Research that ignores the contexts of schools, the Department of Education's general failure to synthesize research across multiple studies, and innovations that are either poorly prescribed or so prescriptive as to demean teachers. NAS noted that many educational innovations are marketed nationally after only short-term evaluations in sites controlled by the developer, leaving unanswered questions about their implementability by third parties and about the endurance of any observed short-term benefits. Demand-side barriers to the use of research in reform include parental complacency with schools, the extended training teachers receive in established instructional approaches during their own K-12 educations, the hectic schedules of teachers which leave little time for consulting research studies and thinking how they might be incorporated into their practice, and the very limited support teachers are often given when asked to adopt an innovation or reform.[42] The study committee recommended more "collaborative relationships" between practitioners and researchers "in pursuit of new understandings and practices that will improve education."[43] These findings are mostly at an intermediate level, between our study's macro focus and the micro focus on how reforms play out in local districts and schools. They tend to complement our lessons, suggesting that reforms be developed and implemented with consideration for teachers' realities and that there be more and better evaluation of reforms before widespread implementation.

Marshall Sashkin and John Egermeier, U.S. Department of Education researchers at the time, identified four strategies widely used to improve schools: fix the parts by transferring innovations into the schools, fix the people through professional training and development, fix the school by developing its capacities to solve problems, and fix the system through systemic reform.[44] They conclude, acknowledging the evidence is not definitive, that systemic reform has the best chance of success, fostering more autonomy and professionalism at the school-site level while holding the staff accountable for results.[45] This approach combines elements of two current education reforms that will be considered in the next chapter—comprehensive school reform and test-based accountability. Several of our studied and relatively successful reforms relied on "fix the parts" or "fix the people" strategies that Sashkin and Egermeier conclude are generally ineffective. Progressive education sought to fix both the curriculum and the pedagogy, professionalization sought to fix the teachers, special education corrected the illegal exclusion of children with disabilities from public schools and the inappropriate services often provided to those who were admitted, compensatory education wanted to fix schools' failure to adapt to the needs of deprived children, and multicultural education intended to fix racist textbooks and school practices. All these "fix" reforms are notable successes in terms of widespread implementation and maintenance, but Sashkin and Egermeier were mainly concerned about improved learning, and our studied reforms have fallen short of the hoped-for improvements in student learning.

Ernest House, who is noted for his evaluations of innovative programs, observes that universities, R&D centers, and businesses are the sources of most education innovations, and school systems, at best, are purchasers of innovation.[46] He concludes that educational innovations are spread largely by personal contacts, not by information dissemination, and that innovations must permeate the rigid internal structure of bureaucratic school systems, which present inertia, if not outright resistance, even when the superintendent or others within the system are advocates. He also notes that teachers are often unconvinced of the efficacy of proposed innovations, that they find the innovations require considerable time and energy to learn, and that there are no rewards when teachers make them work.[47] While House's claim about the sources of educational innovations is probably correct, it was not generally true of the more ambitious reforms reviewed in this book. Universities, R&D centers, and businesses played virtually no role in four of our studied reforms—universal public schooling, secularization, and the initial phases of the professionalization of teaching and special education. Only the progressive education reform, compensatory education reform, and multicultural education came substantially from the sources identified by House—and then only from the universities. House's other conclusions are at a more micro level than the cases studies of this book. His conclusions about teachers do reinforce those of prior cited scholars and his observation about school system inertia is elaborated by the next source.

Seymour Sarason is a clinical psychologist who has extensively consulted with school districts. His *The Predictable Failure of Educational Reform* claims that American schools have been "intractable to change."[48] He asserts what has remained unchanged despite several reform efforts is the gulf in achievement between children of different social classes and races, student disinterest in school learning, and a focus on rote memorization rather than the integration of new ideas that enlarges the personal and social identity of students. Sarason concludes the reforms have not affected these because reformers from outside schools "have nothing resembling a holistic conception of the system that they seek to influence" and even many of the people within the system do not understand the system thoroughly.[49] He goes on to indicate that a necessary condition for successful school reform is a redistribution of power within school systems, giving teachers more influence in the decision-making and students more responsibility and control over their learning, although he adds these will not make every reform successful. Finally, he suggests that if teachers are to foster a more intellectual and collegial environment in the classroom, the teachers themselves need such an environment within the schools.[50] Sarason's concern about the achievement gulf is consistent with what is reported in Chapter 7 and above in this chapter. Sarason addresses school reform at a micro level, which was not examined by our study. Contrary to Sarason's claim about instruction not having changed, our prior chapters have presented considerable evidence that the progressive education reform has changed prevailing instruction moderately, putting less emphasis on rote memorization and recitation and more on fostering student interest and helping students consider the application of new knowledge. His prescription for successful education reform—more discretion for teachers and students—is not new. The professionalization of teaching sought more discretion for teachers and progressive education sought more discretion for students and both partially succeed in providing that, but neither has had a large effect on student achievement.

Robert Slavin has worked single-mindedly for three decades researching and developing instructional strategies and programs to benefit poor and minority children, gaining considerable acclaim first for his work on cooperative learning; then for his Success for All elementary school reading, writing, and languages arts program; and later for his Roots and Wings comprehensive elementary school reform program. He argues that most of the reform efforts of the last quarter of the 20th century have not addressed directly what most needs to be changed in schools—that "student achievement cannot change unless America's teachers use markedly more effective instructional methods."[51] He argues that various instructional programs should be rigorously evaluated and the results should be widely publicized to education decision makers. Three of the seven reforms examined in our study partly aspired to reduce the achievement gap by changing instructional methods—progressive education, special education, and multicultural education—and none have been notable success with that goal. In addition, several innovations during the latter quarter of the 20th century did try to improve the effectiveness of instruction with limited success, including micro-teaching training, computer assisted instruction, and the curriculum and pedagogy guidelines issued by several organizations including the National Council of Teachers of Mathematics and the American Association for the Advancement of Science.

Michael Fullan's extensive review of the literature on educational change, which included some of the literature cited above, concludes, "Neglect of the phenomenology of change—that is, how people actually experience change as distinct from how it might have been intended—is at the heart of the spectacular lack of success of most social reforms."[52] He notes considerable research indicating that teachers tend to be skeptical of innovations (partly because so many innovations have failed), feel overwhelmed by their daily responsibilities, and are concerned about the time and effort needed to learn innovations and implement them in the classroom.[53] Fullan identifies eight factors affecting the initiation of innovation at the local level: existence and quality of innovations, access to them, advocacy from the district administration, teacher advocacy, availability of external change agents to assist in implementation, community pressures for and against the innovation, state or federal policies in support, and whether the bureaucracy pursues innovation to solve educational problems or for extrinsic purposes.[54] Fullan synthesizes 10 guidelines for facilitating change at the local level. Recasting them, they boil down to: 1) Strive to build agreement and buy-in for change through an interchange and synthesis of ideas among the community, administration, and teachers, even though full consensus is unlikely, 2) plan and undertake whatever institutional changes are needed to support instructional innovations being implemented, 3) limit the time spent on needs assessment and program development, otherwise people will approach burnout before implementation begins, 4) provide incentives for change, training, and technical assistance, even though not everyone is likely to fully implement the change—some will reject the change, some will need more assistance than is available, and some will need more time, 5) allow two or three years of practice, reflection, and clarification before expecting substantial change—smooth and swift implementation usually indicates trivial changes or superficial implementation. Although Fullan's guidelines are at the micro level, the first, fourth, and fifth are consistent with our inferred lessons, and the other two do not contradict any of ours.

Expanded Set of Lessons

Six of the eight lessons drawn from the case studies of this book are supported by one or more of the above cited scholars. The only exceptions are the lessons that successful reforms are aided by several changing social, economic, and/or political contexts and that high costs do not necessarily undermine reforms.

While many historians focus on the contexts driving change, most scholars of education reform appear oblivious to the importance of this factor. The prior chapters leave no doubt about the importance of changing contexts to education reforms.

High cost obviously can be an impediment to reform in the short run, but history shows it has not been a barrier in the long run, although that is partly because of the strong economic growth that America has achieved throughout most of the last two centuries.

While the above cited literature does not provide good evidence against any of the lessons inferred from Chapters 2-8, several of those sources suggest two additional lessons, focused at a more micro-level than examined in our case studies—on how reforms play out in local districts and schools. Those lessons are as follows.

Lesson 9: A systems approach is helpful in planning and implementing reforms, giving consideration to interactions with schools' goals, structures, processes, and external relations with society. Schools are complex systems, both internally and as part of larger social systems. Internally there are several operational sub-systems, including those of governance, management, finance, hiring, purchasing, building maintenance, and teaching. Schools must also interface with the local community, their state education agency, federal agencies, teacher preparation institutions, education R&D institutions, the postsecondary education, and employers.[55] If the reform requires simultaneous changes in several of the internal sub-systems or several of the interfaces with the external systems, it will be difficult to carry out.

Most scholars who have examined change efforts within schools have observed that the structure and culture of schools make them resistant to substantial change. That is due to several reasons. Public schools are democratically controlled at three different levels (local, state, and federal) and must serve multiple constituencies—parents, employers, and the larger society—which often have widely divergent opinions. Public education takes place in bureaucracies with many levels of decision-making and authority. Principals usually cannot financially reward or fire their teaching staff. Finally, teachers are trained to be professionals but frequently find themselves to be cogs in a vast bureaucracy.

Lesson 10: Teacher capacity and motivation are important for carrying out classroom reforms. The initial training of teachers for a reform, the availability of subsequent support for them during implementation, and internal or external incentives will facilitate the success of classroom reform. Teachers are the frontline soldiers of such reforms, and for millennia generals have known that the motivation, training, equipment, and logistical support of their troops are important for combat success. Several educational reformers have been sensitive to that reality but others have ignored it. If a reform will add substantial new demands on the time of teachers' without offsetting time savings or increased compensation, successful implementation is likely to be threatened. Several scholars also suggest that opportunities for constructive adaptation or "hybridization" of reforms at the local level can foster morale, stimulate teachers intellectually, enhance capacity, accommodate local variations, and improve the effectiveness of a reform.

Summary of the Lessons

The eight lessons inferred from our case studies and the above two lessons drawn from other literature on school innovation and reform yield a total of ten. To recap, with slight re-ordering they are as follows:

1) **Successful reforms are stimulated and pushed along by several changing social, economic, and/or political contexts** that pose problems or opportunities within society or the schools.

2) **Ambitious changes, once initiated, are more likely to succeed than modest ones**, although they take more effort and time.

3) **Successful reforms offer multiple appeals for various stakeholders,** often with different appeals for parents, educators, business leaders, citizens, and politicians.

4) **A large corps of reform leaders is needed for nationwide success,** highlighting the problems or opportunities, proposing the reform, and managing implementation throughout the states, districts and individual schools.

5) **Federal or state mandates, incentives, and monitoring usually accelerate reforms.**

6) **High costs do not necessarily thwart reforms,** although they may preclude adoption by certain districts at given points in time.

7) **Reliable and favorable information about the reform contributes to success,** including information on the problem or opportunity being addressed, the resources needed for the reform, approaches that facilitate implementation, and the impacts of the reform.

8) **A systems approach is helpful in planning and implementing reforms,** giving consideration to interactions with schools' goals, structures, processes, and the schools' external relations with society.

9) **Teacher capacity and motivation are important for carrying out classroom reforms.**

10) **Persistence is essential—often for 50 or 100 years**, for difficulties and setbacks are inevitable.

Although American education has changed dramatically over the past two centuries it is not without serious shortcomings. The objectives and goals of most reforms detailed in this book have been only partially achieved. In addition, the world is evolving and presenting the United States with new challenges that the schools will be asked to help meet. How might the lessons inferred in this chapter help inform current and future educational reforms? The next chapter will strive to answer that question.

---

[1] U.S. Department of Education, National Center for Education Statistics, *120 Years of American Education: A Statistical Profile* (Washington DC: U.S. Government Printing Office, 1993), 27, 50.

[2] This is a rough estimate based on the following considerations: Massachusetts was known to be a leader in education during the 1700s and 1800s, but Horace Mann's aggressive monitoring of the state's school system in the 1830s found that the school year was about three months during the winter and two during the summer, that the one in ten schools closed earlier than planned because of student rebellions, and that on any given day about half the students were in absent. (See Chapters 2 and 4.) That means the average youth received about 50 days of schooling per year. Clearly not all the students completed the full eight years of elementary school, and it is known that 70 years later only 10-15 percent continued through high school, and only 2 or 3 percent continued through college, so the average years of schooling in 1830 was probably about eight. Multiplying eight years by the 50-days of average attendance per year gives a total of 400 days of schooling. The south clearly trailed the northeastern states in education, but it is not clear by how much. Today the average school year is 178.5 days, average daily attendance is 90 percent, and virtually all students complete 10 years of schooling, 88 percent complete high school, and 29 percent complete four years of college. That means the average days of schooling—not counting post-baccalaureate education—is about 2088 days (178.5 days x .9 attendance rate x 13 average years of schooling). So the country's average days of schooling today is more than five times that of the most educated state in the 1830s. The source of current data is: U.S. Department of Education, National Center for Education Statistics, *Digest of Education Statistics: 2001*(Washington DC: U.S. Government Printing Office, 2002), 17, 49.

[3] U.S. Department of Education, National Center for Education Statistics, *Trends in Academic Progress: Three Decades of Student Performance* (Washington DC: author, 2000), 17, 21.

[4] U.S. Department of Education, National Center for Education Statistics, *Digest of Education Statistics: 2001*(Washington DC: U.S. Government Printing Office, 2002), 161.

[5] Examples are publicly released 12th-grade items from the 1996 National Assessment of Education Progress, available online from http://nces.ed.gov/nationsreportcard/itmrls (click on "Search Options"); retrieved July 27, 2003.

[6] David Tyack, and William Tobin, "The 'Grammar' of Schooling: Why Has It Been So Hard to Change?" *American Educational Research Journal* 31 (Fall, 1994): 455.

[7] David Tyack, and William Tobin, "The 'Grammar' of Schooling: Why Has it Been So Hard to Change?" *American Educational Research Journal* 31 (Fall, 1994): 454-455, 457-459.

[8] David Tyack, and William Tobin, "The 'Grammar' of Schooling: Why Has It Been so Hard to Change?" *American Educational Research Journal* 31 (Fall, 1994): 463-478.

[9] Larry Cuban, "A Fundamental Puzzle of School Reform," *Phi Delta Kappan* 69 (January 1988): 341.

[10] Larry Cuban, "A Fundamental Puzzle of School Reform," *Phi Delta Kappan* 69 (January 1988): 342.

[11] Larry Cuban, "A Fundamental Puzzle of School Reform," *Phi Delta Kappan* 69 (January 1988): 342.

[12] Larry Cuban, "A Fundamental Puzzle of School Reform," *Phi Delta Kappan* 69 (January 1988): 343.

[13] Larry Cuban, "A Fundamental Puzzle of School Reform," *Phi Delta Kappan* 69 (January 1988): 342.

[14] Larry Cuban, *How Teachers Taught: Constancy and Change in American Classrooms: 1880-1990*, 2nd edition (New York: Teachers College Press, 1993), xviii-xix.

[15] Larry Cuban, *How Teachers Taught: Constancy and Change in American Classrooms: 1880-1990*, 2nd edition (New York: Teachers College Press, 1993), 6-8, 145-146.

[16] Michael B. Katz, *Class, Bureaucracy, and Schools: The Illusion of Educational Change in America*, expanded ed. (New York: Praeger, 1975), xviii.

[17] Michael B. Katz, *Class, Bureaucracy, and Schools: The Illusion of Educational Change in America*, expanded ed. (New York: Praeger, 1975), xviii-xix.

[18] Michael B. Katz, *Class, Bureaucracy, and Schools: The Illusion of Educational Change in America*, expanded ed. (New York: Praeger, 1975), 7, 15, 22.

[19] See: James Dyson, *A History of Great Inventions* (New York: Carroll & Graf, 2001), 106; Russell Bourne, *Invention in America* (Golden, CO: Fulcrum Press, 1996), 105; and Kathleen McAuliffe, "The Undiscovered World of Thomas Edison," *The Atlantic Monthly* 276 (December, 1995): 7 when printed from web.

[20] Marcia Angell, *The Truth About the Drug Companies: How They Deceive Us and What To Do About It* (New York: Random House, 2004), 23.

[21] Merrill Goozner, *The $800 Million Pill: The Truth Behind the Cost of New Drugs* (Berkeley, CA: University of California Press, 2004), 165.

[22] Will Durant and Ariel Durant, *The Lessons of History* (New York: Simon & Schuster, 1968), 36.

[23] David H. Fischer, *Historians' Fallacies: Toward a Logic of Historical Thought* (New York: Harper Torchbooks, 1970), 169.

[24] Will Durant and Ariel Durant, *The Lessons of History* (New York: Simon & Schuster, 1968), 34.

[25] Quoted in, Laurence J. Peter, *Peter's Quotations: Ideas for Our Time* (New York: Bantam Books, 1979), 220.

[26] U.S. Department of Education, National Center for Education Statistics, *Digest of Education Statistics: 2001* (Washington DC: U.S. Government Printing Office, 2002), 220.

[27] U.S. Department of Education, National Center for Education Statistics, *Digest of Education Statistics: 2001* (Washington DC: U.S. Government Printing Office, 2002), 90.

[28] The costs are calculated from: President's Commission on Excellence in Special Education, *A New Era: Revitalizing Special Education for Children and Their*

Families (Washington DC: U.S. Department of Education, Office of Special Education and Rehabilitation Services, 2002), 30.

[29] U.S. Department of Education, National Center for Education Statistics, *Digest of Education Statistics: 2001* (Washington DC: U.S. Government Printing Office, 2002), 423, 434.

[30] Richard C. Atkinson and Gregg B. Jackson, eds. *Research and Education Reform: Roles for the Office of Educational Research and Improvement* (Washington DC: National Academy Press, 1992), 130, 154-155.

[31] Richard C. Atkinson and Gregg B. Jackson, eds. *Research and Education Reform: Roles for the Office of Educational Research and Improvement* (Washington DC: National Academy Press, 1992), 79-83.

[32] The What Works Clearinghouse's structure, planned activities, and procedures are described on its website at www.w-w-c.org .

[33] Nicolo Machiavelli, *The Prince*. Translated by W.K. Marriott. Project Guttenberg, 1998. Retrieved from www.gutenberg.org/dirs/etext98/ tprnc11.txt January 11, 2005.

[34] David Tyack and Larry Cuban, *Tinkering Toward Utopia: A Century of Public School Reform* (Cambridge, MA: Harvard University Press, 1995), 57.

[35] David Tyack and Larry Cuban, *Tinkering Toward Utopia: A Century of Public School Reform* (Cambridge, MA: Harvard University Press, 1995), 83.

[36] David Tyack and Larry Cuban, *Tinkering Toward Utopia: A Century of Public School Reform* (Cambridge, MA: Harvard University Press, 1995), 10.

[37] The original study is not readily available. A summary of it is provided in: Milbrey W. McLaughlin, "The Rand Change Agent Study Revisited: Macro Perspectives and Micro Realities," *Educational Researcher*, 19 (December, 1990): 12-13.

[38] Milbrey W. McLaughlin, "The Rand Change Agent Study Revisited: Macro Perspectives and Micro Realities," *Educational Researcher*, 19 (December, 1990): 13.

[39] Milbrey W. McLaughlin, "The Rand Change Agent Study Revisited: Macro Perspectives and Micro Realities," *Educational Researcher*, (December, 1990): 14-15.

[40] David N. Plank and William L. Boyd, "Antipolitics, Education, and Institutional Choice: The Flight from Democracy," *American Educational Research Journal* 31 (Summer, 1994): 264, 277.

[41] Richard C. Atkinson and Gregg B. Jackson, eds. *Research and Education Reform: Roles for the Office of Educational Research and Improvement* (Washington DC: National Academy Press, 1992), 129.

[42] Richard C. Atkinson and Gregg B. Jackson, eds. *Research and Education Reform: Roles for the Office of Educational Research and Improvement* (Washington DC: National Academy Press, 1992), 32, 52, 79-82, 130-134.

[43] Richard C. Atkinson and Gregg B. Jackson, eds. *Research and Education Reform: Roles for the Office of Educational Research and Improvement* (Washington DC: National Academy Press, 1992), 136.

[44] Marshall Sashkin and John Egermeier, *School Change Models and Processes: A Review and Synthesis of Research and Practice* (Washington DC: U. S. Government Printing Office, 1993), 3-16.

[45] Marshall Sashkin and John Egermeier, *School Change Models and Processes: A Review and Synthesis of Research and Practice* (Washington DC: U. S. Government Printing Office, 1993), 13, 17-20.

[46] Ernest R. House, *The Politics of Educational Innovation* (Berkeley, CA: McCutchan Publishing, 1974), 172-174.

[47] Ernest R. House, *The Politics of Educational Innovation* (Berkeley, CA: McCutchan Publishing, 1974), 34-35, 43, 47-49, 56-58, 69, 73.

[48] Seymour B. Sarason, *The Predictable Failure of Educational Reform: Can We Change Course Before It is Too Late?* (San Francisco: Jossey-Bass, 1990), xiii.

[49] Seymour B. Sarason, *The Predictable Failure of Educational Reform: Can We Change Course Before It is Too Late?* (San Francisco: Jossey-Bass, 1990), 4, 26.

[50] Seymour B. Sarason, *The Predictable Failure of Educational Reform: Can We Change Course Before It is Too Late?* (San Francisco: Jossey-Bass, 1990), 52, 87-95, 138, 142.

[51] Robert E. Slavin, "Reforming State and Federal Policies to Support Adoption of Proven Practices," *Educational Researcher* 25 (December, 1996): 4)

[52] Michael G. Fullan, *The New Meaning of Educational Change*, 2nd ed. (New York: Teachers College Press, 1991), 4.

[53] Michael G. Fullan, *The New Meaning of Educational Change*, 2nd ed. (New York: Teachers College Press, 1991), 32-35.

[54] Michael G. Fullan, *The New Meaning of Educational Change*, 2nd ed. (New York: Teachers College Press, 1991), 50-61.

[55] Consortium on the Productivity in the Schools, *Using What We Have To Get the Schools We Need: Productivity Focus on American Education* (Illinois: The Ball Foundation, 1995), 25-33.

10

Prospects of the Early 21st Century Reforms

Gregg B. Jackson

The third quarter of the 20th century saw a whirlwind of educational change in the United States. In 1954, the U.S. Supreme Court banned government induced segregation in public schools and a decades-long struggle for compliance followed. The 1957 Russian launch of Sputnik precipitated the National Defense Education Act (NDEA) that encouraged curriculum revisions, pedagogical changes, and enhanced teacher preparation in the subjects of mathematics, science, engineering, and foreign languages. That sparked efforts to improve the teaching of other subjects. In the 1960s, public television stations were created partly to provide educational programming such as Sesame Street and Nova. The mid-1960s brought compensatory education and then multicultural education reform soon followed. In the late 1960s and early 1970s, open classrooms serving several classes of students in a large space gained a popularity that was short-lived. In the mid-1970s, excitement arose from efforts to identify the instructional strategies of effective teachers and to train other teachers in those strategies by microteaching exercises that involved practicing very specific instructional behaviors. The mid-1970s also brought new life to special education, as noted in Chapter 6.

What effect did this have on student achievement? Several different achievement testing programs showed modest gains from 1950 to about 1965 and then modest declines until the mid-1970s. The Congressional Budget Office found those declines to be "widespread, occurring among many different types of students, on many different tests, in all subject areas, in private as well as public schools, and in all parts of the country"[1] In 1981, incoming President Reagan's Secretary of Education appointed a

National Commission on Excellence in Education. Eighteen months later it issued its report, *A Nation at Risk*, which opened by declaring,

> Our Nation is at risk. Our once unchallenged preeminence in commerce, industry, science, and technological innovation is being overtaken by competitors throughout the world. This report is concerned with only one of the many causes and dimensions of the problem.... The educational foundations of our society are presently being eroded by a rising tide of mediocrity that threatens our very future as a Nation and a people.... We have, in effect, been committing an act of unthinking, unilateral educational disarmament.[2]

The report cited 13 different "indicators of risk" including that thirteen percent of 17-year-olds were functionally illiterate, average achievement test scores had declined over the past three decades, and remedial mathematics courses in 4-year colleges had increased 72 percent between 1975 and 1980.[3] The report also cited 29 findings about problems in American schools, including that 69 percent of recent high school graduates had not taken intermediate algebra, that our high school graduates had received about one-third as many hours of instruction in mathematics beyond arithmetic as students in several other countries, two-thirds of American high school seniors reported doing less than one hour of homework a night, and "the professional working life of teachers is on the whole unacceptable" because of the low pay and lack of influence on educational matters.[4]

Although critics dismissed the report as politically motivated, rhetorical, and misleading, it caught the eye of the public and long held the attention of political leaders in both parties. That was partly due to the bad times the U.S. had suffered immediately preceding the report: a decade of stagnant economic growth, soaring inflation, ballooning trade deficits as Japanese imports captured the consumer electronics market and gained a stronghold in the automotive industry, and the international humiliation suffered when Iranian revolutionaries captured the U.S. embassy staff and our military initiative failed to free them. Most people probably did not recognize that the Commission had excluded from its report all the good news about American public schooling,[5] that many of the identified risks and problems—while real—had existed for a century, that part of the declines was associated with changing demographics of the school population,[6] and that the same indicators revealing declines in achievement starting in 1965 began to show very slowly rising achievement after 1975.[7] Even if this had been widely recognized, it might not have mattered. Americans were worried about the state of their nation. Long-lingering problems appeared to be of increasing importance in a global and information economy. And the report's rhetoric was memorable.

A Nation at Risk provoked an unprecedented series of efforts, at all levels of government, to improve public education. Most of the report's recommendations involved evolutionary improvements in educational resources—more academic coursework, more hours of instruction and homework, and better prepared and remunerated teachers. That spurred several people to move beyond piecemeal efforts to improve instruction in individual subjects to comprehensive and coordinated efforts aimed at improving schools. In addition, there were two unconventional recommendations in the report that sowed the seeds of a different approach to education reform, which would become known as the test-based accountability reform movement. Ironically, what soon became the main education reform initiative of the Reagan administration, school choice, had not been suggested by the report. At the dawn of the 21st century, comprehensive school reform, test-based accountability, and school choice dominated school improvement initiatives in the United States.

What might the ten lessons inferred in Chapter 9 tell us about the prospects for each of these reform initiatives? Are they likely to be adopted widely, implemented as intended, and maintained? Are they likely to be effective in achieving the targeted objectives and goals? And what might be the side effects? Recognition of factors that are likely to propel each reform would allow leaders to make the best use of them. Identification of factors threatening a reform's success might allow reform leaders to counter or compensate for those factors. Resources are always limited, and if certain reforms have better prospects than others, it might be wise to redirect resources from the latter to the former.

In applying the lessons of the past to current reforms, it is important to recall that none of the reforms examined in Chapters 2-8 was established without opponents, problems, and temporary delays. That a current reform faces such difficulties says little about its ultimate potential. The better assessment is to apply the lessons of the past to the undercurrent of each reform rather than to its surface turbulence.

Comprehensive School Reform

Comprehensive school reform is also referred to as "whole school reform," "school wide reform," and "systemic reform." The latter term is also used for integrated reform efforts at the district or state level, which will not be addressed in this chapter. Comprehensive school reform undertakes coordinated changes in the curriculum, instructional approaches, classroom management practices, in-service professional development of teachers, school organization, administrative practices, parental involvement, and student assessment, all of which are directed at clearly articulated learning goals. This is the latest evolution of the resource enhancement approach to education improvement that has been advocated for two centuries, but it differs from prior efforts by replacing piecemeal changes with comprehensive and coordinated school-wide improvements. It was a reaction partly to the disappointing results of prior piecemeal changes and partly to a proliferation of uncoordinated federal and state programs aimed at improving American education. The federal government alone was funding hundreds of educational programs in the early 1990s.[8]

In the late 1980s, several universities, corporations, and non-profit groups undertook the development and demonstration of various models of comprehensive school reform. The models differed dramatically in philosophy and programmatic components. James Comer and colleagues at the Yale Child Study Center created the School Development Program that guides teams of school personnel, parents, and mental health professionals in creating a secure and accepting environment for student learning, drawing on principles from developmental and social psychology. Henry Levin and colleagues at Stanford created the Accelerated Schools program, based on the premise that low achieving students, as well as high achieving ones, will benefit most from enriched instruction that makes use of challenging learning resources and fosters high-level intellectual functioning rather than just basic academic skills. Robert Slavin, Nancy Madden, and associates at Johns Hopkins University created Success for All, which is a highly prescriptive reading, writing, and language arts development program that provides the instructional materials, directions for their use, training, and ongoing technical support. They subsequently developed Roots and Wings, which covers the full elementary school curriculum with a focus on both basic skills, problem-solving, and critical thinking skills.

Lesson 1 from Chapter 9 is that successful reforms are stimulated and pushed along by several changing social contexts. At least four changing contexts played a role in the initiation of comprehensive school reform. One was the loud alarm sounded by *A Nation at Risk* and the underlying concerns about America's apparently waning economic prowess. The second was growing disillusionment with prior piecemeal changes that focused on just one or two aspects of schooling at a time. The post-Sputnik new math, microteaching training, and compensatory education are examples of piecemeal changes. The third changing context was growing disappointment with the small effects of Title I compensatory education programs, which was thought due to the use of pull-out remedial programs that interrupted the participants' other schooling and could not, in one or two hours of special help a week, compensate for the other 23 hours of ineffective instruction.[9] Rotberg and Harvey's 1993 analysis of options for improving Title I concluded that school-wide improvement programs appeared more promising and recommended that schools with more than 50 percent poor students be allowed to use Title I funds for that purpose.[10] Research on unusually effective schools, advocacy of site-based management (allowing principals more discretion over the selection of staff and resources), and the development of the standards movement (discussed in the next section of this chapter) also influenced the development of the comprehensive school reform approach.[11] All these changing contexts, however, are relatively weak in comparison with the ones that pushed the reforms discussed in Chapters 2-8, such as the establishment of a democratic nation, massive immigration, the rise of science and technology, and the civil rights movement.

Lesson 2 is that ambitious school changes, once initiated, are more likely to succeed than modest ones, although they require more effort and time. Comprehensive school reform efforts are moderately ambitious in theory, with their focus on curriculum, instruction, teacher preparation, school organization and management, and student assessment, and their objective of boosting student achievement, particularly that of students who normally have lagged behind. There is, however, considerable variation in the comprehensiveness of models developed. For instance, several models address the entire curriculum, and others focus just on reading and language arts, hoping that improvements in those areas will affect learning in other areas.

Lesson 3 is that successful reforms offer multiple appeals for various stakeholders. Comprehensive school reform appeals to veteran educators and researchers who have long labored to improve educational outcomes with piecemeal approaches that have repeatedly yielded disappointing results. It also appeals to several foundations and corporations, which funded the New American Schools Development Corporation to invite groups not commonly involved in education to propose dramatically new models of schooling in an effort to bring new thinking to the field. Ultimately, however, the models that it funded were not dramatically different from past innovations.[12] Otherwise, the appeal of this reform is limited and it is best known to educators using its models.

Lesson 4 is that a large corps of leaders is needed for nationwide success of an education reform. Comprehensive school reform has several sources of leadership. The federal government has provided leadership in several ways that are described below. State and district officials have often encouraged schools to undertake such reform in attempts to boost achievement. Several of the model developers created substantial organizations to push their models. This reform has marshaled wider leadership within fifteen years than did most of the reforms described in Chapters 2-8.

Lesson 5 is that federal and state mandates, incentives, and monitoring usually accelerate reforms. In this respect, comprehensive school reform appears to be favorably positioned. The 1988 Amendments to Title I permitted schools with at least 75 percent poor children to use their Title I funds for improvements throughout the school. Six years later, partly in response to the Rotberg and Harvey report, Congress lowered the threshold to 50 percent poor children, and then three years later established the Comprehensive School Reform Demonstration program, which has provided several thousand schools, primarily those with lagging student achievement, with at least $50,000 a year for three years, to help implement such reforms.[13] The 1994 reauthorization of Title I also put heavy pressure on participating schools to raise student achievement, as will be discussed below. States added to the pressure with their state accountability reforms. Never before have public educators been under such pressure, and after decades of disappointing fragmented changes, they are eager for "heavy duty" tools that will improve achievement.

Lesson 6 is that high costs do not necessarily thwart reforms, although they may delay adoption by some districts. After initial start-up, most comprehensive school reform models cost an additional $100 to $200 per student per year for a school of 500 pupils.[14] The latter figure is three percent of average per-pupil expenditures. Thus cost should not be a serious impediment unless the United State's economy suffers sustained losses. Even if that happens, the extra funding needed for comprehensive school reform might continue to be provided if policy makers can see results that they think will contribute to economic productivity and competitiveness.

Lesson 7 is that reliable and positive information about a reform helps. Comprehensive school reform model developers have generally provided better information about needed resources and implementation strategies than previously provided for most education innovations. On the other hand, the U.S. Congress misled the country when its conference report for the legislation creating the Comprehensive School Reform Demonstration listed 17 models that that were described as having made impressive "gains in student performance."[15] At that time, there was little evidence of effectiveness for eleven of the listed models.[16] In 1999, Congress established the National Clearinghouse for Comprehensive School Reform, which collected and reported reliable information on these models. A 2003 federally funded meta-analysis of 232 evaluation studies of 29 models reported the effects on achievement were generally small.[17] The authors compared the results to the disappointing ones reported in our Chapter 7 for Title I compensatory education and indicated the average comprehensive reform school "outperformed 55% of the Title I schools."[18] That means that the average comprehensive reform school *equaled or did worse* than 45 percent of Title I schools. The effects were smaller for reading and science achievement than for mathematics. There are three rays of hope in this report. Many of the evaluations were conducted when the models were relatively new, and refinements since may have improved effectiveness. Models that had been used in the evaluated schools for five or more years did considerably better. In addition, several models did considerably better than others, although the researchers concluded only three models currently have a strong body of evidence about their effectiveness and all three of those had small average effects. Since the main appeal of comprehensive school reform was the hope of substantially improved academic achievement, these disappointing evaluation results could weaken support for the reform. On the other hand, the response might be to redirect resources toward those models with the most promising results, to further enhance their effectiveness and improve the evaluation evidence available on them.

Lesson 8 is that a systems approach is helpful in planning and implementing reforms. The comprehensive school reform approach is inherently systemic. It is self-consciously concerned about alignment between the learning goals, in-service teacher preparation, the various school components, and the assessment system. Several models also take into consideration the community context of the targeted schools. External developers are better positioned than individual schools to develop their models systematically. They can devote full-time staff to the development work, while consulting closely with educators who have ongoing teaching and administrative responsibilities. They have tested the models in multiple schools and refined them in light of that experience. The developers' intention to create models that could work in many schools gives them a better chance of achieving that objective than if individual schools had undertaken the development of the models. In effect, the cottage industry approach to school reform that had been widely utilized in the past with little success has been replaced with a corporate-industrial approach. Nevertheless, education is largely delivered through the many teachers in a school, and the delivery inevitably varies some from teacher to teacher and from school to school. Those variations will affect the alignment of the program components.

Lesson 9 is that teacher motivation and capacity are often important for carrying out classroom reforms. Many of the model developers have been sensitive to this. Some require a secret ballot vote of the teachers before agreeing to allow the school to use their model, and that helps assure that there is widespread buy-in at the time of initial implementation. Many provide more training and continuing technical support for school personnel than was common in the past, and these are appreciated by teachers. In addition, the heavy pressures mentioned above to improve student achievement in low-achieving schools have made teachers eager for new tools. On the other hand, the models often require major changes in prior teaching practices, and some experienced educators, who are jaded by a string of prior failed innovations, resist because they doubt the merit of the changes. In addition, several of the models limit the teacher's discretion more than in the past, and that too is not appreciated by many teachers.

Lesson 10 is that persistence is essential—often for 50 or 100 years. It is hard to judge likely persistence in advance. There have been at least two small-scale prior attempts at comprehensive school change that failed. During the 1960s, the Ford Foundation funded 25 projects under its "Comprehensive School Improvement Program," but evaluations later determined that there had been few lasting changes.[19] During the 1970s, the U.S. Office of Education sponsored the "Experimental Schools Program," providing substantial funds to a handful of districts with substantial minority populations that agreed to undertake locally initiated comprehensive changes.[20] Funding was terminated after a half-decade of disappointing results.

Both efforts had required that the schools invent and plan their own comprehensive changes rather than adopt or adapt an existing model, as is the norm in the current comprehensive school reform effort. The currently used models have been developed by external organizations that engage in continual refinement of their model and provide ongoing technical assistance to the school personnel, and that might facilitate persistence in this reform effort.

Four of our ten lessons suggest promising prospects for the comprehensive school reform. This reform has marshaled a large corps of leaders, there are federal and state mandates and incentives supporting the reform, the moderate costs seem widely tolerable, and it uses a systems approach to improving education. On the other hand, three of the lessons suggest the reform is vulnerable. The changing social contexts that are driving this reform appear anemic in comparison those that propelled the reforms examined in Chapters 2-8, the appeal of the reform is limited mostly to educators, and the early evaluation results indicate only modest improvements in student achievement. The other three lessons do not have strongly favorable or unfavorable implications for the reform.

The comprehensive school reform has enough going for it that it will probably spread to more schools, particularly those with low achievement. Implementation is generally more complicated than the *innovations* of the past, but the substantial training and ongoing support for school staff that is offered by several of the model developers may be up to the challenge. The two other ongoing reform efforts discussed below create incentive systems rather than guidance for programmatic changes, and thus comprehensive school reform is the major programmatic reform option available to schools other than return to the piecemeal curriculum and instruction innovations that have disappointed for so long.

On the other hand, the long-term prospects of this reform are shaky. The raison d'etre for the reform is to improve student learning substantially, especially among low-achieving students. The early evaluation results, while not definitive, indicate that many of the models have a long way to go in achieving that objective, and it is unclear whether they will succeed. If several of these models do not accumulate good proof of substantial and sustained achievement gains over the next five years, this reform approach probably will lose favor.

Many of the models have combined multiple components, hoping for additive effects. If refinements along that line continue to prove insufficient, the best hope may be to strive for synergies among the various components. Little is known, however, about how to achieve synergies in education.

Test-Based Accountability

A Nation at Risk's conventional recommendations for enhancing curriculum, increasing the amount of instruction, and improving teaching were accompanied by two recommendations that helped spur a dramatically different approach to educational reform. Recommendation B-3 urged a "nationwide (but not Federal) system of State and local standardized tests" to be "administered at major transition points from one level of schooling to another" to "certify the student's credentials ... identify the need for remedial intervention... and identify the opportunity for advanced or accelerated work."[21] Recommendation D-2 indicated, "Salaries for the teaching profession should be increased ... and performance-based. Salary, promotion, tenure, and retention decisions should be tied to an effective evaluation system ... so that superior teachers can be rewarded, average ones encouraged, and poor ones either improved or terminated."[22]

These were key elements in what became known in the 1980s as the "competency" or "standards" movement and then "performance pay" or "merit pay" movement and finally, with a few added features in the 1990s, as "test-based accountability" or just the "accountability." After more than century of seeking to improve schools with new organization, curriculum, and pedagogy, advocates of accountability proposed a dramatically different approach: set high standards for the performance of students, give the educators discretion in how they go about preparing students to meet the standards, and then reward and/or punish both students and educators according to how well the students meet the standards. The underlying assumption of this proposal is that the shortcomings in American education are primarily the result of vague goals and a lack of incentives for high performance.

There are many possible variations in accountability systems, but most operate at the level of students, teachers, or school administrators. At the first level, accountability systems specify that students must earn passing scores on standardized achievement tests, and if not, the students will be subject to remedial tutoring, summer school, grade repetition, denial of a high school diploma, or other consequences. At the second level, accountability specifies that teachers will be judged by one of the following criteria: the extent to which their students perform above a specified level on the standardized achievement tests, the extent to which their students make progress on the tests over the school year, or a combination of these two criteria.[23] Teachers not meeting the criteria often receive warnings, then are required to participate in additional training, may be denied salary increases, and after several years of failure may be fired. The third level of accountability applies to local school administrators and policy makers—school principals, school district superintendents, and even the school board members who guide the districts. As with teachers, they may be judged by the percentage of students who pass the tests, by students' progress on the tests, or both. They may also be judged partly by dropout rates and other indicators. Persistently poor performing schools may be required to allow parents to transfer their children to other schools, lose part of their funding, be reconstituted (re-staffed), or be closed. Persistently poor performing *districts* may be taken over by the city mayor or the state education agency, disposing of the top administrators and the school board. Most accountability systems also report publicly the achievement test results by schools and districts.

During the 1990s many states adopted accountability provisions.[24] At the close of the 20th century, forty-nine states had curriculum content standards in at least one subject area, forty-three tested students in the 4th grade and 48 did so at the 8th grade, and eighteen required passing scores on a test for high school graduation. In addition, forty-six states publicly reported accountability data by district and 40 reported them by individual school. Thirty-eight states rewarded or sanctioned districts or schools on the basis of their performance.[25] Several states also had provisions that allow districts to reconstitute schools that are persistently not meeting the standards and that allow states to take over districts persistently not meeting the standards.

The federal government has been pushing accountability since the 1988 reauthorization of the Elementary and Secondary Education Act (ESEA) required states to set content standards for Title I student achievement, identify schools not making substantial progress toward those standards, and provide assistance to such schools. Then in 1994, ESEA was amended to require states to develop statewide content standards for all students (not just Title I students) and prepare tests assessing mastery of those standards. President George W. Bush's reauthorization of ESEA, the No Child Left Behind Act of 2001 (NCLB), imposed further accountability on the states, mandating that states administer reading and mathematics skill tests of their choosing annually in grades 3-8 to *all* students; administer tests in science at three grade levels; report the results disaggregated for impoverished students, students with disabilities, students with limited English proficiency, and by race/ethnicity; establish "adequate yearly progress" targets for each of those groups in the state, such that *all* students in each group will meet "challenging State academic achievement standards" in reading, mathematics, and science by the end of the 2013-2014 school year.[26] The legislation also required that schools falling short of the adequate yearly progress targets for two consecutive years must undertake improvement efforts based on instructional programs or approaches that have been scientifically proven effective; that parents of children in schools that have been identified as needing improvement be given the choice of switching their children to a better public school, and that low-income parents in schools failing to meet state standards for at least three of four years be allowed to use the school's per-pupil Title I allotment to obtain compensatory educational services from other public or private sources. In addition, NCLB indicated that schools failing to meet the adequate yearly progress targets for five years might be reconstituted. NCLB imposes more demanding accountability than any state had previously required, particularly in respect to the frequency of testing, the rate of annual yearly progress, and the requirement that *all* students in each of the specified subgroups meet the standards by 2013-2014.

What are the prospects of the test-based accountability reform? This will be assessed in respect to the whole accountability movement and in respect to NCLB of 2001.

Several changing contexts stimulated this reform and continue to push it. There had been a gradual change in American thought about the locus of responsibility for learning, which in the 18th century had been placed primarily on the child and in the 20th century was increasingly placed on educators, as illustrated by the compensatory education reform, which sought to make schools accommodate the learning needs of students not previously well served. Between 1950 and 1980 per-pupil expenditures in constant dollars almost tripled,[27] and the share paid by the states and federal government rose substantially, making those levels of government more concerned about how local school district operations. A growing tradition of evaluating large federal education programs had begun with Robert Kennedy's insistence that there be evaluation of the Title I compensatory education services (see Chapter 7). The newly established National Assessment of Education Progress had shown only small achievement gains since the early 1970s. Policymakers began to lose confidence in education experts as a result of the rapidly rising costs and the many educational change efforts that failed to improve the average academic skills of American youth. In addition, the rising costs made policymakers eager not only to improve the quality of education but also the efficiency and productivity of schools,[28] particularly since decades of research had found small associations between the funding levels of schools (or other school resources) and student achievement.[29] Furthermore, the civil rights movement switched its emphasis from equality of opportunity to equality of results, and that lent moral support to holding educators responsible for student learning. Finally, there was growing disillusionment with government bureaucracy (not just education bureaucracies) and a rising desire to apply market approaches to government operations, a sentiment that helped elect Ronald Reagan as president in 1980 and a sentiment that was shared by the following three presidents.[30] Thus, the accountability reform has been driven by a confluence of several changing contexts, and the lessons of history suggest that contributes to reform success.

Test-based accountability is an ambitious reform effort—at least in theory. Unlike most prior education reforms, it does not focus directly on the organization and instruction of schools, but rather on creating incentives for educators to optimize that organization and instruction. It involves not only standards setting and aligned testing programs but also remedial services when needed, student promotion and graduation policies, teacher remuneration and termination policies, and city or state takeovers of school districts. In the 1980s and 1990s, however, several states set very modest achievement standards for their accountability systems, testing mostly basic skills, not requiring high performance on those skills, and making it easy for schools to exempt low-performing students from testing.

NCLB was more ambitious, aiming to have *all* children meet challenging State academic standards by the year 2014. At the time the legislation was enacted, no public school district in the nation was known to have consistently met the 2014 standards. Most educators and educational experts consider these standards unlikely to be met in the foreseeable future. For instance, no school—not even the best private special education schools—have yet taught all of a representative sample of special education youth to write well-crafted essays, master intermediate algebra, and understand high school physics.

Accountability offers multiple appeals to various stakeholders. Student accountability is attractive to many teachers, with at least 80 percent supporting guidelines for what students should learn and the requirement of passing a standardized test for promotion to the next grade.[31] Teacher accountability appeals to some advocates of low-income and minority students, because they think it will boost educators' efforts to teach those children.[32] Surveys of employers find strong support for standards and accountability.[33] Many state and federal politicians, of both parties, hope accountability will end the long pattern of rising school costs and stagnant test scores. They also like the control that it provides them over schools, without having to micro-manage details of the curriculum and pedagogy about which they have little knowledge. Citizens have strongly supported accountability,[34] but opinion varies considerably depending on the specific issues raised. In a 2003 survey, eighty-four percent believed a school should be judged by improvements in students, but 67-85 percent believed that improvement cannot be judged by a single test and that special education children should not be required to meet the same level of proficiency as set for other students.[35]

Some forms of accountability, however, have encountered strong resistance. Many advocates of the poor and minorities claim that it is unfair to hold all children to the same academic standards when low-income and minority children generally attend schools with lower funding levels and less experienced teachers.[36] They also fear that the pressure placed on schools to raise test scores will result in several detrimental practices: increased classification of students as needing special education so to make them exempt from state testing programs, increased grade retention rates, school staff pressure on weak students to drop out so that they will not be included in the test results, and increased portions of poor and minority students being denied a high school diploma because they do not pass the exit exam.[37] Others fear that schools will expand instructional time on the tested subjects and reduce or eliminate time on other subjects such as the arts, history, and foreign languages, leaving the curriculum as narrowly focused as Chapters 2 and 4 indicated it was in the mid-1800s. In 2003, most teachers strongly opposed holding teachers and schools accountable for each student's achievement, believing that student learning is only partly a function of the teacher's skill and also partly a function of a student's abilities and interests, parental support, and prior instruction. Seventy percent of teachers supported "combat" pay for those working in tough neighborhoods but 62 percent opposed merit pay for those who raise their students' test scores more than expected.[38] Teachers have also found that accountability is constraining their professionalism because when severe sanctions are threatened from high above, the subsequent levels in the education bureaucracy tend to micro-manage the teachers.[39] History suggests that successful reforms offer multiple appeals to several stakeholder groups, and the accountability reform movement has done that, but none of the reforms examined in Chapter 2-8 encountered as much controversy among educators and educational experts as NCLB, except perhaps the secularization of public education.

The accountability reform has garnered considerable leadership at high levels over the past four decades. The leadership has come mostly from politicians of both parties and several policy analysts. The Johnson administration initiated the National Assessment of Education Progress testing program.[40] Above we have seen that each reauthorization of ESEA's Title I, under three different presidents, has added accountability provisions. In addition, in 1989, President George H. Bush convened a National Education Summit of Governors that agreed to establish six National Educational Goals to be achieved by the year 2000, including that students leaving grades 4, 8, and 12 will demonstrate "competency over challenging subject matter including English, mathematics, science, history, and geography."[41] In 1994, President Clinton secured passage of the Goals 2000: Educate America Act, which provided funds to states willing to work toward achieving the national Goals and created the National Education Goals Panel to monitor progress. Governors or legislators in most of the states have successfully pushed for accountability provisions.[42] At the district and school level, the leadership has sometimes been enthusiastic and sometimes reluctant, but the sanctions of public embarrassment and possible job loss have motivated administrators to boost student achievement.

The NCLB 2001 legislation passed with 90 percent of the votes in both the House and Senate.[43] On the other hand, several governors and state legislative leaders, both Republicans and Democrats, subsequently voiced opposition to NCLB 2001, because of its intrusion on state decision-making, because of the burden imposed by the frequent testing, and because the federal funding levels, although increased, appear to fall far short of what will be needed to fully comply with NCLB's provisions.[44] Consequently, NCLB has a narrower leadership base than the former state accountability reforms.

Many states created mandates, incentives, and monitoring for accountability during the 1980s and 1990s. There have also been increasingly strong federal mandates, incentives, and monitoring in support of accountability, with NCLB boosting them further. Partly as a result, this reform has spread nationwide faster than most of the prior reforms examined in this book. Our lessons suggest that top-down pressures help reform, and this is the most top-down education reform in America's history.

The accountability reform will be expensive. It requires the articulation of content standards, the development and refinement of the standardized tests, the administration of the tests and processing of the results, the provision of promised rewards, extra instruction or grade repetition for students doing poorly; new educational programs and training of staff in schools that initially do poorly, the imposition of sanctions against those who repeatedly do poorly, and the hiring of new teachers and administrators to replace those who are terminated for repeatedly poor performance. While expensive, the incremental costs of the state accountability systems are within a range sustained by prior enduring reforms.

NCLB will add far more to the costs. Early estimates of the costs of complying with NCLB in ten states, prepared by several different consultants using different means, ranged from about a 10 percent increase in total expenditures for K-12 education to almost 100 percent increase, with many of the state estimates in the 30-40 percent increase range.[45] The largest portion of the costs is expected to be for the additional services thought necessary to make an honest attempt to help *all* students meet challenging standards. Although the United States has sustained several costly educational reforms in the past, increases of the magnitude estimated for NCLB over a single decade are unprecedented and will be very difficult to fund. On the other hand, NCLB creates unprecedented pressure for dramatic breakthroughs in curriculum and pedagogical effectiveness directed at the tested knowledge and skills, and if those are achieved, the costs may be substantially less than estimated. In addition, the performance goals of NCLB might be scaled back or the timelines extended, and that could moderate the costs.

There is considerable evidence that State accountability systems have raised average test scores a small or modest amount over the first few years of implementation.[46] There is also good reason to think that part of those gains, and perhaps most of them, do not represent real net increases in the children's learning. That is due to several shortcomings in the reported information. Part of the score gains during the first year or two will be from coaching on how to take the tests, rather than from increased mastery of academic skills.[47] Many schools have narrowed their curriculum, cutting back or dropping instruction in foreign languages, history, the arts and health, when those are not tested in their state, and thus students are almost surely learning less than before in the subjects that are not tested.[48] Low achieving students had been increasingly classified for special education or as limited English proficient in states that did not require testing of such students, so that their low scores were not counted,[49] although NCLB seeks to preclude such "gaming the system" by requiring testing and reporting of all children. Federal laws mandate accommodations in testing for special needs students and limited English proficient students, but that can be done over-generously, which would artificially inflate those students scores.[50] For instance, in 2003 a large district in Maryland accommodated third-grade students with disabilities and limited English proficient children on a *reading* test by having the test administrator read the items aloud.[51] Low achieving students in several accountability systems are also dropping out more frequently and in several jurisdictions they are being urged to drop out by school officials who do not want to be dragged down by their low scores.[52] Instances of fraud by teachers and school officials has been detected, and surely more goes undetected, particularly since most states have relatively weak mechanisms for detecting fraud.[53] In addition, statisticians have long known that changes in achievement test scores are relatively unreliable, particularly at the student, classroom and school level, because of measurement error, cohort changes over time, and erratic external influences that the schools cannot control.[54] Several states have been embarrassed by publicly praising schools with unusually large test score gains in one year, only to find several of those schools had small gains, or even losses, in the following year.[55] Furthermore, companies that score the tests have made a number of errors that have been detected, and other errors probably have gone undetected.[56]

For these several reasons, the good news from accountability reforms to date is surely inflated, and this reform, which emphasizes public dissemination of detailed performance data, could easily lose credibility from scandals over the accuracy of the data. Effective accountability requires good counts and that has not yet been achieved by many districts and states. On the other hand, there is also reason to think the potential effects have not been fully realized because of a lags in aligning the curriculum and instruction with the tests being used.[57]

The test-based accountability reform utilizes a systems approach, a system of incentives aimed directly at improving student learning. Rather than specify how to modify the organization, curriculum, pedagogy, and assessment of schools to serve that goal, it creates incentives that encourage districts and schools to change those components in ways that boost achievement. Critics of accountability note that tests do not teach, but that misses the point of advocates who say accountability will focus all levels of educators on improving student learning in the tested subjects, particularly the learning of low performing students.

The accountability reform does not address teacher capability and motivation in the traditional manner of providing training and support for change. Instead, it relies on rewards for strong performance, such as "merit pay," and sanctions, such as required re-training and termination of employment, which are expected to motivate teachers to seek and apply the needed training. In most of the state accountability systems, teachers receive credit for *advancing* students more than they normally would have advanced, and although teachers generally oppose such provisions, they might be motivated by them. Under NCLB 2001, there was initially no such credit for students' progress until they reach the point of meeting the state standards, but in 2007 changes in the regulations did allow for that. Nevertheless, given the ambitious goals of NCLB and the looming deadline of 2013-2014 for compliance by all students, unless the curriculum and pedagogy improve dramatically within the next few years, NCLB will demoralize teachers and administrators in schools with substantial percentages of low-income, minority, and special education students.

Whether there will be persistent pursuit of the accountability reform is difficult to predict. Test-based accountability is not new and its popularity has waxed and waned.[58] Chapter 2 indicated that the Massachusetts General Court passed a bill in 1647 directing town selectmen to monitor parents' fulfillment of their instructional roles. In Chapter 4 we saw that in 1873, the Quincy Massachusetts school board members personally conducted the annual examinations of students and were so appalled by the results that they fired the superintendent. A 1923 book noted, "Survey after survey has revealed unsuspected inadequacy or inefficiency in American education.... Superintendents and teachers have been dismissed, school systems and methods reorganized...."[59] In the 1920s and 1930s, Pittsburgh publicly released test data showing how well individual elementary schools had done in preparing their students for high school.[60] The fact that these antecedents were not long retained, suggests the current accountability reform may not receive the needed persistence. On the other hand, since the 1970s, despite political changes and numerous implementation difficulties, increasing levels of accountability have been adopted by most states and by the federal government. In addition, the reform has two key elements missing in most prior uses of accountability—it is providing advance notification of the standards that are to be met and it usually provides both students and educators with warnings and help in improving their performance before imposing severe sanctions. Accountability is being presented as an improvement system rather than just as negative sanctions, and that may help sustain the reform effort.

Overall, the lessons of two centuries of education reform suggest the accountability reform, excluding the NCLB embodiment, is likely to have staying power, although it does have vulnerability. Five lessons indicate strengths: Several changing contexts are pushing this reform, it has attracted widespread leadership at the state and federal levels, it is supported with state and federal mandates and incentives, it will probably raise costs no more so than several other reforms that have endured, and it applies a systemic approach. The other five lessons do not bode particularly well or ill for the accountability reform.

Since passage of NCLB in 2001, it has overshadowed state accountability systems, even while making use of their state standards and assessments. Consequently, most state and district reform efforts have been redirected to compliance with the more demanding provisions of NCLB. What do the lessons suggest for the prospects of this legislation?

NCLB 2001 is a radical form of accountability. An analogous policy in public health would be to address the problem of cancer deaths in this county with a No Cancer Patient Dead Act that would deny physicians, health clinics, and hospitals receipt of federal funds if *any* of their cancer patients die from the ailment after the year 2014. Both policies create strong incentives to develop dramatically more effective interventions. That might result in reaching the laudable goals within the stated time period, it might result in gratifying progress even though short of the goals, or it might largely fail.

NCLB 2001 is probably overly ambitious. There are dozens of very bright men and women who have devoted most of their lives to developing improved school organizations, cultures, curriculums, and pedagogies that have been aimed at boosting the learning of low-income, minority, special education, and limited English proficient children, all with only modest success—far less success than demanded by NCLB. The NCLB legislation repeatedly called for use of curriculum, instructional strategies, school improvement plans, technical assistance that are "based on scientifically based research,"[61] which is an admirable effort to move away from education faddism, but, as of 2004, no instructional approach has been shown by strong scientific evidence to meet the goals of NCLB.

Perhaps that will change with the mighty incentives of NCLB, but the limited progress of the past may be inherent in the nature of human development. For instance, parents always have had strong incentives for rearing their children well and suffer painful consequences if they fail, but does parenting appear to have become more effective over the past century as a result of those incentives?

NCLB has other vulnerabilities not shared by most prior forms of education accountability. It has a narrower base of leadership. Advocacy for the legislation came primarily from the White House and the bipartisan support of Congress.[62] Several governors and state legislators resent the federal intrusion into their state accountability systems. In addition, only a moderate portion of the people responsible for state and local implementation has become enthusiastic about the reform. Achieving good progress toward the 2014 goals is likely to require unprecedented increases in school spending, mostly to provide considerable extra help to lagging students. NCLB has reduced part of one vulnerability of the accountability movement, by requiring achievement data be reported by various subgroups of children, diminishing the opportunity to "game the system" that several state plans offered by allowing slow learners to be reclassified into categories that were exempt from testing. On the other hand, NCLB does not require dropouts to be reported by subgroups, and allows so much flexibility in reporting dropout that districts and states can create artificial indicators of progress.[63] Finally, NCLB is motivating teachers to improve their instruction, but it is holding them accountable for students' performance without any proven means of meeting the goals, and thus is angering teachers with what they perceive as impossible and unfair demands.[64]

Of the ten lessons of history, three bode well for NCLB--many changing contexts are pushing it, there are strong federal and state incentives for compliance, and it uses a systemic approach. Three of the lessons suggest serious vulnerabilities—it so ambitious as to be probably impossible, it is likely to require unprecedented and perhaps unsustainable cost increases, and it performance standards are angering teachers.

Ultimately, one of three things is likely to happen with NCLB. Necessity can be the mother of invention, and perhaps NCLB will spur educators, corporations, or others to develop new curriculums, instructional approaches, school management procedures, or education delivery mechanisms that work markedly better with students who otherwise have done poorly in school. If not, the standards may be lowered, either to a feasible challenge that stretches students and educators but does not break them, or to an even lower level that will make a sham of the reform. In the first years of NCLB, a few states did reduce their proficiency standards so that a larger percentage of students would be likely to meet them.[65] The third possibility is that federal leaders will "stay the course," without breakthroughs and without adjusting the standards, until there is a four-pronged rebellion: by parents of high achieving students upset about the narrowing of the curriculum in their schools, by advocates of low achieving students angry about the large numbers of students retained in grade repeatedly and then denied graduation, by school officials who are no longer able to fill teaching positions that are doomed to failure, and by taxpayers disillusioned by another reform that has raised costs far more than learning. If such a rebellion occurs against NCLB, it could undermine the entire education accountability reform effort.

Federal leaders could improve the prospects of NCLB with one modification. They could scale back the standards for the various groups of students to levels that scientifically based research suggests are a feasible stretch for those children, and then plan on raising the levels as educational advances might permit. This would require considerable research and effort, but would allow the reform to remain ambitious, while also expanding the potential leadership base, moderating costs, and helping to reverse the resentment of teachers. With that one change, seven of the ten lessons inferred in this book could bode well for NCLB and none would bode ill. In addition, its prospects would be helped if Federal leaders would strive to minimize the several causes of misleading data by requiring measurement of all major objectives of public schooling, by adding provisions to minimize fraud and overly generous accommodations in the testing of special needs children, by defining standards in ways that that take into account the imperfect reliability of the measures used, and by requiring a standard manner of calculating dropout for various subgroups of students.

There has been a conspiracy theory voiced about the accountability reform movement. It contends that the reform leaders, at least those advocating the NCLB provisions, know that those provisions demand the impossible and intend them to discredit the public school system and thereby enflame support for school choice plans, especially publicly funded vouchers that parents could use to pay for private schooling.[66] That some people and organizations supporting NCLB have devoted most of their lives to improving the public education of disadvantaged children tends to counter this theory. These include Kati Haycock at the Education Trust, civil rights attorney William L. Taylor, researcher Paul Hill, Senator Edward Kennedy, and others. On the other hand, support for the conspiracy theory comes from the several state officials ardently pushing school choice who have been unwilling to hold schools of choice accountable in the same manner as they are holding regular public schools accountable.[67] For instance, in 2002, Arizona had 495 charter schools (more than any other state), but it ascertained compliance with various state laws in only 10-20 percent of the schools, and for many where violations were discovered, failed to check for subsequent compliance.[68] Florida has been among the leaders in implementing both accountability and school choice, but its Commissioner of Education announced in 2003 that private schools receiving public vouchers did not need to participate in the state's testing program. He explained that in those schools, "The primary accountability and responsibility lies with the parent,"[69] even though most advocates of accountability have argued that neither parents nor the state can know how well the children are doing without standardized testing.

School Choice[70]

Since the mid-1800s, public education has been managed by public school districts that usually operate multiple schools. Generally, each public school has an attendance zone and all homes in the zone must send their children to that school. Critics explain that has given each school a near-monopoly on providing education to families in the attendance area and they allege this has undermined the effectiveness of public education and its responsiveness to parents' desires.

The School choice reform aims to provide parents with broad freedom in selecting the schools that they think are best for their children. This is expected to improve the quality of education by creating a diversity of schooling approaches that can be matched with the needs of individual students and by requiring competing schools to improve their effectiveness or suffer declining enrollments and closure. It is also proposed as a source of equity, allowing the poor and working classes some degree of choice that the middle class commonly buys with homes in suburban jurisdictions selected for their schools and that the upper class secures with tuition for elite private schools.

There are many forms of school choice. During the 1960s and 1970s, during efforts to desegregate voluntarily, some districts built attractive and distinctive "magnet schools" usually emphasizing the sciences, technology, or the arts, hoping that both black and white families would elect to send their children to those schools. By the late 1970s some districts were allowing parents to select any public school in their district, providing there was space and the move did not exacerbate racial/ethnic isolation. Later several states allowed parents to enroll their children in public schools outside their district, usually with provisions for a transfer of funds to the receiving district to compensate for the cost of educating those who transfer in. In the 1990s, charter schools and voucher programs gained prominence and they constitute the main thrust of the choice reform movement during the opening of the 21st century. While in theory choice is applicable to children of all socio-economic strata, most charter school and voucher options implemented to date have been targeted primarily to urban minority children who otherwise would have to attend public schools with generally low achievement levels.

Charter schools are operated by private groups with public school district funding and oversight. They are usually open to all children living within the district. Many charter schools try to provide distinctive instructional environments—anything from boot camps to progressive education. If there are more applicants than can be handled at a given school, they are usually selected by lottery. The first charter schools were established in Minnesota in 1991, and by 2003 there were almost 685,000 children attending 2,700 charter schools throughout the country.[71]

District or state voucher plans give parents the option of using public funds to pay tuition costs at private schools. Usually the voucher amount is less than or equal to the district or state per capita expenditure, and if it does not cover the full tuition costs of the selected private school, the parents must make up the difference. In 1990, Milwaukee began the first major voucher program, serving 1,000 disadvantaged children. Cleveland followed in 1995. Florida adopted the first state demonstration plan in 1999, and the following year offered vouchers to all special education students in the state.[72] In addition, at the opening of the 21st century, there were reportedly about 46,000 disadvantaged children throughout the country who had received vouchers provided by private donors to help them attend private schools.[73]

What do the lessons of history suggest for the choice reform effort? The analysis will focus on charter schools and voucher programs.

Several changing contexts pushed this reform. Two had stimulated the test-based accountability reform: The alarms of *A Nation at Risk* and the

1975-1985 ebb in public opinion toward public schools. Three other changing contexts had influence. The 1960s and 1970s brought desegregation to many public school districts and that sparked increased interest in private schools among white families who opposed that change. In 1980, Ronald Reagan campaigned for the presidency promising to free the country from burdensome federal regulations and return it to laissez faire markets. The economy improved during his presidency, giving credibility to market mechanisms. Finally, three groups of scholars published books with elaborate statistical analyses that found, after controlling for family characteristics and student's initial achievement, private and Catholic high schools had higher achievement than did public high schools.[74] Although this research had several methodological weaknesses and the differences in achievement were small,[75] these books reinforced interest in vouchers. These five changing contexts, however, were modest and transient in comparison to those that drove most of the reforms discussed in Chapters 2-8. While concerns about student achievement and public school effectiveness have continued, opposition to desegregation has abated over time and the scholarly books that helped stimulate the choice reform are almost forgotten. This reform is currently lacking strong push from changing contexts.

School choice is an ambitious reform on two counts and that adds to its chances of success. First it is using a dramatically different approach for spurring improvements in K-12 education—competitive market forces. Second, if vouchers worth the full public per-pupil expenditure are made available to all families in the country, that would change the organization and control of our schooling more than any time since the establishment of universal public schooling the mid-1800s. It is possible that public schools would cease to exist and all children would attend an expanded array of private schools, leaving states only to disburse the vouchers and exercise regulatory functions in respect to safety and health, civil rights, core curriculum requirements, and perhaps achievement standards. It is more likely that unlimited choice would result in a mixed system of public and private schools, with the excellent public schools retaining a share of the market and some mediocre or weak public schools remaining where the only other options would require long transportation times.

School choice offers diverse appeals, but has also sparked strong opposition. It appeals to Americans' love of freedom. It appeals to those who are frustrated by prior reforms' failure to boost substantially student achievement. It appeals to some poor and to some racial and ethnic minorities, who think that their children have been trapped in failing public schools and see it as allowing them the same access to private schooling that more affluent citizens have always enjoyed.[76] Charter schools appeal to families that want a distinctive school culture for their children within a public system. Parents sending their children to religious schools, or desiring to do so, generally support voucher programs because they would subsidize the tuition costs. Many in the business community think that making schools subject to market competition will improve the quality of schooling.

Despite their many appeals, vouchers have drawn fierce opposition from some stakeholders. The teachers' unions fear they will weaken or destroy public schools, exacerbate socio-economic stratification in America, and undermine the unionization of teachers.[77] The American Civil Liberties Union opposes public funds going to religious schools, which accounted for 84 percent of the enrollment in private K-12 schools at the close of the century.[78] Others fear that vouchers will dissolve what little social cohesion the country has, separating students by family background and fostering schools that teach bigotry and hatred.[79] Gallup polls between 1970 and 1986 found the country just about evenly split between those who supported voucher plans and those who opposed them, but non-whites, Catholics, and those who felt public schools were failures supported vouchers by about a 5 to 3 margin.[80] During comparable polls taken each year in the late 1990s through 2003, support for vouchers had dropped moderately, bouncing between 34-46 percent.[81] In a 1999 survey of parents, 48 percent were very satisfied with their child's attendance zone public school, 62 were very satisfied with their child's chosen public school, and 79 percent were very satisfied with their child's private school.[82] While the appeals are broad, the substantial opposition to vouchers will slow and maybe prevent the widespread adoption of them.

The leadership ranks of the choice reform have broadened gradually. The initial advocates of vouchers were a few academics, business leaders, and conservative politicians. Over the past two decades community leaders in several jurisdictions have worked to establish voucher programs. African American leaders secured the landmark Milwaukee demonstration, and subsequently formed the Black Alliance for Educational Options.[83] Albert Shanker, the long-time president of the American Federation of Teachers, opposed vouchers, but in 1988 began advocating for teacher-led charter schools and continued to support them until his death.[84] Groups of teachers, parents, and youth workers have established charter schools. Non-profit organizations, comprehensive school reform model developers, and businesses have also done so. Starting a charter school is a complicated matter, involving a petition to the regulatory entity, the securing of physical facilities, the planning of curriculum and pedagogy, the hiring of the teachers, and the recruitment of students. That 2,700 charter schools were established in one decade is testimony to expanding leadership of this reform.

School choice has received moderate support from the federal government. In the 1970s the federal government has provided modest funding for public magnet schools that admit students from throughout a district. Three of the four last presidents of the United States, all Republicans, urged federally supported voucher programs, and those efforts undoubtedly gave support to the reform, even though Congress rejected most of their proposals. The 1994 amendments of the Elementary and Secondary Education Act established a Charter Schools Program that has provided competitively awarded grants for planning and establishing charter schools and credit enhancement mechanisms to aid in the acquisition of facilities.[85] For fiscal year 2003, the appropriation was a modest $199 million.[86] The NCLB legislation of 2001 requires that parents of children in persistently poorly performing schools be offered the option of switching to other public schools and vouchers for private compensatory education services. In addition, most federal funding available to K-12 schools can be used in public schools of choice and charter schools even though it is not specifically targeted to them. Nevertheless, federal support for choice has been modest in comparison with federal support for compensatory education and special education.

Over the past three decades, many governors and state legislatures have provided mandates and incentives for charter schools and public school choice options, but only a very few have done so for vouchers. At the turn of the century, 32 states had adopted legislation permitting or requiring at least one form of public school choice, 36 had adopted legislation for charter schools, but only three had legislation for vouchers—Wisconsin, Ohio, and Florida.[87]

A universal voucher system, offering vouchers for all youth with a value equivalent to the per-capita public school expenses would add about 15-20 percent to the total cost of public education. That increase is primarily because almost all of the 11 percent of students who attend private schools at their family's personal expense would opt to receive the vouchers.[88] The rest of the increase would come from administering the voucher program, setting minimum standards for all schools and monitoring compliance, the additional transportation expenses as students fan out in more directions, and from inefficiencies in operating public school districts with presumably shrunken enrollments.[89] These additional costs are less than resulted from at least three of the long sustained reforms described in this book—universal public education, the professionalization of teaching, and special education. In addition, the social cost would be only about half the estimated total, because parents who currently send their children to private schools would save on tuition expenses when they receive vouchers.

Advocates have asserted that vouchers could dramatically lower total costs because private schools have average per pupil expenditures that are

62 percent those of public schools.[90] That comparison is misleading. Most private schools do not provide special education, which all public school systems provide and which is almost three times as expensive as regular education. Private school tuition rates do not include auxiliary expenses—for books, uniforms, busing, extracurricular activities, and the supplemental donations that parents and then graduates are pressured to make. Finally, most private schools are subsidized by their sponsoring churches, which probably would not be willing to subsidize the education of large numbers of non-members' children.[91]

Widespread adoption of charter schools would increase the cost of public education by only a small amount. While the start-up costs of charter schools are substantial, so are the start-up costs for regular public schools. The operating costs of charter schools generally do not have to exceed those of regular schools. If the system adds charter schools and does not close some regular schools, there will be modestly increased overhead costs per student, but those could be mitigated by closing some of the regular schools. Thus costs are not likely to be a serious impediment to the choice reform.

The school choice reform effort has been highly political, probably more politicized than any of the reforms detailed in this book except the universal public school initiative and the secularization of public education. As a result, there has been considerable conflicting information, some of it clearly false or misleading. In addition, opponents of vouchers have rigorously opposed even limited demonstrations that would test them. There has been so much biased information about choice, both pro and con, that the credibility of all information on this topic has been cast in doubt, and that does not bode well for the reform.

An independent evaluation of the first four years of the Milwaukee public voucher program for low-income families, in which 80 percent of the children attended just three private schools, found that participation doubled over three years, parents were considerably more satisfied with the private schools than the public ones from which they withdrew their children, and overall achievement had not changed significantly.[92] A three-year evaluation of the Cleveland voucher program found that public school students made slightly larger gains than those using vouchers to attend private schools.[93] An evaluation of privately funded voucher programs in Dayton, New York City, and Washington DC, using an experimental design, found no achievement gains for the full group of studied participants over a three year period, although Black students' achievement increased 6.6 percentile points, and many of the parents receiving vouchers reported being more satisfied with the private schools[94] It should be noted that these voucher programs were seriously limited in ways that are likely to have reduced whatever positive effects could be achieved: All involved vouchers worth considerably less than some private schools' tuition, constraining the choice available to participating low-income families; all were offered to only a small portion of the students in a given community; and the two publicly funded programs were subject to repeated political and legal challenges, leaving the fate of the programs in question and thus dissuading investments to expand existing private schools or establish new ones. A review of the research and evaluation in 2000 concluded that "empirical evidence is not sufficiently compelling to justify either strong advocacy or opposition to large-scale voucher programs."[95] A 2002 review of the evaluations of charter schools found modest gains in some cases, modest losses in others, and several cases with no differences.[96] The same review also found the effects of charter schools on improving public schools was mixed. Another review of both the voucher and charter evaluations concluded that overall there was only a weak suggestion of enhanced student achievement, at least at this early point in these demonstrations.[97] A broader review of 25 research studies on the effects of competition among schools on public student achievement found that there was a small positive effect.[98] For example, schools near the top of the competitiveness scale had average achievement scores about four percentile points higher than schools near the bottom of the competitiveness scale.

Choice relies on market system incentives to make schools more effective or more appealing to parents. In market systems, parents select the schools that they think will best serve their objectives, and if they are unsatisfied with the results they move the child to another school. Thus choice is a bottom-up form of accountability, whereas test-based accountability is top-down form of accountability. As we have seen, a systems approach generally aids a reform effort, but there is a question about whether the market system, which has contributed so much to technological development and industrial productivity in this country, will have similar effects on schools. Several proponents of choice have warned that the particular structure of a choice system is likely to influence the impacts on student learning and the possible undesirable side effects.[99] From Adam Smith on, scholars of market mechanisms have recognized that various conditions can impair the efficiency with which the "invisible hand" of a market guides the production and consumption of goods and services.

Textbook discussions of "market failures" commonly mention situations in which there are few sellers, considerable product differentiation, information asymmetries, or the involvement of important public goods.[100] In metropolitan areas there can be several public and several private schools that are within a tolerable commute of most families, but on the fringes of suburbs and in rural areas, there will not be enough children to support more than one school. Product differentiation reduces the need for schools to compete even though it is likely to enhance parental satisfaction. For example, if a Muslim school, a Jewish school, and a Catholic School were on adjoining property in the middle of a community, very few parents would give consideration to sending their children to all three schools, and thus there would be little actual competition among the schools. In addition, markets work best when both the buyers and sellers have good information. Parents prefer schools that will maximize the overall development and life chances of their children, but that is hard to judge and thus parents often rely on indicators such as the reputation of a school, average SAT scores, the college-going rate of graduates, and the colleges to which the graduates have gone. Private schools commonly report the latter indicators to interested parents, but the Educational Testing Service does not verify the accuracy of their reports and in 1993 an official of the organization told this author that one Educational Testing Service study addressing other matters had discovered some misrepresentations in private schools' reports of average SAT scores.[101] Finally, schools provide both private benefits to families and public benefits to employers, the community, and the nation. Markets are unlikely to maximize public benefits, although the public interest can be protected by government regulation of the market, as states have done for more than a century by imposing minimum safety and academic standards on private schools.[102]

There are longstanding examples of markets in areas of education other than K-12 education and they offer conflicting signals. There is a vibrant market in American colleges and universities that are among the best and most expensive in the world. Many metropolitan areas have markets in postsecondary occupational training that have been found to promote deceptive advertising and sustain ineffective providers.[103] Finally, many metropolitan areas have markets in after-school music lessons, but this writer is unaware of any indication that two centuries of competition in this field has resulted in dramatic improvements in effectiveness or efficiency of instruction, particularly for students who have difficulty learning to play a musical instrument. Taking into consideration all these factors, it is unclear whether the market system used by the choice reform will result in substantial improvements in the quality or efficiency of K-12 education.

The choice reform does nothing directly to improve teachers' capacity to teach, but rather it provides incentives intended to spur administrators and teachers to maximize their effectiveness. As indicated above, many teachers fear that choice may undermine their job and that fear may motivate teachers to be more effective. Teachers' opinions are mixed on charter schools. In several locations public school teachers have been energized by joining together to establish and run such schools. There is also preliminary evidence that test scores have increased slightly in some jurisdictions where regular public schools must compete with charter schools for students.[104]

Whether there will be persistent support for the choice reform is unclear. Proposals for K-12 school vouchers have repeatedly arisen and then faded over the past two centuries. Our Chapter 2 indicates that Thomas Jefferson submitted, without success, a series of proposals for a public school system in Virginia that included vouchers to permit the most academically able boys of poor families to continue into high school and college. Chapter 2 also describes how, in the early 1800s, some cities provided funding to private schools, but when Catholics sought a share of the funds, fierce conflict ensued and the practice was terminated. In response to court ordered desegregation, Alabama, Louisiana, Mississippi, and Virginia established voucher programs intended to help white students move to all-white private schools, but federal courts declared the plans illegal.[105] In the early 1970s, the Nixon administration tried to fund voucher experiments, but only one district agreed to participate, Alum Rock, California, and it imposed conditions that seriously comprised the short-live demonstration.[106] Despite the notable demonstrations of voucher programs in Milwaukee and Cleveland, both with expanding enrollments over the years, an effort to include a school voucher provision in the No Child Left Behind bill failed, although a provision for vouchers to be used for compensatory education services was enacted. With such a checkered history, it is hard to know if sufficient persistence will be mustered in behalf of vouchers.

On the other hand, efforts to expand public school choice options and charter schools have steadily increased. Since the late 1800s, several large cities have operated one or two schools that specialize in the arts or sciences and have been open to the most talented students throughout the city. Progressive educators in the late 1800s and early 1900s urged that children have more choice in what they studied and how they studied it, and in response high schools introduced elective courses, which remain to this day. It has already been mentioned that magnet schools were introduced to foster voluntary desegregation and that over the past few decades some districts and states have allowed voluntary transfers to other public schools. More recently, a number of large public high schools have been subdivided into several small schools, each with a distinctive program, among which students can choose. Finally, charter schools expanded rapidly during the last decade of the 20th century. By 1999, sixteen percent of public school students attended a public school other the one of their attendance zone[107] and a larger percentage had the option available to them. School choice options were most common in the western states and least common in the northeastern states.[108]

The lessons of Chapter 9 send very mixed signals for the choice reform. Three lessons bode well for it: Its ambitious nature, the substantial corps of leaders that has been marshaled over the past decade, and costs that would be within the range of several other sustained reforms. Two lessons bode ill for the reform: The lack of strong changing social contexts to push the reform and the lack of reliable information about the reform and about the schools from which families have to choose. That leaves five other lessons that offer ambivalent implications for the success of this reform—more than for the other reforms analyzed in this chapter.

There is not much that reformers can do about the lack of changing contexts pushing this reform, except to keep their eye open for an emerging one that might help. On the other hand, reformers could address the lack of reliable information by establishing mechanisms that provide parents with easy access to accurate and thorough information on each school that they might want to choose among, including private ones, if a voucher program is in operation. That information would include the philosophy and goals of the school, the knowledge and skills covered in the curriculum, the qualifications of teachers, the pedagogy used, the rules and disciplinary practices, school building code and health regulation compliance, and student outcomes. The latter would include transfers rates out to other schools, dropout rates, absolute levels and gains in state test scores, the average SAT and ACT scores, and the postsecondary education achieved by graduates.[109] False or misleading advertising could be prohibited and violations penalized. Parents should be allowed to visit and observe schools that they are considering for their children. There should also be a means for parents to file complaints against schools, a mechanism for investigating and judging those complaints, and a procedure to report publicly those schools that have been repeatedly subject to validated complaints. These changes would allow parents to make more informed choices than is possible today.

Conclusions

All three of the main American education reform efforts at the dawn of the 21st century appear to have a mix of promise and shortcoming when judging their prospects by the lessons distilled from Chapters 2-9. The test-based accountability reform has the most indicators of success, but, ironically, the NCLB version of that reform has the most indicators of failure. The above discussion suggests ways in which the prospects of each of these reforms could be improved.

Both the accountability and choice reforms rely heavily on incentive systems to improve student learning, but there is reason to doubt that better motivated principals and teachers can currently achieve large improvements in learning even if they make skillful use of the best available school organization, administration, curriculums, and instructional techniques. This writer has never seen evidence, in thirty years of reading the research literature, that any teacher can consistently cut 25 percent off the time needed for a representative sample of lagging students to master complex knowledge or skills. If the very best teachers cannot do that, what reason is there to think that powerful incentives will make other teachers capable of it? Consequently, the best hope for these reforms is that they will stimulate the development of markedly more effective instruction.

---

[1] Congressional Budget Office, Congress of the United States, *Trends in Educational Achievement* (Washington DC: Author, 1986), xv.

[2] National Commission on Excellence in Education, *A Nation At Risk* (Washington DC: U.S. Government Printing Office, 1983), 5.

[3] National Commission on Excellence in Education, *A Nation At Risk* (Washington DC: U.S. Government Printing Office, 1983), 8-9.

[4] National Commission on Excellence in Education, *A Nation At Risk* (Washington DC: U.S. Government Printing Office, 1983), 18-23.

[5] Charles W. Fowler, "Only Masochists Could Accept the Findings of the Excellence Commission," *American School Board Journal* 170 (September, 1983), 43-46, 49.

[6] Congressional Budget Office, Congress of the United States, *Educational Achievement: Explanations and Implications of Recent Trends* (Washington DC: Author, 1987), xii, 32-33.

[7] Congressional Budget Office, Congress of the United States, *Trends in Educational Achievement* (Washington DC: Author, 1986), xvi, 31-84.

[8] United States General Accounting Office, *Federal Education Funding: Multiple Programs and Lack of Data Raise Efficiency and Effectiveness Concerns* (Washington DC: Author, 1997), 1, 8-10.

[9] Iris C. Rotberg and James J. Harvey, *Federal Policy Options for Improving the Education of Low-Income Students* (Santa Monica, CA: RAND, 1993), 20.

[10] Iris C. Rotberg and James J. Harvey, *Federal Policy Options for Improving the Education of Low-Income Students* (Santa Monica, CA: RAND, 1993), 31-38.

[11] Marshall S. Smith and Jennifer O'Day, "Systemic School Reform," in *The Politics of Curriculum and Testing: The 1990 Yearbook of the Politics of Education Association*, ed. Susan Fuhrman and Betty Malen (Philadelphia, PA: Falmer Press, 1991).

[12] Richard C. Atkinson and Gregg B. Jackson, eds., *Research and Education Reform: Roles for the Office of Educational Research and Improvement* (Washington, DC: National Academy Press, 1992), 105-106.

[13] U.S. Department of Education, Office of Elementary and Secondary Education, "About CSR," undated. Retrieved August 18, 2003 at http://www.ed.gov/offices/OESE/compreform/2pager.html

[14] Calculated from: Northwest Regional Educational Laboratory and The National Clearinghouse for Comprehensive School Reform, *The Catalog of School Reform Models,* retrieved 12/22/03 from http://www.nwrel.org/scpd/catalog/printversion.shtml

[15] U.S. Department of Education, *Guidance On the Comprehensive School Reform Demonstration Program* (Washington DC: author, October 4 1999), Appendix A. H.R. No 390 (105th Congress 1st Session), 32, 38, 96-99, 106-109.

[16] American Institutes for Research, *An Educator's Guide to Schoolwide Reform* (Washington DC: American Association of School Administrators, 1999), 3-6 [Retrieved August 22, 03 at http://www.aasa.org/issues_and_insights

/district_organization/Reform/index.htm] Three of the seventeen models were judged to have strong evidence of effectiveness and three were judged to have promising evidence. The rest were judged to have marginal, weak or no evidence of positive effects.

[17] The overall effect size was a small 0.15 for all studies and 0.09 for those judged strongest methodologically. Geoffrey D. Borman, Gina M. Hewes, Laura T Overman, and Shelly Brown, "Comprehensive School Reform and Achievement: A Meta-Analysis," *Review of Educational Research* 73 (Summer, 2003), 125-230.

[18] Geoffrey D. Borman, Gina M. Hewes, Laura T Overman, and Shelly Brown, "Comprehensive School Reform and Achievement: A Meta-Analysis," *Review of Educational Research* 73 (Summer, 2003), 125-230. pg 164-165.

[19] Ford Foundation, *A Foundation Goes to School* (New York: Author, 1972).

[20] See: Peter Cowden and David K Cohen, *Divergent Worlds of Practice: The Federal Reform of Local Schools in the Experimental Schools Program* (Cambridge, MA: Center for the Study of Public Policy, 1981) [ERIC Document ED217541]; Robert E. Herriott and Neal G. Gross, eds. *The Dynamics of Planned Educational Change: Case Studies and Analyses* (Berkeley CA: McCutchan Publishing, 1979).

[21] National Commission on Excellence in Education, *A Nation At Risk* (Washington DC: U.S. Government Printing Office, 1983), 28.

[22] National Commission on Excellence in Education, *A Nation At Risk* (Washington DC: U.S. Government Printing Office, 1983), 30.

[23] U.S. Department of Education, National Center for Education Statistics, *Overview and Inventory of State Education Reforms: 1990 to 2000* (Washington DC: author, 2003), 27.

[24] National Conference of State Legislatures, "Education Program: Shifting Roles in Governance," (Washington DC: author, undated), retrieved 03/25/04 from http://www.ncsl.org/programs/educ/k12Gov.htm.

[25] U.S. Department of Education, National Center for Education Statistics, *Overview and Inventory of State Education Reforms: 1990 to 2000* (Washington DC: author, 2003), 9, 13, and 21.

[26] Public Law No. 107-110, Title I. The description of the law was taken from the following: Wayne Riddle *Education for the Disadvantaged: Overview of ESEA Title I-A Amendments Under the No Child Left Behind Act,* Washington DC: Congressional Research Service, 2003); and "The No Child Left Behind Act of 2001" (January 7, 2002) [which is described as the "Executive Summary of the No Child Left Behind Act of 2001"] retrieved 08/29/03 from www.ed.gov/nclb/overview/intro/execsumm. html]

[27] U.S. Department of Education, National Center for Education Statistics, *Digest of Education Statistics: 2001* (Washington DC: U.S. Government Printing Office, 2002), 49.

[28] Consortium On Productivity In the Schools, *Using What We Have To Get the Schools We Need: A Productivity Focus for American Education* (Illinois: Ball Foundation, 1995).

[29] See the following: James S. Coleman, et. al., *Equality of Educational Opportunity* (Washington DC: U.S. Government Printing Office, 1966); Christopher Jencks, et. al., *Inequality: A Reassessment of the Effect of Family and Schooling in America* (New York: Basic Books, 1972); Eric Hanushek, "The Economics of Schooling: Production and Efficiency in Public Schools," *Journal of Economic Literature* 24 (September 1986), 1141-1177.

[30] Reforms of the federal government during the Clinton administration focused more on reducing bureaucratic regulations and making federal agencies accountable to the public than did federal government reforms during the prior Bush and Reagan administrations. See: Paul C. Light, *The tides of Reform: Making Government Work: 1945-1995* (New Haven, CT: Yale University Press, 1997), 132-135.

[31] Jean Johnson, and Ann Duffett, *Where We Are Now: 12 Things You Need to Know about Public Opinion and Public Schools* (New York: Public Agenda, 2003), 8-9.

[32] For instance: advocate Kati Haycock and her Education Trust, civil rights attorney William L. Taylor, researcher Paul Hill, Senator Edward Kennedy, and others. In November 2003, The Education Trust assembled 100 African American and Latino school superintendents who spoke out in support of NCLB. Source for latter: Lynn Olson, "In ESEA Wake, School Data Flowing Forth," *Education Week* (December 10, 2003), retrieved 12/12/03 from www.edweek.org/ew/ewstory.cfm?slug= 15NCLB.h23

[33] Jean Johnson, and Ann Duffett, *Where We Are Now: 12 Things You Need to Know about Public Opinion and Public Schools* (New York: Public Agenda, 2003), 8-9, 12-13.

[34] See: Jean Johnson and Ann Duffett, *Where We Are Now: 12 Things You Need to Know about Public Opinion and Public Schools* (New York: Public Agenda, 2003), 8-9; Lorraine M. McDonnell, "Accountability As Seen Through a Political Lens," in *Making Sense of Test-Based Accountability in Education*, eds. Laura S. Hamilton, Brian M. Stecher, and Stephen P. Klein (Santa Monica, CA: RAND, 2002). Pg 109

[35] See: Jean Johnson and Ann Duffett, *Where We Are Now: 12 Things You Need to Know about Public Opinion and Public Schools* (New York: Public Agenda, 2003), 12-13; Lowell C. Rose and Alec M. Gallup, "The 35th Annual Phi Delta Kappa/Gallup Poll of the Public's Attitudes Toward the Public Schools" (Bloomington, IN: 2003), retrieved 03/26/04 from http://www.pdkintl.org/kappan/k0309pol.htm.

[36] See: John Gehring, "Massachusetts Sued Over Graduation Tests," *Education Week* (October 2, 2002); Mary Ann Zehr, "Federal Judge Rules That Texas Exit Exam Is Constitutional," Education Week (January 19, 2000).

[37] Mary Ann Zehr, "Texas Exit Exam Under Challenge In Federal Court," *Education Week* (September 29, 1999).

[38] See: Steve Farkas, Jean Johnson, and Ann Duffett, *Stand By Me: What Teachers Really Think about Unions, Merit Pay and Other Professional Matters* (Public Agenda, 2003), 13-16, 25-26; Greg Toppo, "No. 2 Teachers Union Soften Stance Against No Child Left Behind Law: But AFT Says It Still Has Serious Reservations," *USA Today* (July 10, 2003).

[39] Jennifer O'Day, Catherine Bitter, Michael Kirst, Martin Carnoy, Elisabeth Woody, Melissa Buttles, Bruce Fuller, and David Ruenzel, *Assessing California's Accountability System: Successes, Challenges, and Opportunities for Improvement* (Philadelphia, PA: Center for Policy Research in Education, 2004), 9-10.

[40] Hugh Davis Graham, *The Uncertain Triumph* (Chapel Hill: The University of North Carolina Press, 1984), 115.

[41] Wayne Riddle, James Stedman, and Paul Irwin, *National Education Goals: Federal Policy Issues* (Washington DC: Congressional Research Service, The Library of Congress, 1991), 2.

[42] See: Ulrich Boser, "Pressure Without Support," *Education Week* 20(17) (January 11, 2001), 68-84; Diane Massell, Michael Kirst, and Margaret Hoppe, "Persistence and

Change: Standards-Based Systemic Reform in Nine States," *CPRE Policy Briefs* [RB-21] (March 1997), 3-5.

[43] "Bill Summary & Status for the 107th Congress: H.R.1,". (Washington DC: The Library of Congress, undated), Retrieved 01/10/04 from the "Thomas" legislation reporting system at http://thomas.loc.gov/cgi-bin/bdquery/z?d107:HR00001:@@@S|TOM:/bss/d107query.html.

[44] See: Eric Kelderman, "State Republicans Assail Bush Education Law," (Washington DC: Stateline.org, January 28, 2004); retrieved 02/09/04 from www.stateline.org/stateline/?pa=story&sa=showStoryInfor&id= 347004 ; "Lawmakers Want Out of No Child Act," *Honolulu Advertiser* (April 3, 2 003); Paul Manna, "Leaving No Child Behind," in *Political Education: National Policy Comes of Age*, by Christopher T. Cross (New York: Teachers College Press, 2004), 126-143. 133-136,141-142

[45] William J. Mathis, "No Child Left Behind: Costs and Benefits," *Phi Delta Kappan* 84 (May 2003), 679-686. Some dramatically lower cost estimates have been publicized, but they have focused just on the costs of testing and reporting the test data, which will be a small part of the total if most low-achieving students are to be boosted to the state proficiency standards.

[46] Most, but not all, studies of accountability have indicated that it does raise achievement test scores some, but usually only a small amount. See: Audrey L. Amrein and David C. Berliner, "The Impact of High-Stakes Tests on Student Academic Performance" (Tempe, AZ: Education Policy Research Unit, Arizona State University, 2002); Martin Carnoy and Susanna Loeb, "Does External Accountability Affect Student Outcome? A cross-State Analysis," *Educational Evaluation and Policy Analysis* 24 (Winter 2002), 305-331; Robert L. Linn, Eva L. Baker, and Damaian W. Betebenner, "Accountability Systems: Implications of Requirements of the No Child Left Behind Act of 2001," *Educational Researcher* 31 (August/September 2002), 3-16; pgs 5-8 Margaret E. Raymond and Eric A. Hanushek, "Shopping for Evidence Against School Accountability" *Education Next* (Summer, 2003), retrieved December 23, 2003 from http://www.educationnext.org/unabridged/20033/; Brian M. Stecher and Laura S. Hamilton, "Putting Theory to the Test: Systems of 'Educational Accountability' Should be Held Accountable," *RAND Review* 26 (Spring 2002), 17-23; pg 19-20 and Herbert J.Walberg, "Real Accountability," in *Our Schools & Our Future: Are We Still At Risk*, ed. Paul E. Peterson (Stanford, CA: Hoover Institution Press, 2003), 305-328. pg 314-315.

[47] Brian M. Stecher and Laura S. Hamilton, "Putting Theory to the Test: Systems of 'Educational Accountability' Should be Held Accountable," *RAND Review* 26 (Spring 2002), 17-23. pg 20

[48] See: Linda Darling-Hammond, "Standards and Assessments: Where We Are and What We Need," *Teachers College Record* (February 2003), retrieved March 8, 2003 from www.tcrecord.org/Content.aps? ContentID=11109 pg. 3; David M. Herszenhorn, "Basic Skills Forcing Cuts in Art Classes,' *New York Times* (July 23, 2003); Kathleen K. Manzo, "Arts, Foreign Languages Getting Edged Out," *Education Week* (November 5, 2003), 3; National Association of State Boards of Education, "The Complete Curriculum: Ensuring a Place for the Arts and Foreign Languages in American's Schools (Alexandria, VA: author, 2003); Brian M. Stecher and Laura S. Hamilton, "Putting Theory to the Test: Systems of 'Educational Accountability' Should be Held Accountable," *RAND Review* 26 (Spring 2002), 17-23. pg 20

[49] See Lynn Olson, "NAEP Exclusion Rates Continue to Bedevil Policymakers" *Education Week* (May 28, 2003), 5.

[50] See: U.S. Department of Education, National Center for Education Statistics, *Overview and Inventory of State Education Reforms: 1990 to 2000* (Washington DC: author, 2003), 29; Charles Stansfield and Charlene Rivera, "How Will English Language Learners Be Accommodated in State Assessment? ?"in *Assessment in Educational Reform: Both Means and Ends*, ed. Robert W Lissitz and William D. Schafer (Boston: Allyn and Bacon, 2002), 124-144; Gerald Tindal, "How Will Assessments Accommodate Students with Disabilities?" in *Assessment in Educational Reform: Both Means and Ends*, ed. Robert W Lissitz and William D. Schafer (Boston: Allyn and Bacon, 2002), 101-123..

[51] Andrew Trotter, "Testing aid for some students leads to scoring flap in Md.," *Education Week (October 22, 2003), 12.*

[52] See: James S. Catterall, *Standards and School Dropouts: A National Study of Minimum Competency Test* (Los Angeles, CA: Center for Research on Evaluation, Standards, and Student Testing, University of California, 1988); Linda Darling-Hammond, "Standards and Assessments: Where We Are and What We Need," *Teachers College Record* (February 2003), 4-7, retrieved March 8, 2003 at www.tcrecord.org/Content.aps? ContentID=11109 ; Tamar Lewin and Jennifer Medina, "To Cut Failure Rate, Schools Shed Students," *New York Times* (July 31, 2003), A1; Christopher B. Swanson, "The New Math on Graduation Rates," *Education Week* (July 28, 2004).

[53] See: Jeff Archer, "Houston Case Offers Lesson on Dropouts: Lack of Accurate Figures Called National Problem, *Education Week* (September 44, 2003), 1, 14-17; David J. Hoff, "New York Teachers Caught Cheating on State Tests," *Education Week* (November 6, 2003), 27; Brian A Jacob and Steven D. Levitt, "Rotten Apples: An Investigation of the Prevalence and Predictors of Teacher Cheating," (unpublished paper, about 2003). Michael Gormley, "Disturbing New Trend: Teachers Who Cheat," *Associated Press* (October 27, 2003).

[54] See: Henry S. Dyer, Robert L. Linn, and Michael J. Patton, "A Comparison of Four Methods of Obtaining Discrepancy Measures Based on Observed and Predicted School System Means on Achievement Tests," *American Educational Research Journal* 6 (November 1969), 591-605; Robert E. Klitgaard and George Hall, *Are There Unusually Effective Schools?* (unknown source, 1973) [Judging by reports on related topics with similar dates, this report was probably published by RAND, in Santa Monica, CA]; Robert L. Linn, Eva L. Baker, and Damaian W. Betebenner, "Accountability Systems: Implications of Requirements of the No Child Left Behind Act of 2001," *Educational Researcher* 31 (August/September 2002), 3-16. pg. 12-13

[55] See: Thomas J. Kane and Douglas O. Staiger, "Volatility in School Test Scores: Implications for Test-Based Accountability Systems" in *Brookings Papers on Education Policy:* 2002, ed. Diane Ravitch (Washington DC: Bookings Institutions Press), 235-283; and Robert L. Linn, Eva L. Baker, and Damaian W. Betebenner, "Accountability Systems: Implications of Requirements of the No Child Left Behind Act of 2001," *Educational Researcher* 31 (August/September 2002), 3-16; pgs 12-13

[56] See: U.S. General Accounting Office, *Title I: Education Needs to Monitor States' Scoring of Assessments* (Washington DC: author, 2002), 4; Kathleen Rhoades and George Madaus, *Errors in Standardized Tests: A Systemic Problem* (Boston: National Board on Educational Testing and Public Policy, Boston College, 2003).

[57] Susan H. Fuhrman, ed. *From the Capitol to the Classroom: Standards-based Reform in the States: One Hundredth Yearbook of the National Society for the Study of Education, Part II* (Chicago, IL: University of Chicago Press, 2001.
[58] Gregg B. Jackson, "Accounting for Accountability," *Phi Delta Kappan* [to be published in fall 2008 or spring 2009].
[59] Otis W. Caldwell and Stuart A .Courtis, *Then and Now in Education: 1845-1923* (New York: World Book Company, 1923), v.
[60] Daniel P. Resnick and Lauren B. Resnick, "Standards, Curriculum, and Performance: A Historical and Comparative Perspective," *Educational Researcher* 14 (April 1985), 5-20. pg. 11
[61] Public Law 107-1010. For instance, see: Sec. 1114(b)(1)(B)(ii) and Sec. 1116(b)(3)(A)(i), (b)(4)(C), and (b)(7)(C)(iv)(II).
[62] Paul Manna, "Leaving No Child Left Behind," in *Political Education: National Policy Comes of Age*, by Christopher T. Cross (New York: Teachers College Press, 2004), 126-143.
[63] Christopher B. Swanson, "The New Math on Graduation Rates," *Education Week* (July 28, 2004).
[64] See: American Federation of Teachers, "AFT On Meeting the Challenges of No Child Left Behind Act" (Washington DC: author, August 2003), retrieved 03/26/04 from http://www.aft.org/esea/downloads/ NCLB_general.pdf; National Education Association, "NEA Annual Meeting Takes Aim at 'No Child Left Behind' Flaws: Members Are Mobilized to Fix and Fund the Law's Laudable Goals," [News Release] (Washington DC: author, July 6, 2003), retrieved 03/26/2003 from http://www.nea.org/newsreleases/2003/nr030706.html; National Education Association, "National Education Association to Challenge Provisions of No Child Left Behind Act: Litigation to Focus On the Impact of Unfunded Mandates" [News Release] (Washington DC: author, July 2, 2003) retrieved 03/26/04 from http://www.nea.org/newsreleases/2003/nr030702.html; and Sandra Feldman, letter to Honorable Judd Gregg and others in the U.S. Congress, February 4, 2004, retrieved 03/26/04 from http://www.aft.org/esea/downloads/ESEA04 ImplementationLettertocommittee.pdf
[65] W. James Popham, "The 'No Child' Noose Tightens—But Some States Are Slipping It," *Education Week* (24 September 2004), 48.
[66] Maine Education Association president, Rob Walker is one of several who have alleged this. See "ESEA Stinks" (undated) [retrieved 03/08/03 from www.maine.nea.org/dir2/esea_st inks.htm]
[67] See: Katrina Bulkley and Jennifer Fisler, "A Decade of Charter Schools: From Theory to Practice" (CPRE Policy Briefs, RB-350 University of Pennsylvania, April 2002), 4-6, Caroline Hendrie, "New Scrutiny For Sponsors Of Charter Schools," *Education Week* (20 November 2002): 1, 18.
[68] Pat Kossan, "Report Rips Oversight of Charters," *The Arizona Republic*, August 13, 2003.
[69] "School Double Standard" *St. Petersburg Times* [Florida] August 3, 2003. Retrieved August 22, 2003 at www.sptimes.com/2003/08/03/School_ double_standar.shtml.
[70] The author acknowledges that the discussion of the school choice reform was informed, with permission, by Michael T. Luekens' class paper, "Tuition Vouchers: A History of the Use of Public Funds for Private Schooling" (The George Washington University, 2000).

[71] Center for Educational Reform, *The National Charter School Directory*. Retrieved October 28, 2003 at www.edreform.com
[72] Terry M. Moe, "The Politics of the Status Quo," in *Our Schools and Our Future: Are We Still At Risk*, ed. Paul E. Peterson (Stanford, CA: Hoover Institution Press, 2003), 177-210. pgs 198-199
[73] Computed from: John E Chubb, "Real Choice," in *Our Schools and Our Future: Are We Still At Risk?* Paul E. Peterson ed. (Stanford, CA: Hoover Institution Press, 2003), 329-361. pg 338-339
[74] The books were: James S. Coleman, Thomas Hoffer, and Sally Kilgore, *High School Achievement: Public, Catholic and Private Schools Compared* (New York: Basic Books, 1982); James S. Coleman and Thomas Hoffer, *Public and Private High Schools: The Impact of Communities* (New York: Basic Books, 1987); John E. Chubb and Terry M. Moe, *Politics, Markets, and America's Schools* (Washington DC: The Brookings Institution, 1990).
[75] Gene V. Glass, "Are Data Enough?" review of "Politics, Markets, and America's Schools," by John E. Chubb and Terry M. Moe, *Educational Researcher* 20 (April 1991): 24-27.
[76] See: The Black Alliance for Educational Options [http://www.baeo.org/home/index.php]; Karla Scoon Reid, "Minority Paretns Quietly Embrace School Choice," *Education Week* (December 5, 2001).
[77] See: American Federation of Teachers, "What You Need to Know About Vouchers," (retrieved online July 28, 2004 from http://www.aft.org/pubs-reports/psrp_reporter/2000/backtoschool/vouchers.htm; National Education Association, "Vouchers" (retrieved online July 28, 2004 at www.nea.org/vouchers; National Education Association, "NEA On Vouchers: Opposed" (retrieved online July 28, 2004 at www.new.org/vouchers/vouchposition.html.
[78] See: Terry M. Moe, "The Politics of the Status Quo," in *Our Schools and Our Future: Are We Still At Risk*, ed. Paul E. Peterson (Stanford, CA: Hoover Institution Press, 2003), 177-210; p. 196; percentage was calculated from: U.S. Department of Education, National Center for Education Statistics, *Digest of Education Statistics: 2001* (Washington DC: U.S. Government Printing Office, 2002), 71.
[79] National Working Commission on Choice in K-12 Education, *School Choice: Doing It the Right Way Makes a Difference* (Washington DC: The Brown Center on Education Policy, The Brookings Institute, 2004), 23 & 33.
[80] David W. Kirkpatrick, *Choice In Schooling: A Case for Tuition Vouchers* (Chicago: Loyola University Press, 1990), 150-151.
[81] Lowell C. Rose and Alec M. Gallup, "The 35th Annual Phi Delta Kappan/Gallup Poll of the Public's Attitudes Toward The Public Schools," *Phi Delta Kappan* (2003), retrieved 08/22/03 from www.pdkintl.org/kappan/k0309pol.htm
[82] U.S. Department of Education, National Center for Education Statistics, *The Condition of Education: 2001* (Washington DC: U.S. Government Printing Office, 2001), 68.
[83] See The Black Alliance for Educational Options' web site at http://www.baeo.org/home/index.php
[84] John E. Chubb, "Real Choice," in *Our Schools and Our Future: Are We Still At Risk?* ed. Paul E. Peterson (Stanford, CA: Hoover Institution Press, 2003), 329-361. pg 344
[85] [Lost Reference]
[86] David P. Smole, *School Choice: Current Legislation* (Washington DC: Congressional Research Service, 2003): 6-7.

[87] U.S. Department of Education, National Center for Education Statistics, *Overview and Inventory of State Education Reforms: 1990 to 2000* (Washington DC: author, 2003), x. 98, 100.

[88] Computed from: U.S. Department of Education, National Center for Education Statistics, *Digest of Education Statistics: 2008* (Washington DC: U.S. Government Printing Office, 2008), 13.

[89] Paul T. Hill, *Administrative Costs of Education Voucher Programs* (Seattle, WA: Center on Reinventing Public Education, University of Washington, 2003).

[90] Computed from: U.S. Department of Education, National Center for Education Statistics, *Digest of Education Statistics: 2001* (Washington DC: U.S. Government Printing Office, 2002), 12 and 34.

[91] Henry M. Levin, "The Economics of Educational Choice," *Economics of Education Review* 10 (1991) 137-158. 152

[92] John E. Witte, "The Milwaukee Voucher Experiment," *Educational Evaluation and Policy Analysis* 20 (Winter 1998): 229-251.

[93] Scott Stephens, "Public School Kids Edge Out Voucher Peers," *The Plain Dealer*, 16 April 2003.

[94] William G. Howell and Paul E. Peterson, *The Education Gap: Vouchers and Urban Schools* (Washington DC: Brookings Institution Press, 2002), xiv-xv, 146-147, 153-154.

[95] Patrick J. McEwan, "The Potential Impact of Large-Scale Voucher Programs," *Review of Educational Research* 70 (Summer 2000): 103-149. p. 103

[96] Katrina Bulkley and Jennifer Fisler, "A Decade of Charter Schools: From Theory to Practice" (CPRE Policy Briefs, RB-35 University of Pennsylvania, April 2002), 7-8.

[97] Brian P. Gill, P. Michael Timpane, Karen E. Ross, and Dominic J. Brewer, *Rhetoric Versus Reality: What We Know and What We Need to Know About Vouchers and Charter Schools* (Santa Monica, CA: RAND, 2001).

[98] Clive R. Belfield and Henry M. Levin, "The Effects of Competition Between Schools on Educational Outcomes: A Review for the United States, *Review of Educational Research* 72 (Summer 2002) 279-341, 294-295.

[99] John E. Coons and Stephen D. Sugarman, *Scholarships for Children* (Berkeley, CA: Institute of Governmental Studies Press, University of California, Berkeley, 1992), vii; National Working Commission on Choice in K-12 Education, *School Choice: Doing It the Right Way Makes a Difference* (Washington DC: The Brown Center on Education Policy, The Brookings Institute, 2004), 19-36.

[100] See: Henry M. Levin, "The Economics of Educational Choice," *Economics of Education Review* 10 (1991) 137-158; Paul A. Samuelson and William D. Nordhaus, *Economics*, 13th ed. (New York: McGraw-Hill, 1989), 566-573, 750-751; David L. Weimer and Aidan R. Vining, *Policy Analysis: Concepts and Practices* (Englewood Cliffs, NJ: Prentice-Hall, 1989), 39-88.

[101] The name of the ETS official and the date of the telephone conversation have long since been lost.

[102] Henry M. Levin, "The Economics of Educational Choice," *Economics of Education Review* 10 (1991) 137-158.

[103] See: Federal Interagency Committee on Education, *Toward a Federal Strategy for Protection of the Consumer of Education* (Washington DC: U. S. Department of Health, Education, and Welfare, 1975); Gregg B. Jackson and Stephanie Castelli, *Where to Get Jobs Training in the DC Area* (Washington, D.C.: Washington Center for the Study of Services, 1979); U.S. Federal Trade Commission, Bureau of

Consumer Protection, *Proprietary Vocational and Home Study Schools* (Washington DC: Government Printing Office, 1976).

[104] Caroline M. Hoxby, *School Choice and School Productivity (Or Could School Choice Be a Tide That Lifts All Boats?)* (Cambridge, MA: National Bureau of Economic Research, 2002). Note that these results should be considered preliminary because the analyses were conducted in only two states and no controls were made for other policy changes that may have been implemented during the periods studied.

[105] Paul E. Peterson, "The New Politics of Choice," in *Learning From the Past: What History Teaches Us About School Reform*, ed. Diane Ravitch and Maris A Vinovskis (Baltimore, MD: Johns Hopkins University Press, 1995), 217-240. pgs 229

[106] See: David Kirkpatrick, *Choice in Schooling: A Case for Tuition Vouchers* (Chicago, IL: Loyola University Press, 1990) chapters 7-9; Paul E. Peterson, "The New Politics of Choice," in *Learning From the Past: What History Teaches Us About School Reform*, ed. Diane Ravitch and Maris A Vinovskis (Baltimore, MD: Johns Hopkins University Press, 1995), 217-240. pgs 231-232.

[107] Computed from: U.S. Department of Education, National Center for Education Statistics, *The Condition of Education: 2002* (Washington DC: U.S. Government Printing Office, 2002), 89.

[108] U.S. Department of Education, National Center for Education Statistics, *The Condition of Education: 2002* (Washington DC: U.S. Government Printing Office, 2002), 176.

[109] See: Education Commission of the States, *A State Policy Maker's Guide to Public School Choice* (Denver, CO: author, 1989); National Working Commission on Choice in K-12 Education, *School Choice: Doing It the Right Way Makes a Difference* (Washington DC: The Brown Center on Education Policy, The Brookings Institute, 2004), 6 & 32; John E. Coons and Stephen D. Sugarman, *Scholarships for Children* (Berkeley, CA: Institute of Governmental Studies Press, University of California, Berkeley, 1992), 28.

Author Bios

Beth Antunez is an assistant director of Educational Issues at the American Federation of Teachers, where she acts as a liaison to state and local unions as they work to implement the No Child Left Behind Act. Prior to joining the AFT, Ms. Antunez worked at the Council for the Great City Schools and the National Clearinghouse for Bilingual Education. She began her career as a third grade teacher in Compton, California.

Nina de las Alas is a research associate at the Council of Chief State School Officers. She provides technical assistance to state education agencies in the areas of education reform and accountability and she manages several National Science Foundation-funded studies of teacher professional development programs. She recently co-authored *Does Teacher Professional Development Have Effects on Teaching and Learning? Analysis of Evaluation Findings from Programs for Mathematics and Science Teachers in 14 States* (available at www.ccsso.org/publications). She is also a writer and editor for the Support for School Improvement e-Newsletter at (http://communities.ccsso.org/web/ssinews).

Gregg B. Jackson is Associate Professor Emeritus of Education Policy and Public Policy at The George Washington University. Prior to joining GWU, he held senior research positions at the U.S. Commission on Civil Rights, the International City Management Association, the National Research Council, and the U.S. Congressional Office of Technology Assessment. His research interests include education reform, equity, and technology applications. His forthcoming "Accounting for Accountability" in *Phi*

Delta Kappan (vol. 90), examines the history of high-stakes accountability in American education.

John Yoshito Jones is an educational consultant residing in Texas. He assists American and Japanese teachers to collaborate on sustainable development initiatives in schools. He recently completed a doctoral degree in Educational Theory and Policy at Pennsylvania State University. His dissertation was titled "Intelligent Design and Education Policy: The Case of Kansas," and is available through ProQuest.

Sean B. Kelly is a Workforce Development Analyst at the U.S. Department of Labor. He helps administer the Workforce Investment Act--an initiative to prepare the workforce of the 21st century. He provides assistance to states in using the flexibility available under the law to create system reform. Prior to joining the Department of Labor, he worked for the workforce investment system sponsored by the District of Columbia and the AFL-CIO. There, he developed and led training programs for dislocated workers, and pre-apprenticeship programs for the building trades.

Maria Soledad Mackinnon is a knowledge management officer at the Global Environment Facility Evaluation Office (GEF EO), responsible for effective dissemination. Previously, Ms Mackinnon worked as a consultant on education and science and technology for the World Bank and the Inter-American Development Bank. She began her career as a teacher and teacher educator in Uruguay. She is a co-author of "Education, Science and Technology in Latin America and the Caribbean: A Statistical Compendium of Indicators" available at (www.iadb.org/sds/publication/publication_4357_e.htm). She also has contributed several articles to TechKnowlogia (http://www.techknowlogia.org/).

Daniel C. Padolsky currently teaches writing at Anglo-American University in Prague and also teaches cultural studies and English at the Bohemia Institute of the Czech Republic. His "Education and Society: The Roots of Civic Disengagement" was published by *The New Presence: The Prague Journal of Central European Affairs*. He is also the author of "Civic disengagement in the Czech Republic" at (http://comm-org.wisc.edu/papers2003/padolsky.htm).

www.ingramcontent.com/pod-product-compliance
Lightning Source LLC
Chambersburg PA
CBHW021804220426
43662CB00006B/170